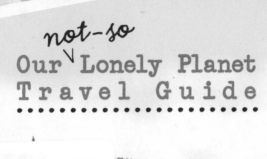

Our not-so Lonely Planet
Travel Guide

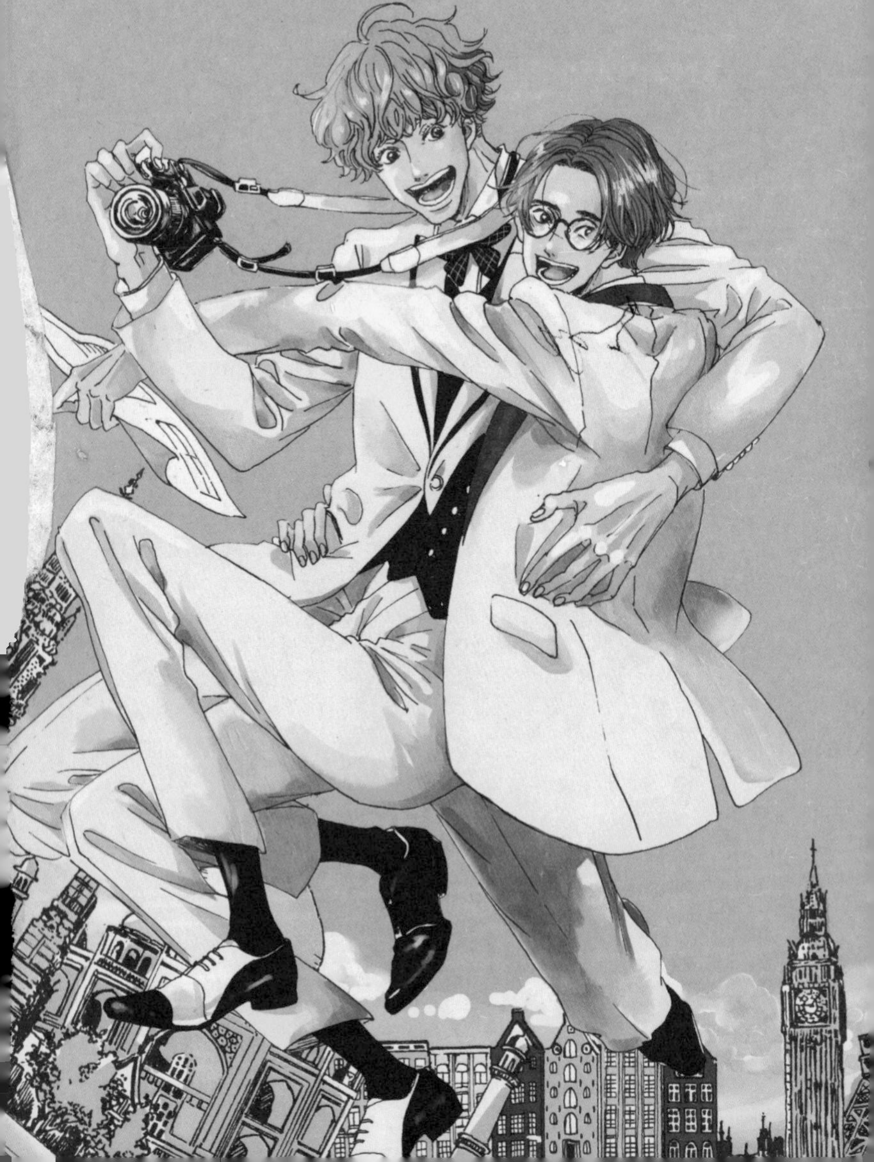

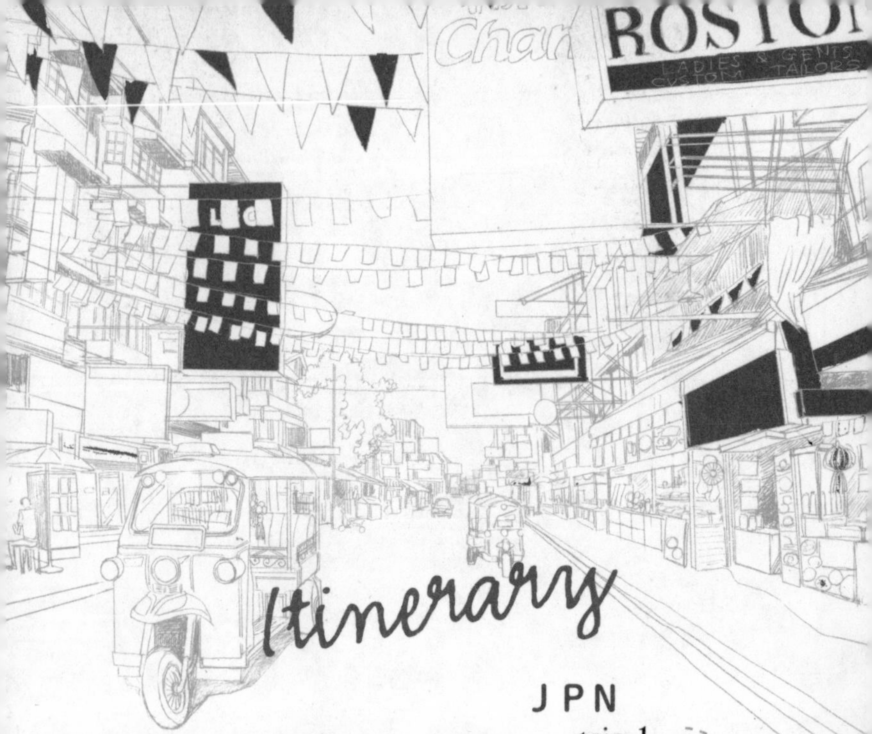
LADIES & GENTS
CUSTOM TAILORS

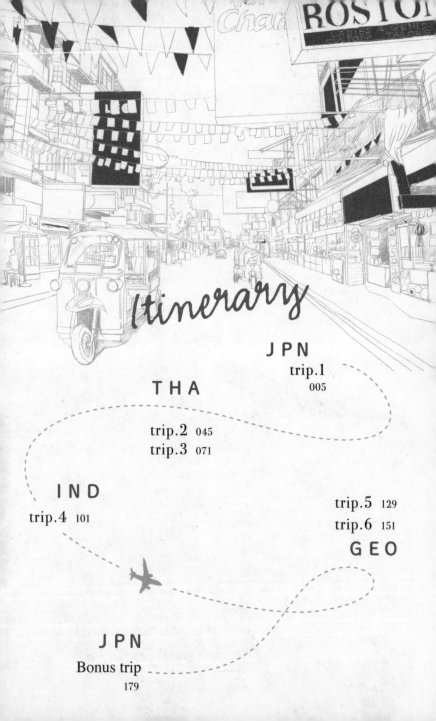

Itinerary

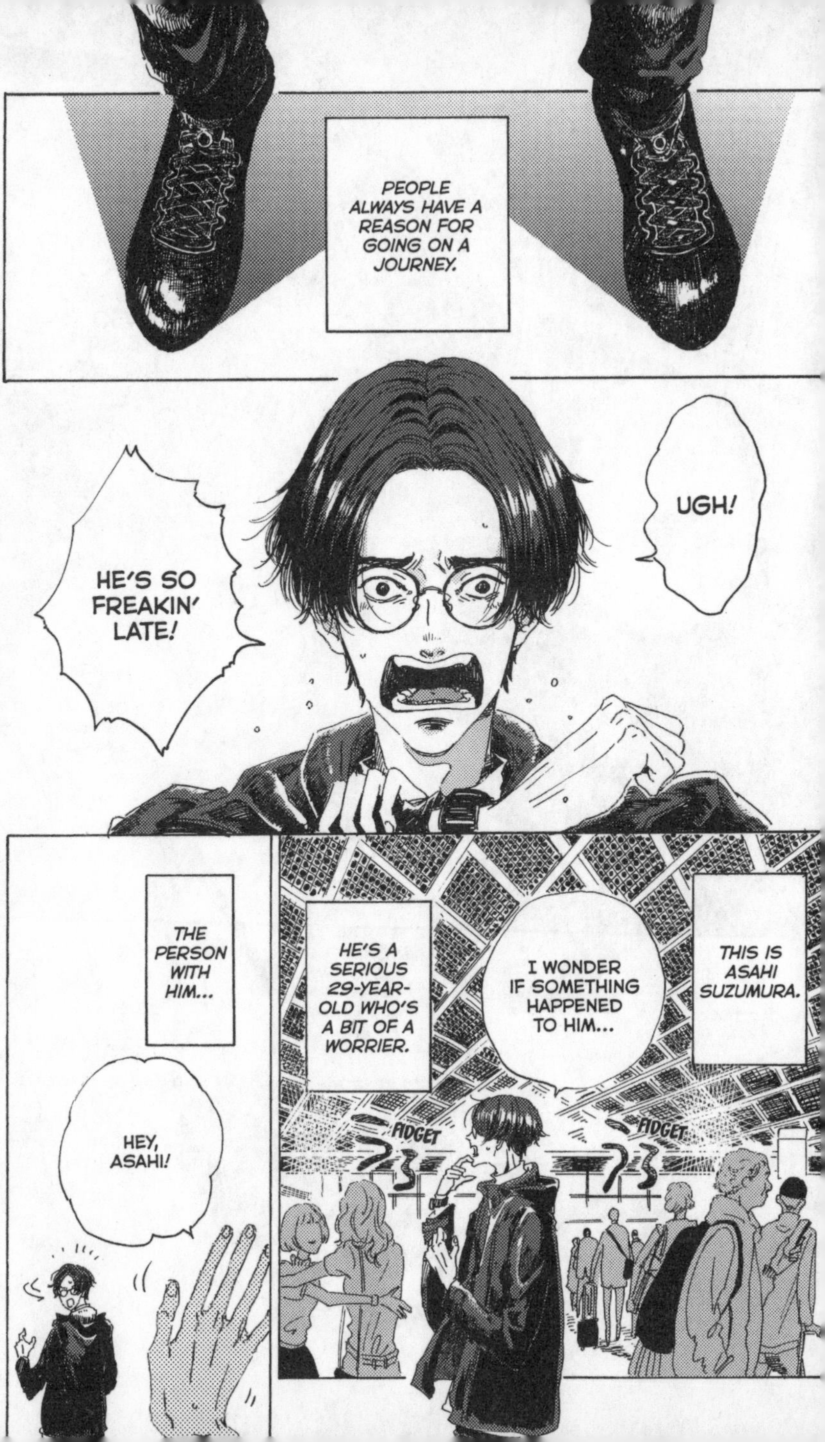
PEOPLE ALWAYS HAVE A REASON FOR GOING ON A JOURNEY.
UGH!
HE'S SO FREAKIN' LATE!
THIS IS ASAHI SUZUMURA.
I WONDER IF SOMETHING HAPPENED TO HIM...
HE'S A SERIOUS 29-YEAR-OLD WHO'S A BIT OF A WORRIER.
FIDGET
FIDGET
THE PERSON WITH HIM...
HEY, ASAHI!

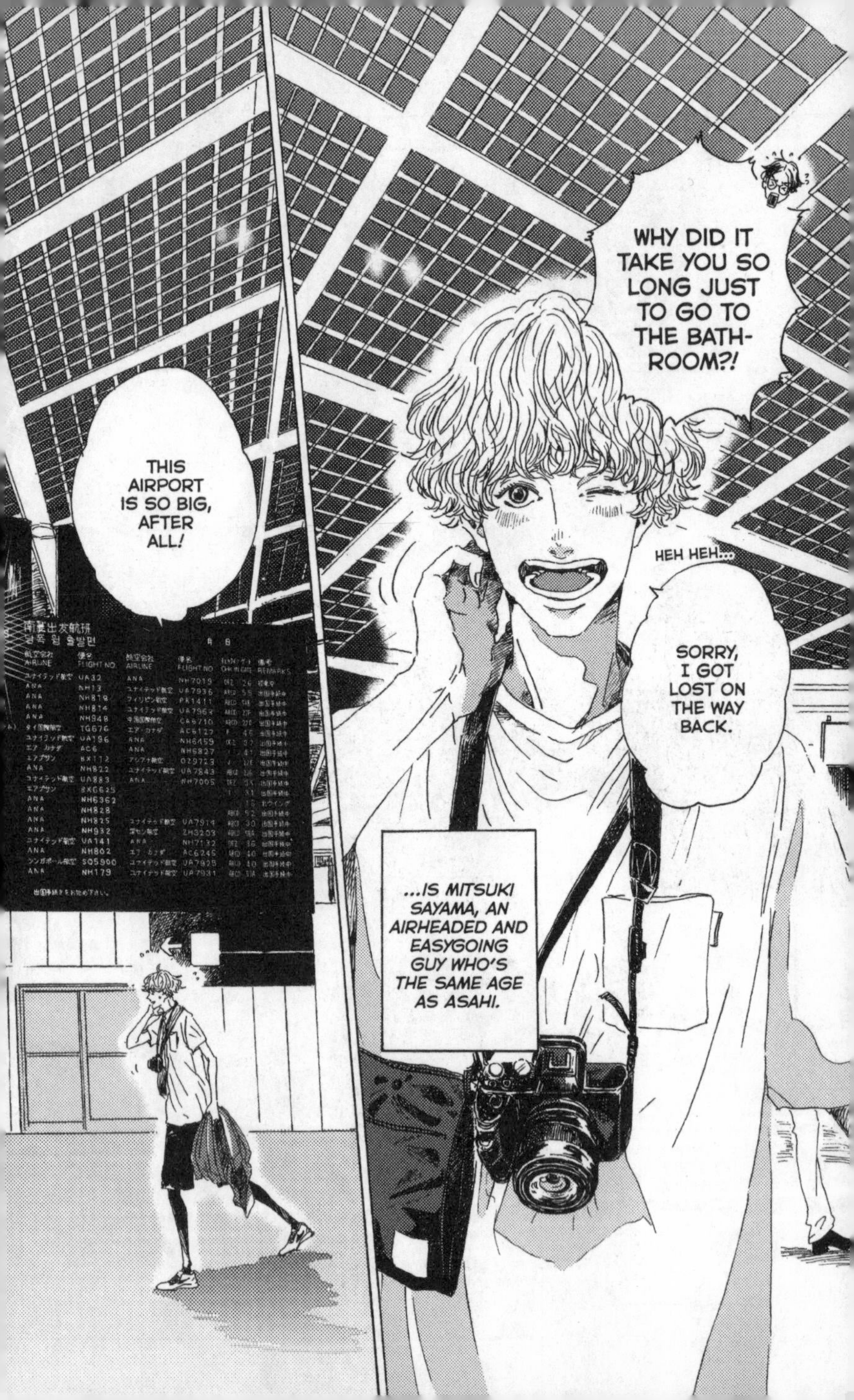
WHY DID IT TAKE YOU SO LONG JUST TO GO TO THE BATH-ROOM?!
HEH HEH...
SORRY, I GOT LOST ON THE WAY BACK.
...IS MITSUKI SAYAMA, AN AIRHEADED AND EASYGOING GUY WHO'S THE SAME AGE AS ASAHI.
THIS AIRPORT IS SO BIG, AFTER ALL!

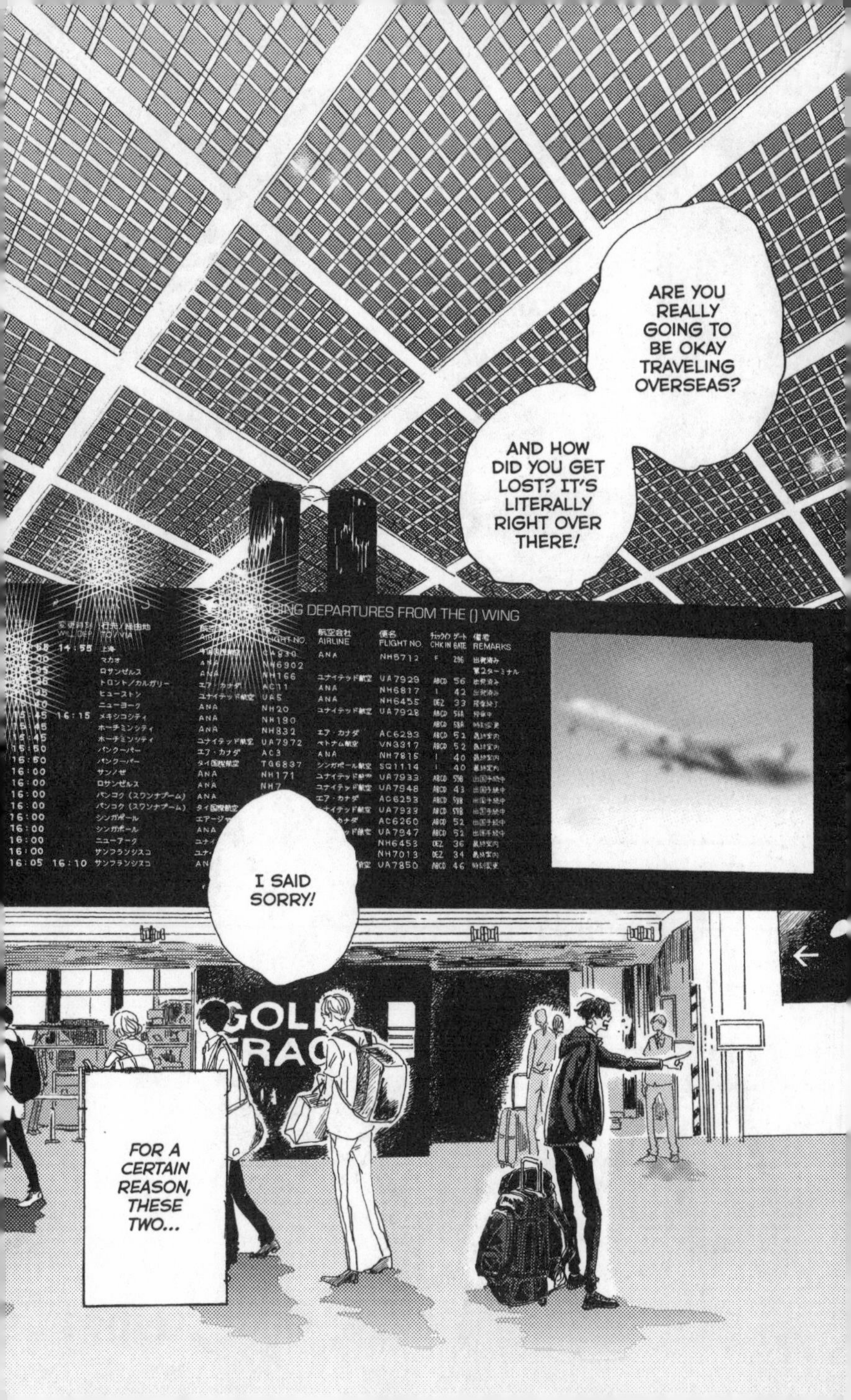
ARE YOU REALLY GOING TO BE OKAY TRAVELING OVERSEAS?
AND HOW DID YOU GET LOST? IT'S LITERALLY RIGHT OVER THERE!
I SAID SORRY!
FOR A CERTAIN REASON, THESE TWO...

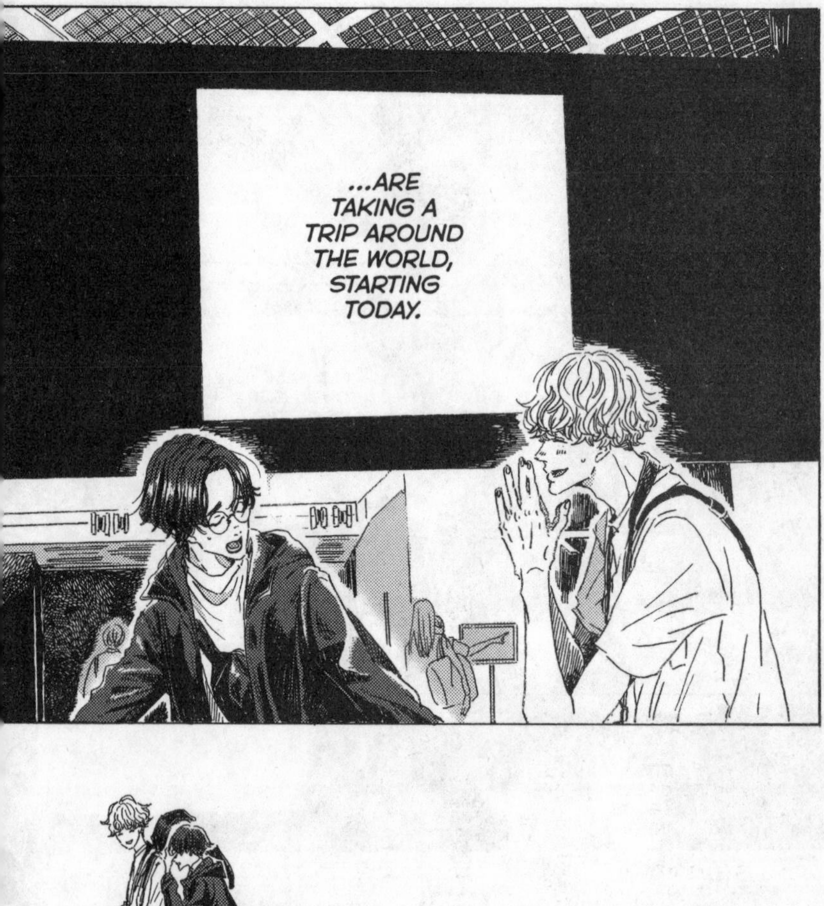
...ARE TAKING A TRIP AROUND THE WORLD, STARTING TODAY.

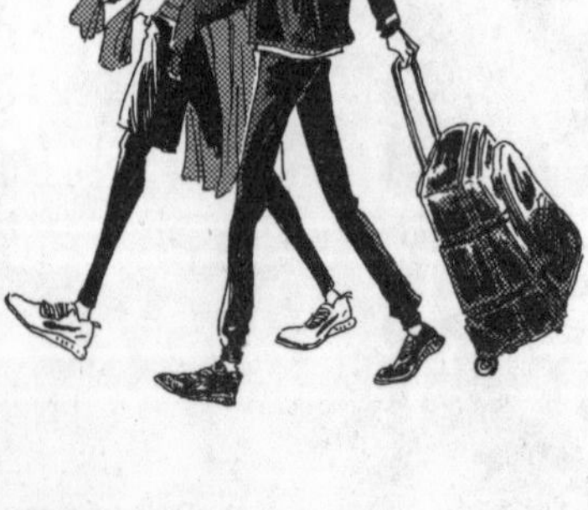

trip. 1

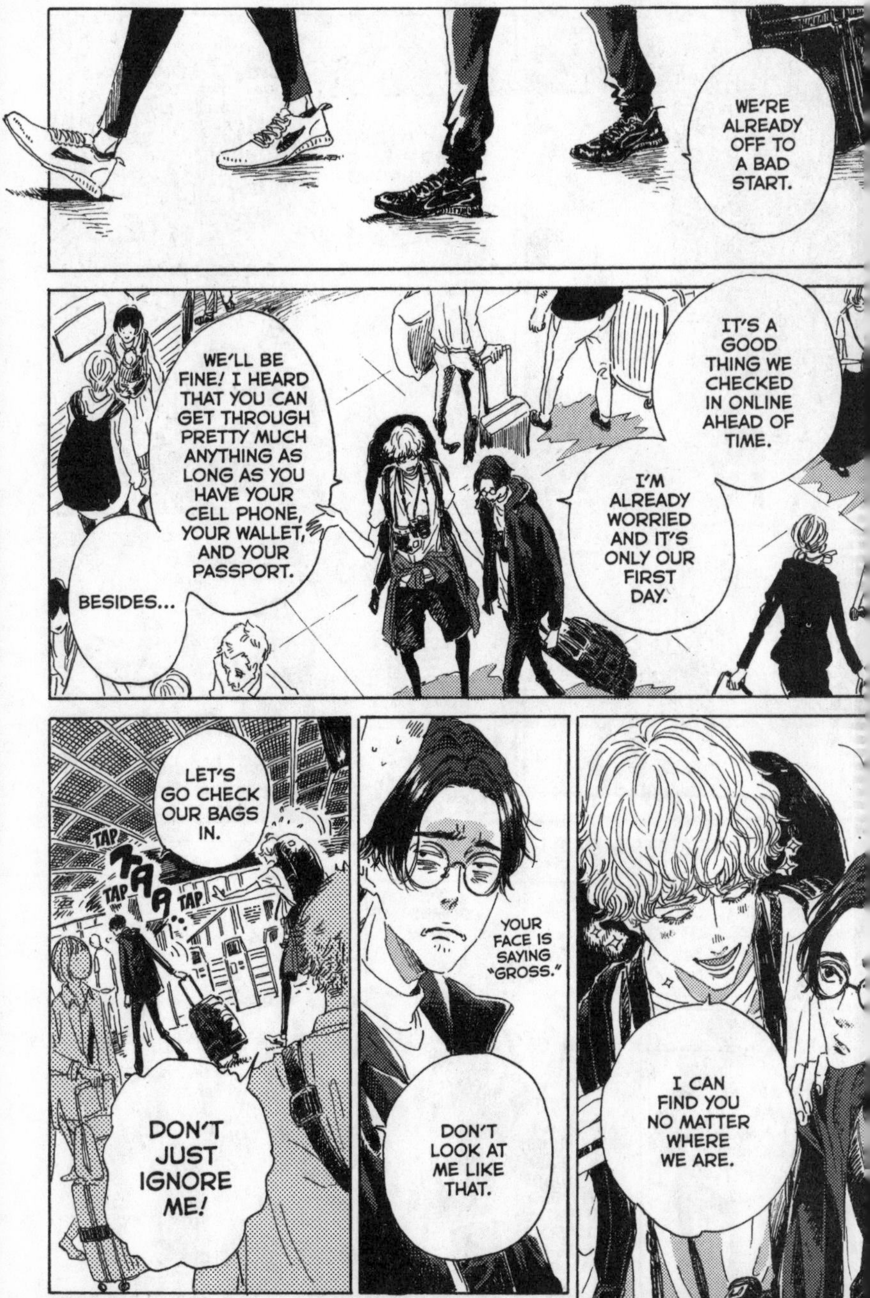
WE'RE ALREADY OFF TO A BAD START.
IT'S A GOOD THING WE CHECKED IN ONLINE AHEAD OF TIME.
I'M ALREADY WORRIED AND IT'S ONLY OUR FIRST DAY.
WE'LL BE FINE! I HEARD THAT YOU CAN GET THROUGH PRETTY MUCH ANYTHING AS LONG AS YOU HAVE YOUR CELL PHONE, YOUR WALLET, AND YOUR PASSPORT.
BESIDES...
I CAN FIND YOU NO MATTER WHERE WE ARE.
YOUR FACE IS SAYING "GROSS."
DON'T LOOK AT ME LIKE THAT.
LET'S GO CHECK OUR BAGS IN.
TAP
TAP
TAP
DON'T JUST IGNORE ME!

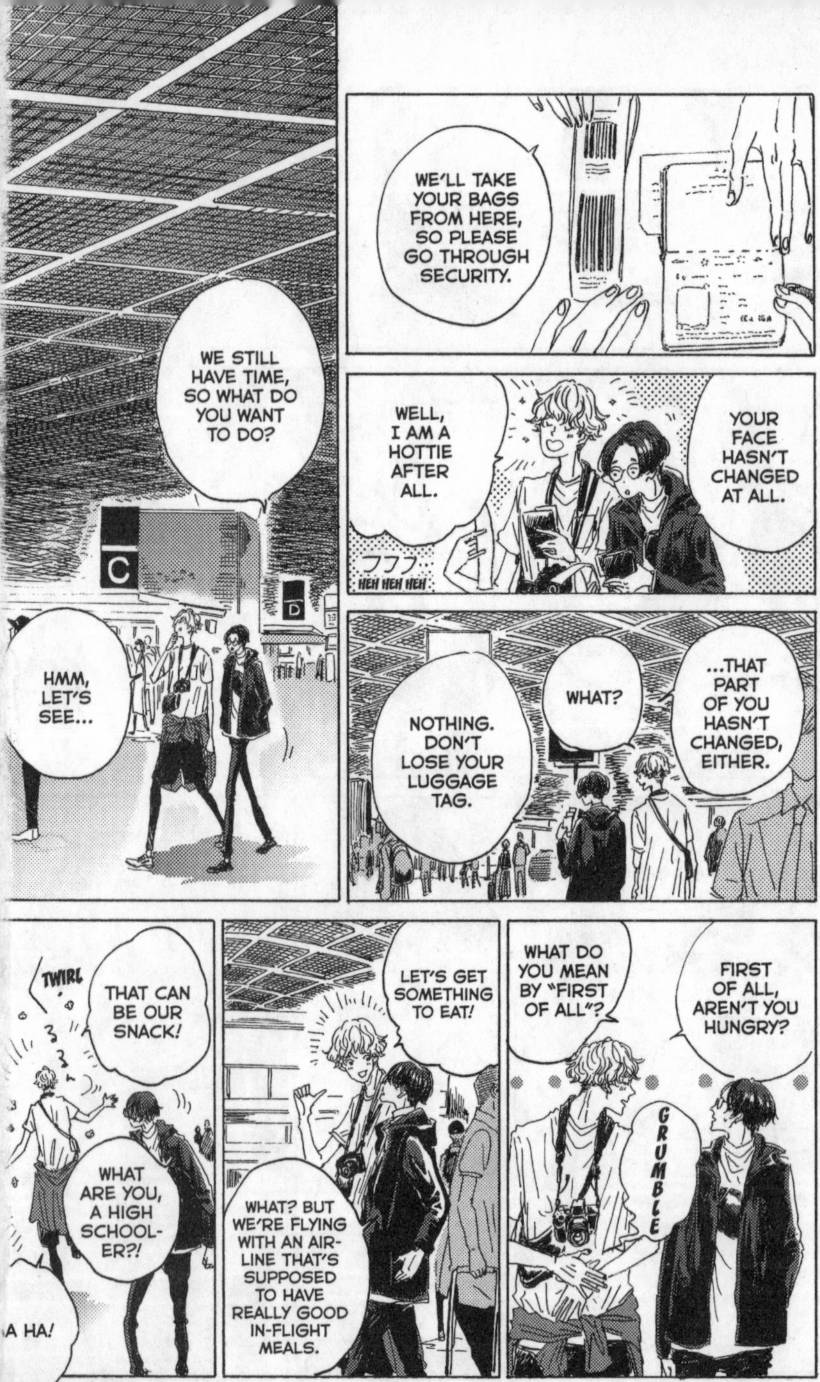

WE'LL TAKE YOUR BAGS FROM HERE, SO PLEASE GO THROUGH SECURITY.
YOUR FACE HASN'T CHANGED AT ALL.
WELL, I AM A HOTTIE AFTER ALL.
フフフ
HEH HEH HEH
...THAT PART OF YOU HASN'T CHANGED, EITHER.
WHAT?
NOTHING. DON'T LOSE YOUR LUGGAGE TAG.
WE STILL HAVE TIME, SO WHAT DO YOU WANT TO DO?
C
D
HMM, LET'S SEE...
FIRST OF ALL, AREN'T YOU HUNGRY?
WHAT DO YOU MEAN BY "FIRST OF ALL"?
GRUMBLE
LET'S GET SOMETHING TO EAT!
WHAT? BUT WE'RE FLYING WITH AN AIR-LINE THAT'S SUPPOSED TO HAVE REALLY GOOD IN-FLIGHT MEALS.
TWIRL
THAT CAN BE OUR SNACK!
WHAT ARE YOU, A HIGH SCHOOL-ER?!
A HA!

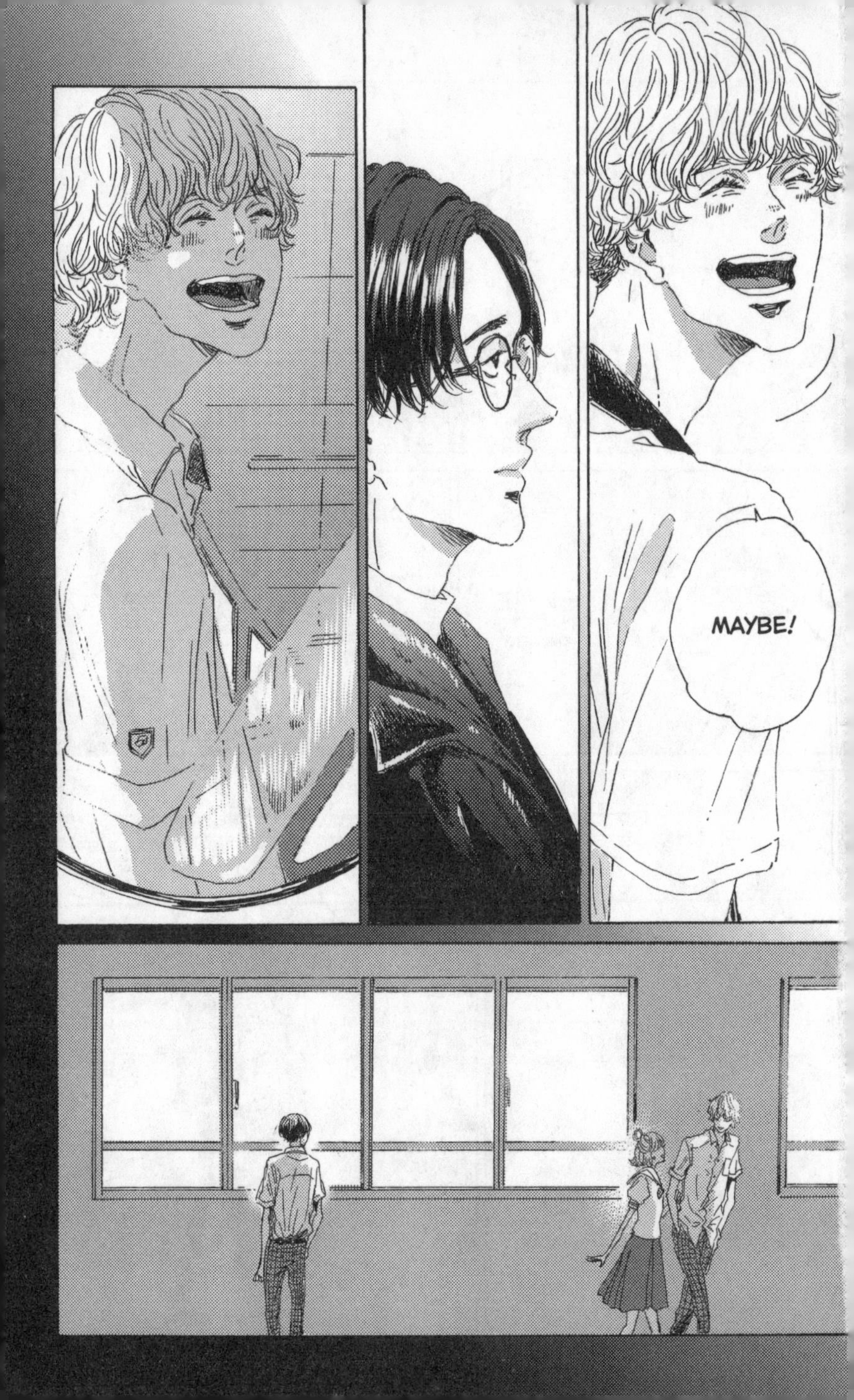
MAYBE!

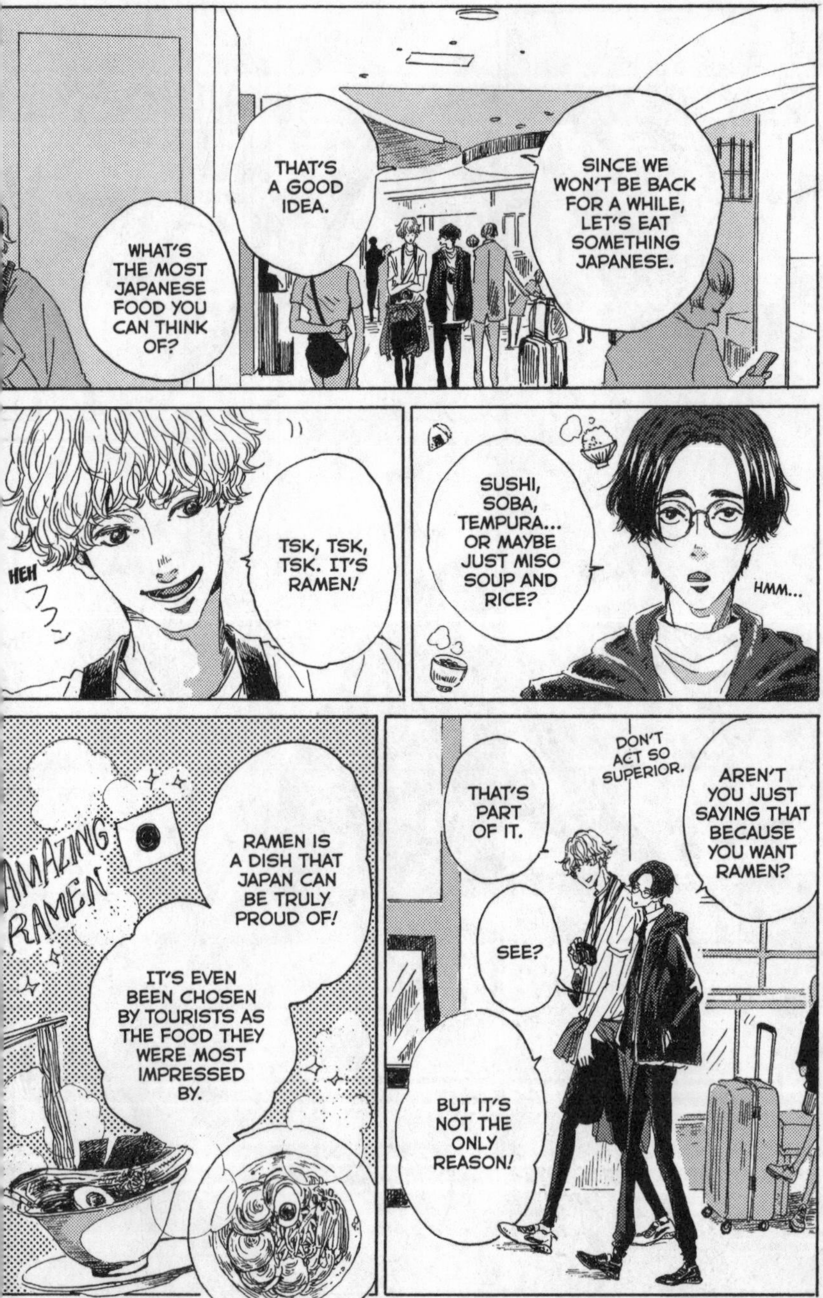
SINCE WE WON'T BE BACK FOR A WHILE, LET'S EAT SOMETHING JAPANESE.
THAT'S A GOOD IDEA.
WHAT'S THE MOST JAPANESE FOOD YOU CAN THINK OF?
SUSHI, SOBA, TEMPURA... OR MAYBE JUST MISO SOUP AND RICE?
HMM...
TSK, TSK, TSK. IT'S RAMEN!
HEH
AREN'T YOU JUST SAYING THAT BECAUSE YOU WANT RAMEN?
DON'T ACT SO SUPERIOR.
THAT'S PART OF IT.
SEE?
BUT IT'S NOT THE ONLY REASON!
RAMEN IS A DISH THAT JAPAN CAN BE TRULY PROUD OF!
AMAZING RAMEN
IT'S EVEN BEEN CHOSEN BY TOURISTS AS THE FOOD THEY WERE MOST IMPRESSED BY.

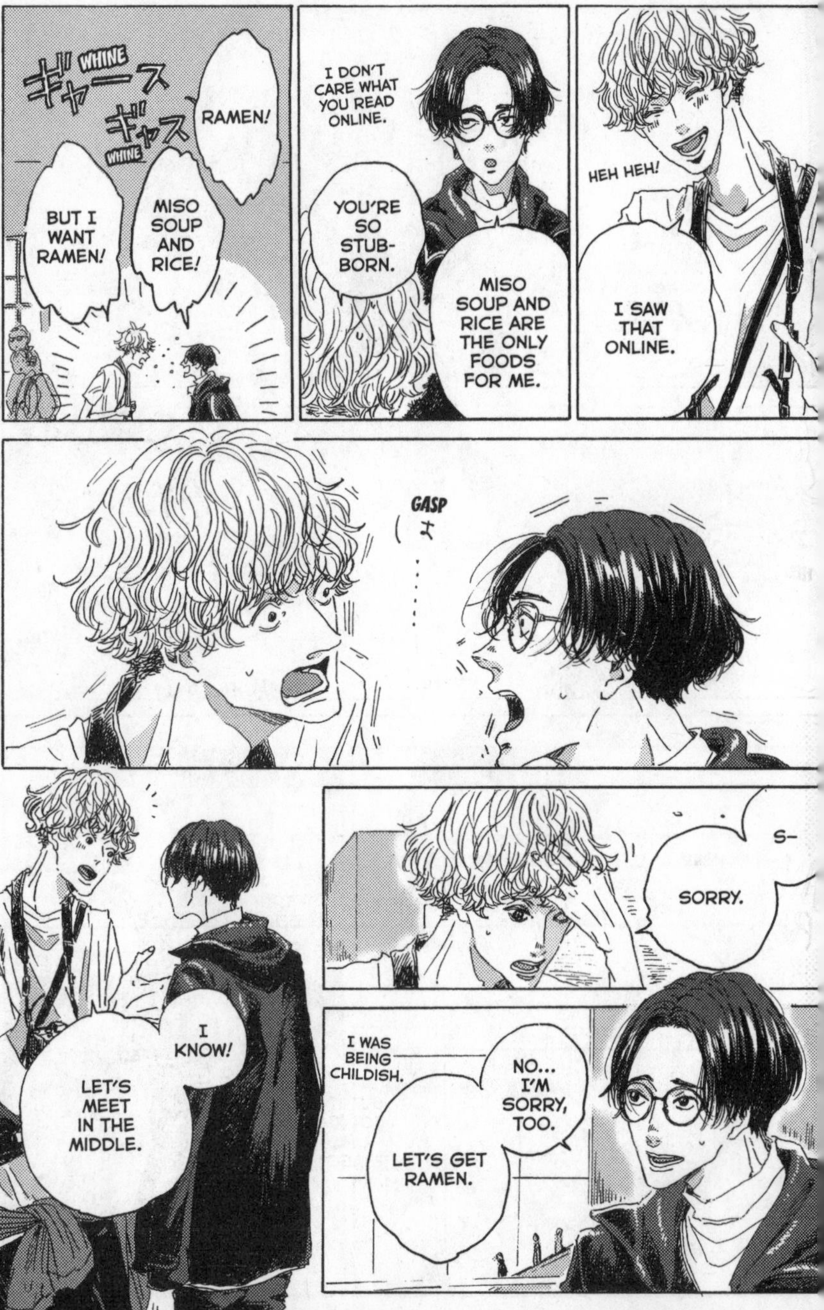
HEH HEH!
I SAW THAT ONLINE.
MISO SOUP AND RICE ARE THE ONLY FOODS FOR ME.
I DON'T CARE WHAT YOU READ ONLINE.
YOU'RE SO STUBBORN.
ギャース WHINE
ギャス WHINE
RAMEN!
MISO SOUP AND RICE!
BUT I WANT RAMEN!
GASP
.....
S-
SORRY.
NO... I'M SORRY, TOO.
I WAS BEING CHILDISH.
LET'S GET RAMEN.
I KNOW!
LET'S MEET IN THE MIDDLE.

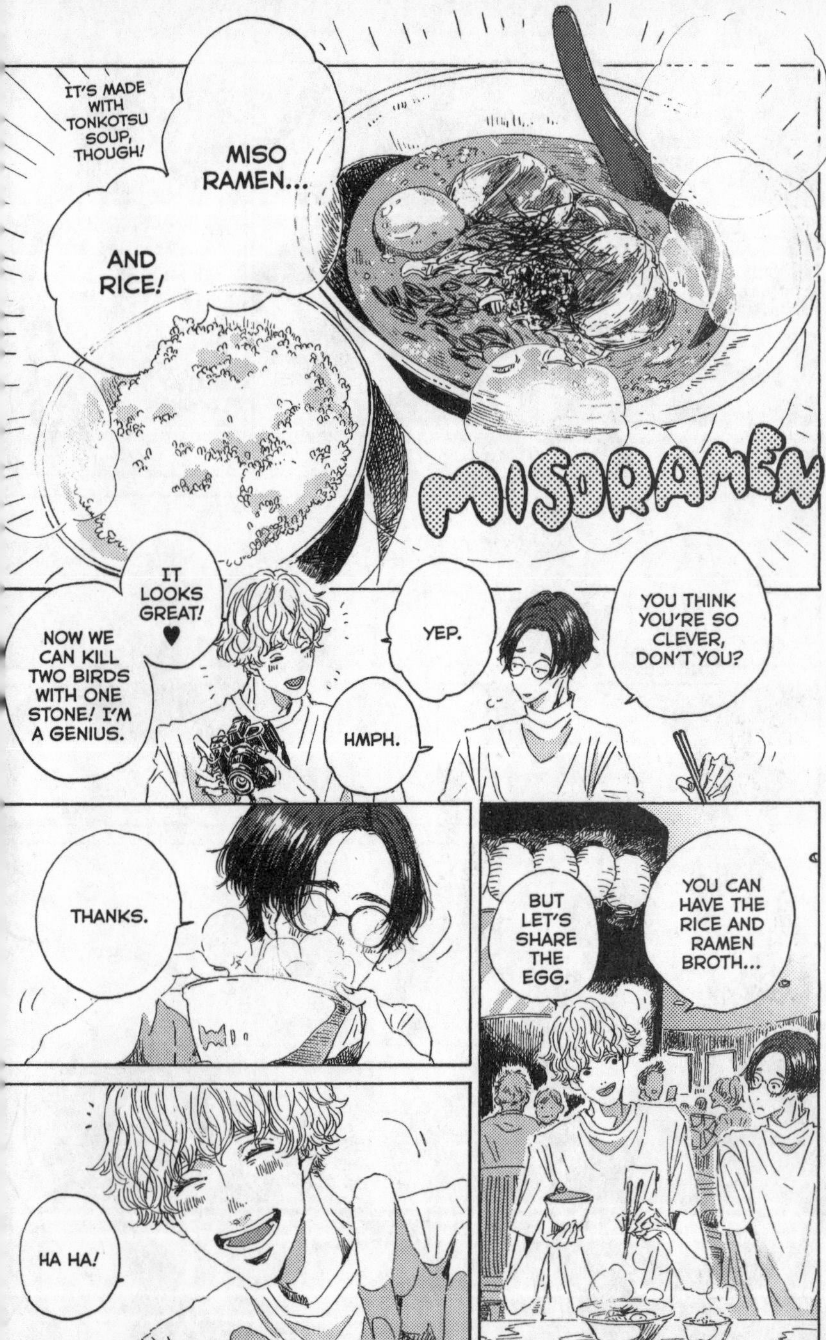
MISO RAMEN...
AND RICE!
IT'S MADE WITH TONKOTSU SOUP, THOUGH!
MISORAMEN
YOU THINK YOU'RE SO CLEVER, DON'T YOU?
YEP.
HMPH.
IT LOOKS GREAT! ♥
NOW WE CAN KILL TWO BIRDS WITH ONE STONE! I'M A GENIUS.
YOU CAN HAVE THE RICE AND RAMEN BROTH...
BUT LET'S SHARE THE EGG.
THANKS.
HA HA!

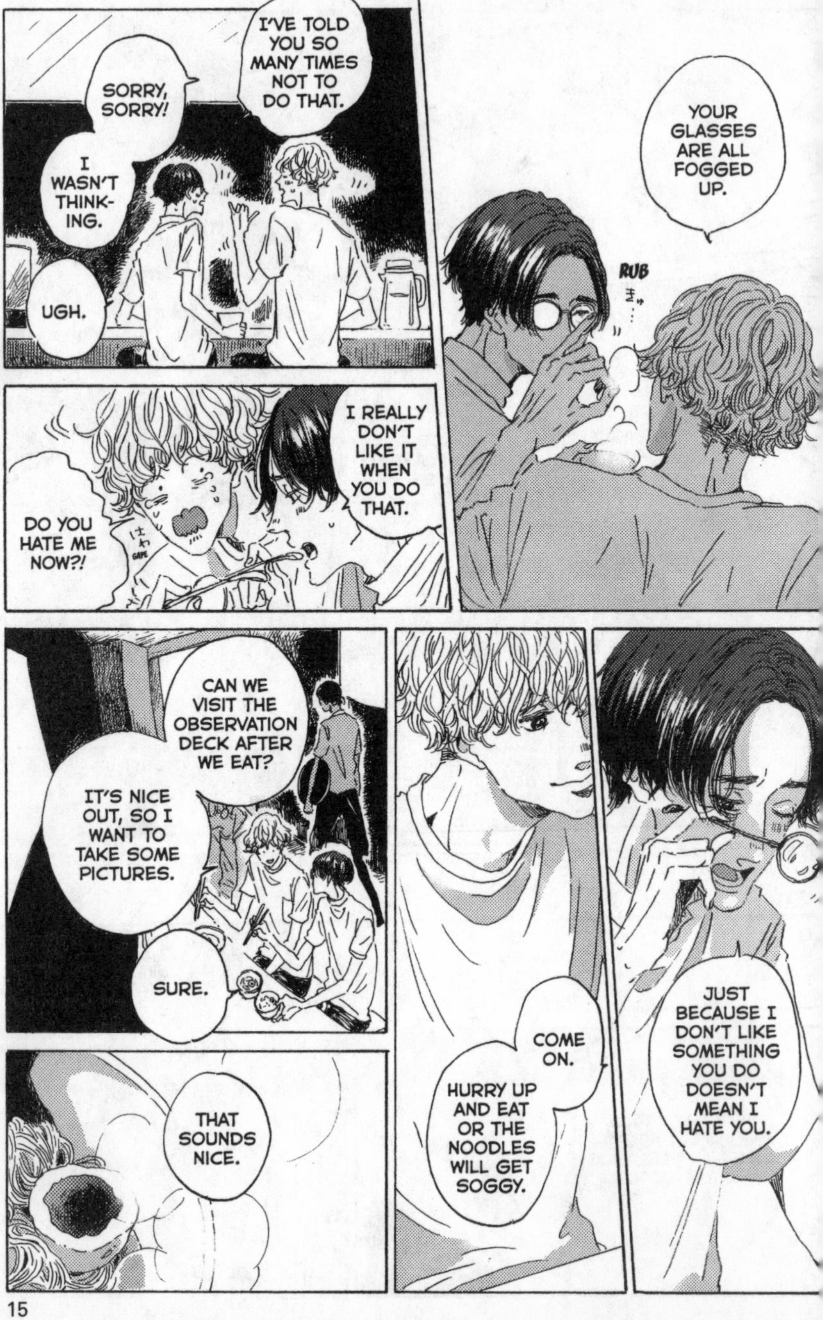
YOUR GLASSES ARE ALL FOGGED UP.
RUB
I'VE TOLD YOU SO MANY TIMES NOT TO DO THAT.
SORRY, SORRY!
I WASN'T THINKING.
UGH.
I REALLY DON'T LIKE IT WHEN YOU DO THAT.
GAPE
DO YOU HATE ME NOW?!
JUST BECAUSE I DON'T LIKE SOMETHING YOU DO DOESN'T MEAN I HATE YOU.
COME ON.
HURRY UP AND EAT OR THE NOODLES WILL GET SOGGY.
CAN WE VISIT THE OBSERVATION DECK AFTER WE EAT?
IT'S NICE OUT, SO I WANT TO TAKE SOME PICTURES.
SURE.
THAT SOUNDS NICE.

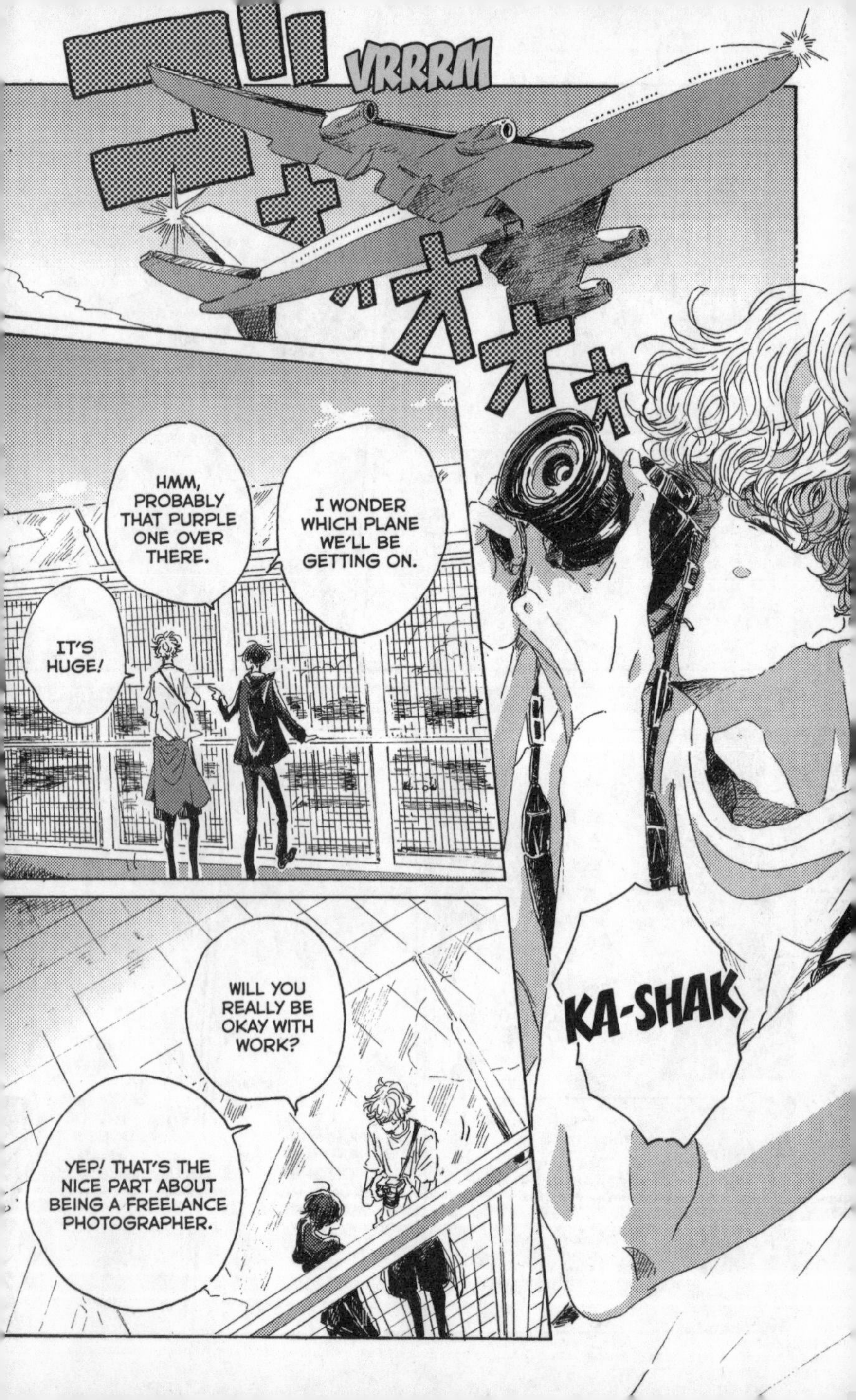
VRRRM
KA-SHAK
I WONDER WHICH PLANE WE'LL BE GETTING ON.
HMM, PROBABLY THAT PURPLE ONE OVER THERE.
IT'S HUGE!
WILL YOU REALLY BE OKAY WITH WORK?
YEP! THAT'S THE NICE PART ABOUT BEING A FREELANCE PHOTOGRAPHER.

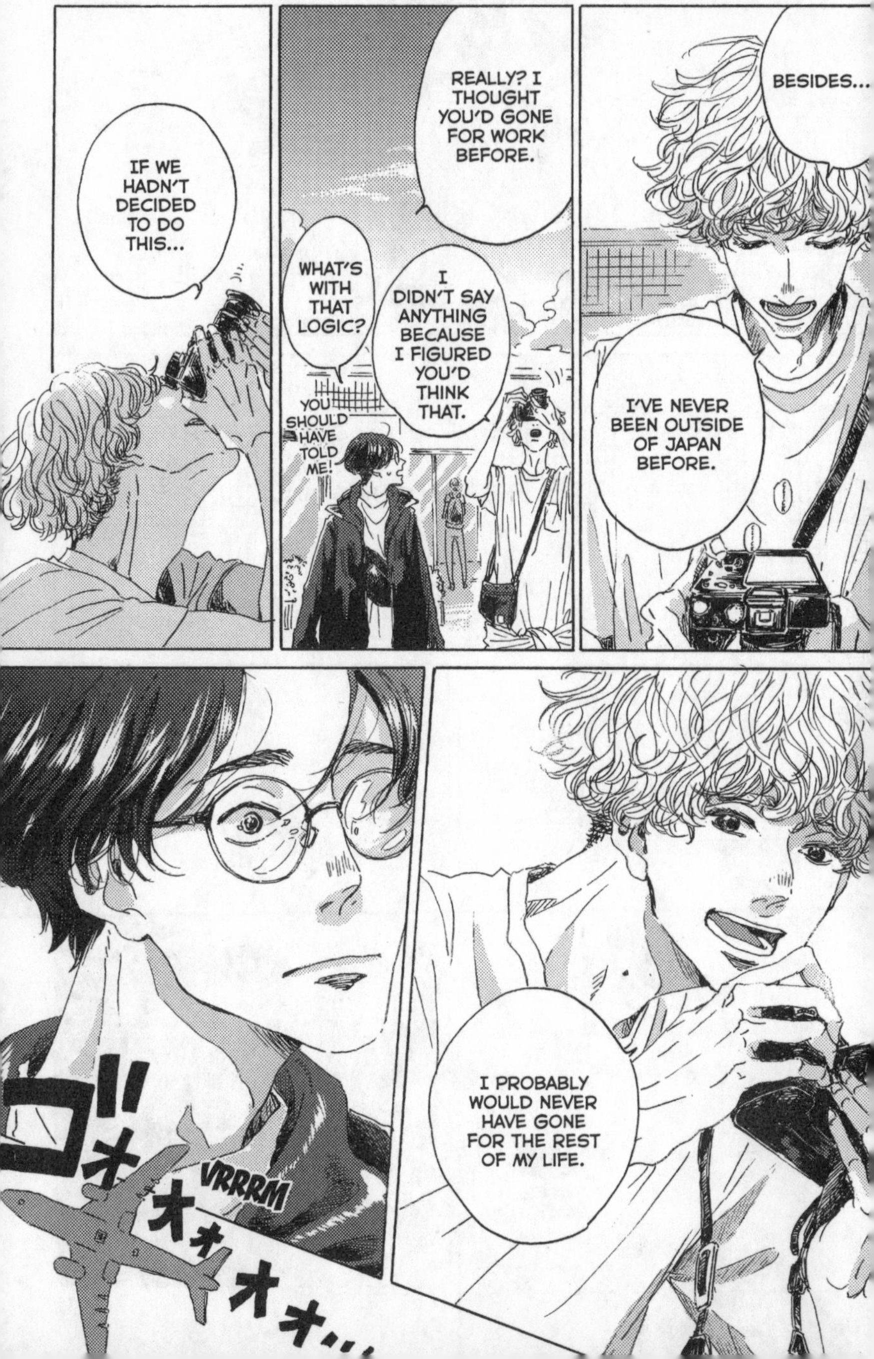
BESIDES...
I'VE NEVER BEEN OUTSIDE OF JAPAN BEFORE.
REALLY? I THOUGHT YOU'D GONE FOR WORK BEFORE.
YOU SHOULD HAVE TOLD ME!
I DIDN'T SAY ANYTHING BECAUSE I FIGURED YOU'D THINK THAT.
WHAT'S WITH THAT LOGIC?
IF WE HADN'T DECIDED TO DO THIS...
I PROBABLY WOULD NEVER HAVE GONE FOR THE REST OF MY LIFE.
VRRRM

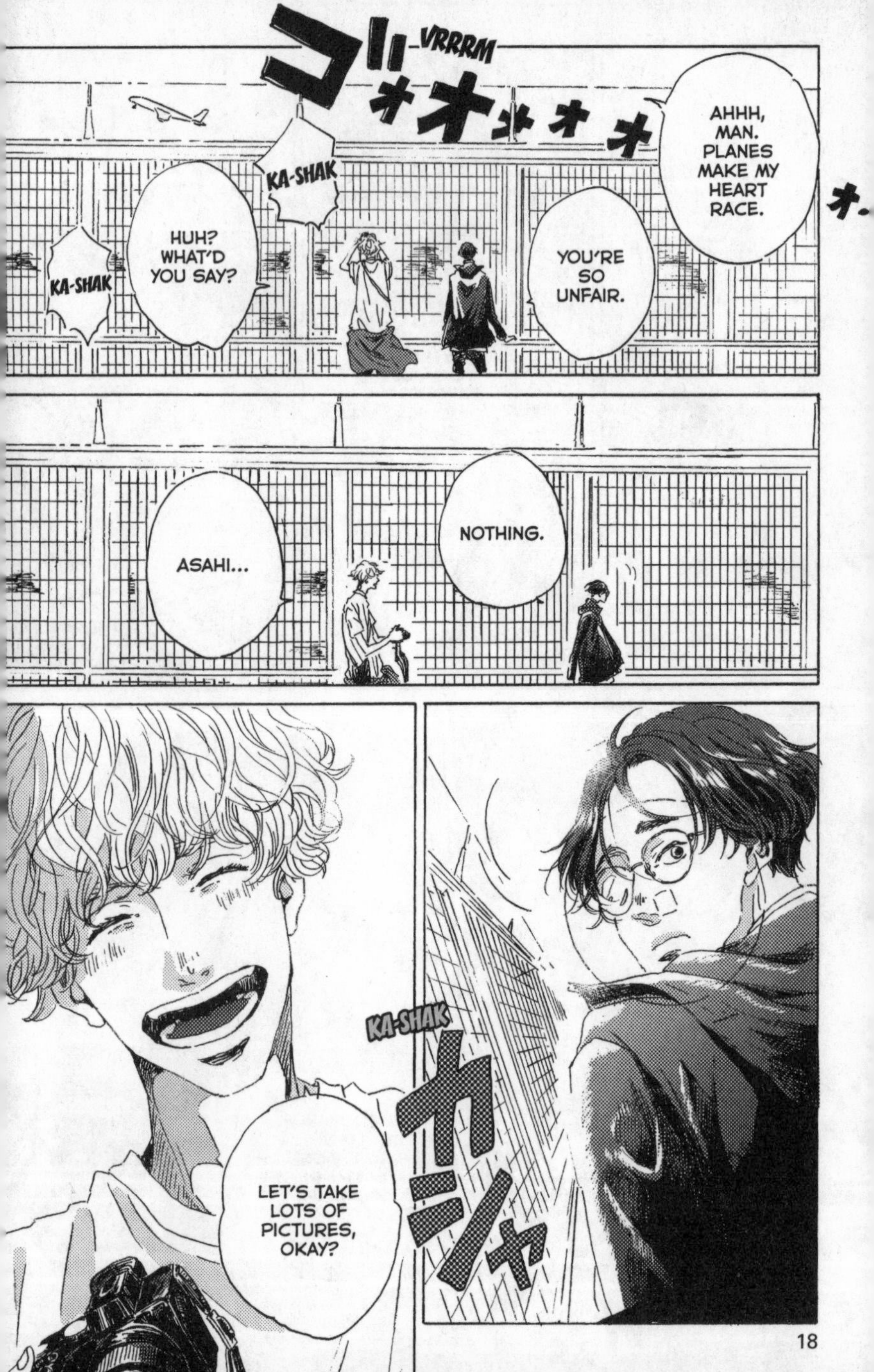
VRRRM
AHHH, MAN. PLANES MAKE MY HEART RACE.
YOU'RE SO UNFAIR.
KA-SHAK
HUH? WHAT'D YOU SAY?
KA-SHAK
NOTHING.
ASAHI...
KA-SHAK
LET'S TAKE LOTS OF PICTURES, OKAY?

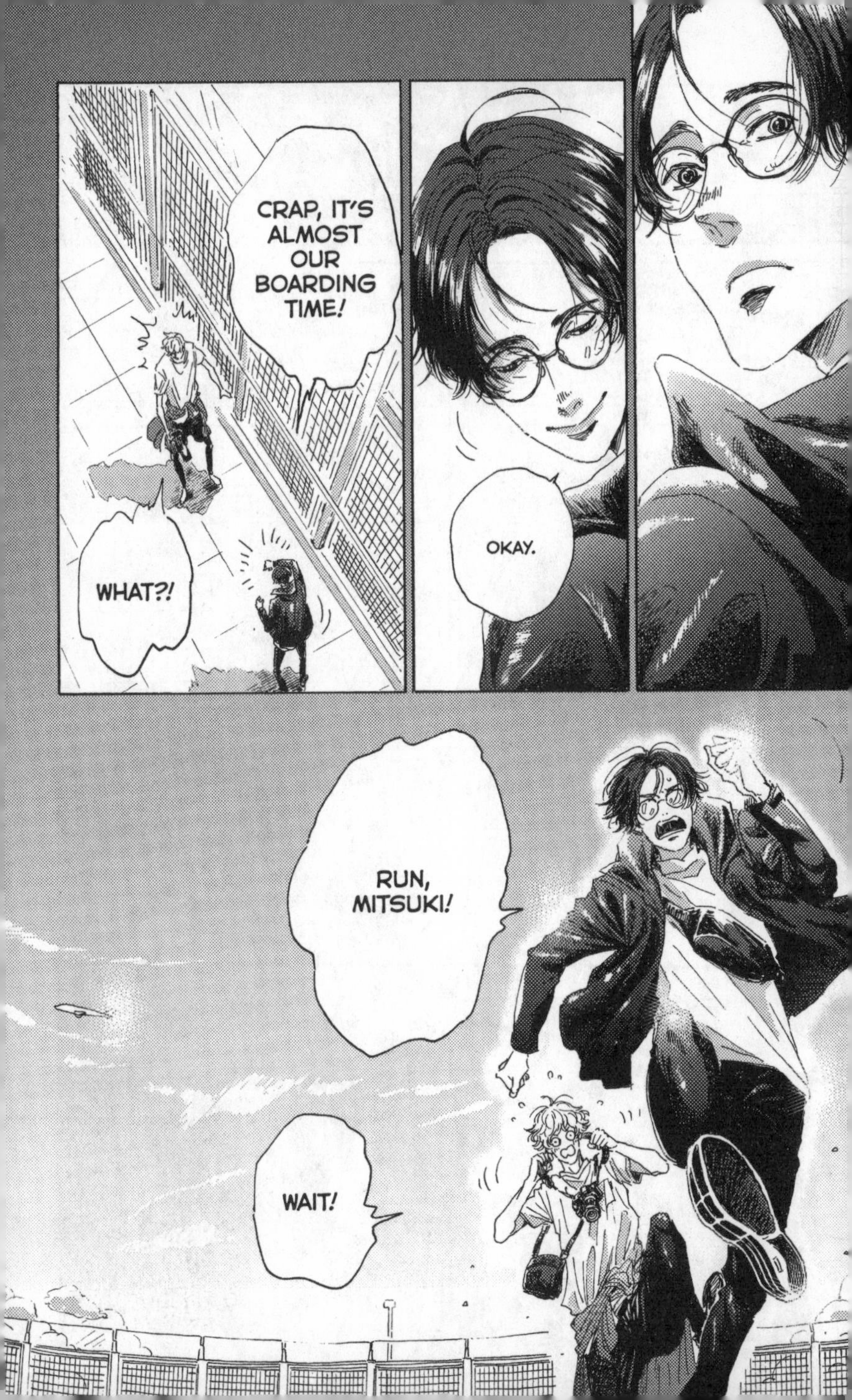
OKAY.
CRAP, IT'S ALMOST OUR BOARDING TIME!
WHAT?!
RUN, MITSUKI!
WAIT!

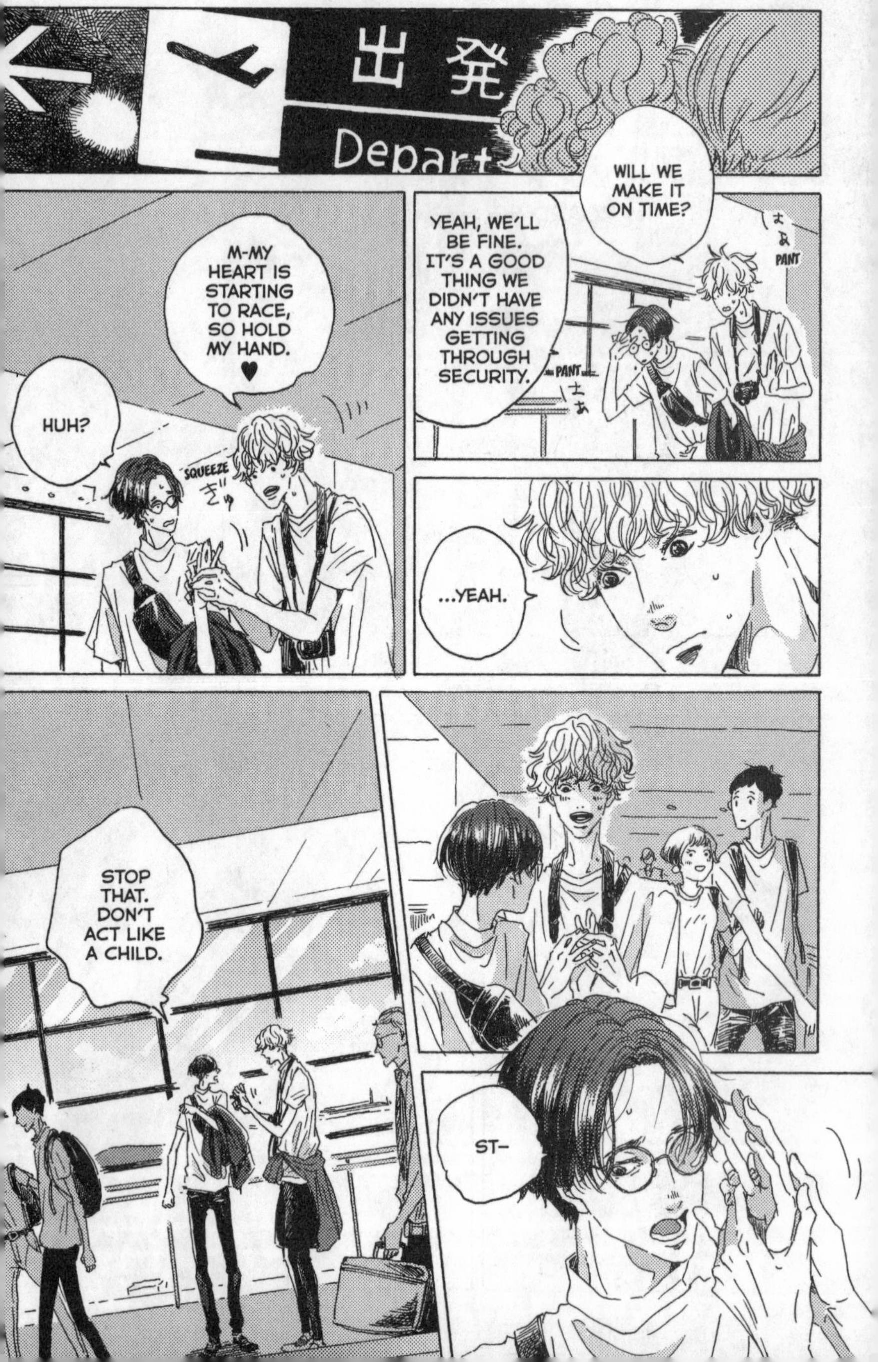
出発
Depart
WILL WE MAKE IT ON TIME?
はぁ
PANT
YEAH, WE'LL BE FINE. IT'S A GOOD THING WE DIDN'T HAVE ANY ISSUES GETTING THROUGH SECURITY.
PANT
はぁ
...YEAH.
M-MY HEART IS STARTING TO RACE, SO HOLD MY HAND. ♥
HUH?
SQUEEZE
ぎゅ
ST-
STOP THAT. DON'T ACT LIKE A CHILD.

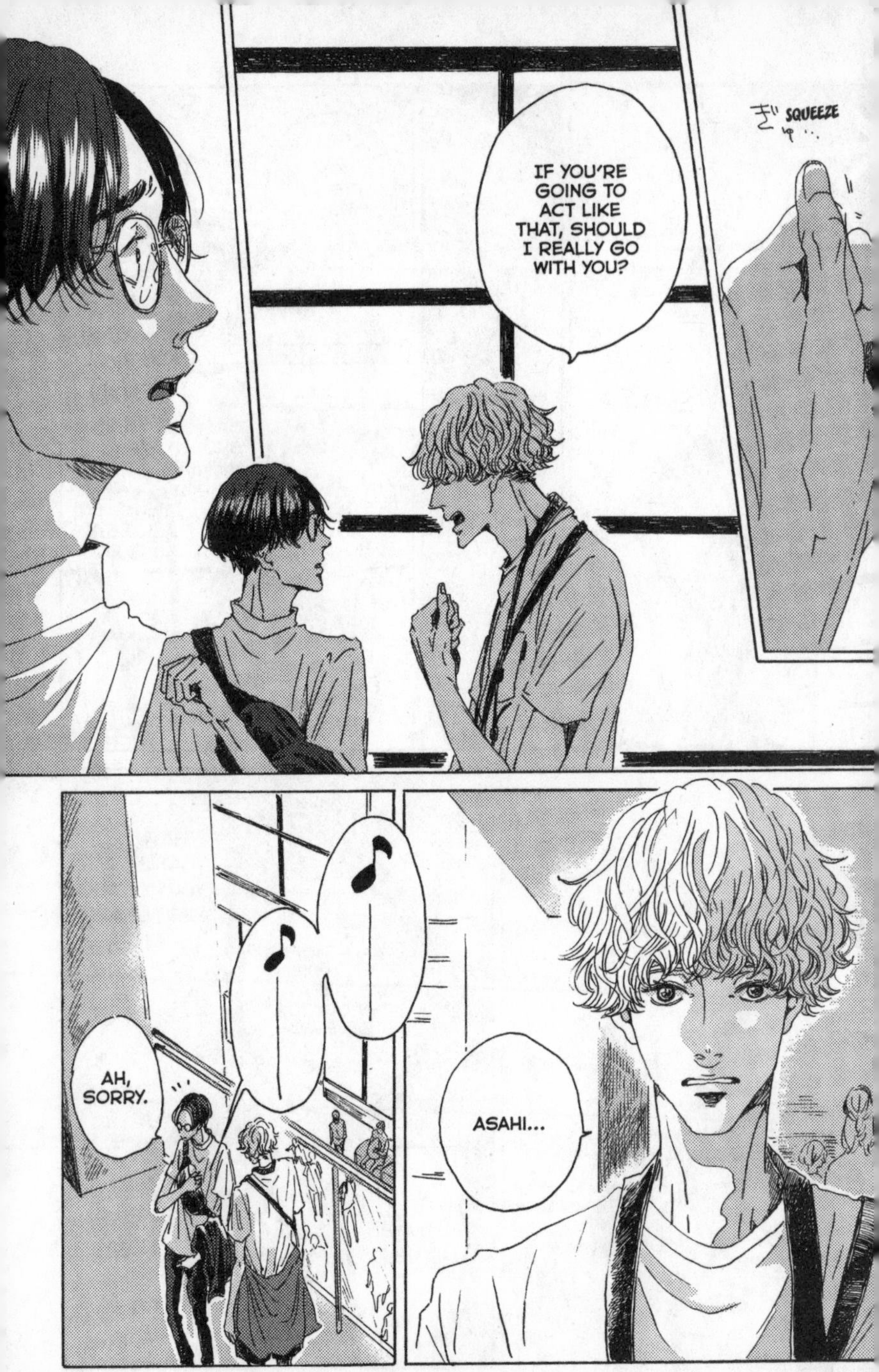
ぎゅ… SQUEEZE
IF YOU'RE GOING TO ACT LIKE THAT, SHOULD I REALLY GO WITH YOU?
ASAHI...
AH, SORRY.

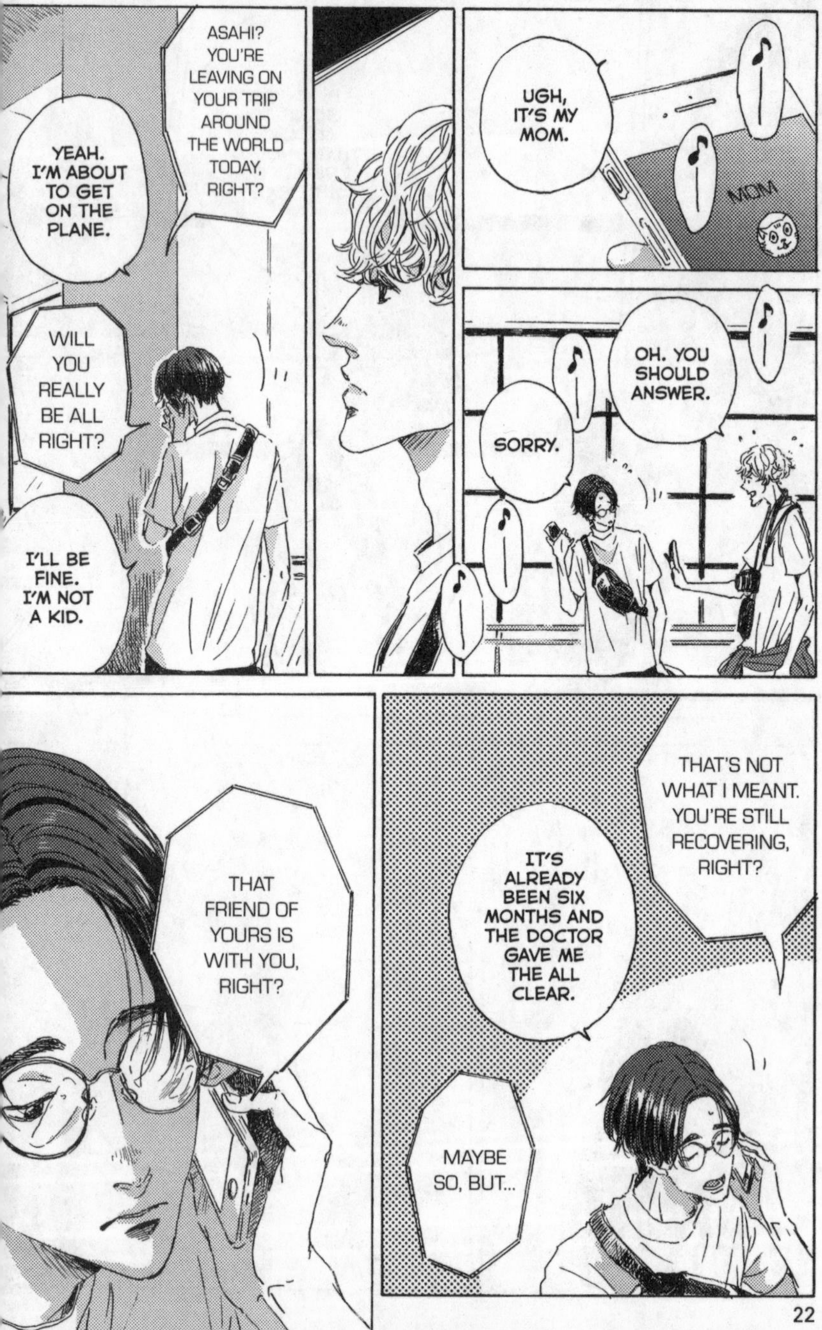
UGH, IT'S MY MOM.
MOM
OH. YOU SHOULD ANSWER.
SORRY.
ASAHI? YOU'RE LEAVING ON YOUR TRIP AROUND THE WORLD TODAY, RIGHT?
YEAH. I'M ABOUT TO GET ON THE PLANE.
WILL YOU REALLY BE ALL RIGHT?
I'LL BE FINE. I'M NOT A KID.
THAT'S NOT WHAT I MEANT. YOU'RE STILL RECOVERING, RIGHT?
IT'S ALREADY BEEN SIX MONTHS AND THE DOCTOR GAVE ME THE ALL CLEAR.
MAYBE SO, BUT...
THAT FRIEND OF YOURS IS WITH YOU, RIGHT?

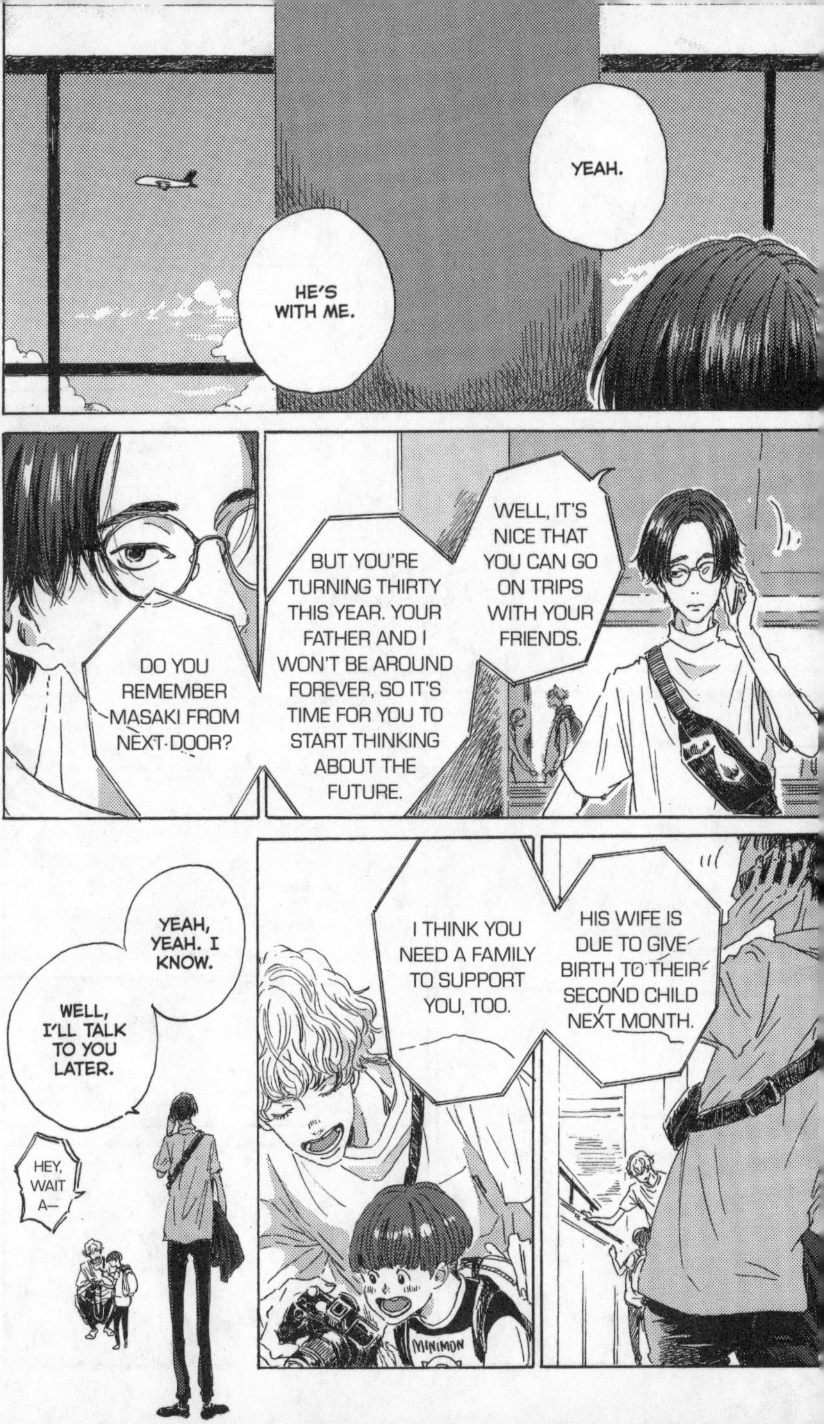
YEAH.
HE'S WITH ME.
WELL, IT'S NICE THAT YOU CAN GO ON TRIPS WITH YOUR FRIENDS.
BUT YOU'RE TURNING THIRTY THIS YEAR. YOUR FATHER AND I WON'T BE AROUND FOREVER, SO IT'S TIME FOR YOU TO START THINKING ABOUT THE FUTURE.
DO YOU REMEMBER MASAKI FROM NEXT DOOR?
HIS WIFE IS DUE TO GIVE BIRTH TO THEIR SECOND CHILD NEXT MONTH.
I THINK YOU NEED A FAMILY TO SUPPORT YOU, TOO.
YEAH, YEAH. I KNOW.
WELL, I'LL TALK TO YOU LATER.
HEY, WAIT A—
MINIMON

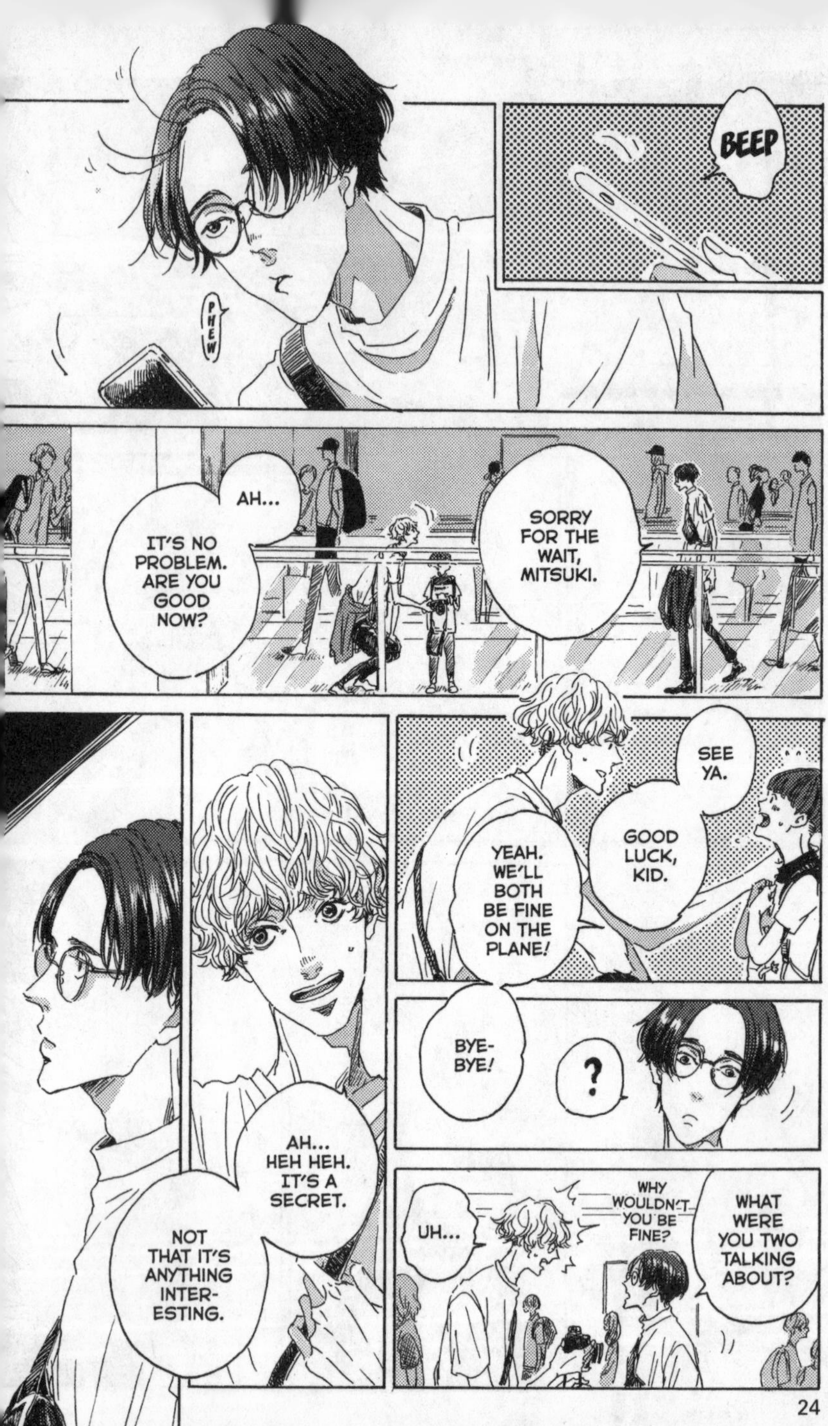
BEEP
PHEW
SORRY FOR THE WAIT, MITSUKI.
AH...
IT'S NO PROBLEM. ARE YOU GOOD NOW?
SEE YA.
GOOD LUCK, KID.
YEAH. WE'LL BOTH BE FINE ON THE PLANE!
BYE-BYE!
?
WHAT WERE YOU TWO TALKING ABOUT?
WHY WOULDN'T YOU BE FINE?
UH...
AH... HEH HEH. IT'S A SECRET.
NOT THAT IT'S ANYTHING INTER-ESTING.

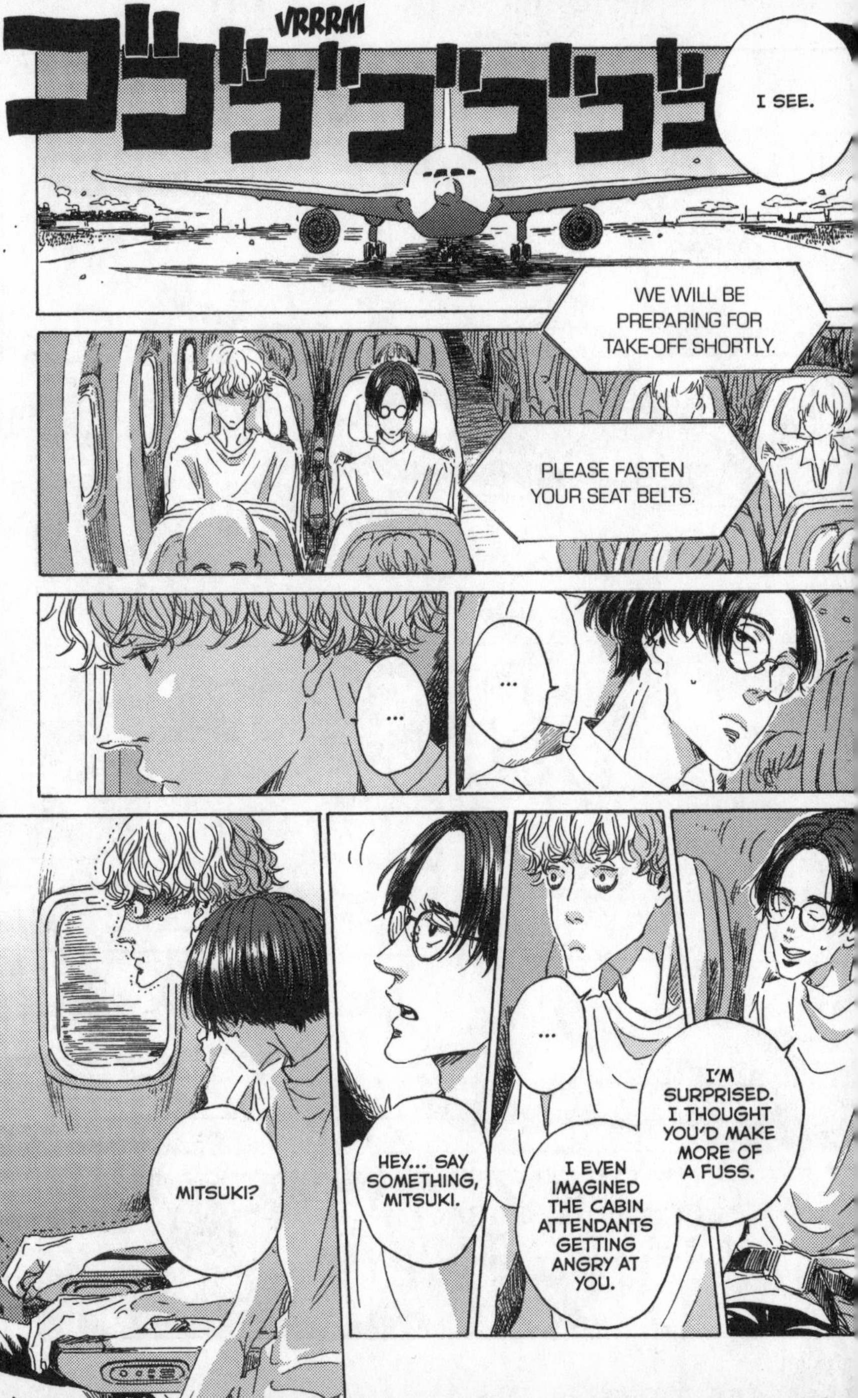
I SEE.
VRRRM
WE WILL BE PREPARING FOR TAKE-OFF SHORTLY.
PLEASE FASTEN YOUR SEAT BELTS.
...
...
I'M SURPRISED. I THOUGHT YOU'D MAKE MORE OF A FUSS.
...
I EVEN IMAGINED THE CABIN ATTENDANTS GETTING ANGRY AT YOU.
HEY... SAY SOMETHING, MITSUKI.
MITSUKI?

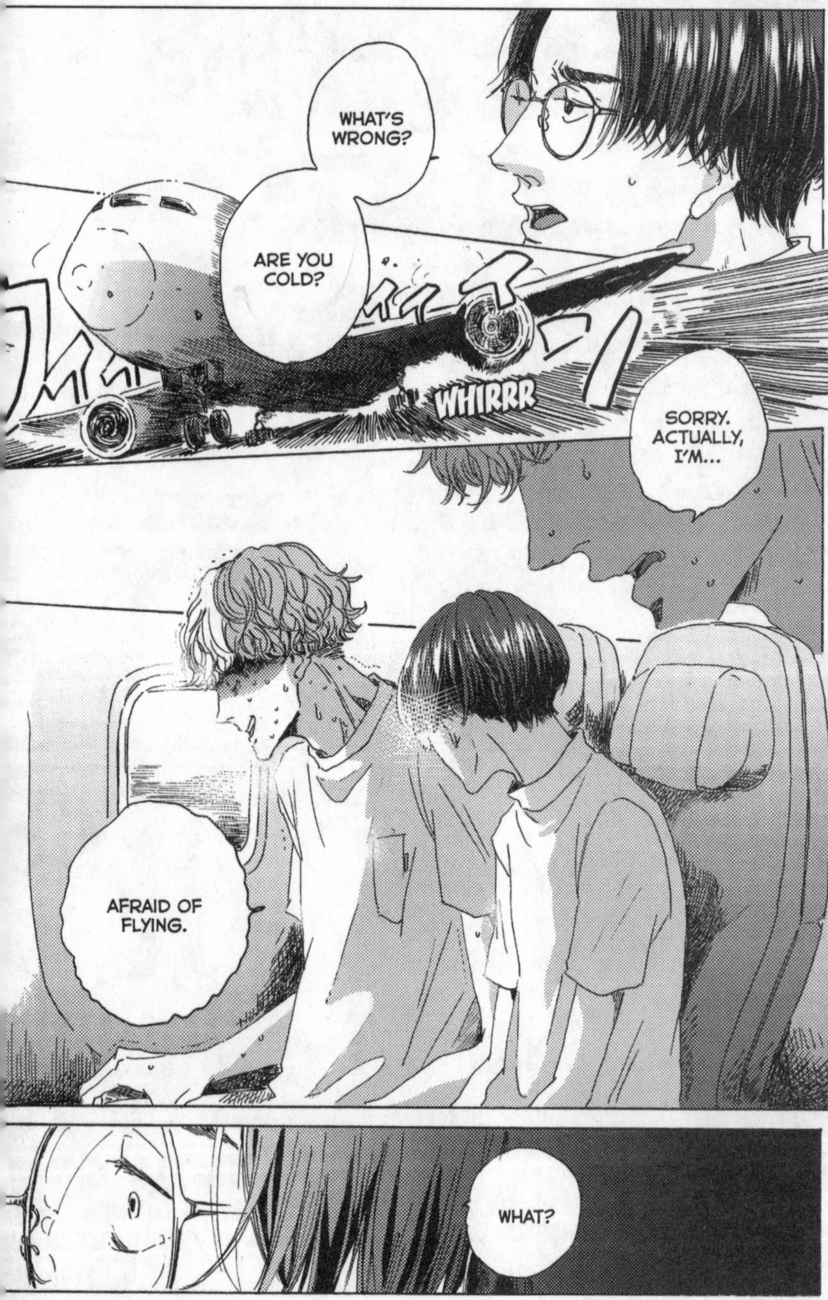
WHAT'S WRONG?
ARE YOU COLD?
WHIRRR
SORRY. ACTUALLY, I'M...
AFRAID OF FLYING.
WHAT?

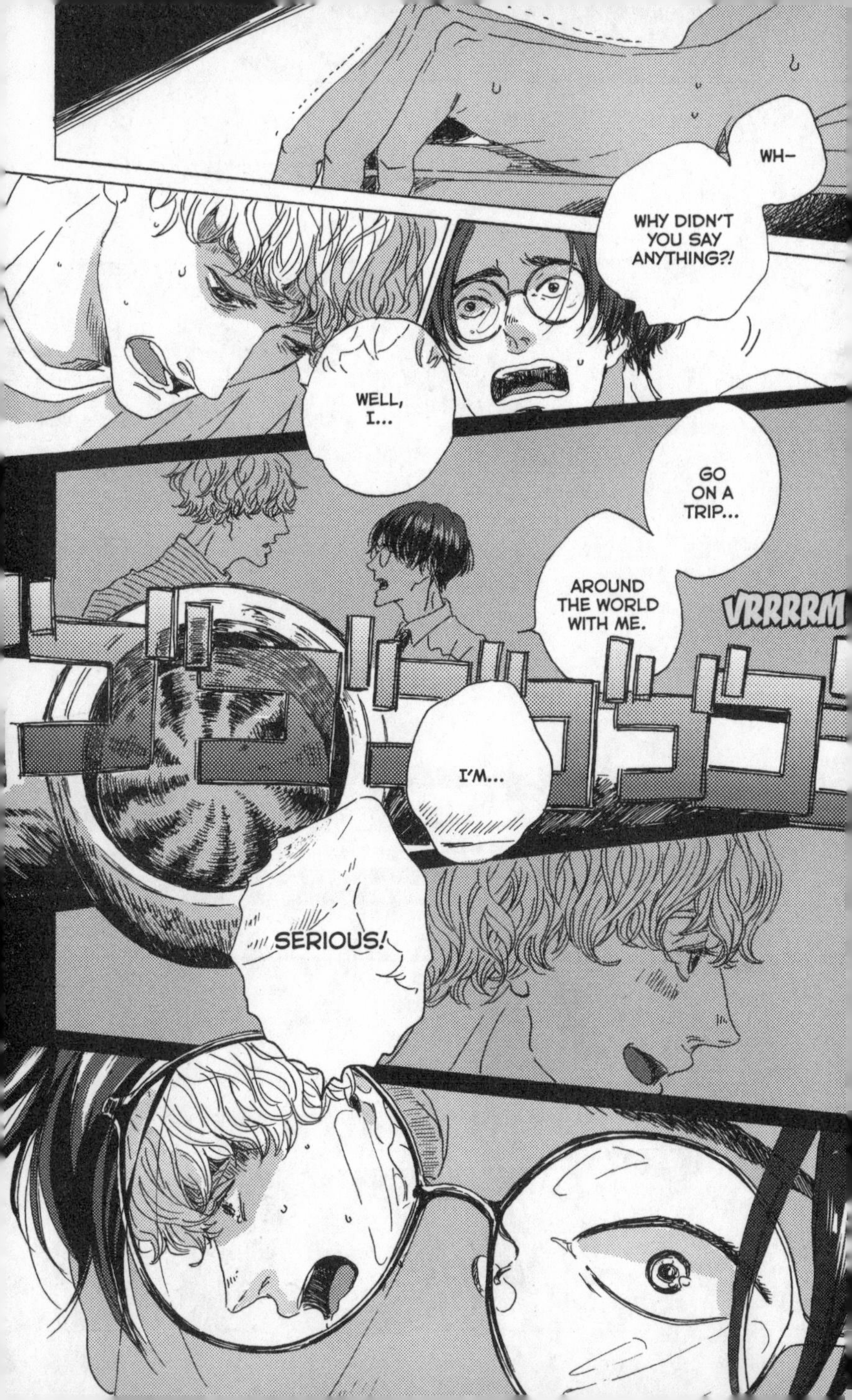
WH-
WHY DIDN'T YOU SAY ANYTHING?!
WELL, I...
GO ON A TRIP...
AROUND THE WORLD WITH ME.
VRRRRM
I'M...
SERIOUS!

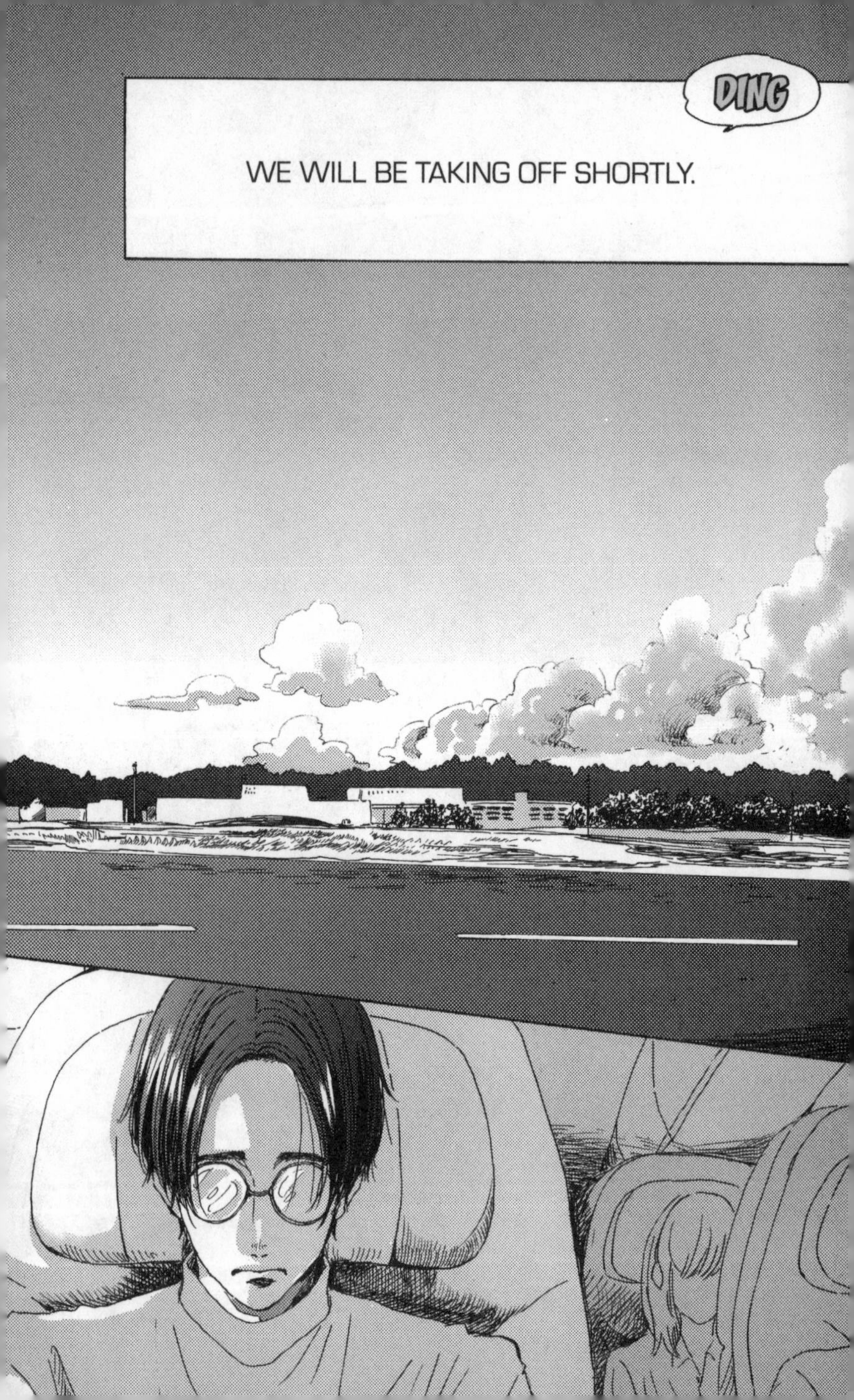
DING
WE WILL BE TAKING OFF SHORTLY.

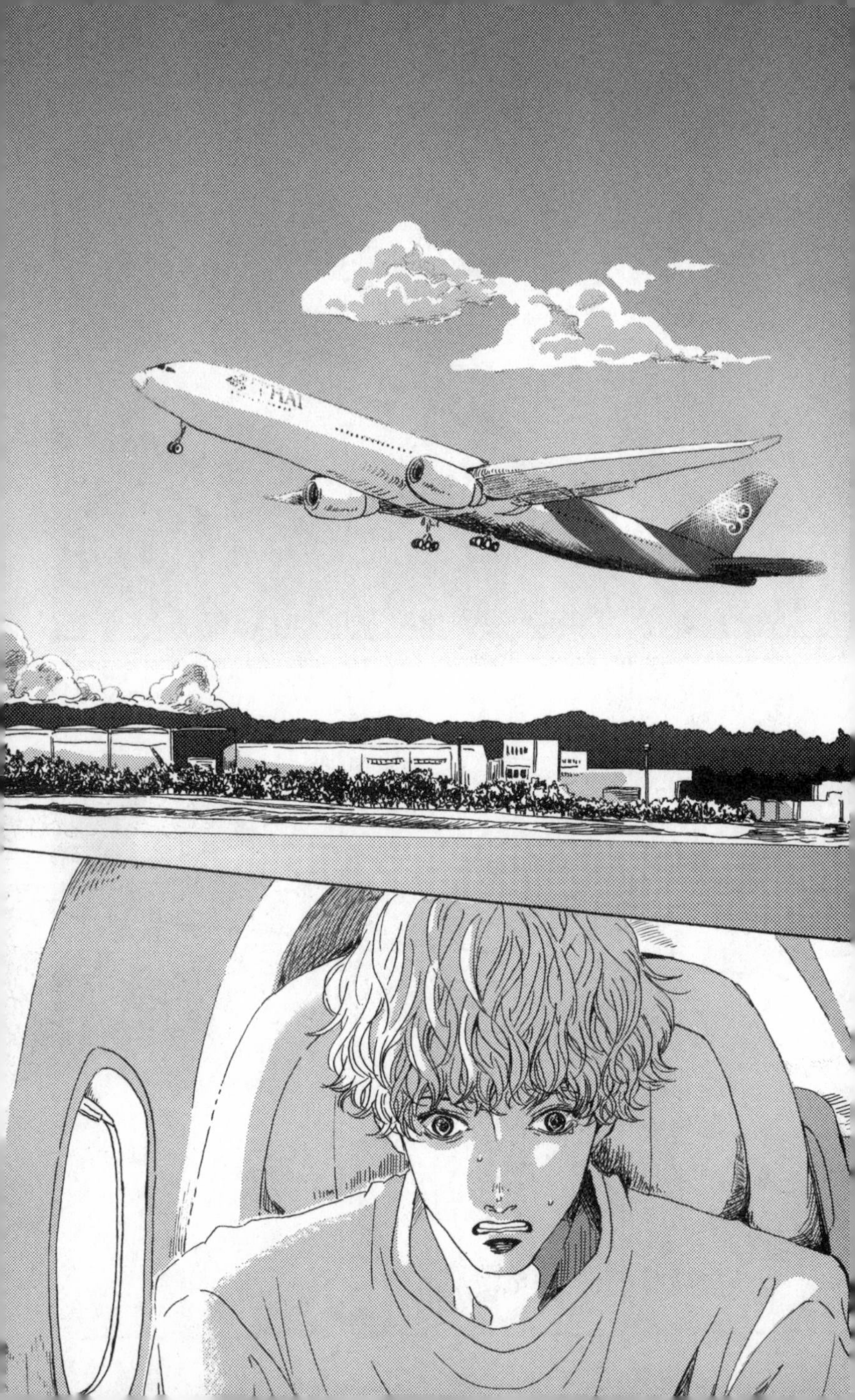

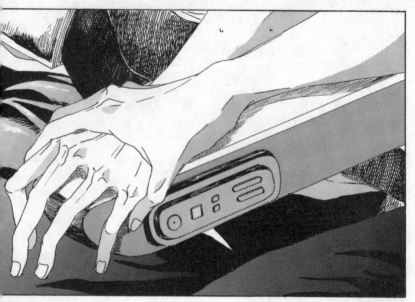

IF WE DIE,
IT'LL BE
TOGETHER.

DON'T
WORRY.

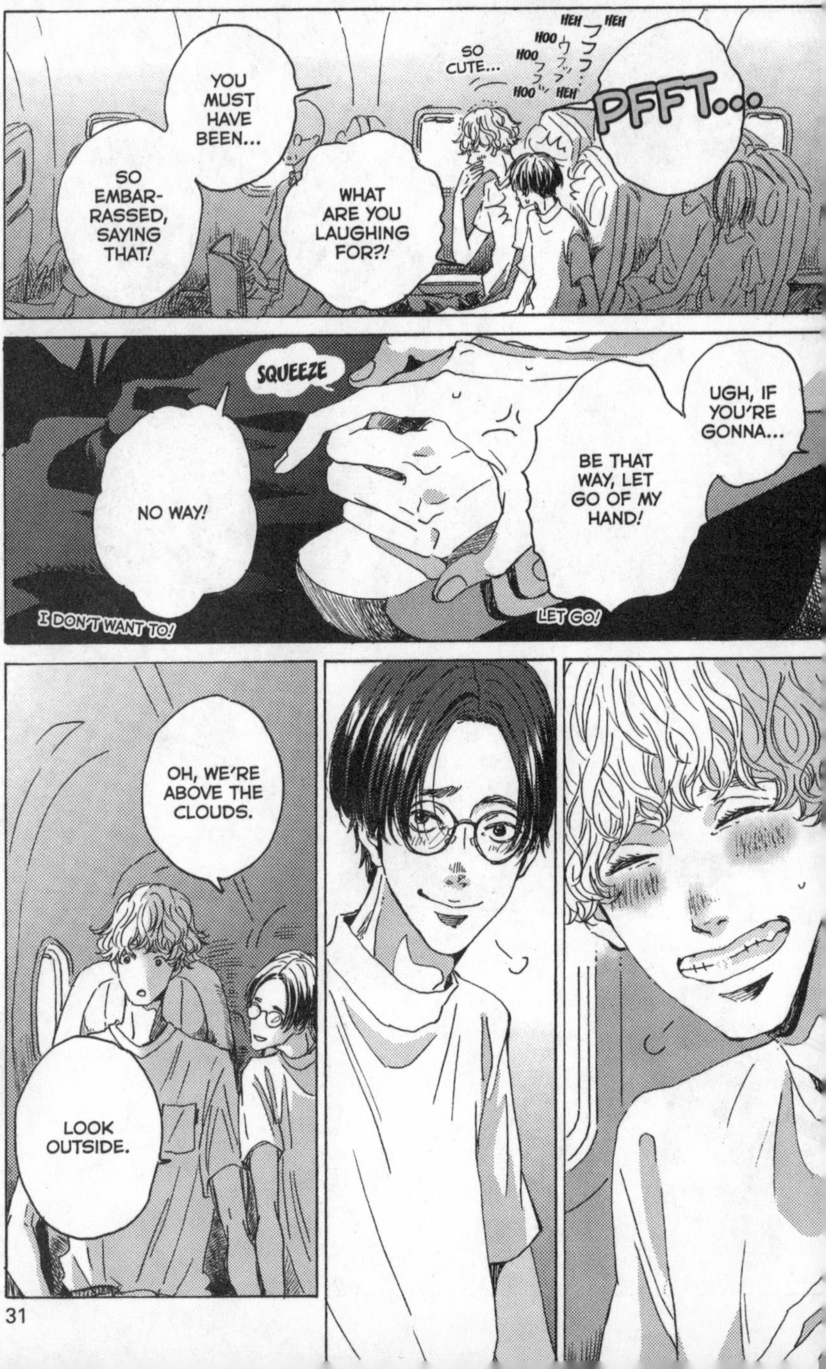
HEH HEH
HOO HOO HOO HEH
PFFT...
SO CUTE...
WHAT ARE YOU LAUGHING FOR?!
YOU MUST HAVE BEEN...
SO EMBARRASSED, SAYING THAT!
UGH, IF YOU'RE GONNA...
BE THAT WAY, LET GO OF MY HAND!
LET GO!
SQUEEZE
NO WAY!
I DON'T WANT TO!
OH, WE'RE ABOVE THE CLOUDS.
LOOK OUTSIDE.

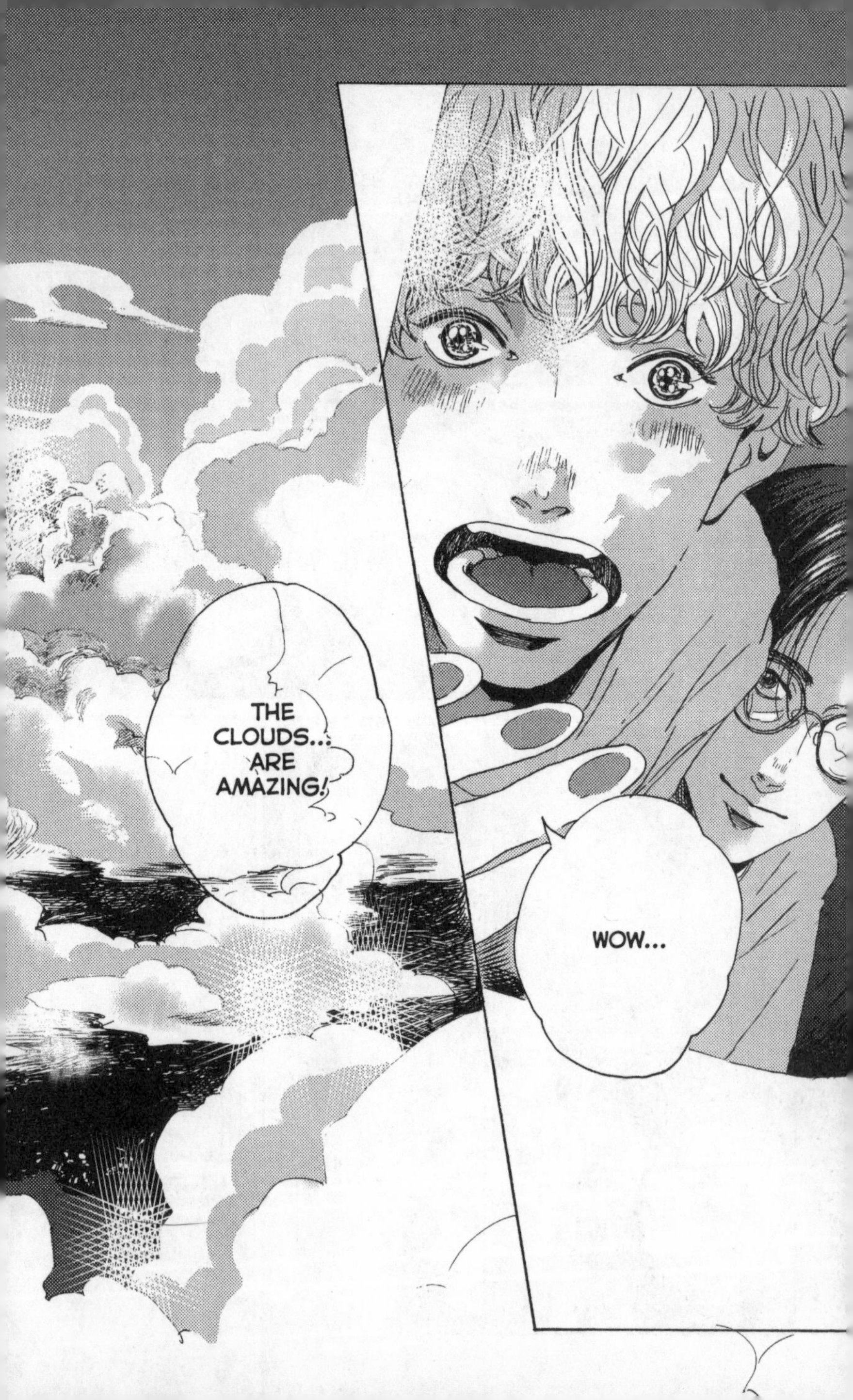
WOW...
THE CLOUDS... ARE AMAZING!

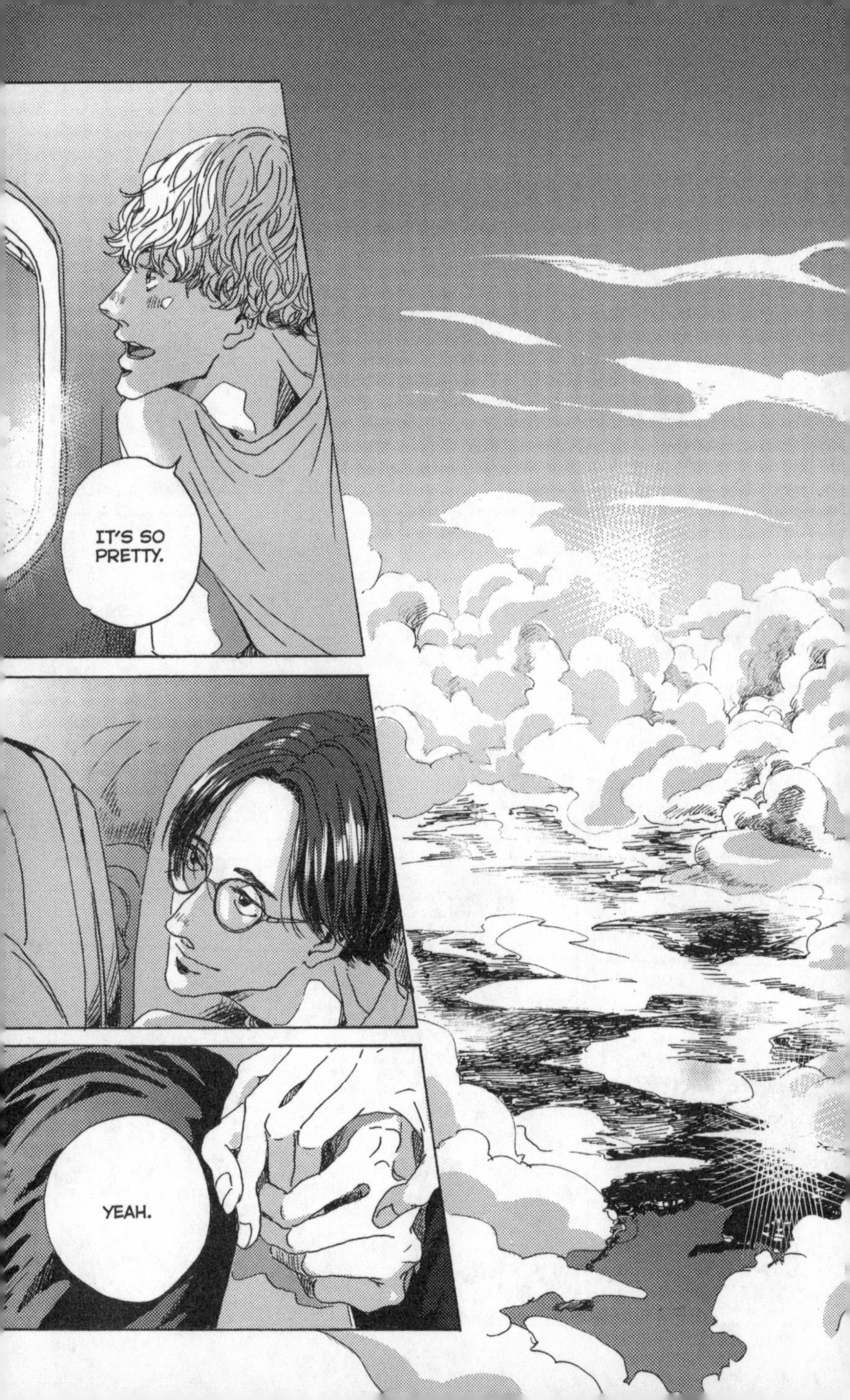
IT'S SO PRETTY.
YEAH.

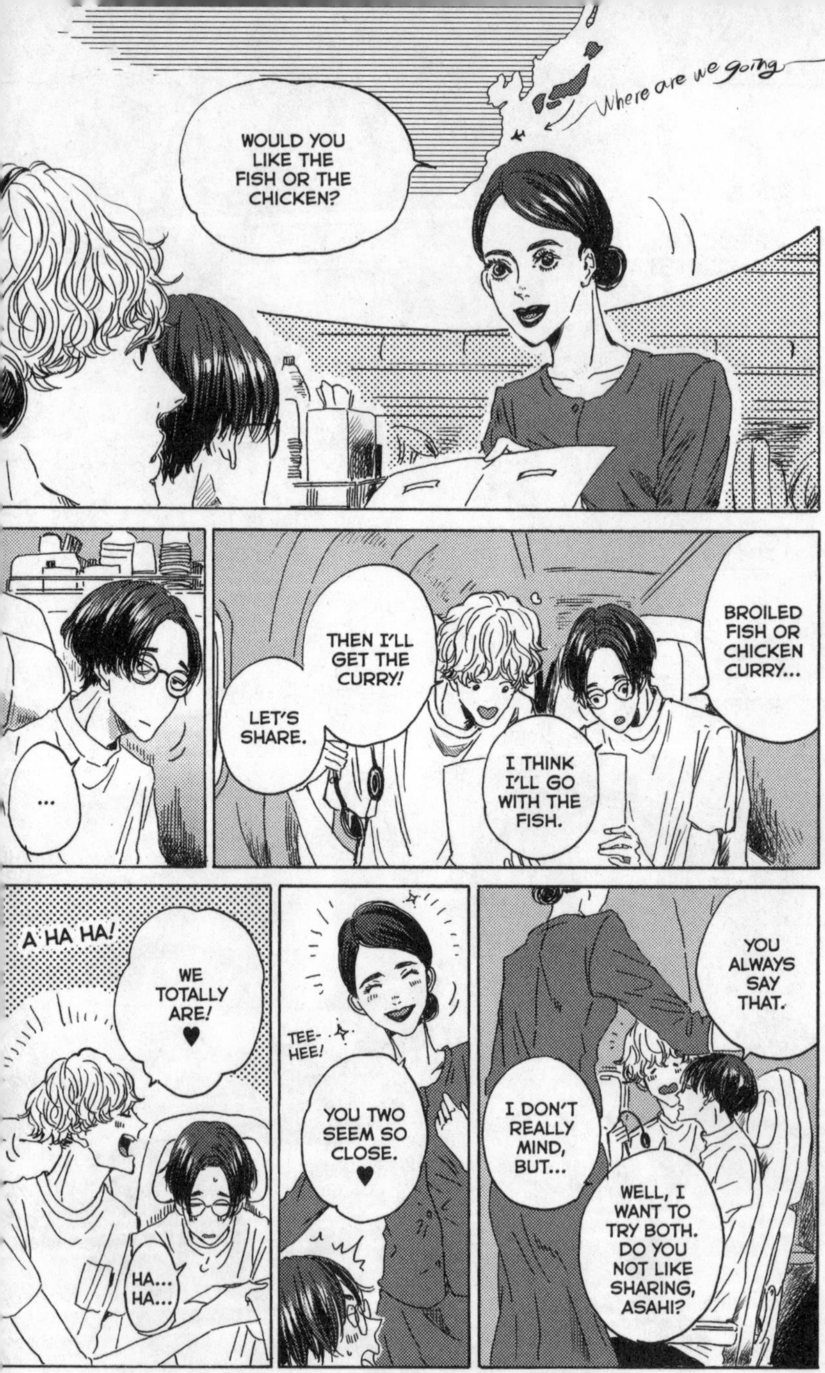
Where are we going
WOULD YOU LIKE THE FISH OR THE CHICKEN?
BROILED FISH OR CHICKEN CURRY...
I THINK I'LL GO WITH THE FISH.
THEN I'LL GET THE CURRY!
LET'S SHARE.
...
YOU ALWAYS SAY THAT.
I DON'T REALLY MIND, BUT...
WELL, I WANT TO TRY BOTH. DO YOU NOT LIKE SHARING, ASAHI?
TEE-HEE!
YOU TWO SEEM SO CLOSE. ♥
A HA HA!
WE TOTALLY ARE! ♥
HA... HA...

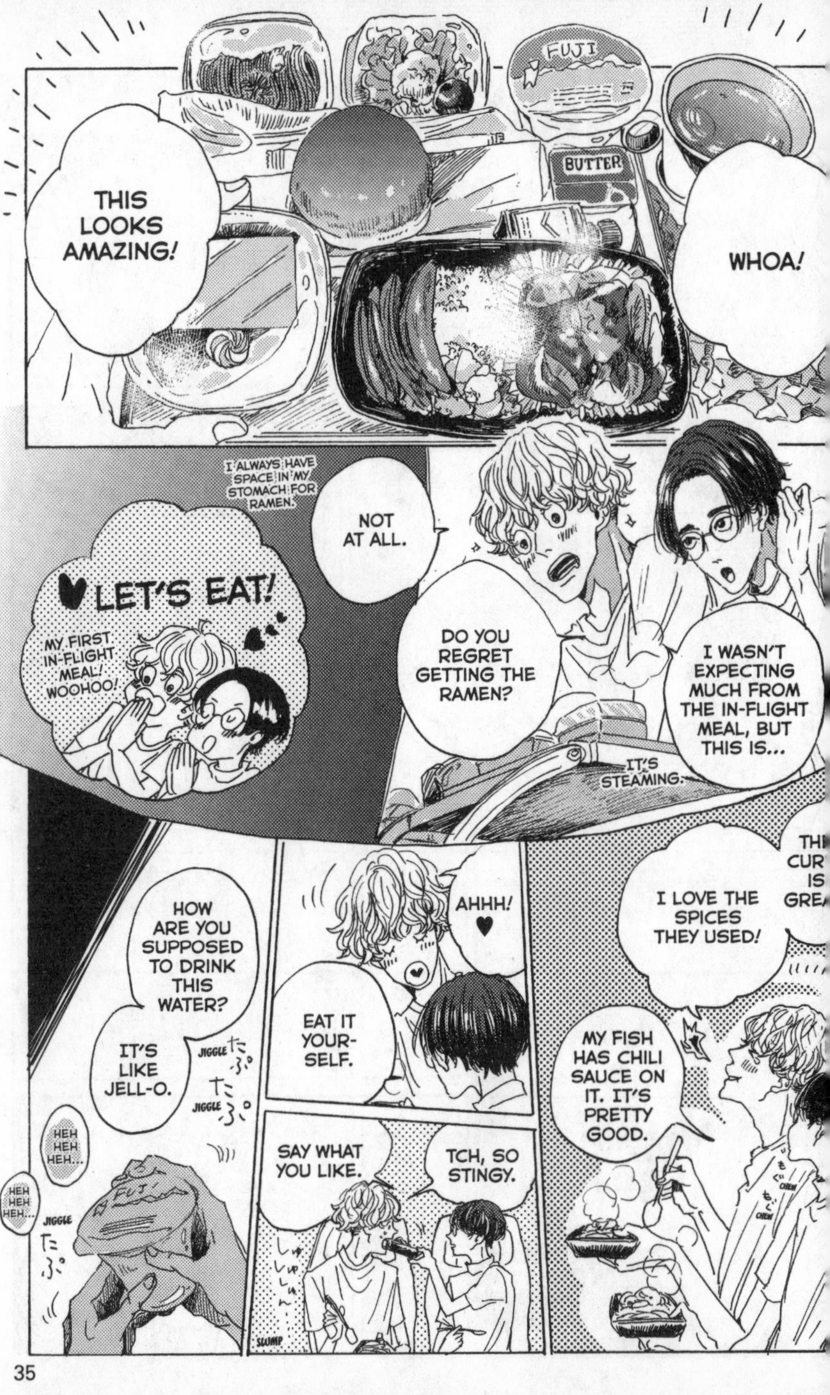
WHOA!
THIS LOOKS AMAZING!
I WASN'T EXPECTING MUCH FROM THE IN-FLIGHT MEAL, BUT THIS IS...
IT'S STEAMING.
DO YOU REGRET GETTING THE RAMEN?
NOT AT ALL.
I ALWAYS HAVE SPACE IN MY STOMACH FOR RAMEN.
♥ LET'S EAT!
MY FIRST IN-FLIGHT MEAL! WOOHOO!
I LOVE THE SPICES THEY USED!
MY FISH HAS CHILI SAUCE ON IT. IT'S PRETTY GOOD.
CHEW
CHEW
AHHH! ♥
EAT IT YOURSELF.
TCH, SO STINGY.
SAY WHAT YOU LIKE.
SLUMP
HOW ARE YOU SUPPOSED TO DRINK THIS WATER?
IT'S LIKE JELL-O.
JIGGLE
JIGGLE
HEH HEH HEH...
HEH HEH HEH...
JIGGLE

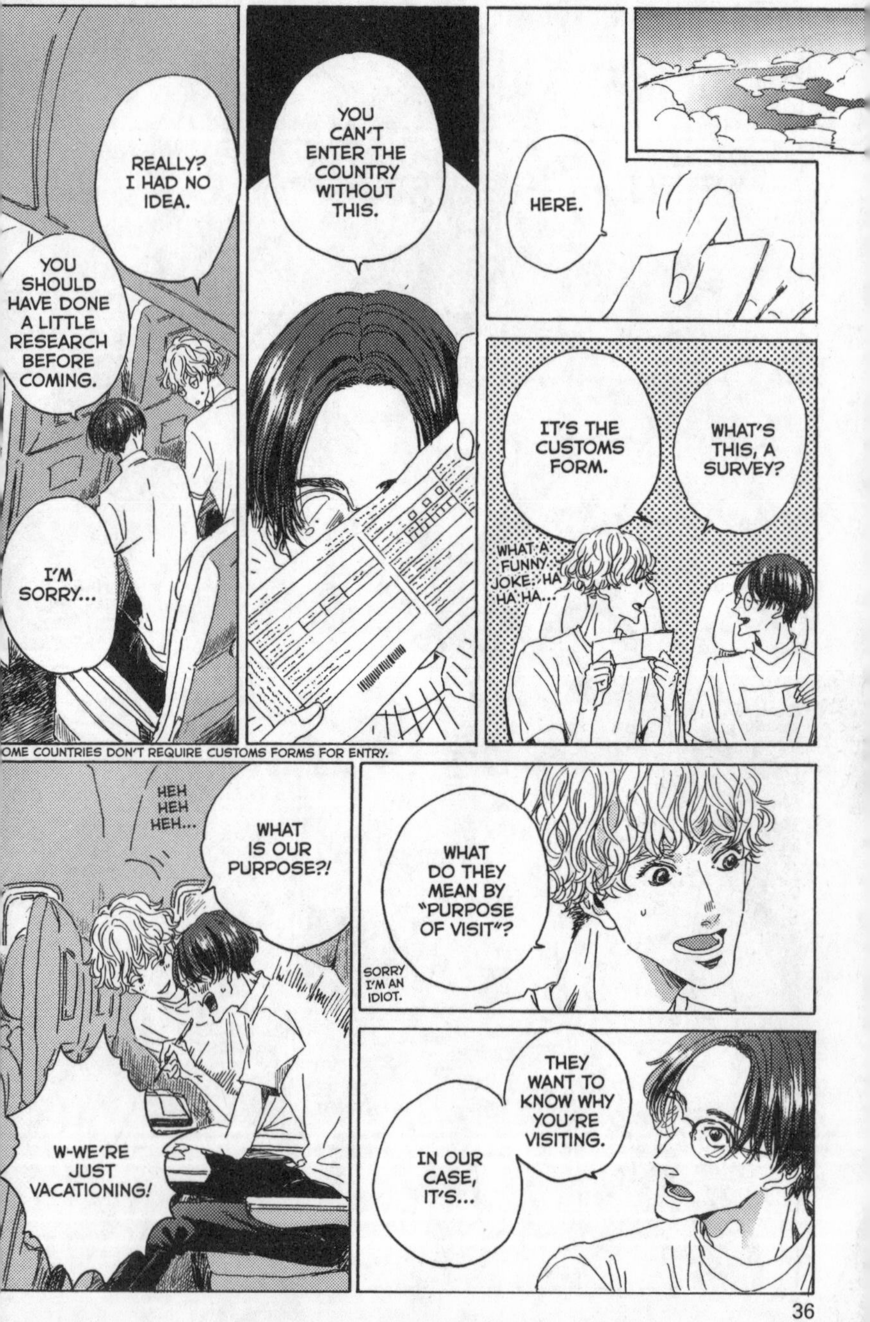
HERE.
WHAT'S THIS, A SURVEY?
IT'S THE CUSTOMS FORM.
WHAT A FUNNY JOKE. HA HA HA...
YOU CAN'T ENTER THE COUNTRY WITHOUT THIS.
REALLY? I HAD NO IDEA.
YOU SHOULD HAVE DONE A LITTLE RESEARCH BEFORE COMING.
I'M SORRY...
WHAT DO THEY MEAN BY "PURPOSE OF VISIT"?
SORRY I'M AN IDIOT.
THEY WANT TO KNOW WHY YOU'RE VISITING.
IN OUR CASE, IT'S...
WHAT IS OUR PURPOSE?!
HEH HEH HEH...
W-WE'RE JUST VACATIONING!

OME COUNTRIES DON'T REQUIRE CUSTOMS FORMS FOR ENTRY.

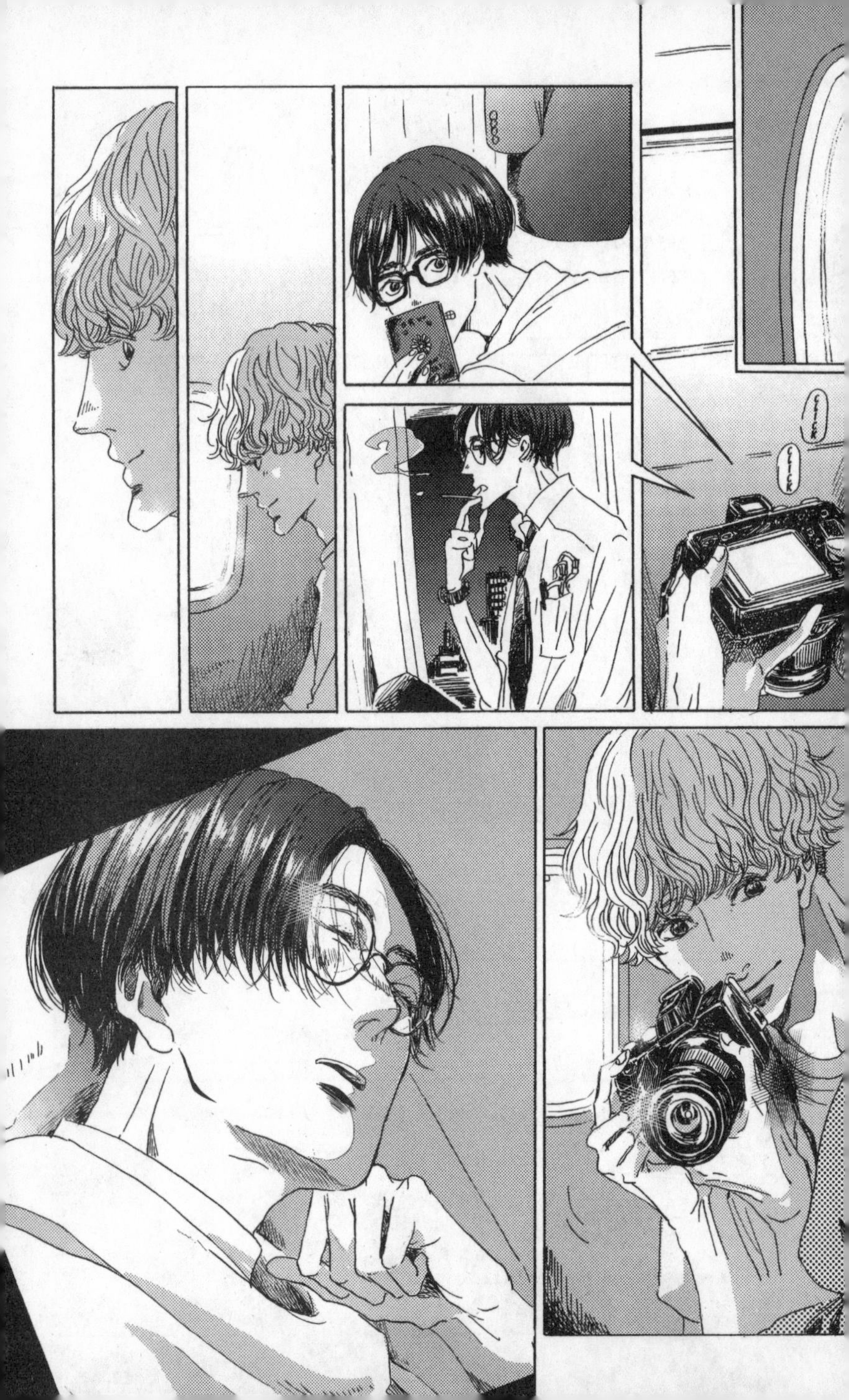
CLICK
CLICK

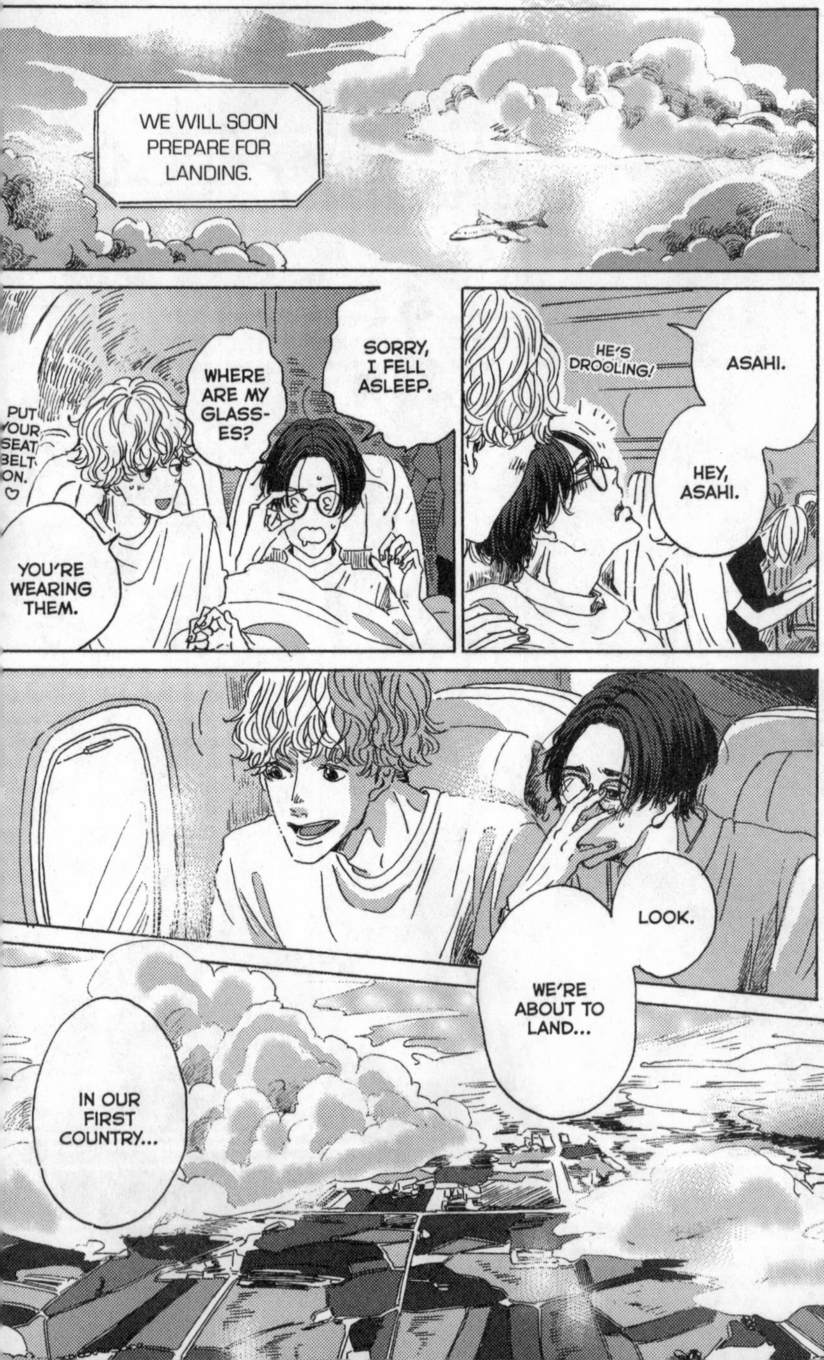
WE WILL SOON PREPARE FOR LANDING.
ASAHI.
HEY, ASAHI.
HE'S DROOLING!
SORRY, I FELL ASLEEP.
WHERE ARE MY GLASSES?
PUT YOUR SEAT BELT ON. ♡
YOU'RE WEARING THEM.
LOOK.
WE'RE ABOUT TO LAND...
IN OUR FIRST COUNTRY...

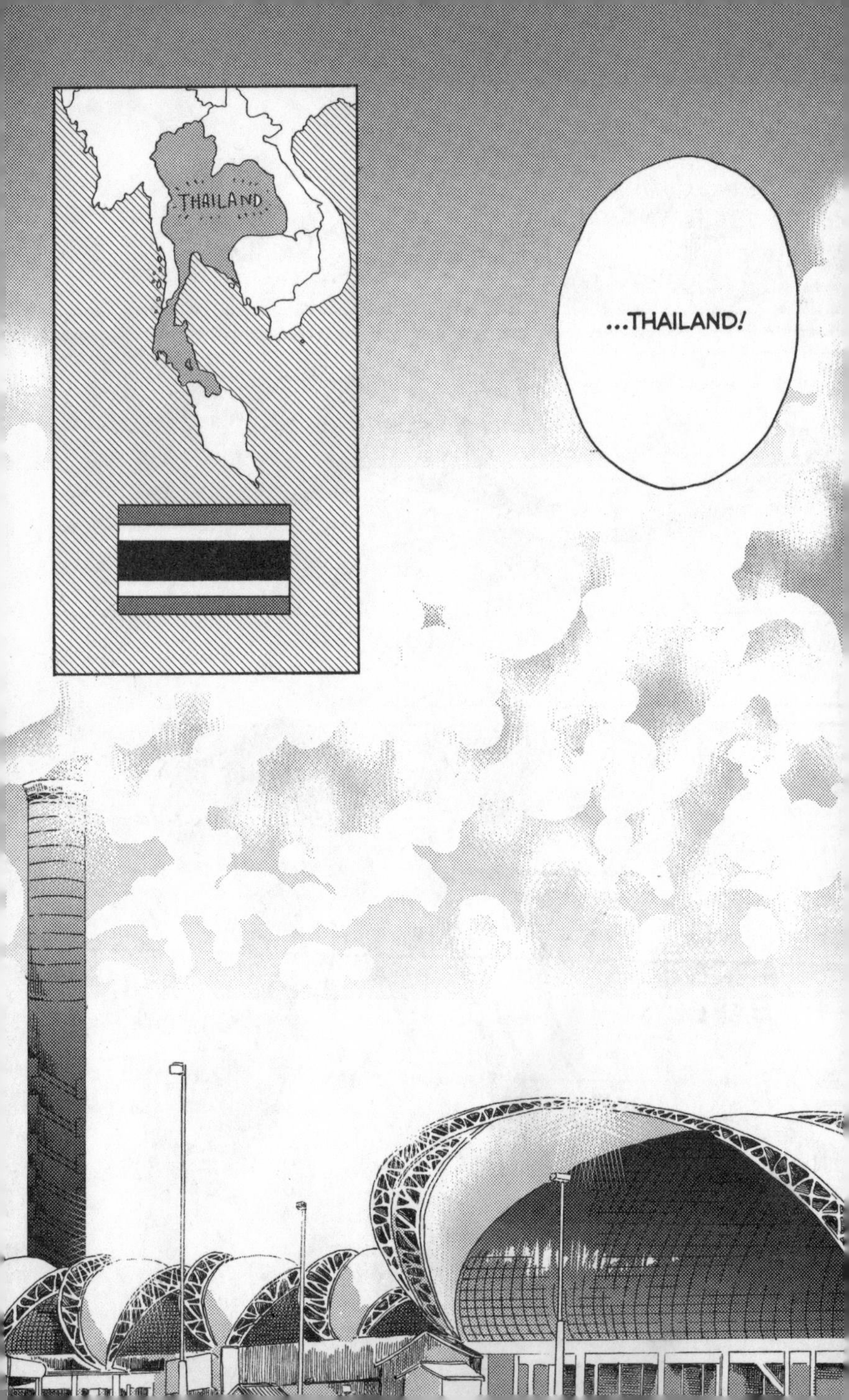
...THAILAND!
THAILAND

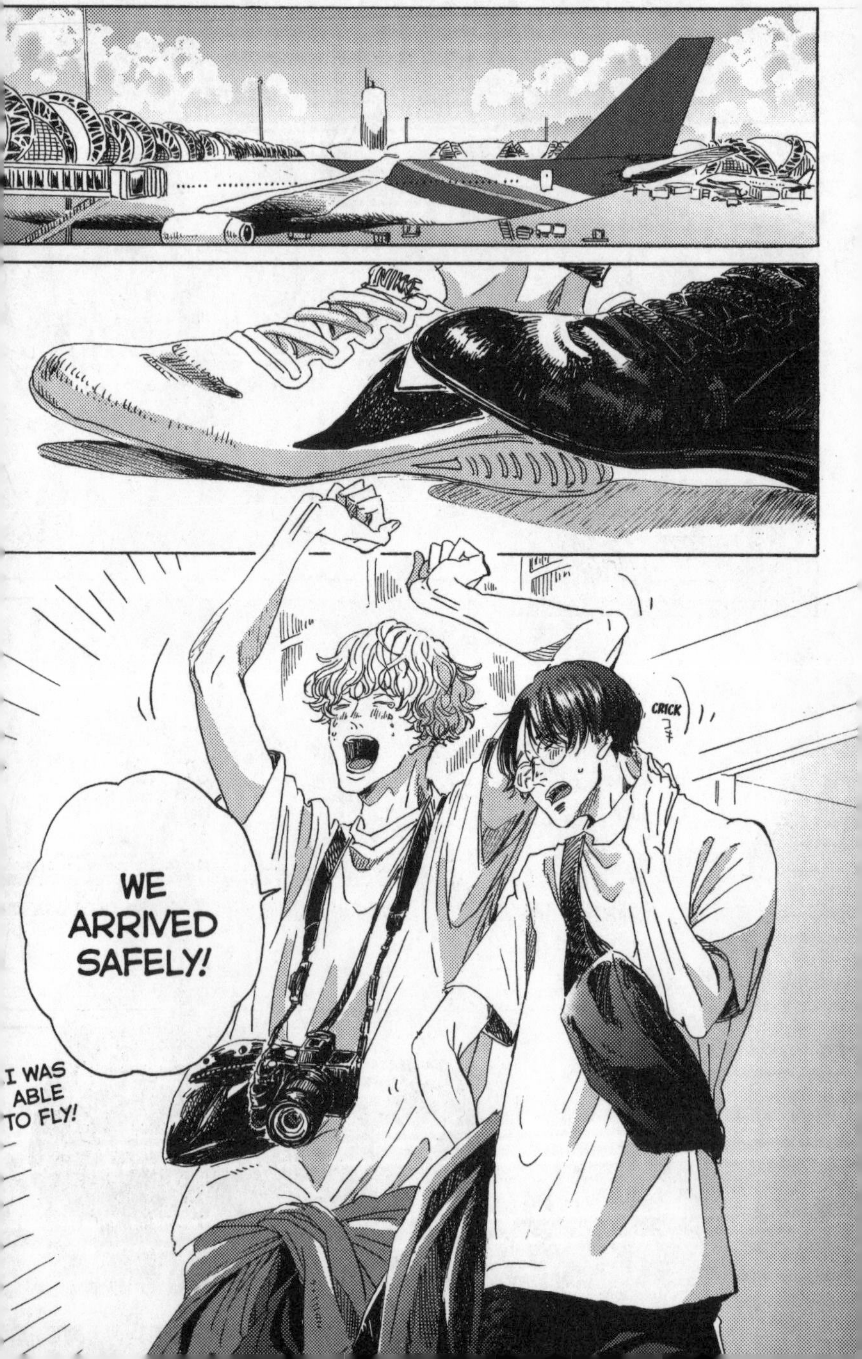
CRICK
コキ
WE ARRIVED SAFELY!
I WAS ABLE TO FLY!

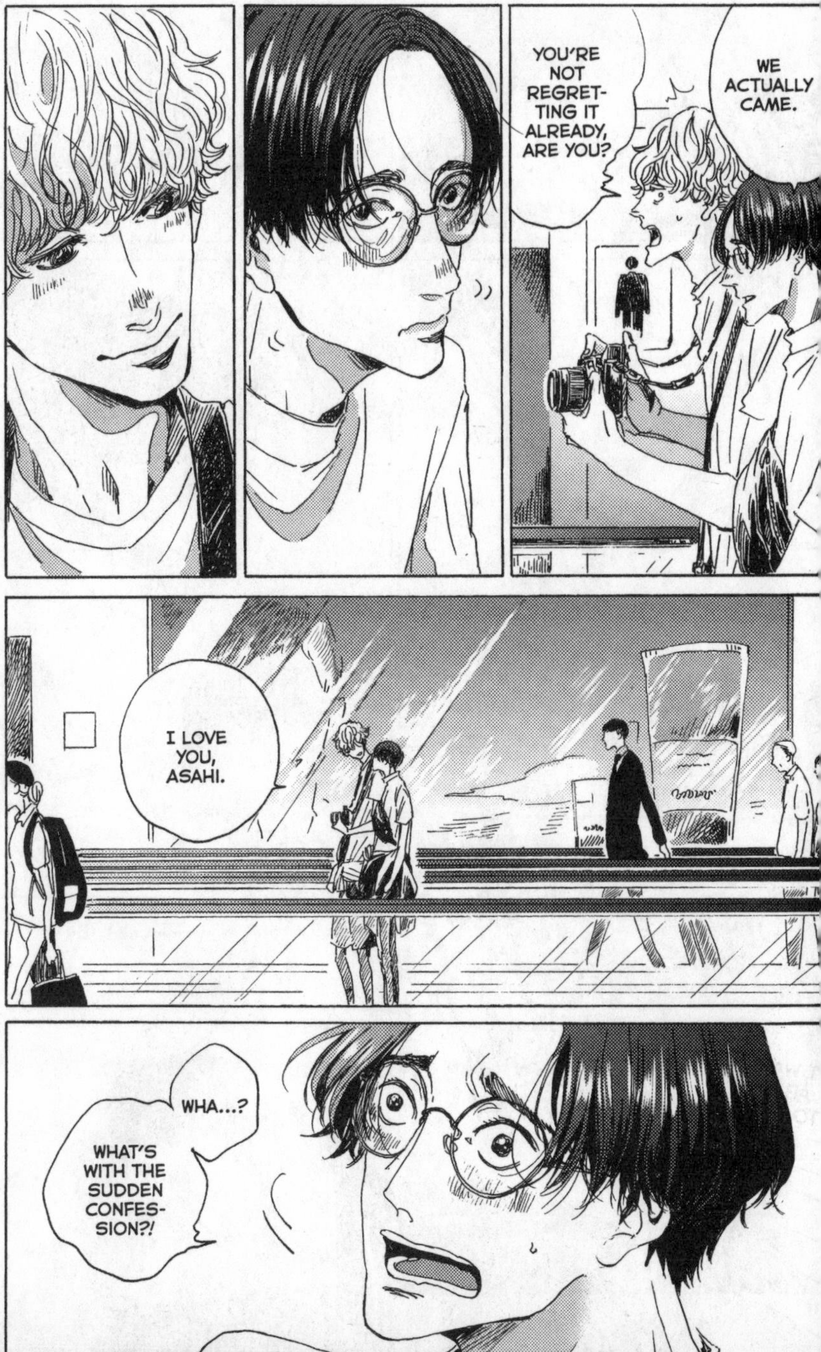
WE ACTUALLY CAME.
YOU'RE NOT REGRETTING IT ALREADY, ARE YOU?
I LOVE YOU, ASAHI.
WHA...?
WHAT'S WITH THE SUDDEN CONFESSION?!

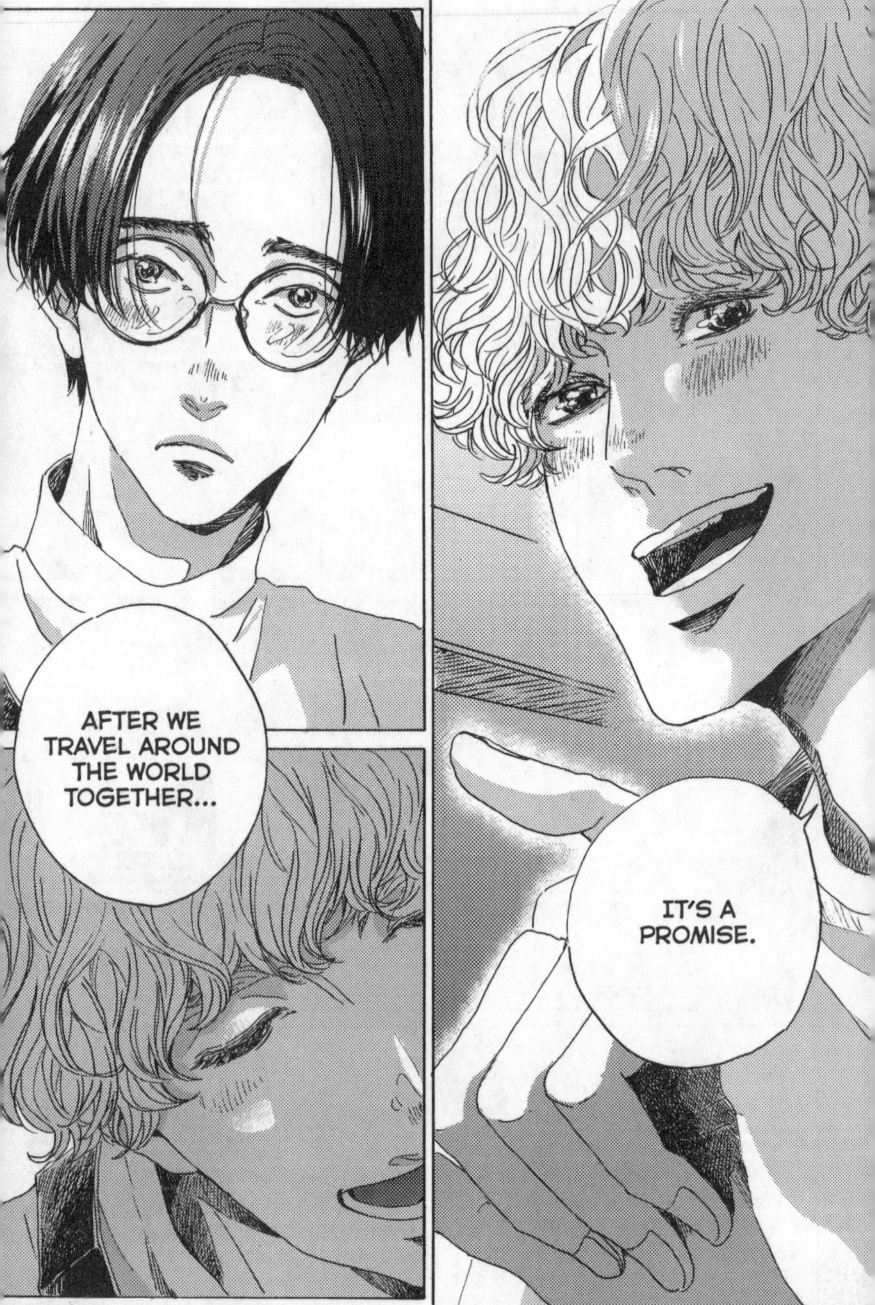
IT'S A PROMISE.
AFTER WE TRAVEL AROUND THE WORLD TOGETHER...

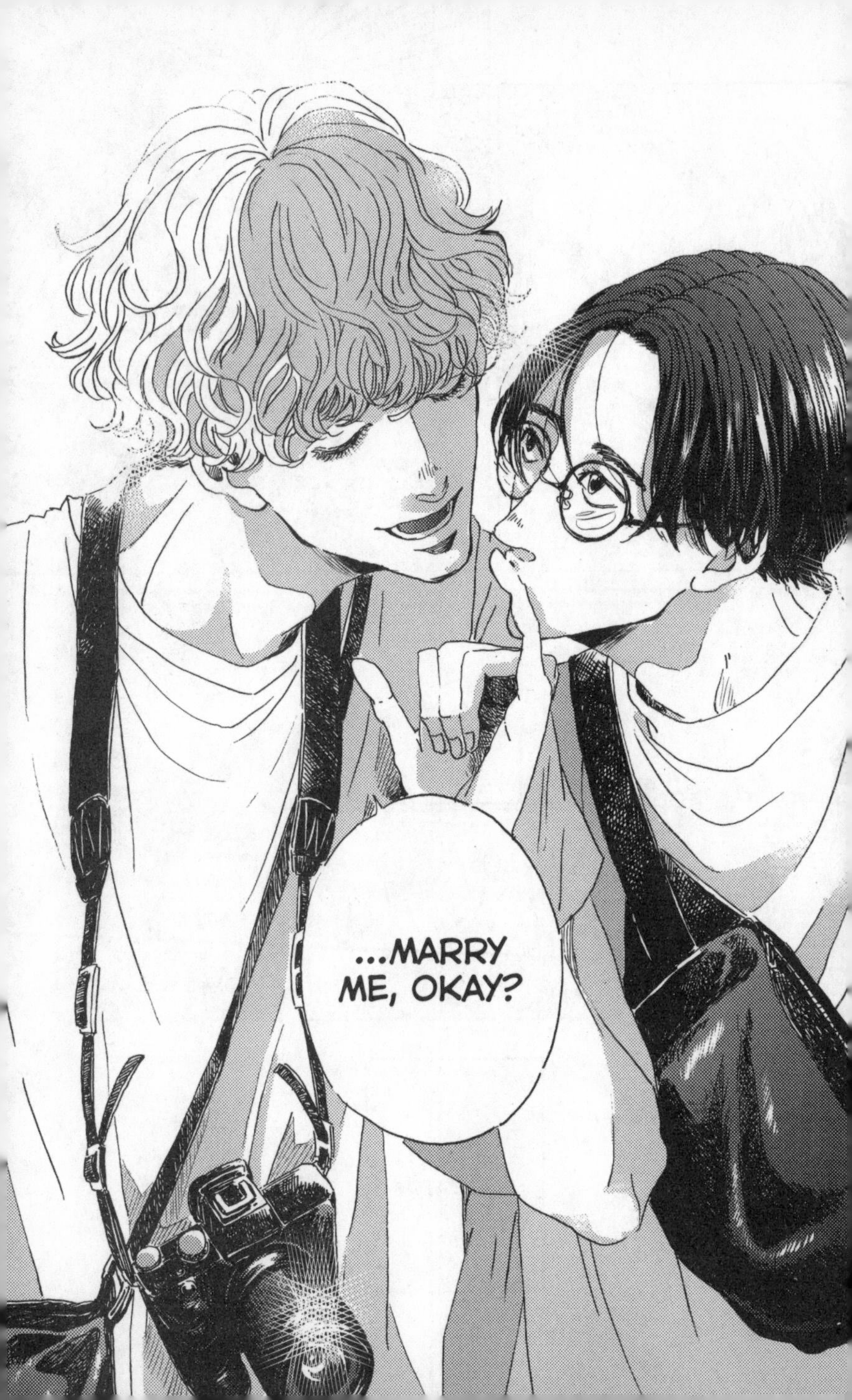
...MARRY ME, OKAY?

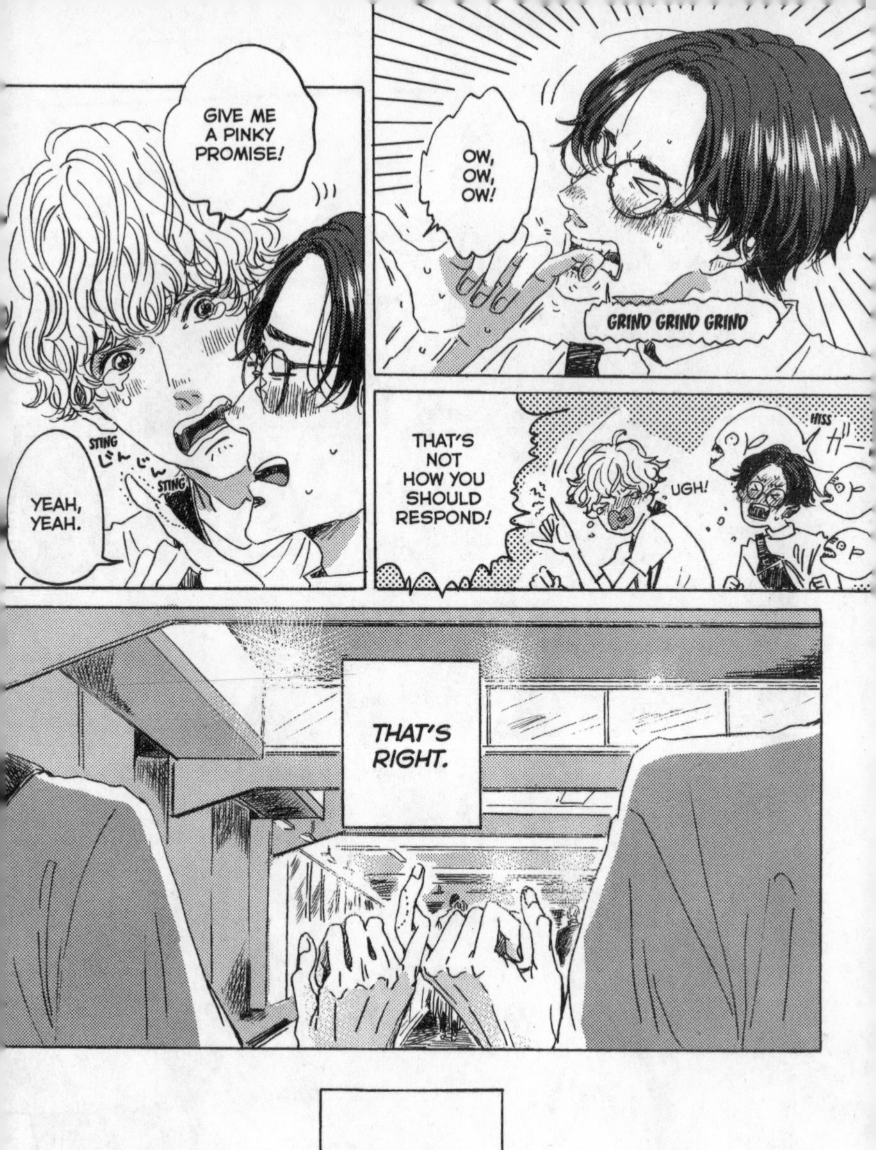

OW, OW, OW!
GRIND GRIND GRIND
THAT'S NOT HOW YOU SHOULD RESPOND!
UGH!
HISS
ガー
GIVE ME A PINKY PROMISE!
STING
じんじん
STING
YEAH, YEAH.
THAT'S RIGHT.
THIS IS THE REASON FOR THEIR JOURNEY.

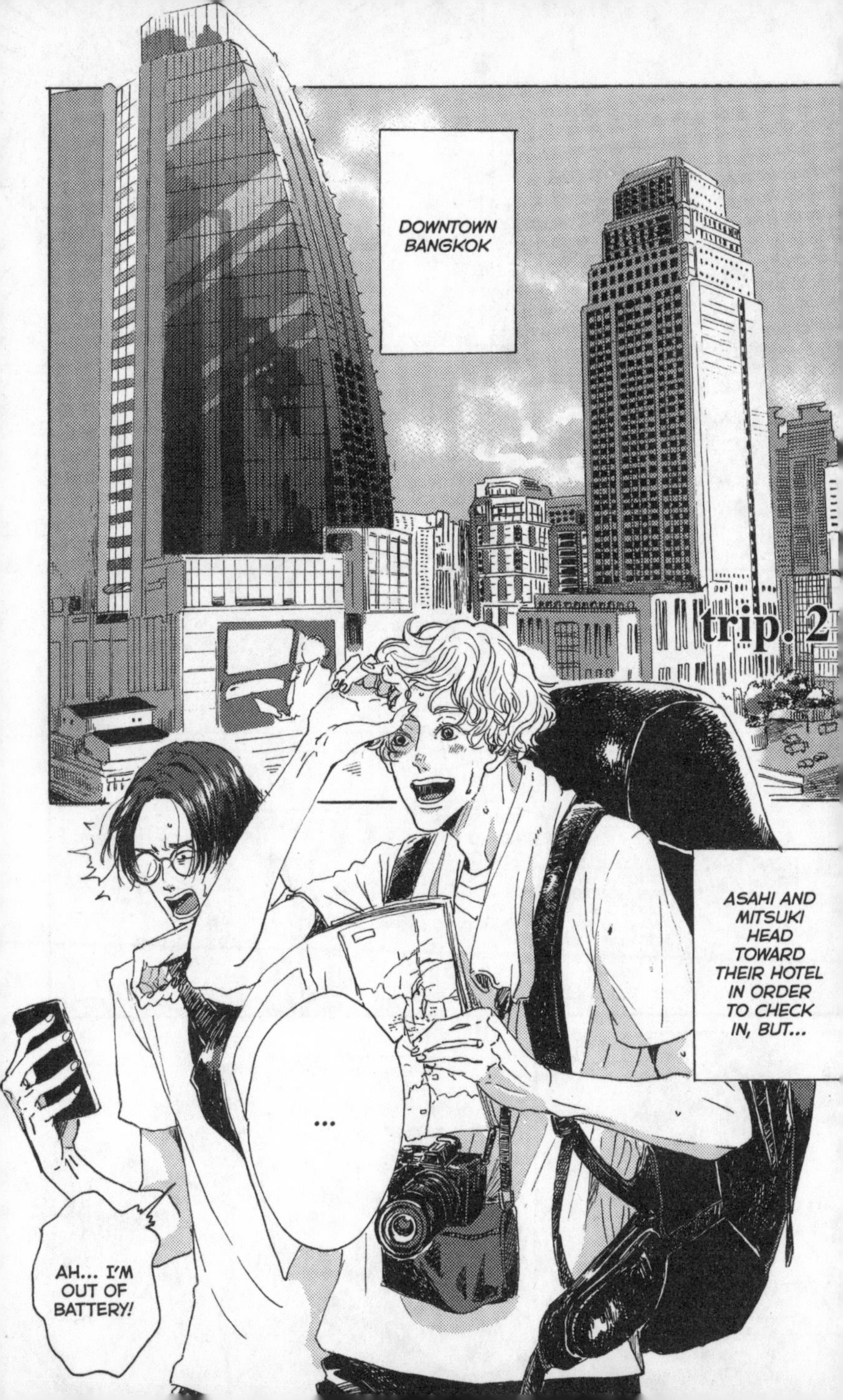
DOWNTOWN BANGKOK
trip. 2
ASAHI AND MITSUKI HEAD TOWARD THEIR HOTEL IN ORDER TO CHECK IN, BUT...
...
AH... I'M OUT OF BATTERY!

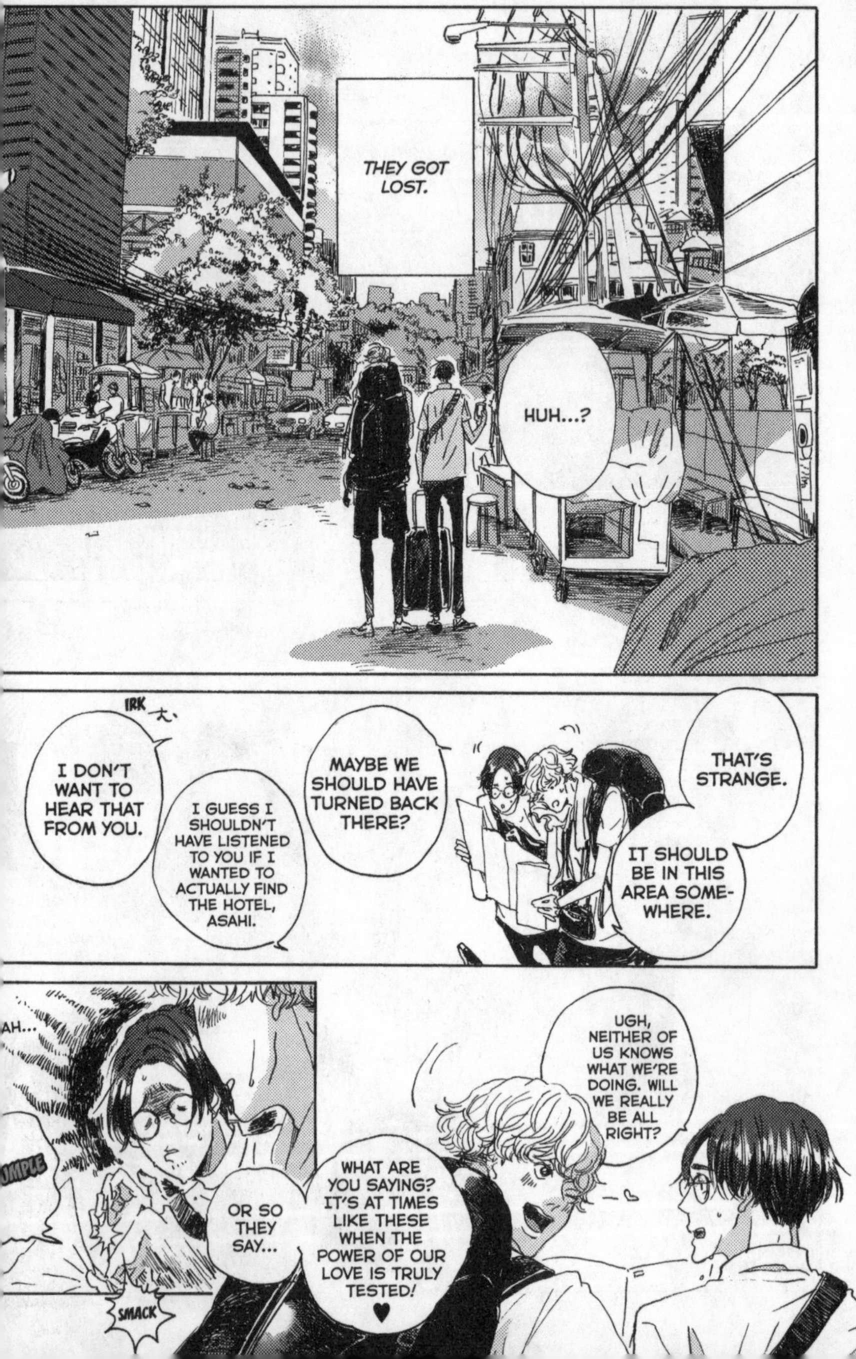
THEY GOT LOST.
HUH...?
THAT'S STRANGE.
IT SHOULD BE IN THIS AREA SOME-WHERE.
MAYBE WE SHOULD HAVE TURNED BACK THERE?
I GUESS I SHOULDN'T HAVE LISTENED TO YOU IF I WANTED TO ACTUALLY FIND THE HOTEL, ASAHI.
IRK
I DON'T WANT TO HEAR THAT FROM YOU.
UGH, NEITHER OF US KNOWS WHAT WE'RE DOING. WILL WE REALLY BE ALL RIGHT?
WHAT ARE YOU SAYING? IT'S AT TIMES LIKE THESE WHEN THE POWER OF OUR LOVE IS TRULY TESTED! ♥
AH...
OR SO THEY SAY...
SMACK

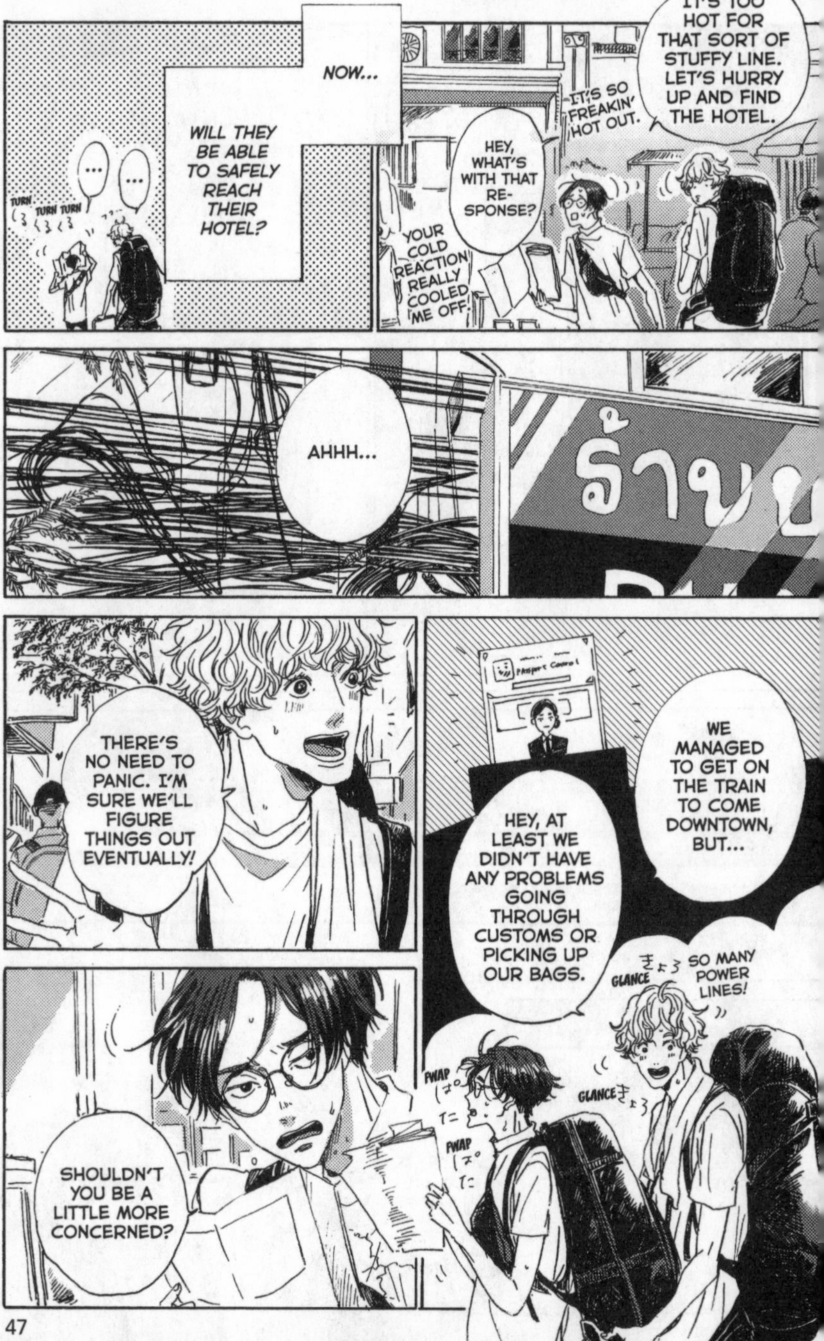
IT'S TOO HOT FOR THAT SORT OF STUFFY LINE. LET'S HURRY UP AND FIND THE HOTEL.
IT'S SO FREAKIN' HOT OUT.
HEY, WHAT'S WITH THAT RE-SPONSE?
YOUR COLD REACTION REALLY COOLED ME OFF.
NOW...
WILL THEY BE ABLE TO SAFELY REACH THEIR HOTEL?
...
...
TURN くる
TURN TURN くるくる
AHHH...
WE MANAGED TO GET ON THE TRAIN TO COME DOWNTOWN, BUT...
HEY, AT LEAST WE DIDN'T HAVE ANY PROBLEMS GOING THROUGH CUSTOMS OR PICKING UP OUR BAGS.
GLANCE きょろ
SO MANY POWER LINES!
GLANCE きょろ
FWAP ぱた
FWAP ぱた
THERE'S NO NEED TO PANIC. I'M SURE WE'LL FIGURE THINGS OUT EVENTUALLY!
SHOULDN'T YOU BE A LITTLE MORE CONCERNED?

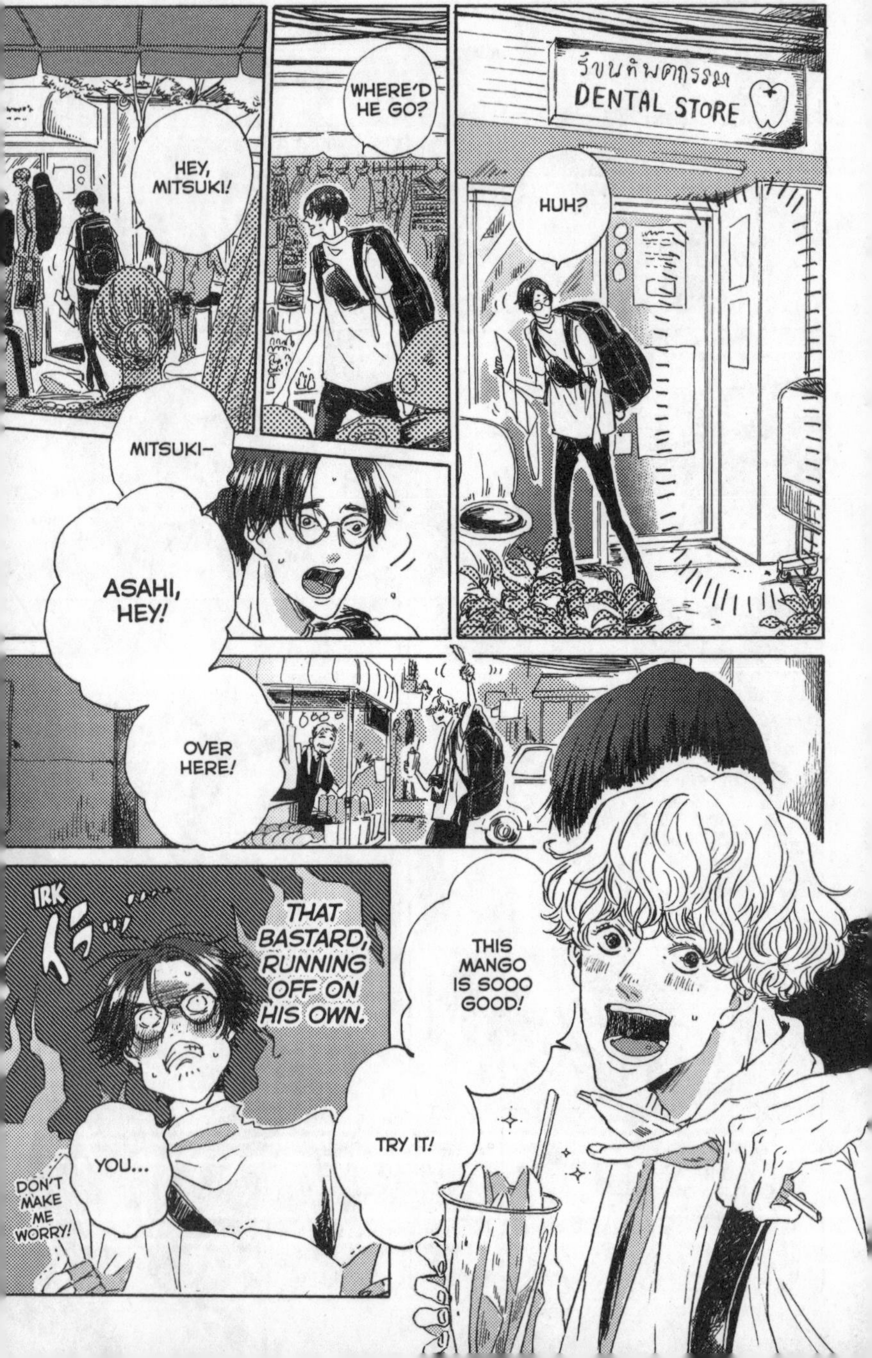
DENTAL STORE
HUH?
WHERE'D HE GO?
HEY, MITSUKI!
MITSUKI–
ASAHI, HEY!
OVER HERE!
THIS MANGO IS SOOO GOOD!
TRY IT!
IRK
THAT BASTARD, RUNNING OFF ON HIS OWN.
YOU...
DON'T MAKE ME WORRY!

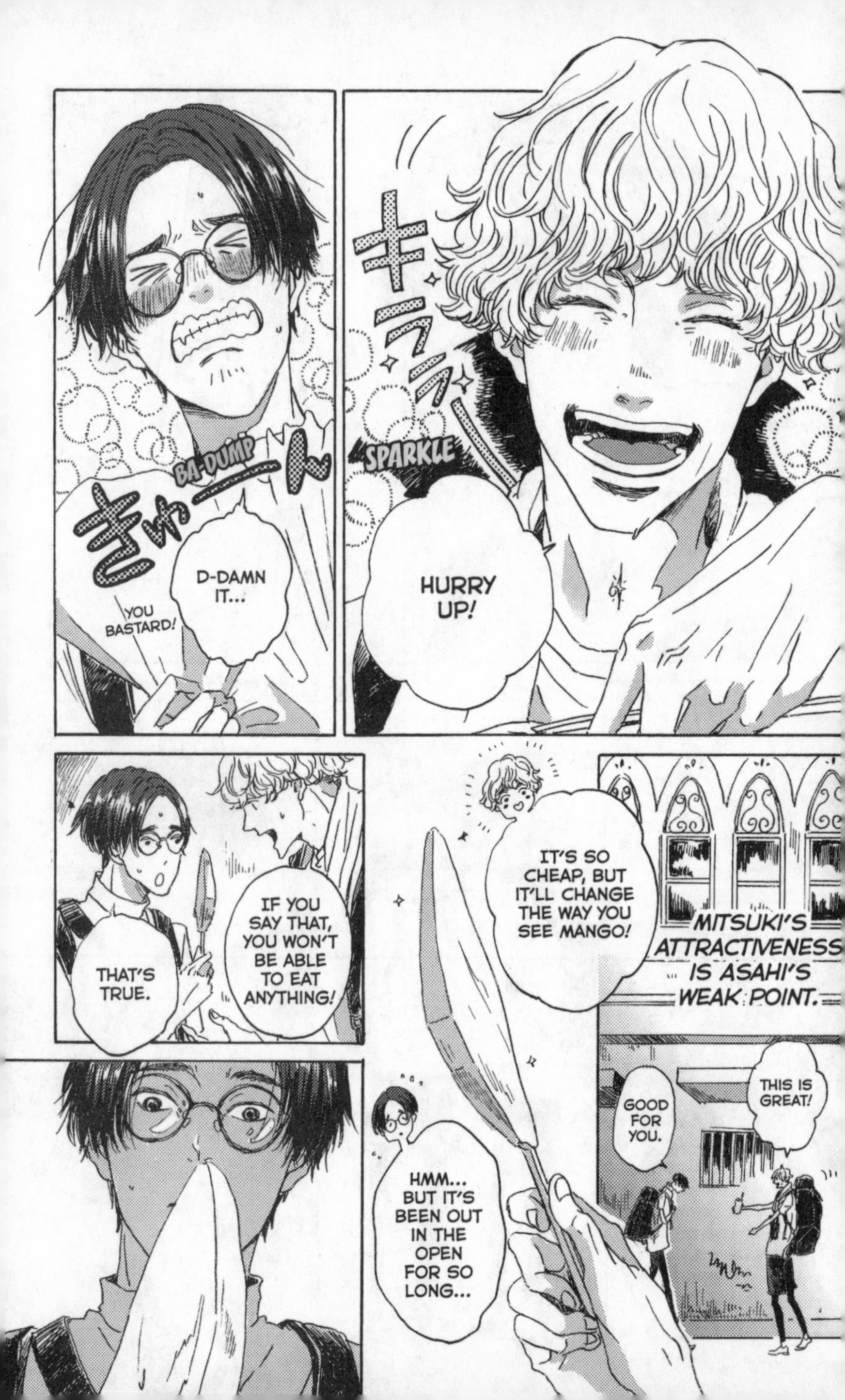
SPARKLE
HURRY UP!
BA-DUMP
D-DAMN IT...
YOU BASTARD!
MITSUKI'S ATTRACTIVENESS IS ASAHI'S WEAK POINT.
IT'S SO CHEAP, BUT IT'LL CHANGE THE WAY YOU SEE MANGO!
IF YOU SAY THAT, YOU WON'T BE ABLE TO EAT ANYTHING!
THAT'S TRUE.
THIS IS GREAT!
GOOD FOR YOU.
HMM... BUT IT'S BEEN OUT IN THE OPEN FOR SO LONG...

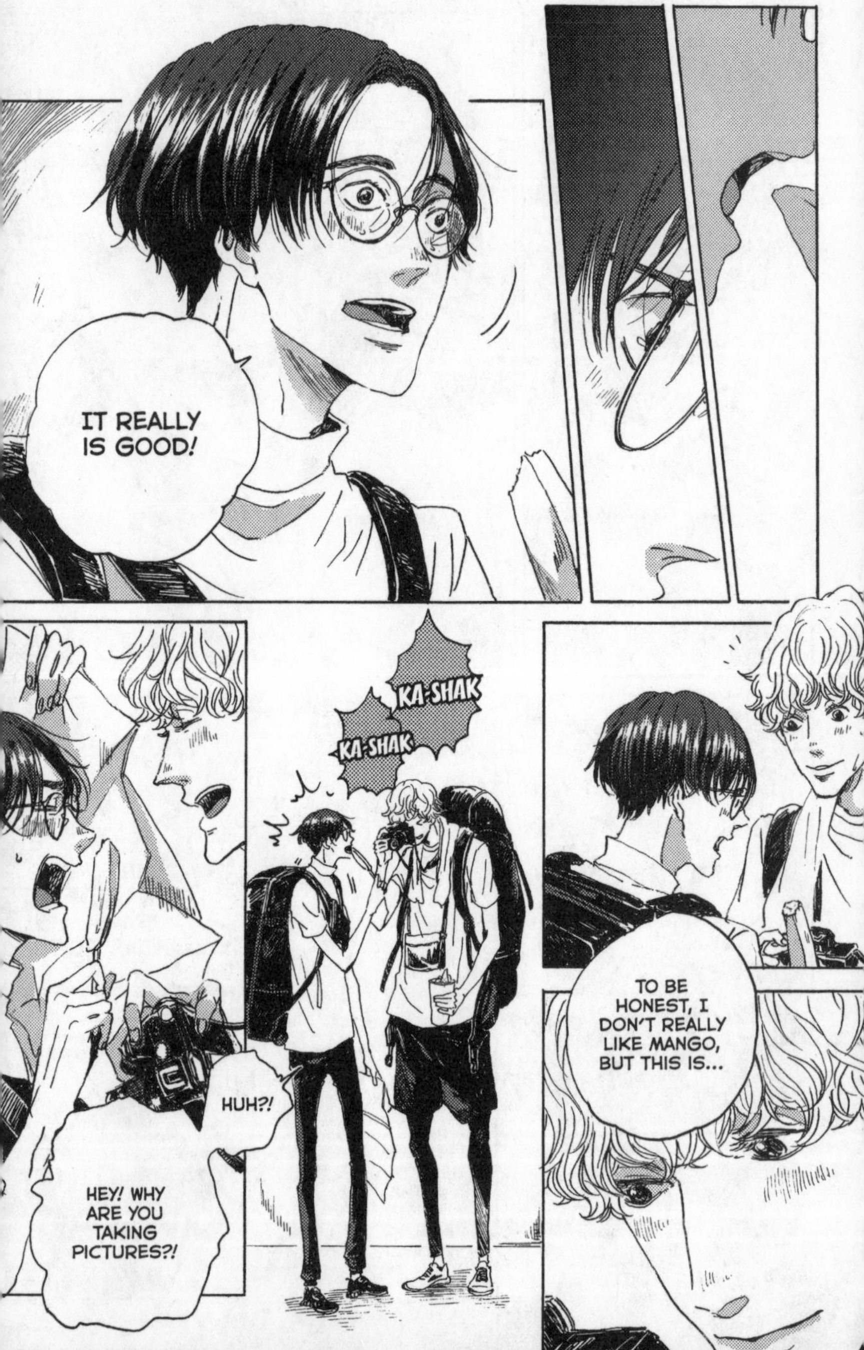
IT REALLY IS GOOD!
TO BE HONEST, I DON'T REALLY LIKE MANGO, BUT THIS IS...
KA-SHAK
KA-SHAK
HUH?!
HEY! WHY ARE YOU TAKING PICTURES?!

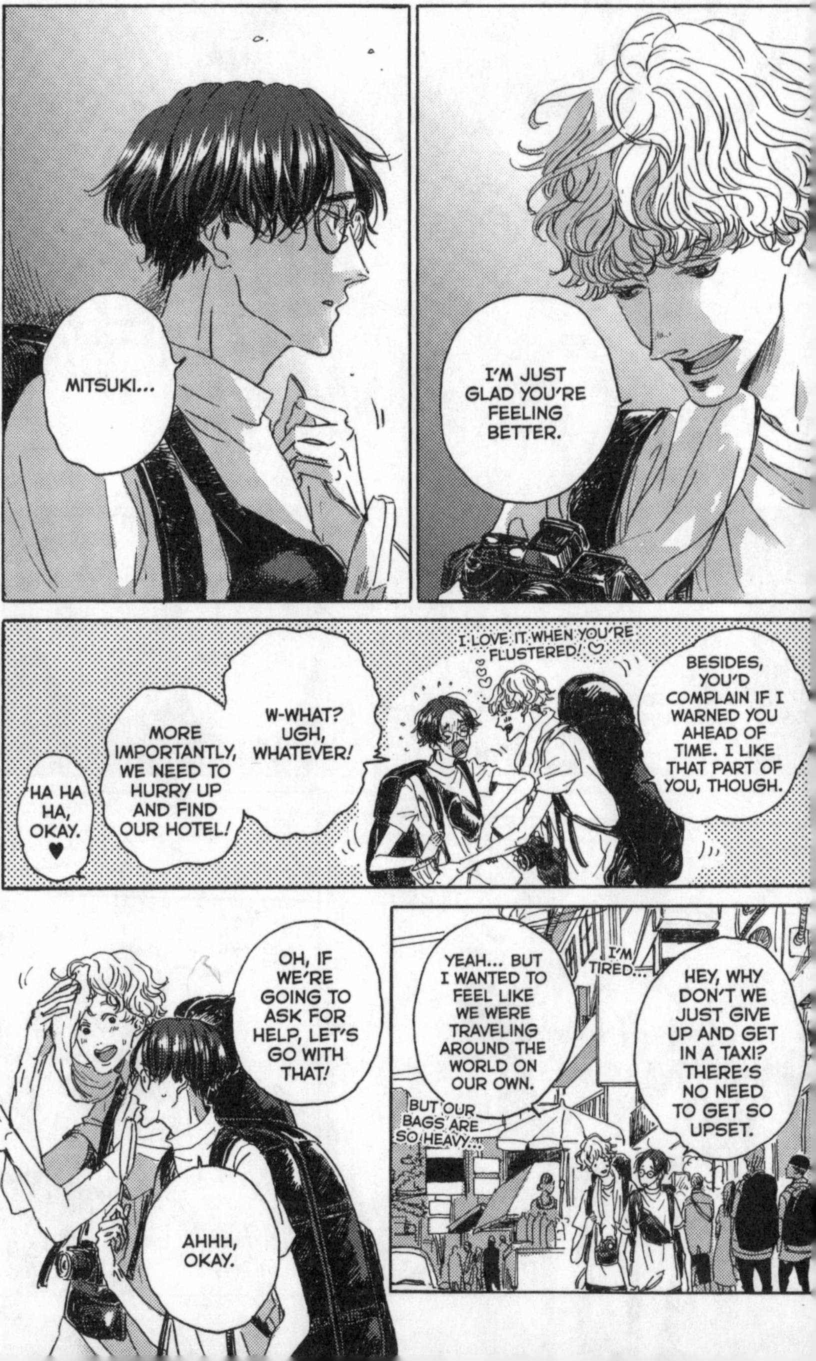
I'M JUST GLAD YOU'RE FEELING BETTER.
MITSUKI...
BESIDES, YOU'D COMPLAIN IF I WARNED YOU AHEAD OF TIME. I LIKE THAT PART OF YOU, THOUGH.
I LOVE IT WHEN YOU'RE FLUSTERED! ♡
W-WHAT? UGH, WHATEVER!
MORE IMPORTANTLY, WE NEED TO HURRY UP AND FIND OUR HOTEL!
HA HA HA, OKAY. ♥
HEY, WHY DON'T WE JUST GIVE UP AND GET IN A TAXI? THERE'S NO NEED TO GET SO UPSET.
I'M TIRED...
YEAH... BUT I WANTED TO FEEL LIKE WE WERE TRAVELING AROUND THE WORLD ON OUR OWN.
BUT OUR BAGS ARE SO HEAVY...
OH, IF WE'RE GOING TO ASK FOR HELP, LET'S GO WITH THAT!
AHHH, OKAY.

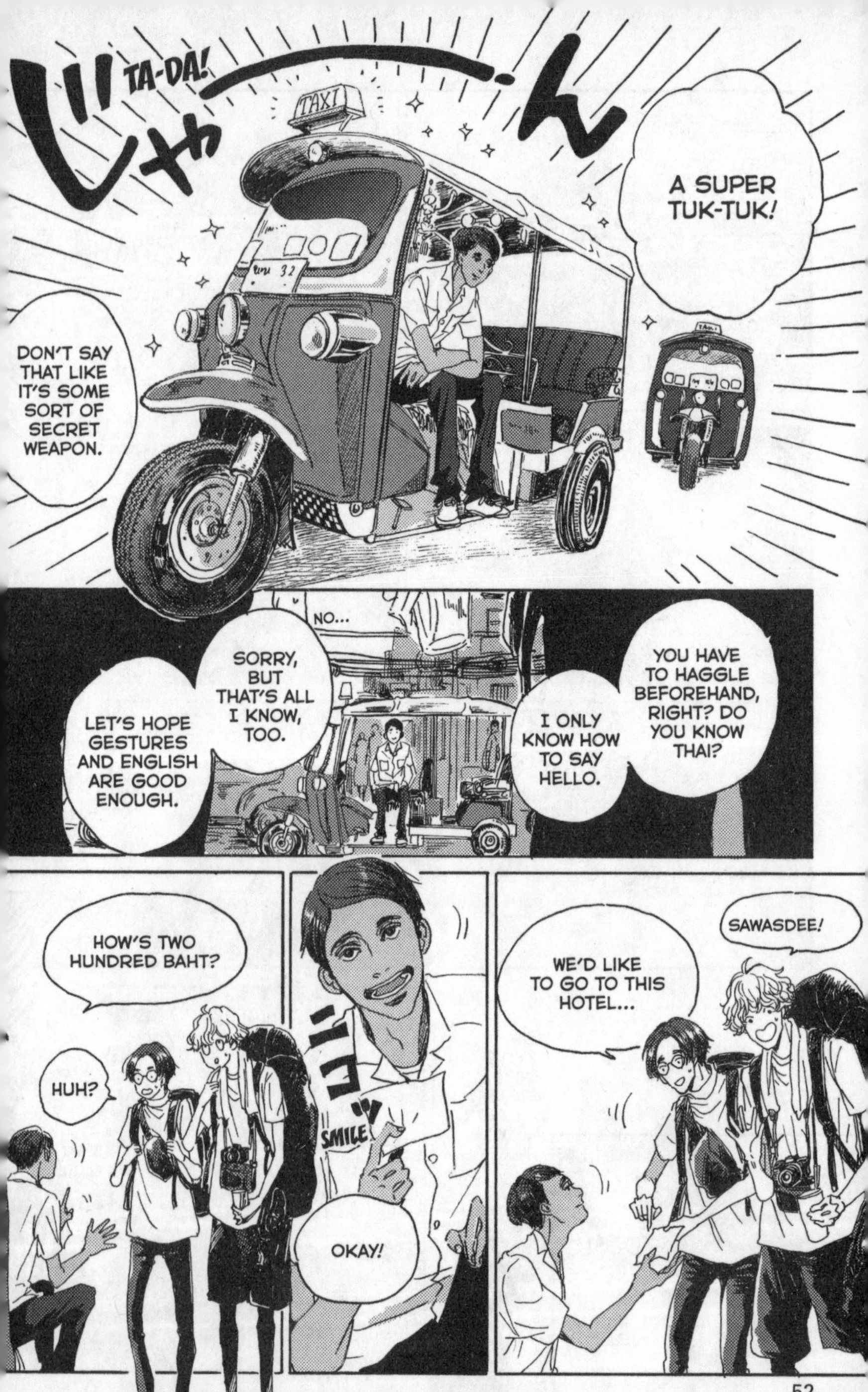
TA-DA!
A SUPER TUK-TUK!
DON'T SAY THAT LIKE IT'S SOME SORT OF SECRET WEAPON.
YOU HAVE TO HAGGLE BEFOREHAND, RIGHT? DO YOU KNOW THAI?
I ONLY KNOW HOW TO SAY HELLO.
NO...
SORRY, BUT THAT'S ALL I KNOW, TOO.
LET'S HOPE GESTURES AND ENGLISH ARE GOOD ENOUGH.
SAWASDEE!
WE'D LIKE TO GO TO THIS HOTEL...
SMILE
OKAY!
HOW'S TWO HUNDRED BAHT?
HUH?

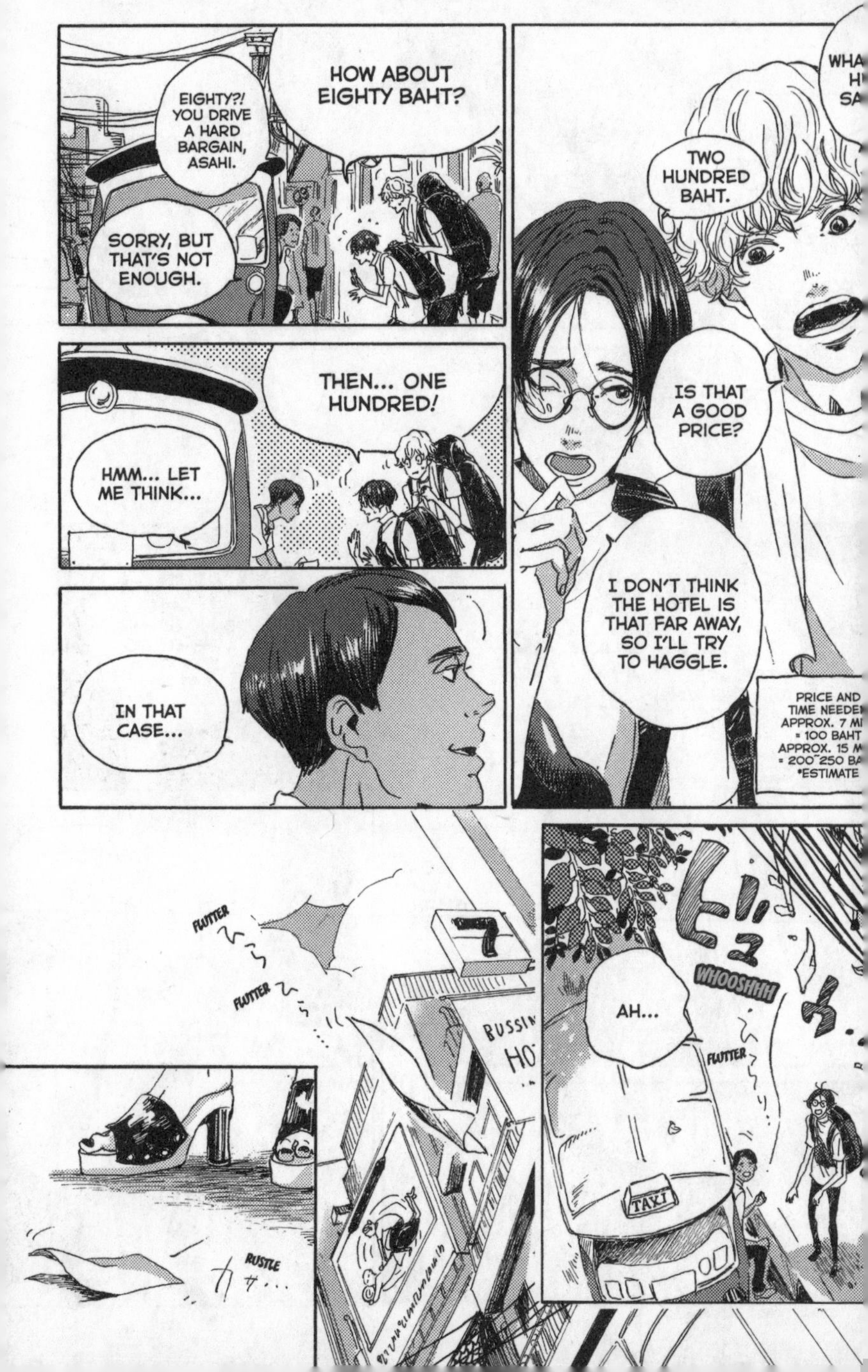
TWO HUNDRED BAHT.
IS THAT A GOOD PRICE?
I DON'T THINK THE HOTEL IS THAT FAR AWAY, SO I'LL TRY TO HAGGLE.
PRICE AND TIME NEEDE APPROX. 7 MI = 100 BAHT APPROX. 15 M = 200~250 BA *ESTIMATE
HOW ABOUT EIGHTY BAHT?
EIGHTY?! YOU DRIVE A HARD BARGAIN, ASAHI.
SORRY, BUT THAT'S NOT ENOUGH.
THEN... ONE HUNDRED!
HMM... LET ME THINK...
IN THAT CASE...
WHOOSHHH
AH...
FLUTTER
TAXI
FLUTTER
FLUTTER
BUSSIN HO
RUSTLE

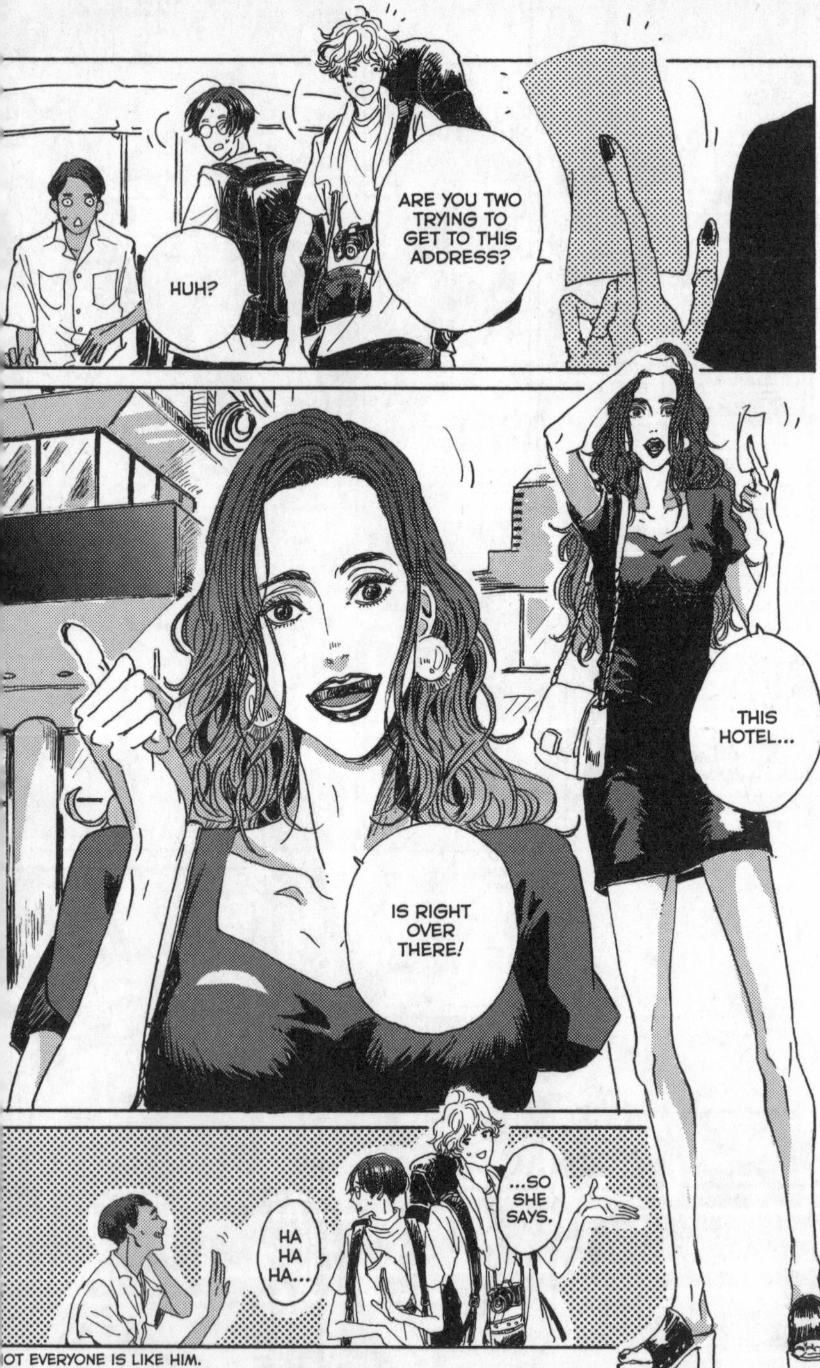
ARE YOU TWO TRYING TO GET TO THIS ADDRESS?
HUH?
THIS HOTEL...
IS RIGHT OVER THERE!
...SO SHE SAYS.
HA HA HA...

OT EVERYONE IS LIKE HIM.

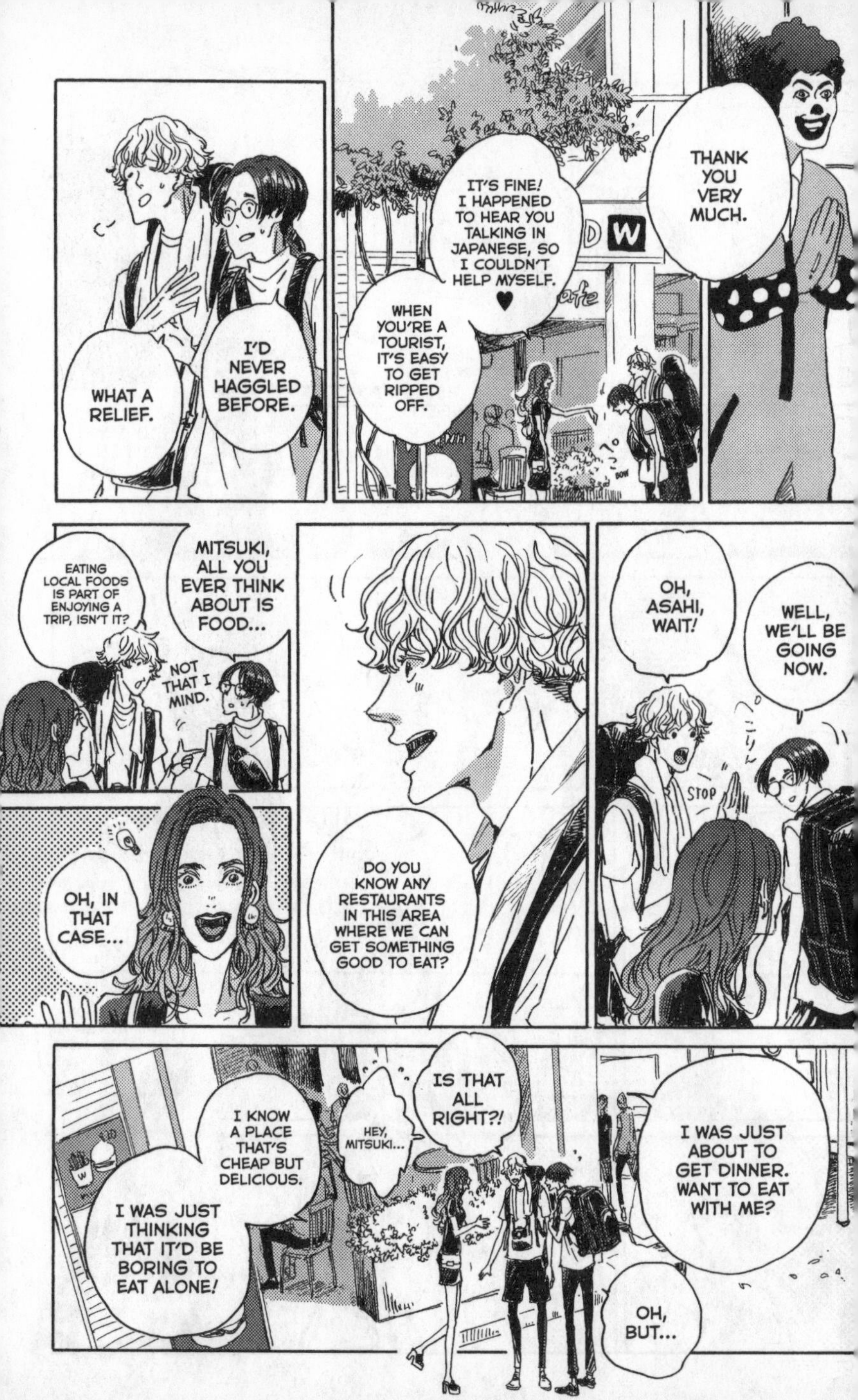
THANK YOU VERY MUCH.
IT'S FINE! I HAPPENED TO HEAR YOU TALKING IN JAPANESE, SO I COULDN'T HELP MYSELF. ♥
WHEN YOU'RE A TOURIST, IT'S EASY TO GET RIPPED OFF.
BOW
I'D NEVER HAGGLED BEFORE.
WHAT A RELIEF.
WELL, WE'LL BE GOING NOW.
OH, ASAHI, WAIT!
STOP
DO YOU KNOW ANY RESTAURANTS IN THIS AREA WHERE WE CAN GET SOMETHING GOOD TO EAT?
MITSUKI, ALL YOU EVER THINK ABOUT IS FOOD...
NOT THAT I MIND.
EATING LOCAL FOODS IS PART OF ENJOYING A TRIP, ISN'T IT?
OH, IN THAT CASE...
I WAS JUST ABOUT TO GET DINNER. WANT TO EAT WITH ME?
OH, BUT...
IS THAT ALL RIGHT?!
HEY, MITSUKI...
I KNOW A PLACE THAT'S CHEAP BUT DELICIOUS.
I WAS JUST THINKING THAT IT'D BE BORING TO EAT ALONE!

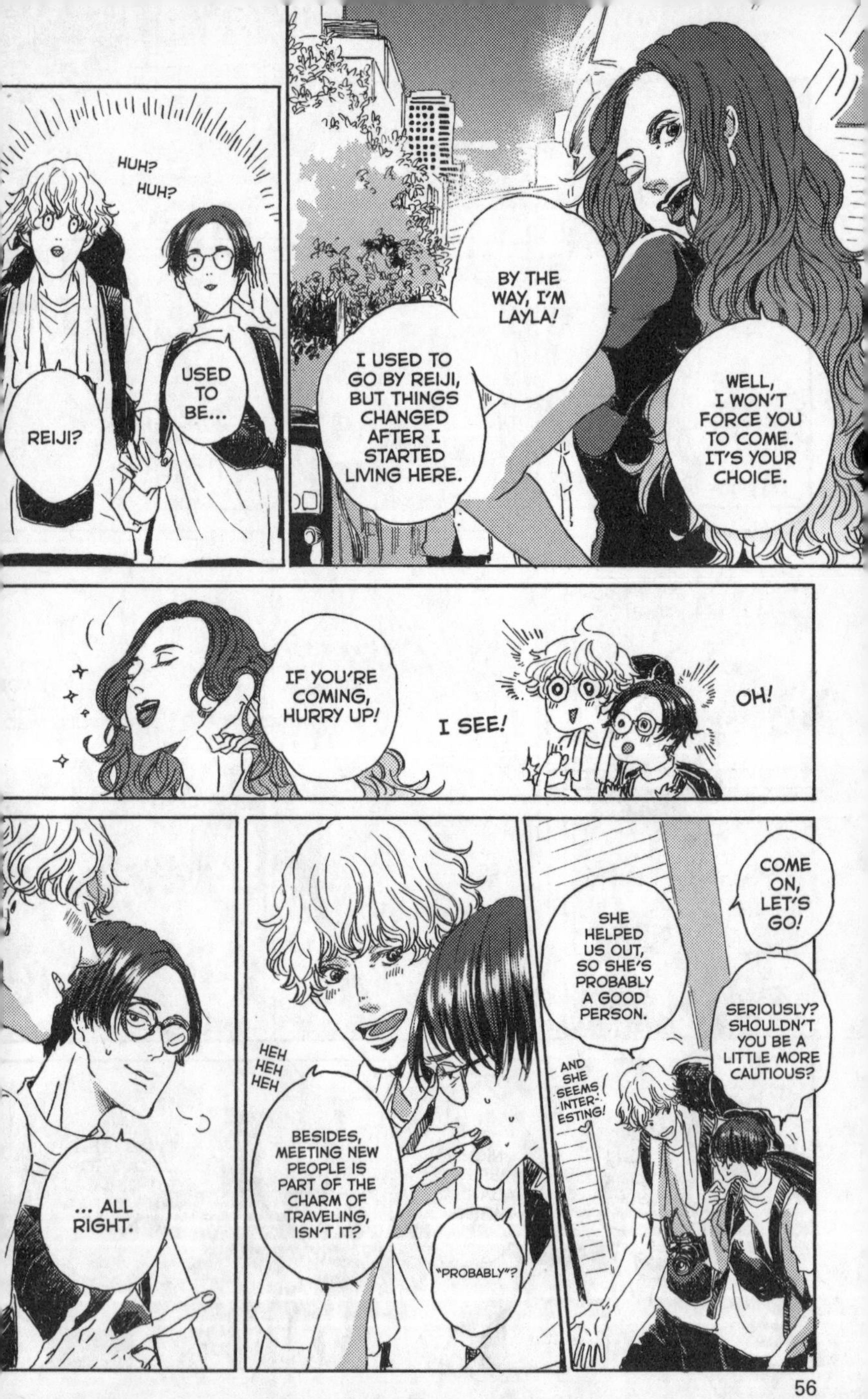
WELL, I WON'T FORCE YOU TO COME. IT'S YOUR CHOICE.
BY THE WAY, I'M LAYLA!
I USED TO GO BY REIJI, BUT THINGS CHANGED AFTER I STARTED LIVING HERE.
HUH? HUH?
REIJI?
USED TO BE...
OH!
I SEE!
IF YOU'RE COMING, HURRY UP!
COME ON, LET'S GO!
SERIOUSLY? SHOULDN'T YOU BE A LITTLE MORE CAUTIOUS?
SHE HELPED US OUT, SO SHE'S PROBABLY A GOOD PERSON.
AND SHE SEEMS INTER-ESTING!
"PROBABLY"?
HEH HEH HEH
BESIDES, MEETING NEW PEOPLE IS PART OF THE CHARM OF TRAVELING, ISN'T IT?
... ALL RIGHT.

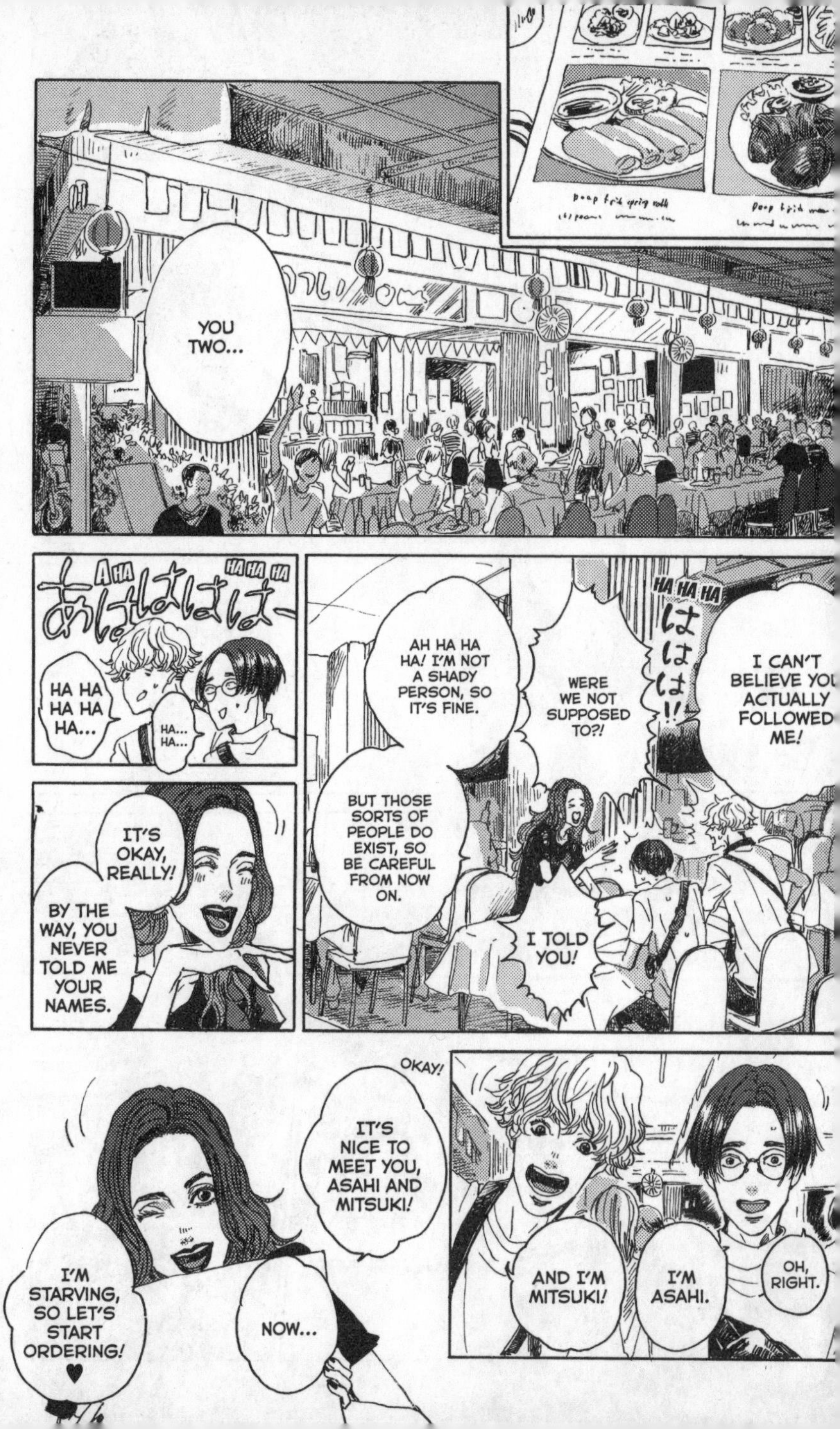
YOU TWO...
I CAN'T BELIEVE YOU ACTUALLY FOLLOWED ME!
HA HA HA
ははは!!
WERE WE NOT SUPPOSED TO?!
AH HA HA HA! I'M NOT A SHADY PERSON, SO IT'S FINE.
BUT THOSE SORTS OF PEOPLE DO EXIST, SO BE CAREFUL FROM NOW ON.
I TOLD YOU!
A HA HA HA HA
あはははは
HA... HA...
HA HA HA HA HA...
IT'S OKAY, REALLY!
BY THE WAY, YOU NEVER TOLD ME YOUR NAMES.
OH, RIGHT.
I'M ASAHI.
AND I'M MITSUKI!
OKAY!
IT'S NICE TO MEET YOU, ASAHI AND MITSUKI!
NOW...
I'M STARVING, SO LET'S START ORDERING! ♥

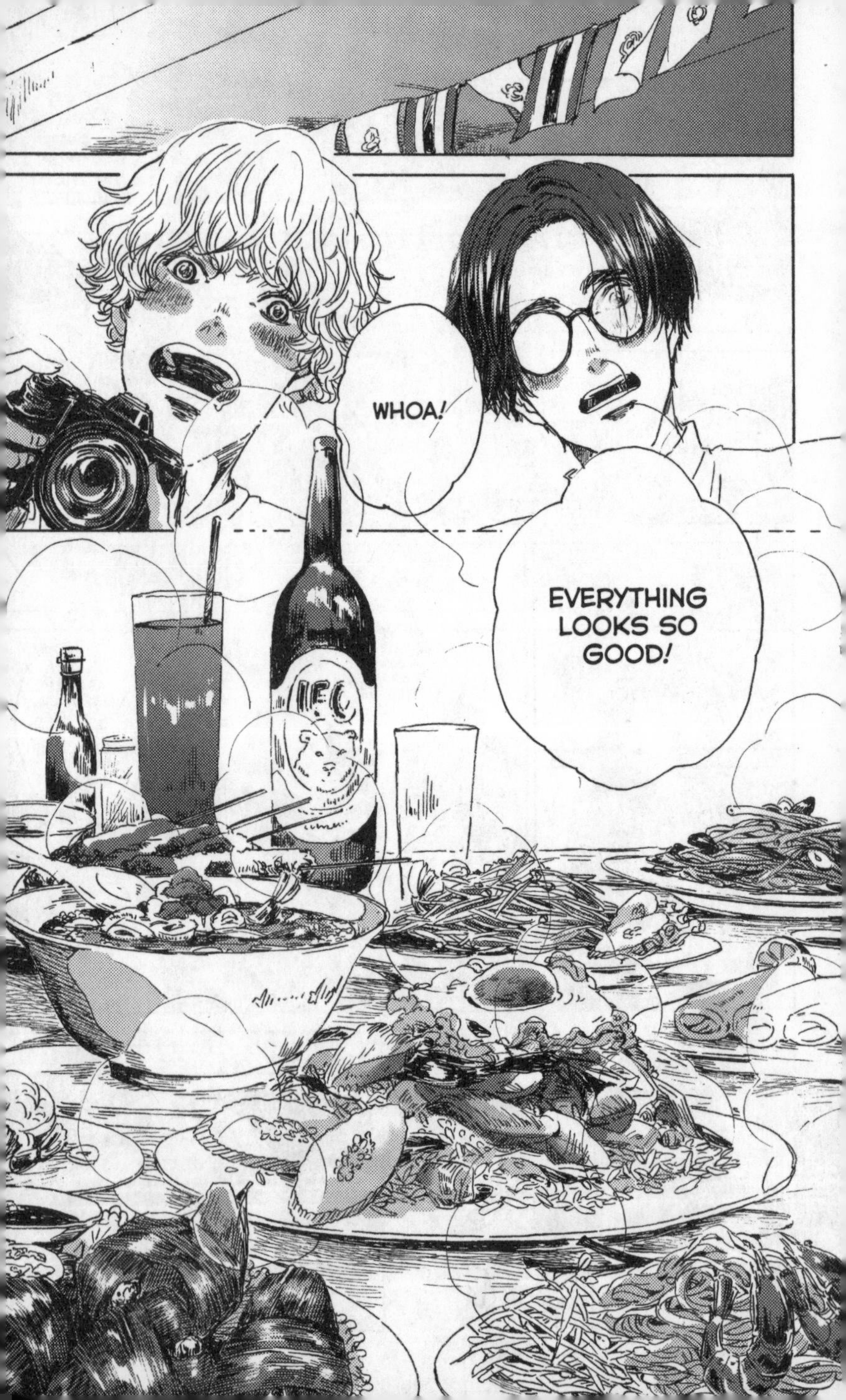
WHOA!
EVERYTHING LOOKS SO GOOD!

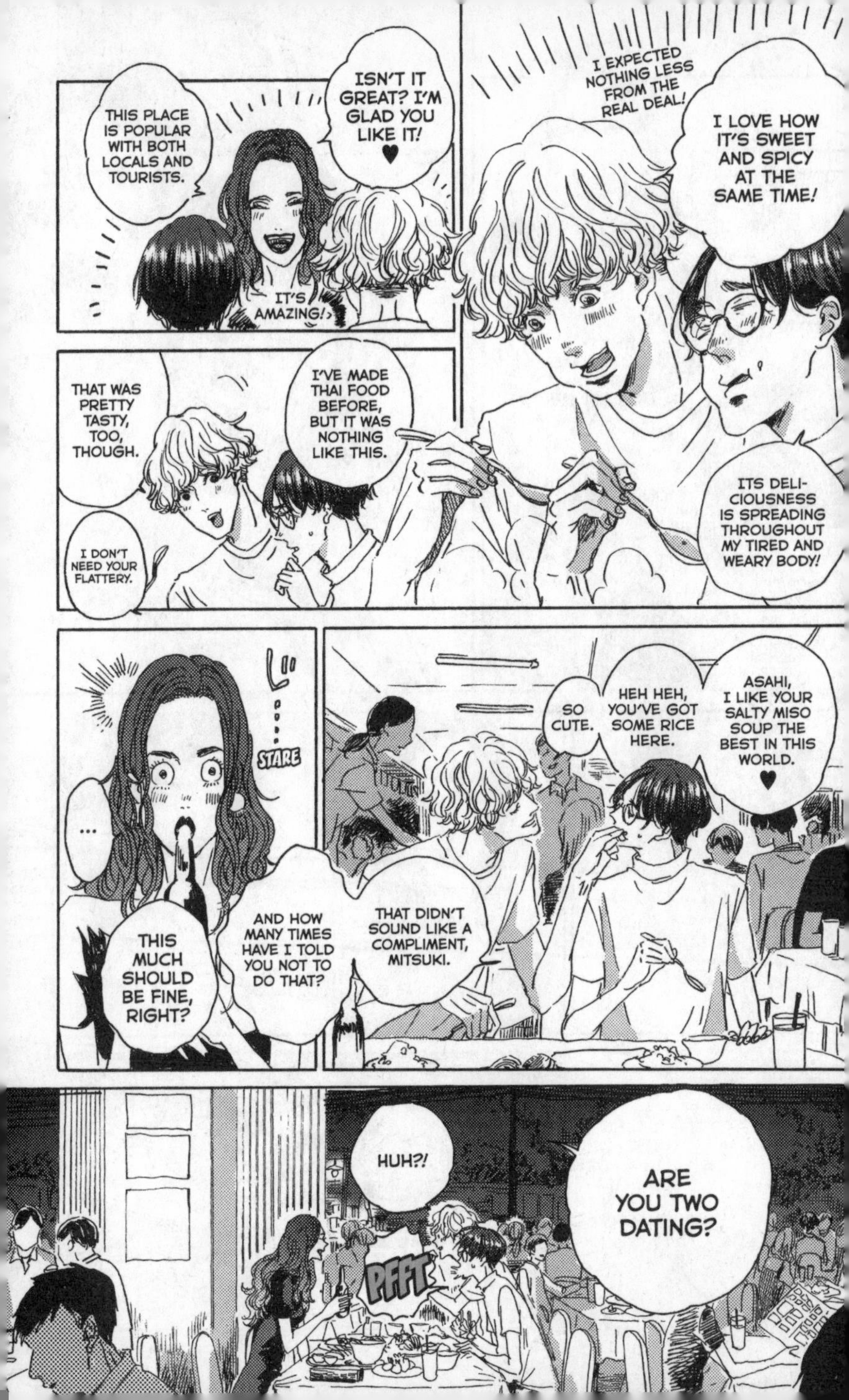
I EXPECTED NOTHING LESS FROM THE REAL DEAL!
I LOVE HOW IT'S SWEET AND SPICY AT THE SAME TIME!
ITS DELICIOUSNESS IS SPREADING THROUGHOUT MY TIRED AND WEARY BODY!
ISN'T IT GREAT? I'M GLAD YOU LIKE IT! ♥
THIS PLACE IS POPULAR WITH BOTH LOCALS AND TOURISTS.
IT'S AMAZING!
I'VE MADE THAI FOOD BEFORE, BUT IT WAS NOTHING LIKE THIS.
THAT WAS PRETTY TASTY, TOO, THOUGH.
I DON'T NEED YOUR FLATTERY.
ASAHI, I LIKE YOUR SALTY MISO SOUP THE BEST IN THIS WORLD. ♥
HEH HEH, YOU'VE GOT SOME RICE HERE.
SO CUTE.
THAT DIDN'T SOUND LIKE A COMPLIMENT, MITSUKI.
AND HOW MANY TIMES HAVE I TOLD YOU NOT TO DO THAT?
STARE
...
THIS MUCH SHOULD BE FINE, RIGHT?
ARE YOU TWO DATING?
HUH?!
PFFT

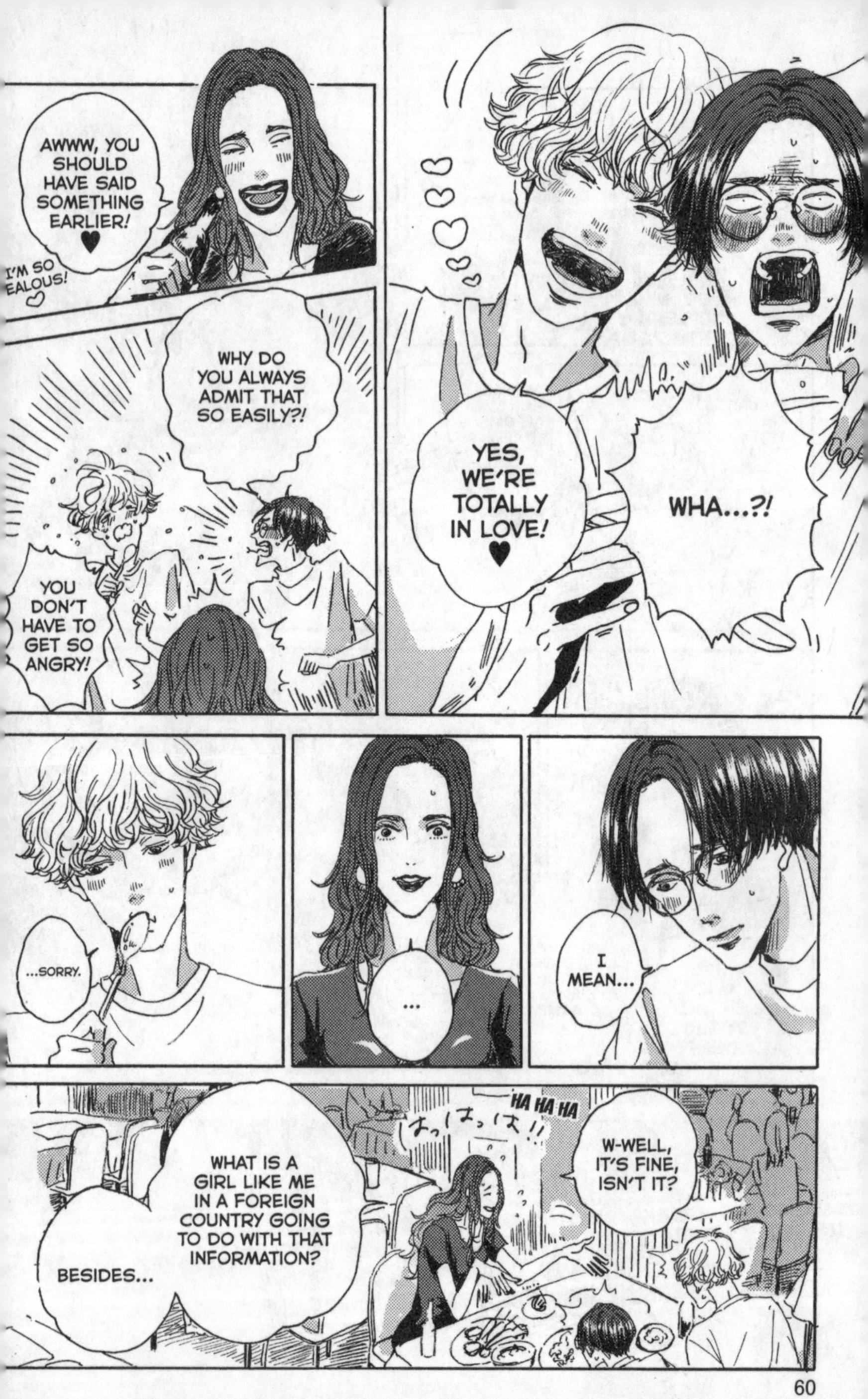
YES, WE'RE TOTALLY IN LOVE! ♥
WHA...?!
AWWW, YOU SHOULD HAVE SAID SOMETHING EARLIER! ♥
I'M SO EALOUS! ♡
WHY DO YOU ALWAYS ADMIT THAT SO EASILY?!
YOU DON'T HAVE TO GET SO ANGRY!
I MEAN...
...
...SORRY.
W-WELL, IT'S FINE, ISN'T IT?
HA HA HA
はっはっは!!
BESIDES...
WHAT IS A GIRL LIKE ME IN A FOREIGN COUNTRY GOING TO DO WITH THAT INFORMATION?

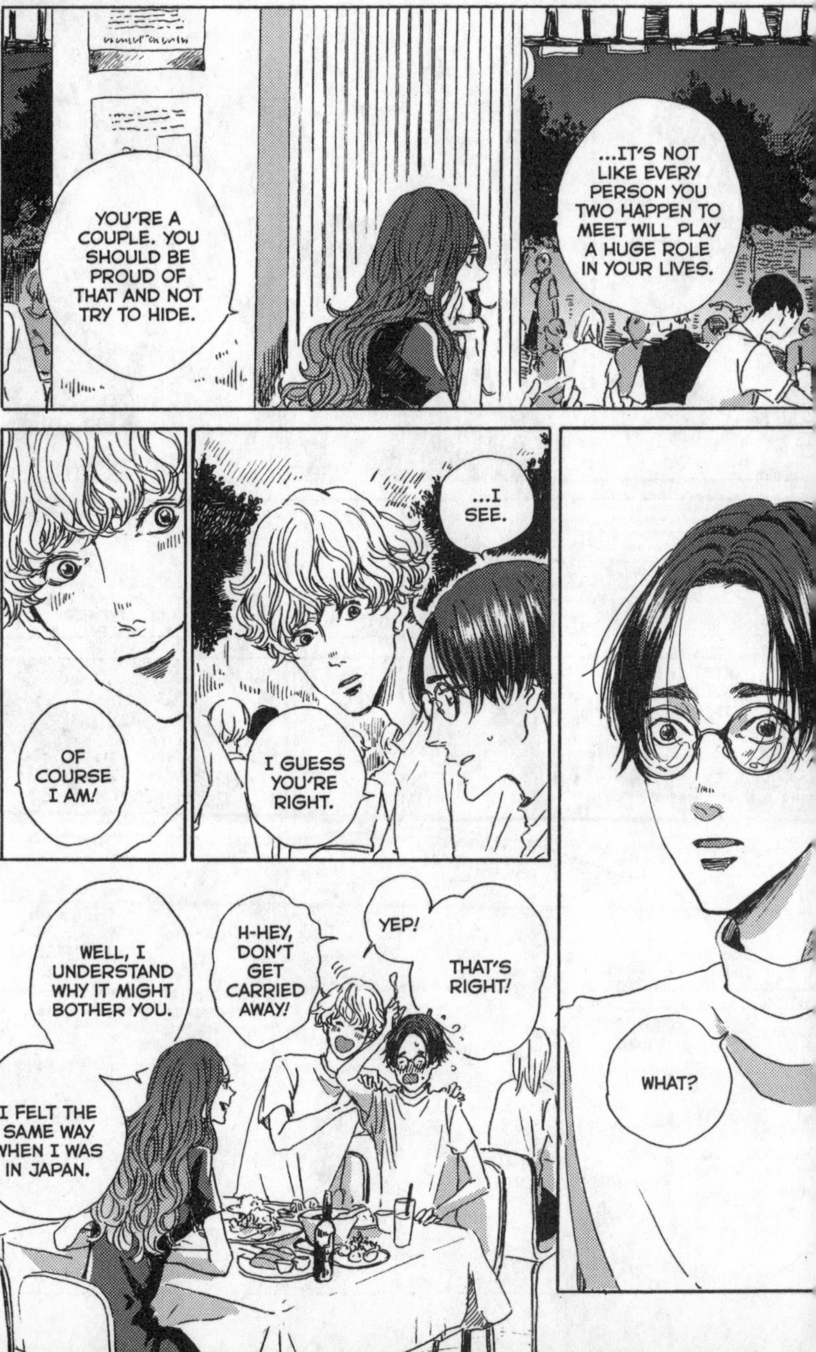
...IT'S NOT LIKE EVERY PERSON YOU TWO HAPPEN TO MEET WILL PLAY A HUGE ROLE IN YOUR LIVES.
YOU'RE A COUPLE. YOU SHOULD BE PROUD OF THAT AND NOT TRY TO HIDE.
WHAT?
...I SEE.
I GUESS YOU'RE RIGHT.
OF COURSE I AM!
YEP!
THAT'S RIGHT!
H-HEY, DON'T GET CARRIED AWAY!
WELL, I UNDERSTAND WHY IT MIGHT BOTHER YOU.
I FELT THE SAME WAY WHEN I WAS IN JAPAN.

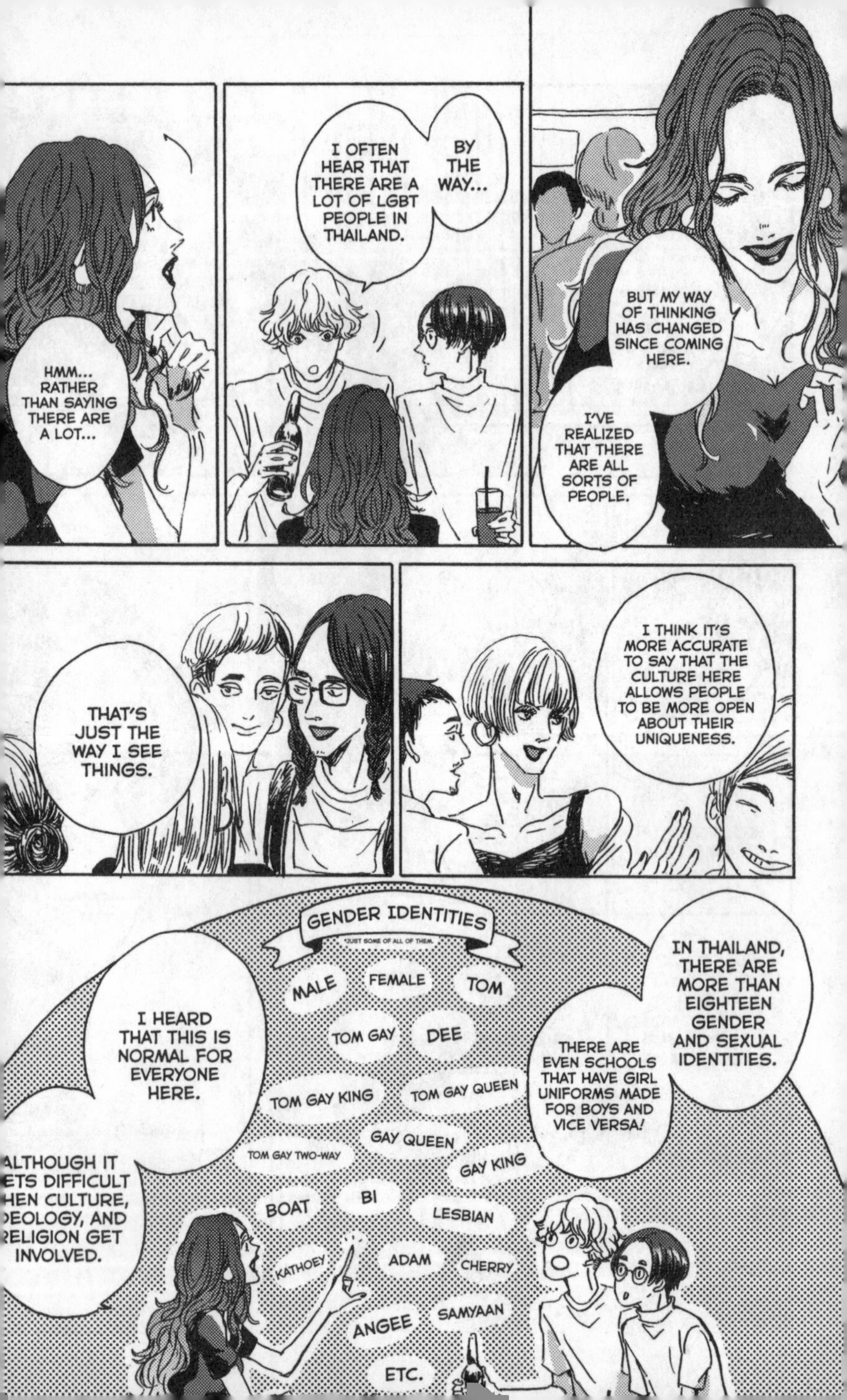
BUT MY WAY OF THINKING HAS CHANGED SINCE COMING HERE.
I'VE REALIZED THAT THERE ARE ALL SORTS OF PEOPLE.
BY THE WAY...
I OFTEN HEAR THAT THERE ARE A LOT OF LGBT PEOPLE IN THAILAND.
HMM... RATHER THAN SAYING THERE ARE A LOT...
I THINK IT'S MORE ACCURATE TO SAY THAT THE CULTURE HERE ALLOWS PEOPLE TO BE MORE OPEN ABOUT THEIR UNIQUENESS.
THAT'S JUST THE WAY I SEE THINGS.
IN THAILAND, THERE ARE MORE THAN EIGHTEEN GENDER AND SEXUAL IDENTITIES.
THERE ARE EVEN SCHOOLS THAT HAVE GIRL UNIFORMS MADE FOR BOYS AND VICE VERSA!
GENDER IDENTITIES
*JUST SOME OF ALL OF THEM.
MALE
FEMALE
TOM
TOM GAY
DEE
TOM GAY KING
TOM GAY QUEEN
TOM GAY TWO-WAY
GAY QUEEN
GAY KING
BOAT
BI
LESBIAN
KATHOEY
ADAM
CHERRY
ANGEE
SAMYAAN
ETC.
I HEARD THAT THIS IS NORMAL FOR EVERYONE HERE.
ALTHOUGH IT ETS DIFFICULT HEN CULTURE, DEOLOGY, AND ELIGION GET INVOLVED.

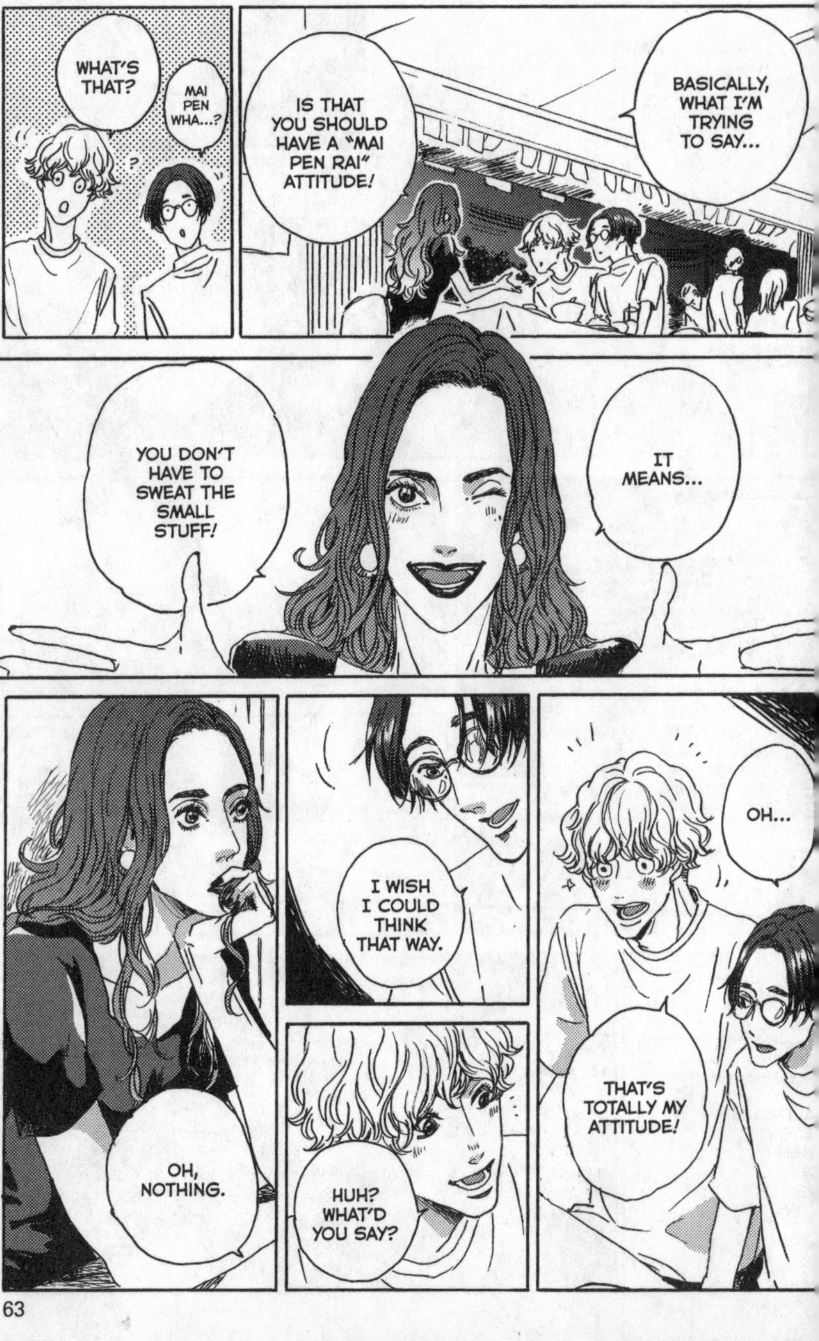
BASICALLY, WHAT I'M TRYING TO SAY...
IS THAT YOU SHOULD HAVE A "MAI PEN RAI" ATTITUDE!
MAI PEN WHA...?
WHAT'S THAT?
IT MEANS...
YOU DON'T HAVE TO SWEAT THE SMALL STUFF!
OH...
THAT'S TOTALLY MY ATTITUDE!
I WISH I COULD THINK THAT WAY.
HUH? WHAT'D YOU SAY?
OH, NOTHING.

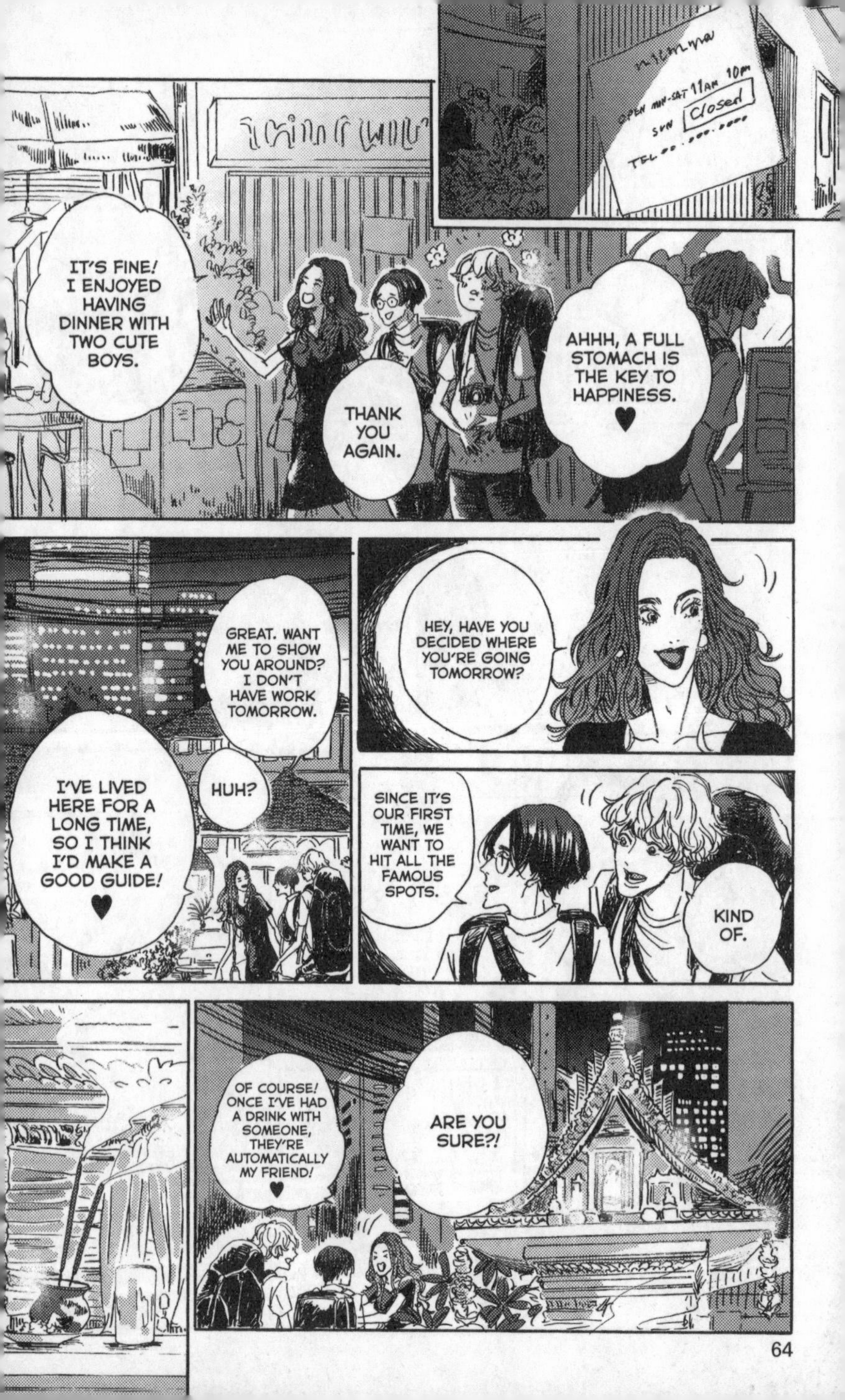
OPEN MON-SAT 11AM 10PM
SUN Closed
AHHH, A FULL STOMACH IS THE KEY TO HAPPINESS. ♥
THANK YOU AGAIN.
IT'S FINE! I ENJOYED HAVING DINNER WITH TWO CUTE BOYS.
HEY, HAVE YOU DECIDED WHERE YOU'RE GOING TOMORROW?
KIND OF.
SINCE IT'S OUR FIRST TIME, WE WANT TO HIT ALL THE FAMOUS SPOTS.
GREAT. WANT ME TO SHOW YOU AROUND? I DON'T HAVE WORK TOMORROW.
HUH?
I'VE LIVED HERE FOR A LONG TIME, SO I THINK I'D MAKE A GOOD GUIDE! ♥
ARE YOU SURE?!
OF COURSE! ONCE I'VE HAD A DRINK WITH SOMEONE, THEY'RE AUTOMATICALLY MY FRIEND! ♥

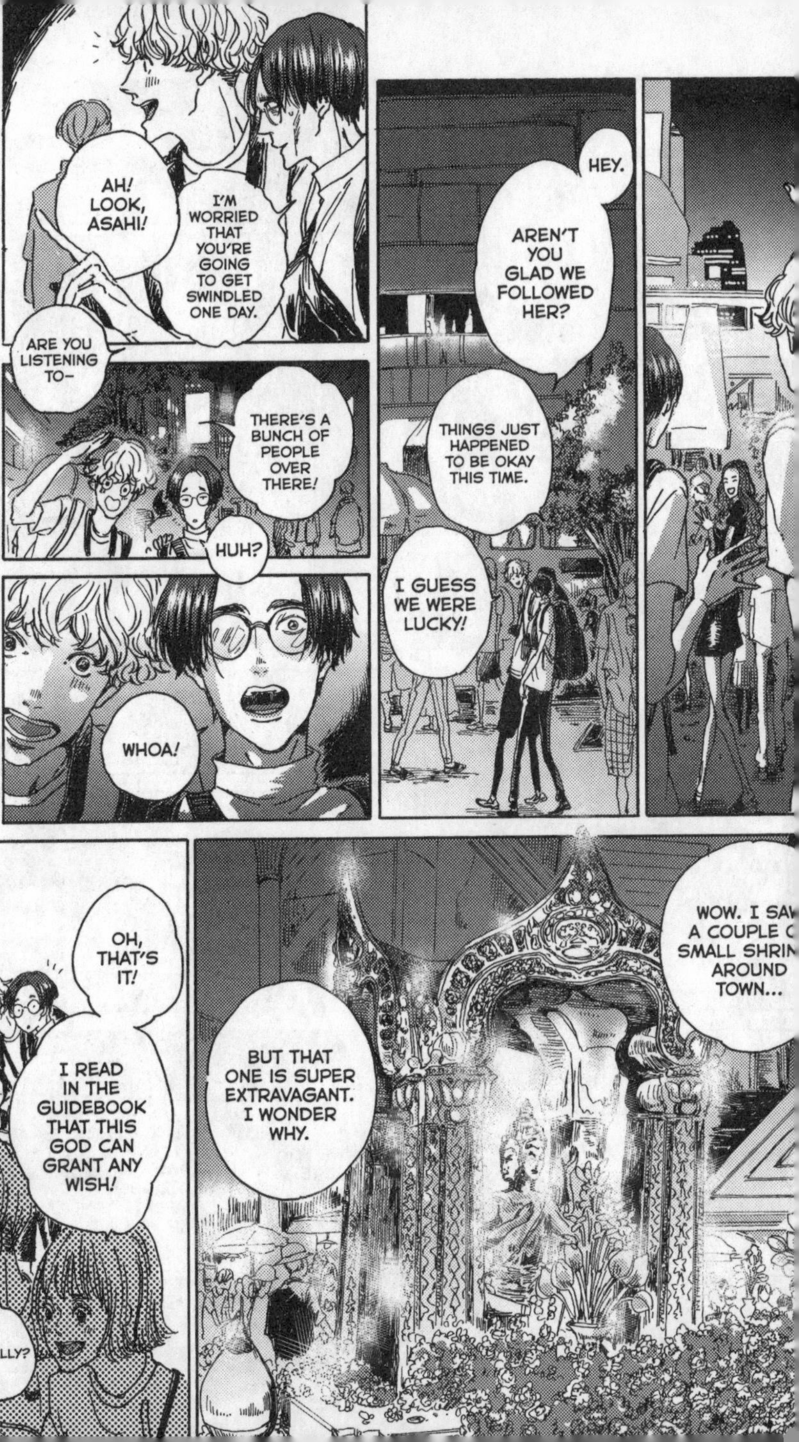
HEY.
AREN'T YOU GLAD WE FOLLOWED HER?
THINGS JUST HAPPENED TO BE OKAY THIS TIME.
I GUESS WE WERE LUCKY!
I'M WORRIED THAT YOU'RE GOING TO GET SWINDLED ONE DAY.
AH! LOOK, ASAHI!
ARE YOU LISTENING TO–
THERE'S A BUNCH OF PEOPLE OVER THERE!
HUH?
WHOA!
WOW. I SAW A COUPLE O SMALL SHRIN AROUND TOWN...
BUT THAT ONE IS SUPER EXTRAVAGANT. I WONDER WHY.
OH, THAT'S IT!
I READ IN THE GUIDEBOOK THAT THIS GOD CAN GRANT ANY WISH!
REALLY?

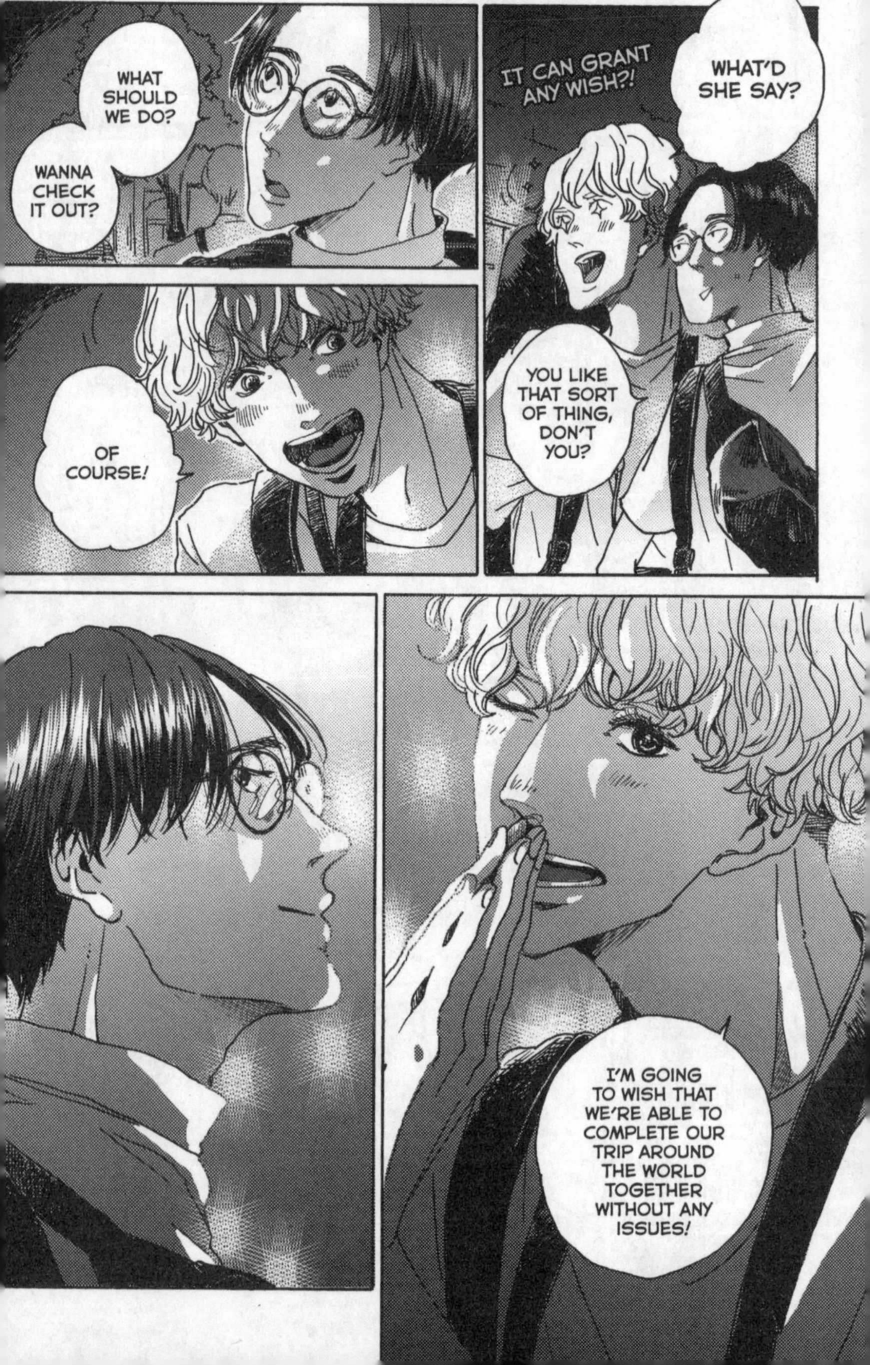
WHAT'D SHE SAY?
IT CAN GRANT ANY WISH?!
YOU LIKE THAT SORT OF THING, DON'T YOU?
WHAT SHOULD WE DO?
WANNA CHECK IT OUT?
OF COURSE!
I'M GOING TO WISH THAT WE'RE ABLE TO COMPLETE OUR TRIP AROUND THE WORLD TOGETHER WITHOUT ANY ISSUES!

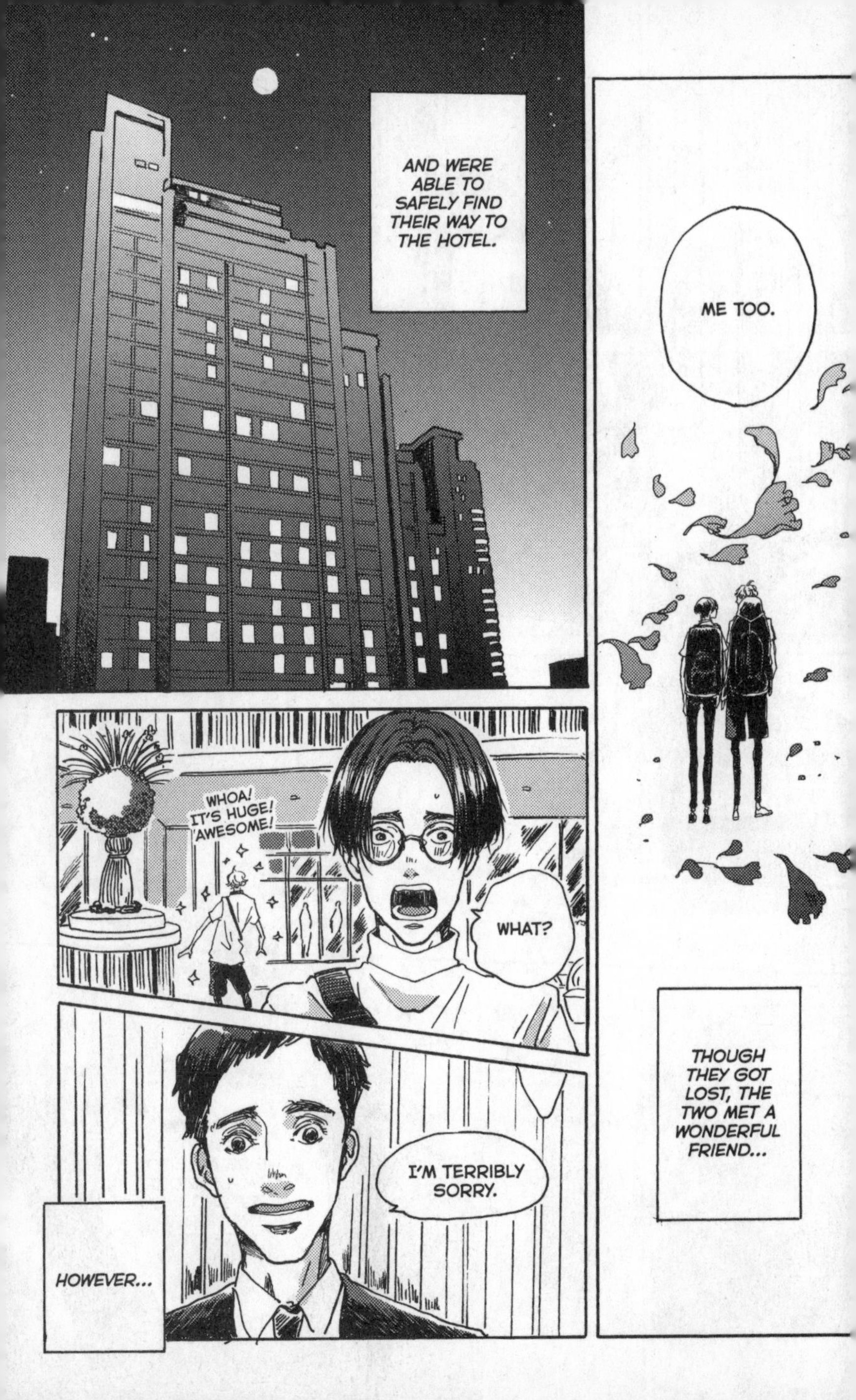
ME TOO.
THOUGH THEY GOT LOST, THE TWO MET A WONDERFUL FRIEND...
AND WERE ABLE TO SAFELY FIND THEIR WAY TO THE HOTEL.
WHOA! IT'S HUGE! AWESOME!
WHAT?
I'M TERRIBLY SORRY.
HOWEVER...

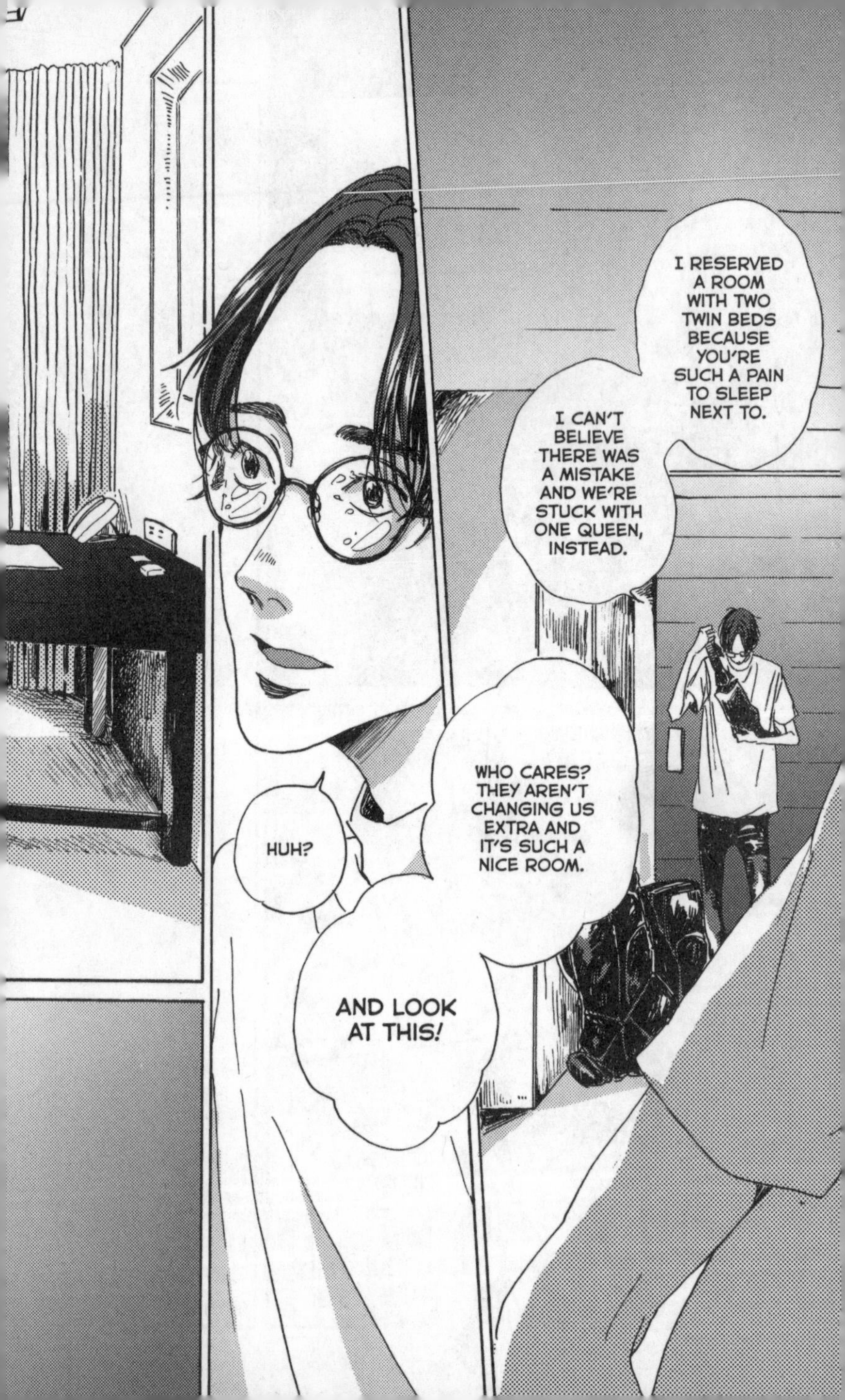
I RESERVED A ROOM WITH TWO TWIN BEDS BECAUSE YOU'RE SUCH A PAIN TO SLEEP NEXT TO.
I CAN'T BELIEVE THERE WAS A MISTAKE AND WE'RE STUCK WITH ONE QUEEN, INSTEAD.
WHO CARES? THEY AREN'T CHANGING US EXTRA AND IT'S SUCH A NICE ROOM.
HUH?
AND LOOK AT THIS!

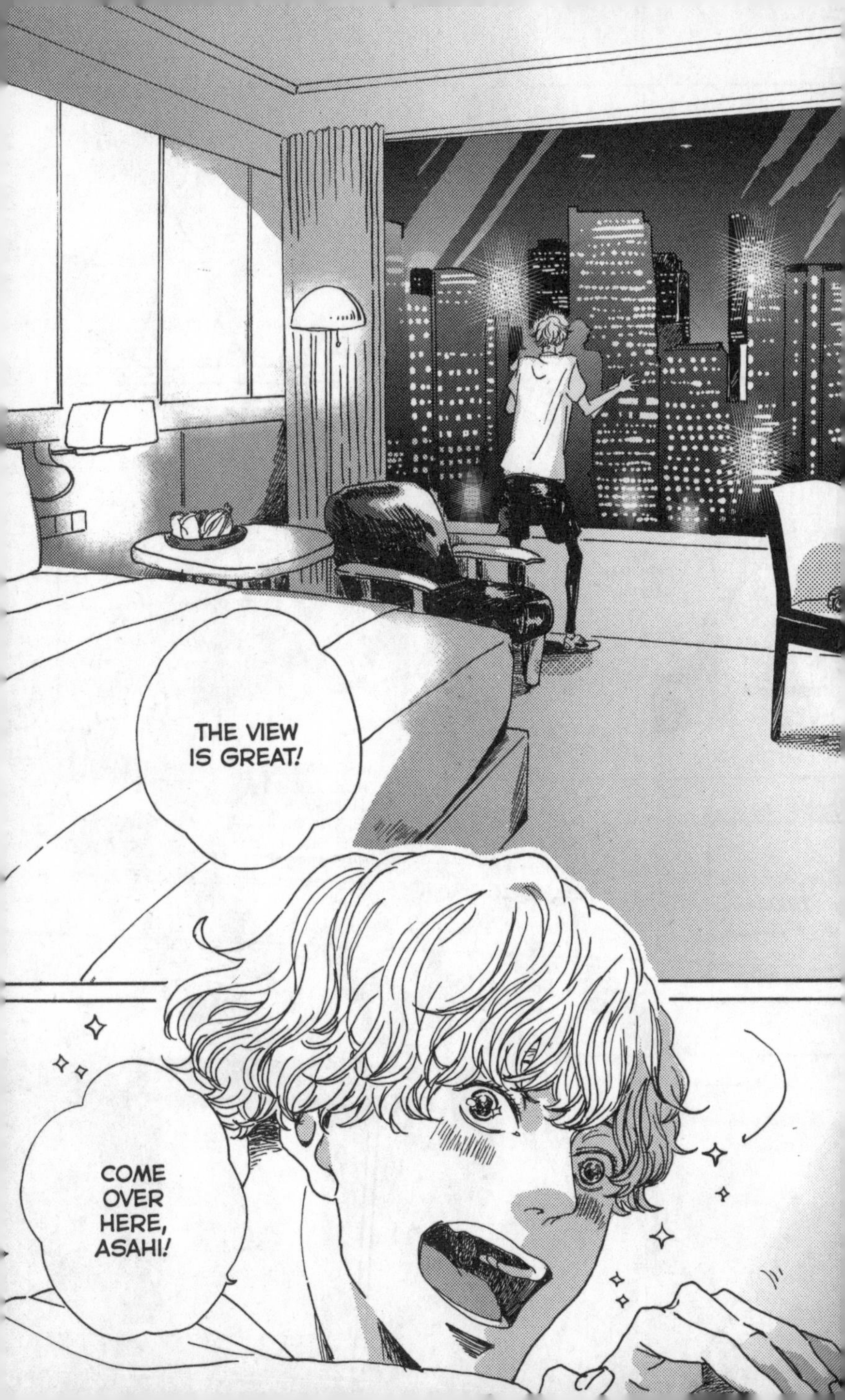
THE VIEW IS GREAT!
COME OVER HERE, ASAHI!

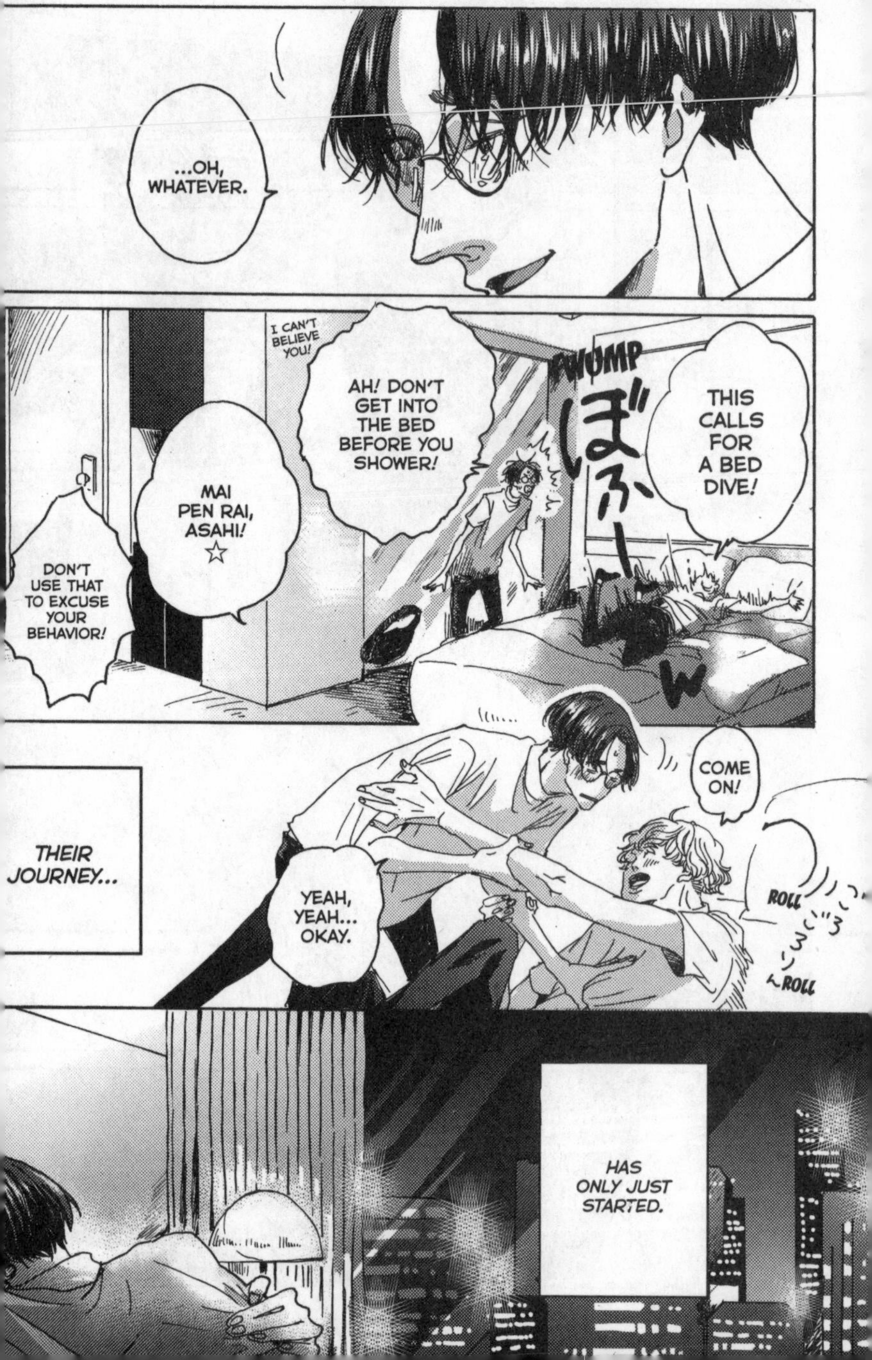
...OH, WHATEVER.
THIS CALLS FOR A BED DIVE!
FWOMP
ぼふー
AH! DON'T GET INTO THE BED BEFORE YOU SHOWER!
I CAN'T BELIEVE YOU!
MAI PEN RAI, ASAHI! ☆
DON'T USE THAT TO EXCUSE YOUR BEHAVIOR!
COME ON!
ROLL
ROLL
YEAH, YEAH... OKAY.
THEIR JOURNEY...
HAS ONLY JUST STARTED.

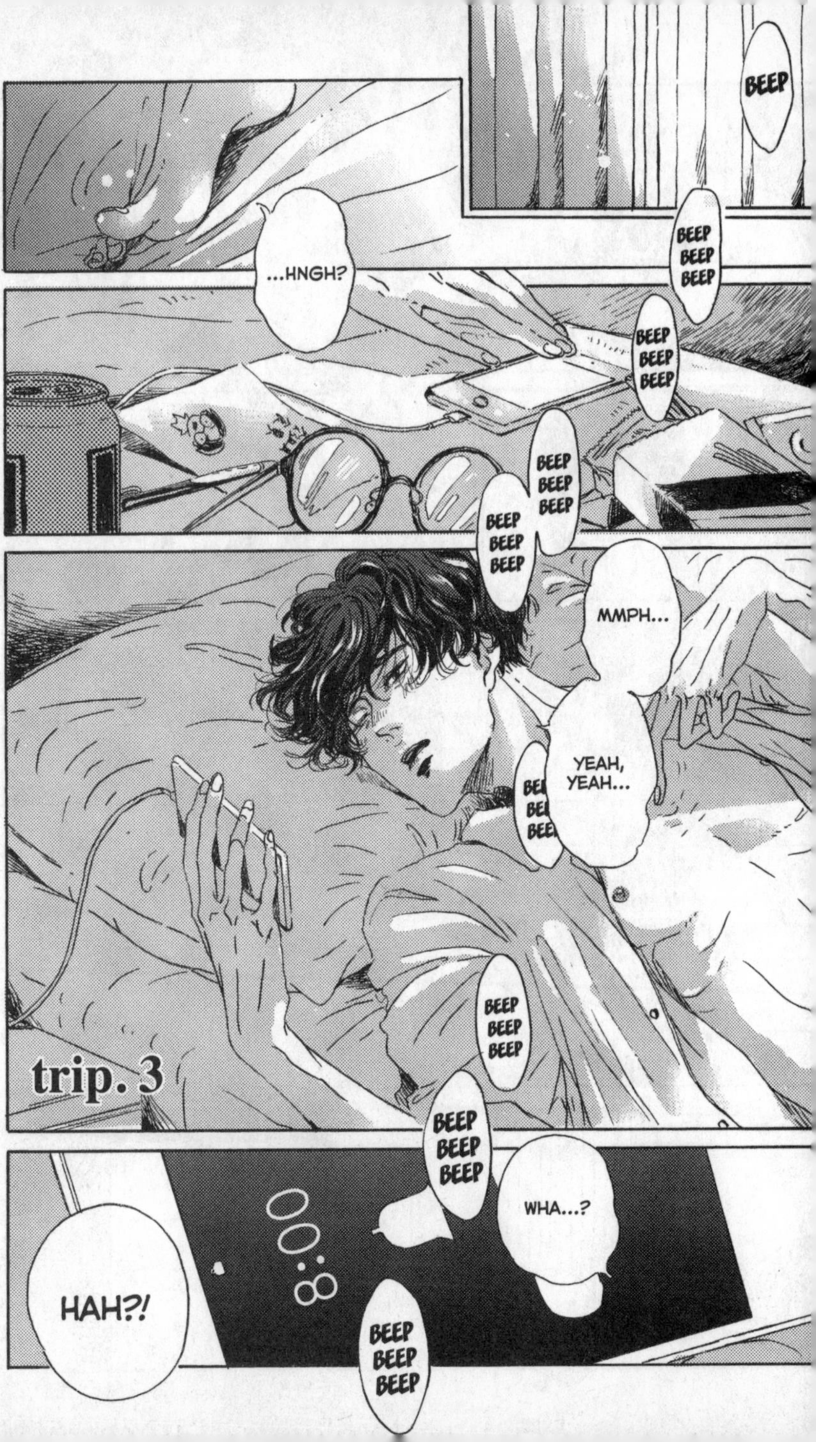
BEEP
BEEP BEEP BEEP
...HNGH?
BEEP BEEP BEEP
BEEP BEEP BEEP
BEEP BEEP BEEP
MMPH...
YEAH, YEAH...
BEEP BEEP BEEP
trip. 3
BEEP BEEP BEEP
WHA...?
8:00
HAH?!
BEEP BEEP BEEP

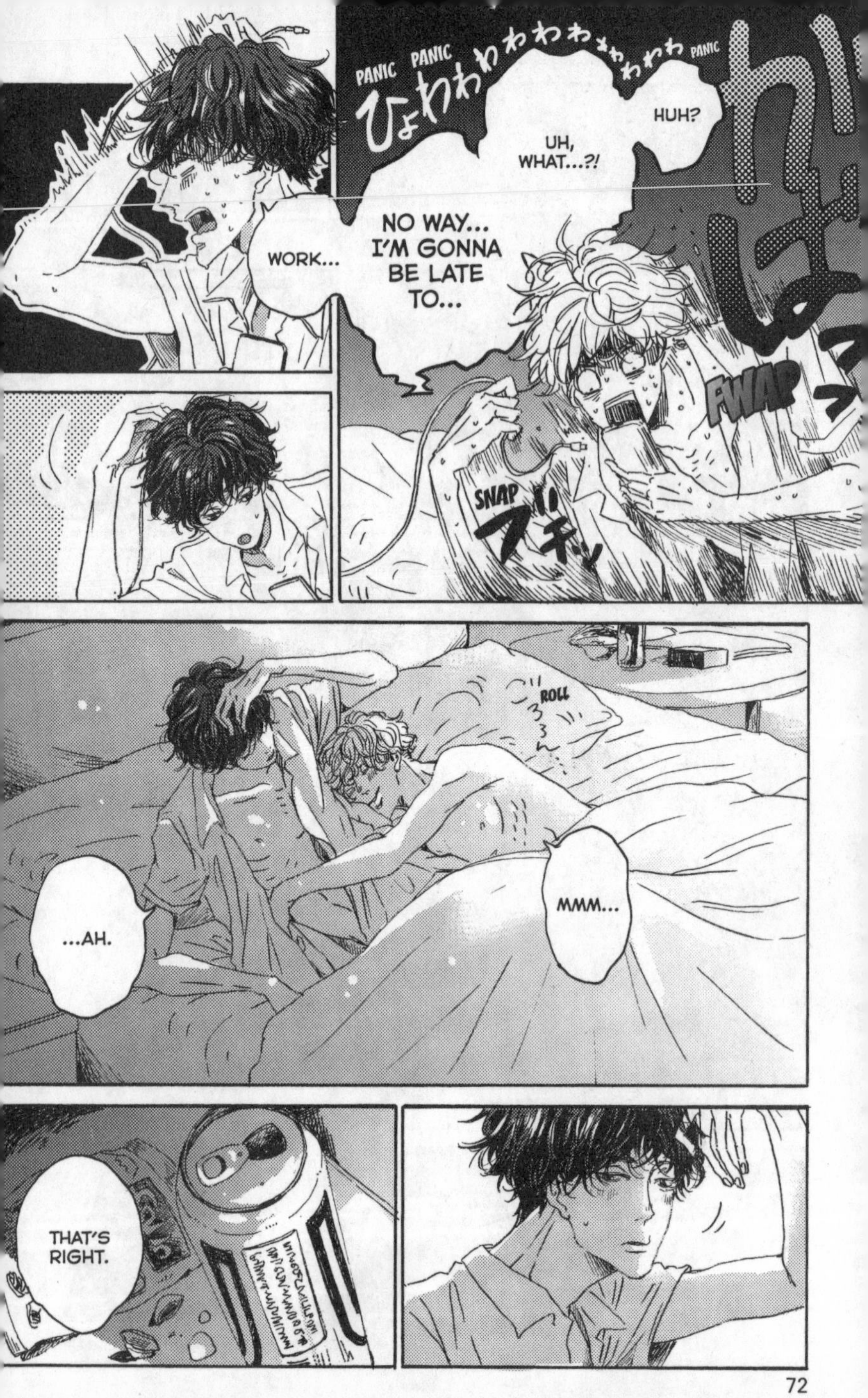
PANIC PANIC
ひょわわわわわ
PANIC
HUH?
UH, WHAT...?!
FWAP
SNAP
ブチッ
NO WAY... I'M GONNA BE LATE TO...
WORK...
ROLL
MMM...
...AH.
THAT'S RIGHT.

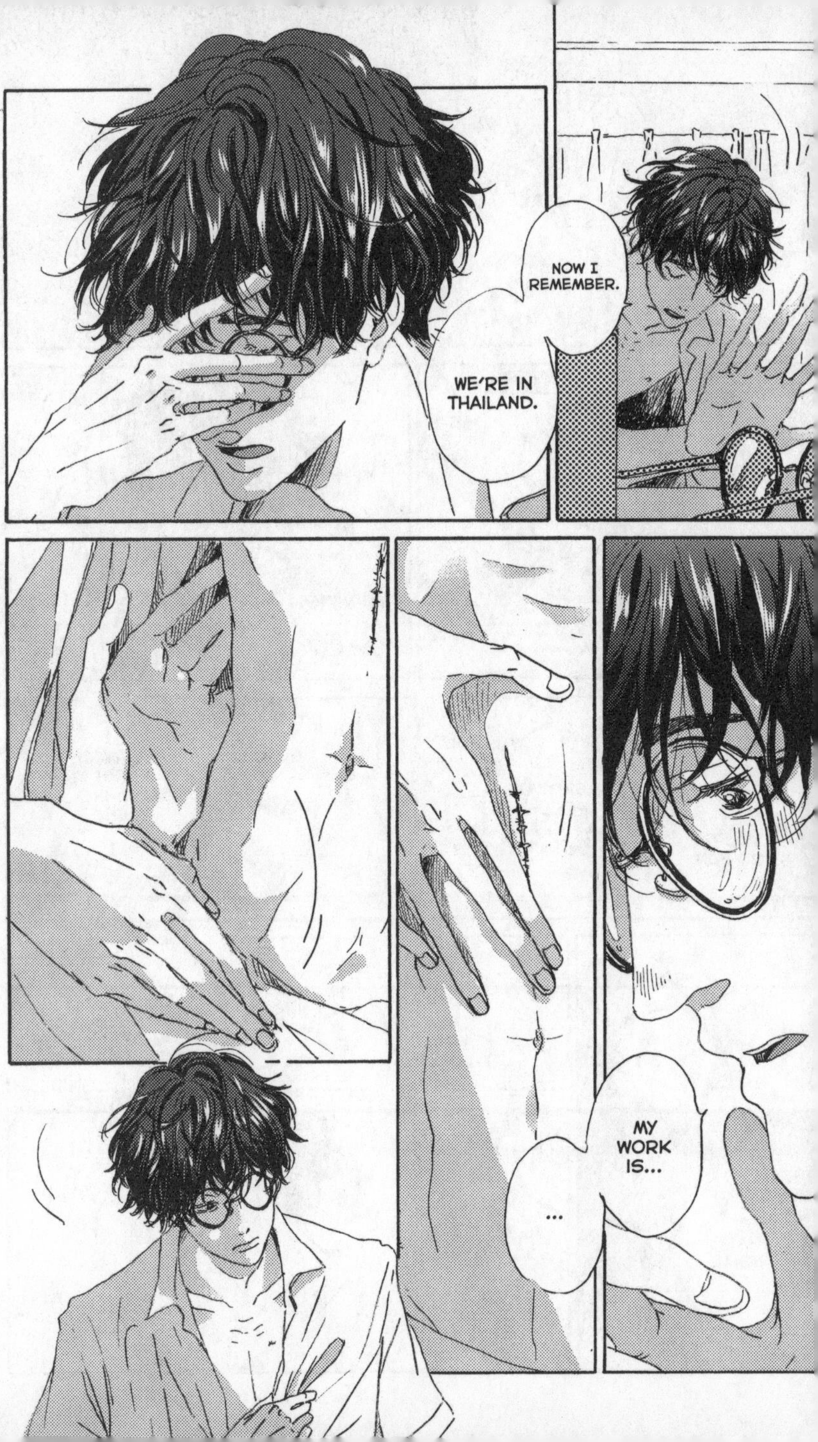
NOW I REMEMBER.
WE'RE IN THAILAND.
MY WORK IS...
...

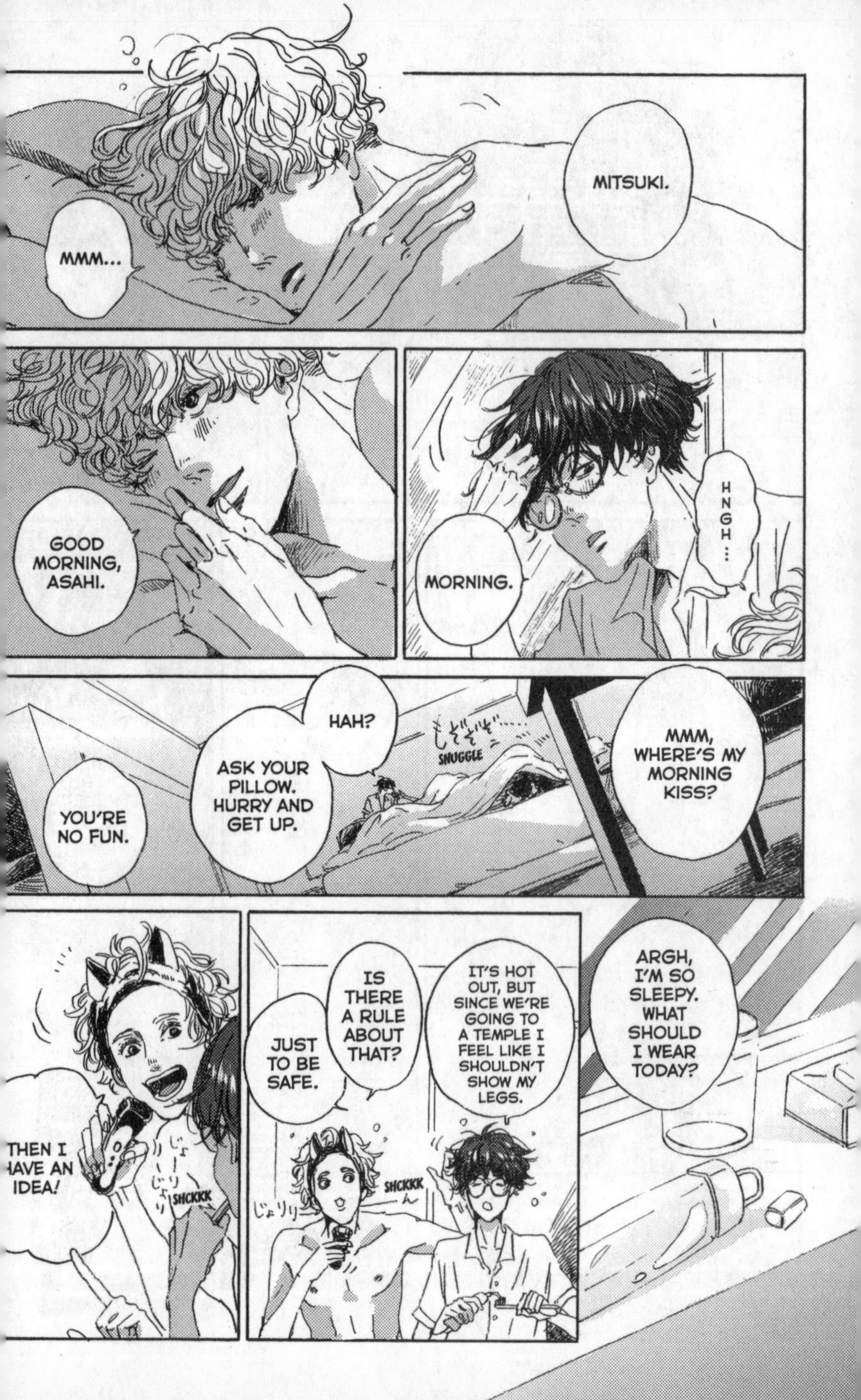
MITSUKI.
MMM...
HNGH...
MORNING.
GOOD MORNING, ASAHI.
MMM, WHERE'S MY MORNING KISS?
SNUGGLE
HAH?
ASK YOUR PILLOW. HURRY AND GET UP.
YOU'RE NO FUN.
ARGH, I'M SO SLEEPY. WHAT SHOULD I WEAR TODAY?
IT'S HOT OUT, BUT SINCE WE'RE GOING TO A TEMPLE I FEEL LIKE I SHOULDN'T SHOW MY LEGS.
IS THERE A RULE ABOUT THAT?
JUST TO BE SAFE.
SHCKKK
SHCKKK
THEN I HAVE AN IDEA!

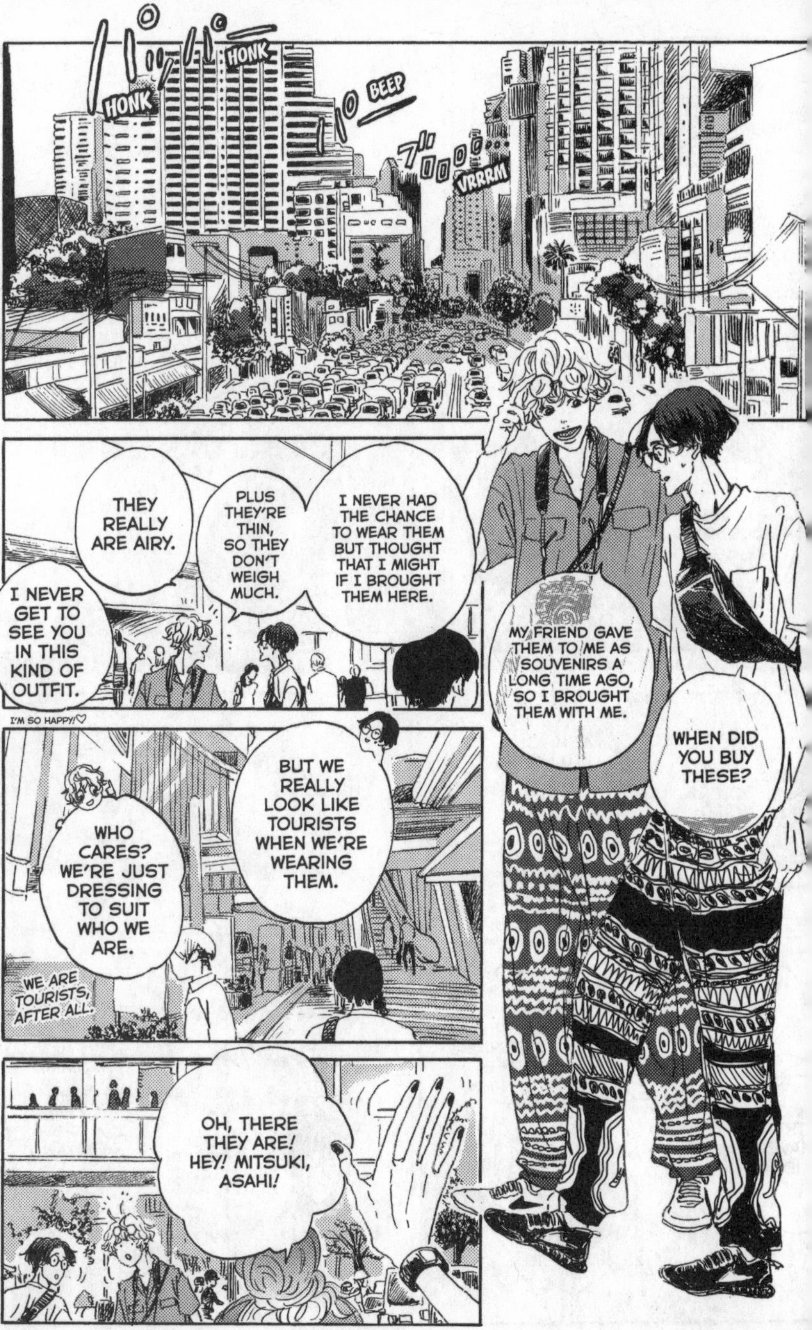
HONK
HONK
BEEP
VRRRM
WHEN DID YOU BUY THESE?
MY FRIEND GAVE THEM TO ME AS SOUVENIRS A LONG TIME AGO, SO I BROUGHT THEM WITH ME.
I NEVER HAD THE CHANCE TO WEAR THEM BUT THOUGHT THAT I MIGHT IF I BROUGHT THEM HERE.
PLUS THEY'RE THIN, SO THEY DON'T WEIGH MUCH.
THEY REALLY ARE AIRY.
I NEVER GET TO SEE YOU IN THIS KIND OF OUTFIT.
I'M SO HAPPY!♡
BUT WE REALLY LOOK LIKE TOURISTS WHEN WE'RE WEARING THEM.
WHO CARES? WE'RE JUST DRESSING TO SUIT WHO WE ARE.
WE ARE TOURISTS, AFTER ALL.
OH, THERE THEY ARE! HEY! MITSUKI, ASAHI!

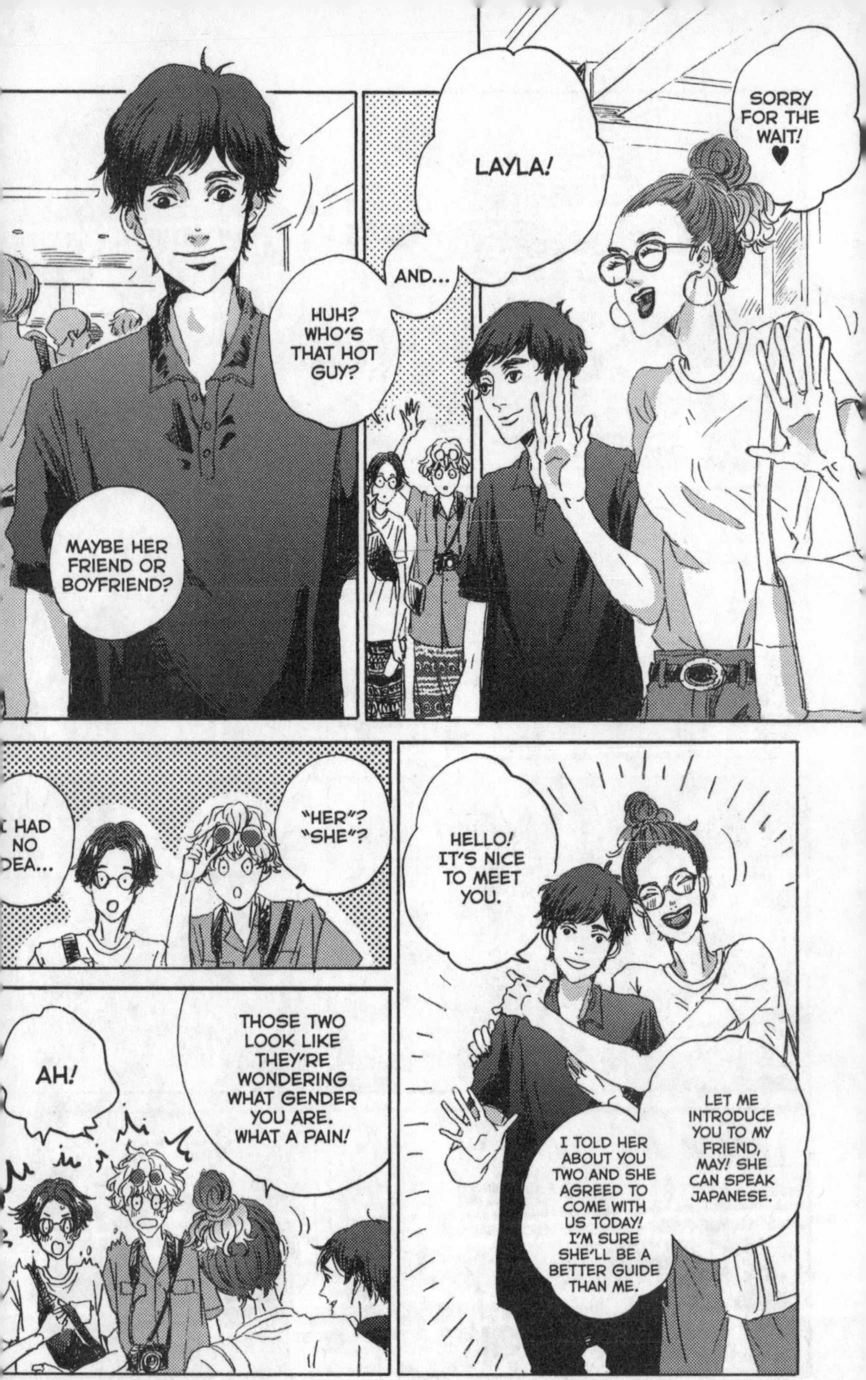
SORRY FOR THE WAIT! ♥
LAYLA!
AND...
HUH? WHO'S THAT HOT GUY?
MAYBE HER FRIEND OR BOYFRIEND?
HELLO! IT'S NICE TO MEET YOU.
LET ME INTRODUCE YOU TO MY FRIEND, MAY! SHE CAN SPEAK JAPANESE.
I TOLD HER ABOUT YOU TWO AND SHE AGREED TO COME WITH US TODAY! I'M SURE SHE'LL BE A BETTER GUIDE THAN ME.
"HER"? "SHE"?
HAD NO DEA...
THOSE TWO LOOK LIKE THEY'RE WONDERING WHAT GENDER YOU ARE. WHAT A PAIN!
AH!

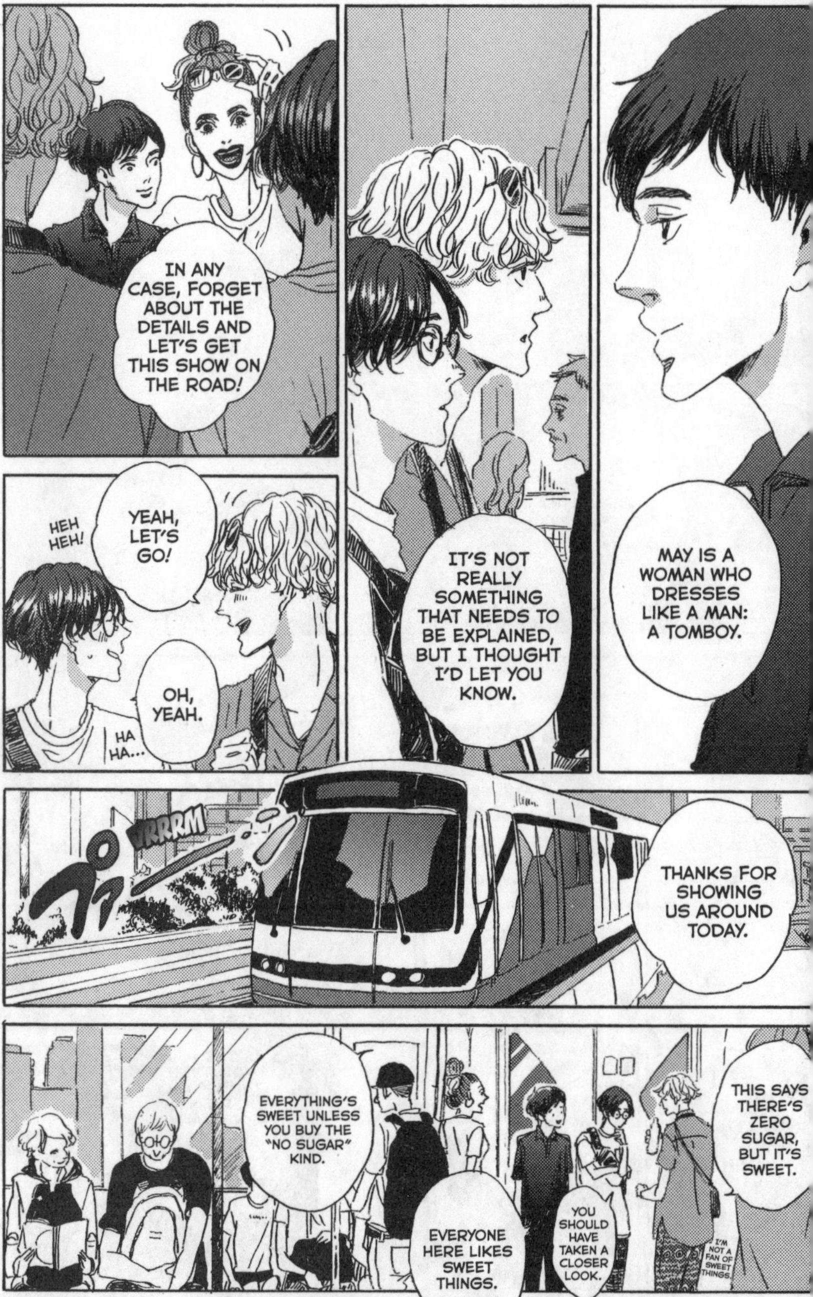
MAY IS A WOMAN WHO DRESSES LIKE A MAN: A TOMBOY.
IT'S NOT REALLY SOMETHING THAT NEEDS TO BE EXPLAINED, BUT I THOUGHT I'D LET YOU KNOW.
IN ANY CASE, FORGET ABOUT THE DETAILS AND LET'S GET THIS SHOW ON THE ROAD!
YEAH, LET'S GO!
HEH HEH!
OH, YEAH.
HA HA...
THANKS FOR SHOWING US AROUND TODAY.
VRRRM
THIS SAYS THERE'S ZERO SUGAR, BUT IT'S SWEET.
I'M NOT A FAN OF SWEET THINGS.
YOU SHOULD HAVE TAKEN A CLOSER LOOK.
EVERYONE HERE LIKES SWEET THINGS.
EVERYTHING'S SWEET UNLESS YOU BUY THE "NO SUGAR" KIND.

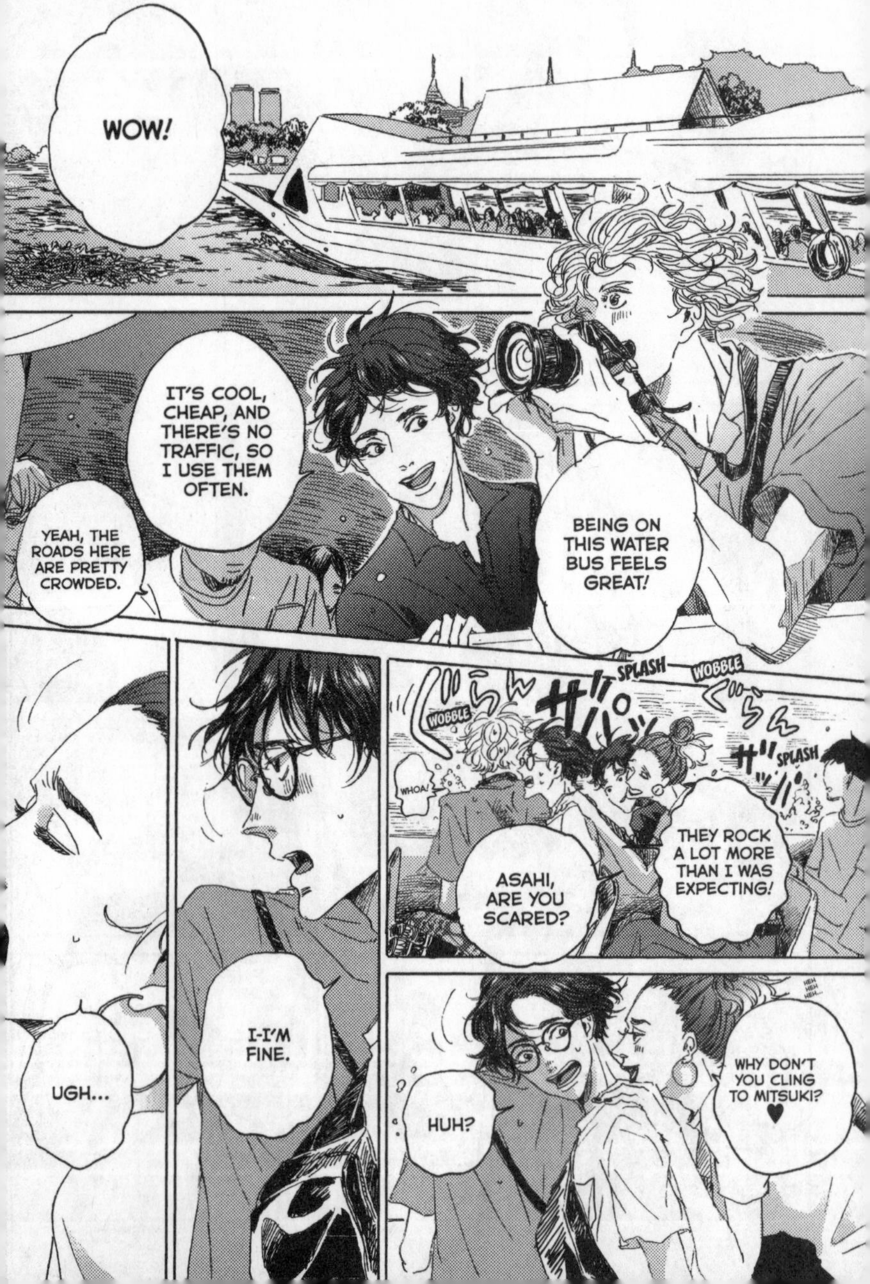
WOW!
BEING ON THIS WATER BUS FEELS GREAT!
IT'S COOL, CHEAP, AND THERE'S NO TRAFFIC, SO I USE THEM OFTEN.
YEAH, THE ROADS HERE ARE PRETTY CROWDED.
WOBBLE
SPLASH
WOBBLE
SPLASH
WHOA!
THEY ROCK A LOT MORE THAN I WAS EXPECTING!
ASAHI, ARE YOU SCARED?
HEH HEH HEH...
WHY DON'T YOU CLING TO MITSUKI? ♥
HUH?
I-I'M FINE.
UGH...

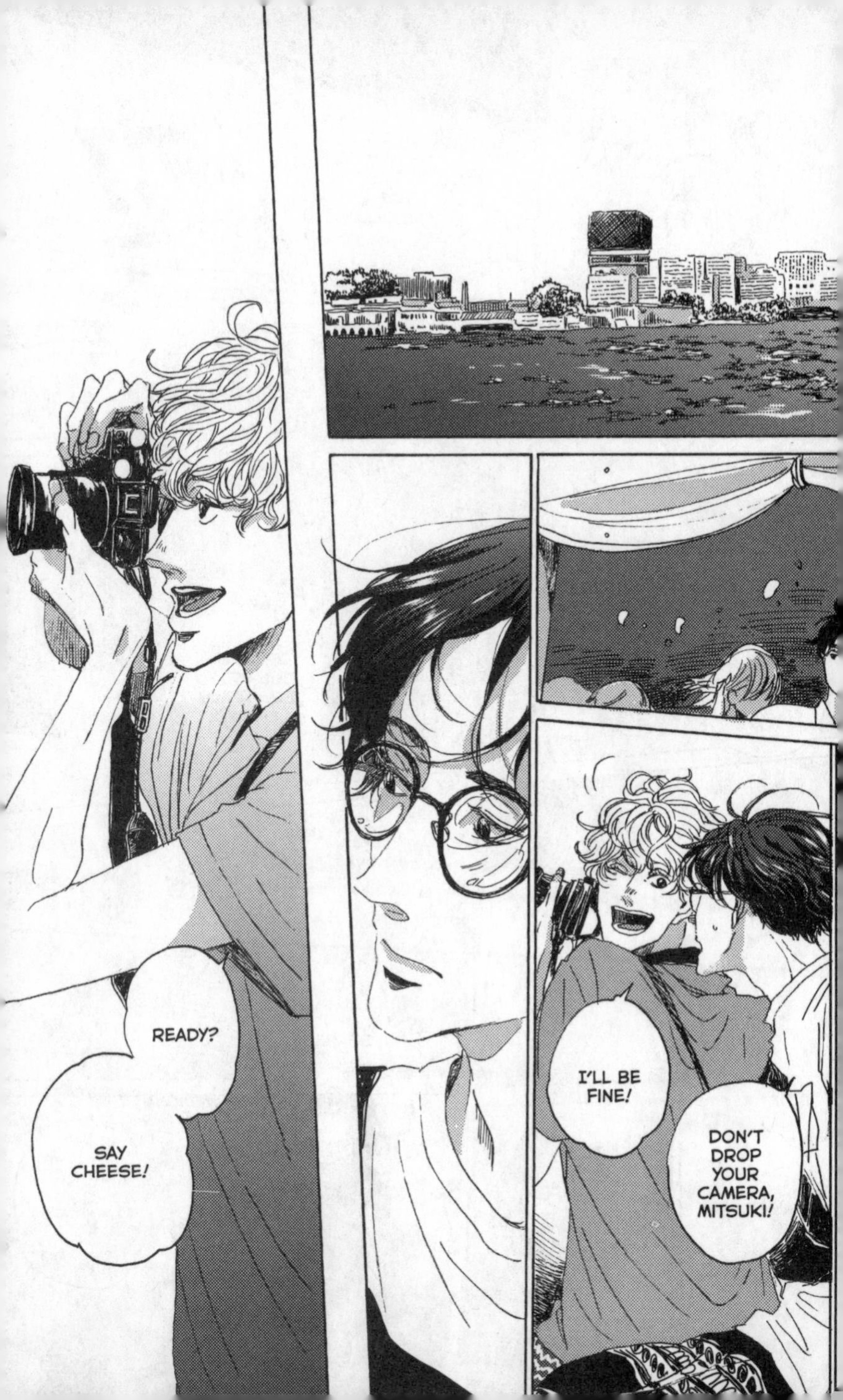
DON'T DROP YOUR CAMERA, MITSUKI!
I'LL BE FINE!
READY?
SAY CHEESE!

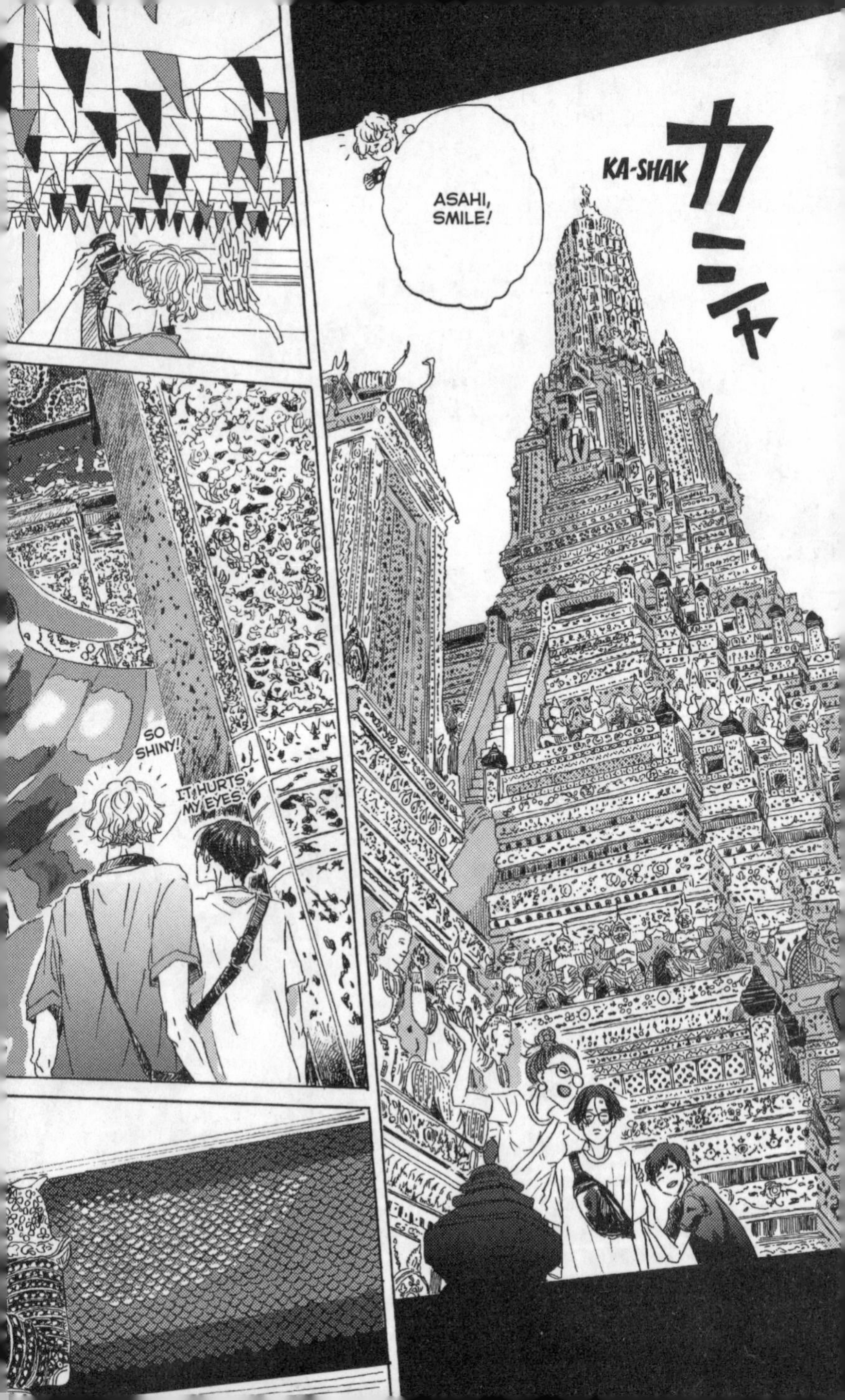
ASAHI, SMILE!
KA-SHAK
カシャ
SO SHINY!
IT HURTS MY EYES.

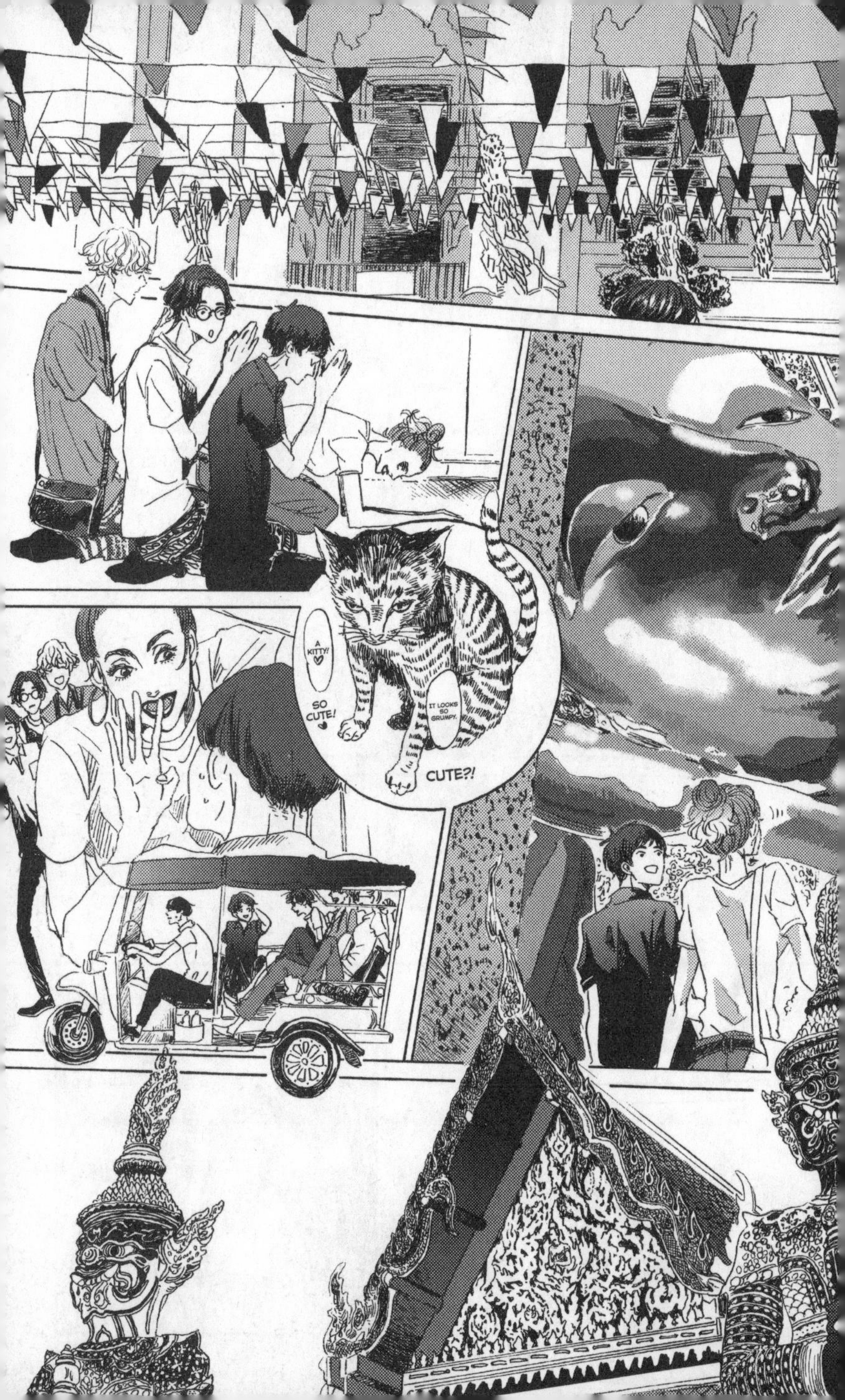
A KITTY! ♥
SO CUTE! ♥
IT LOOKS SO GRUMPY.
CUTE?!

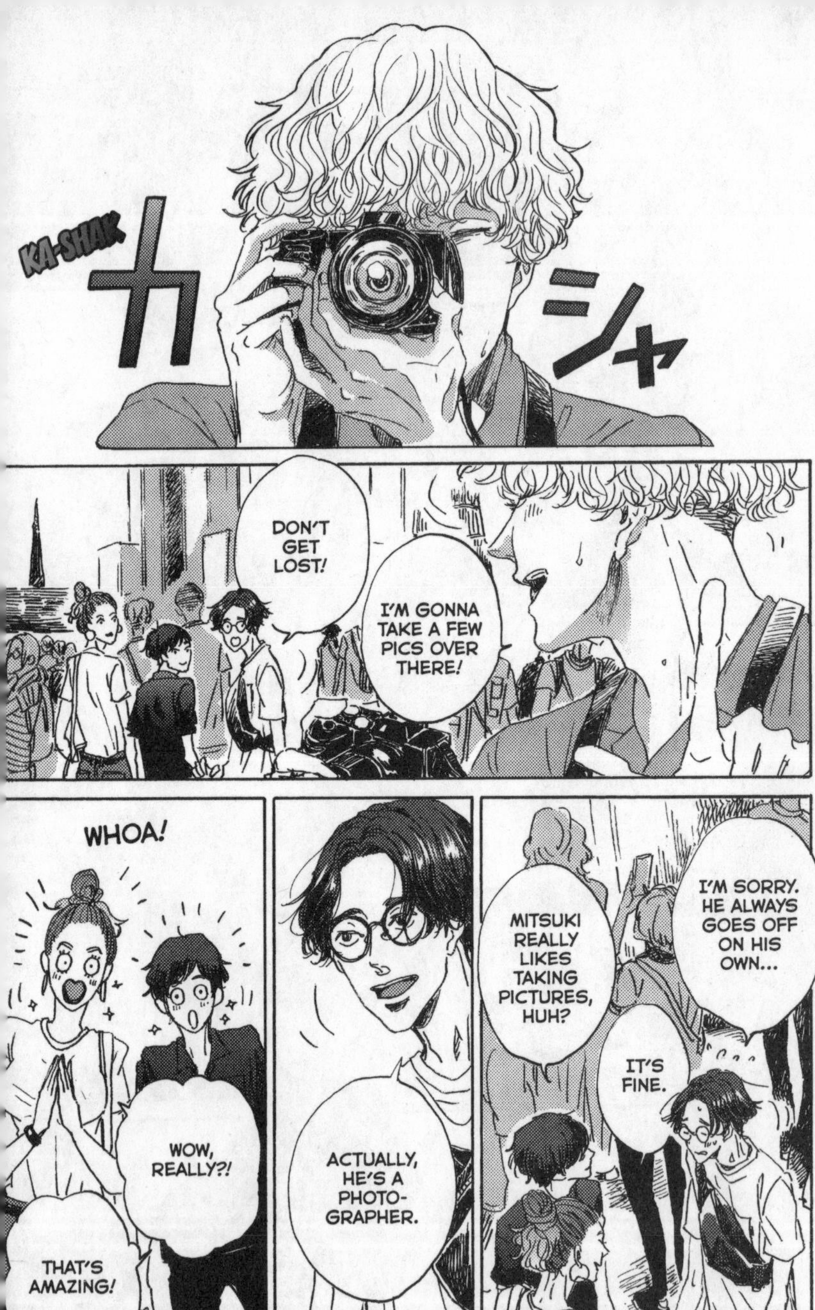
KA-SHAK
カシャ
I'M GONNA TAKE A FEW PICS OVER THERE!
DON'T GET LOST!
I'M SORRY. HE ALWAYS GOES OFF ON HIS OWN...
MITSUKI REALLY LIKES TAKING PICTURES, HUH?
IT'S FINE.
ACTUALLY, HE'S A PHOTO-GRAPHER.
WHOA!
WOW, REALLY?!
THAT'S AMAZING!

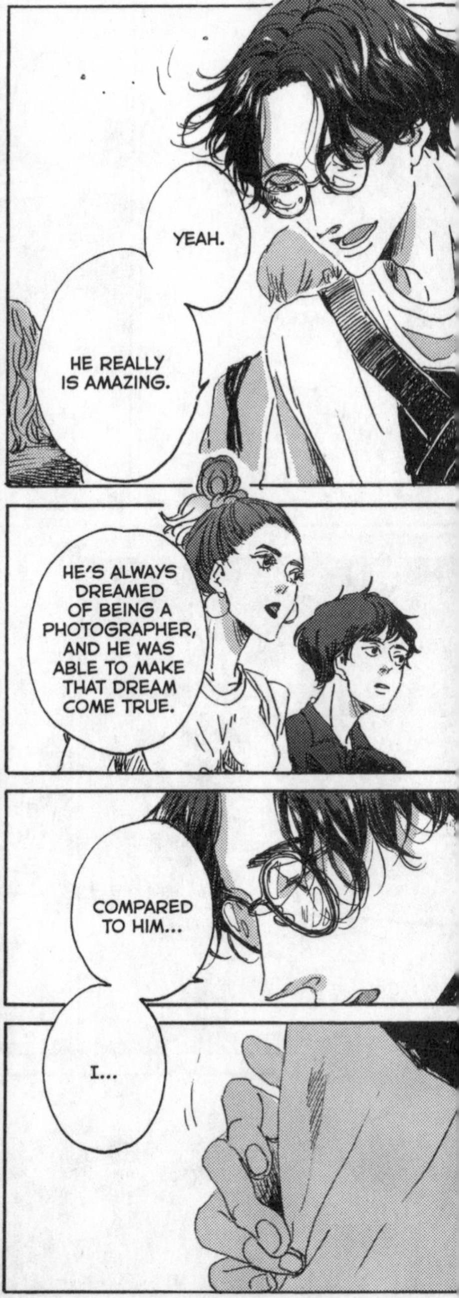
YEAH.
HE REALLY IS AMAZING.
HE'S ALWAYS DREAMED OF BEING A PHOTOGRAPHER, AND HE WAS ABLE TO MAKE THAT DREAM COME TRUE.
COMPARED TO HIM...
I...
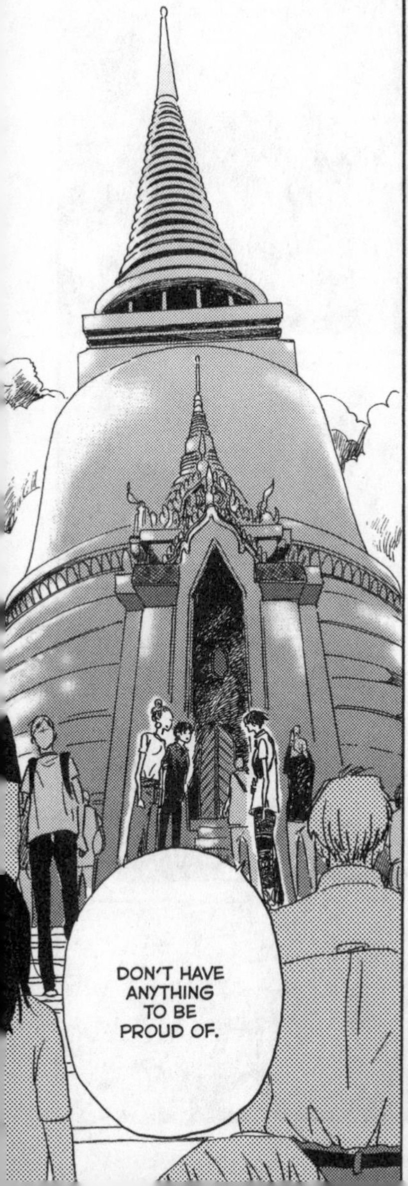
DON'T HAVE ANYTHING TO BE PROUD OF.

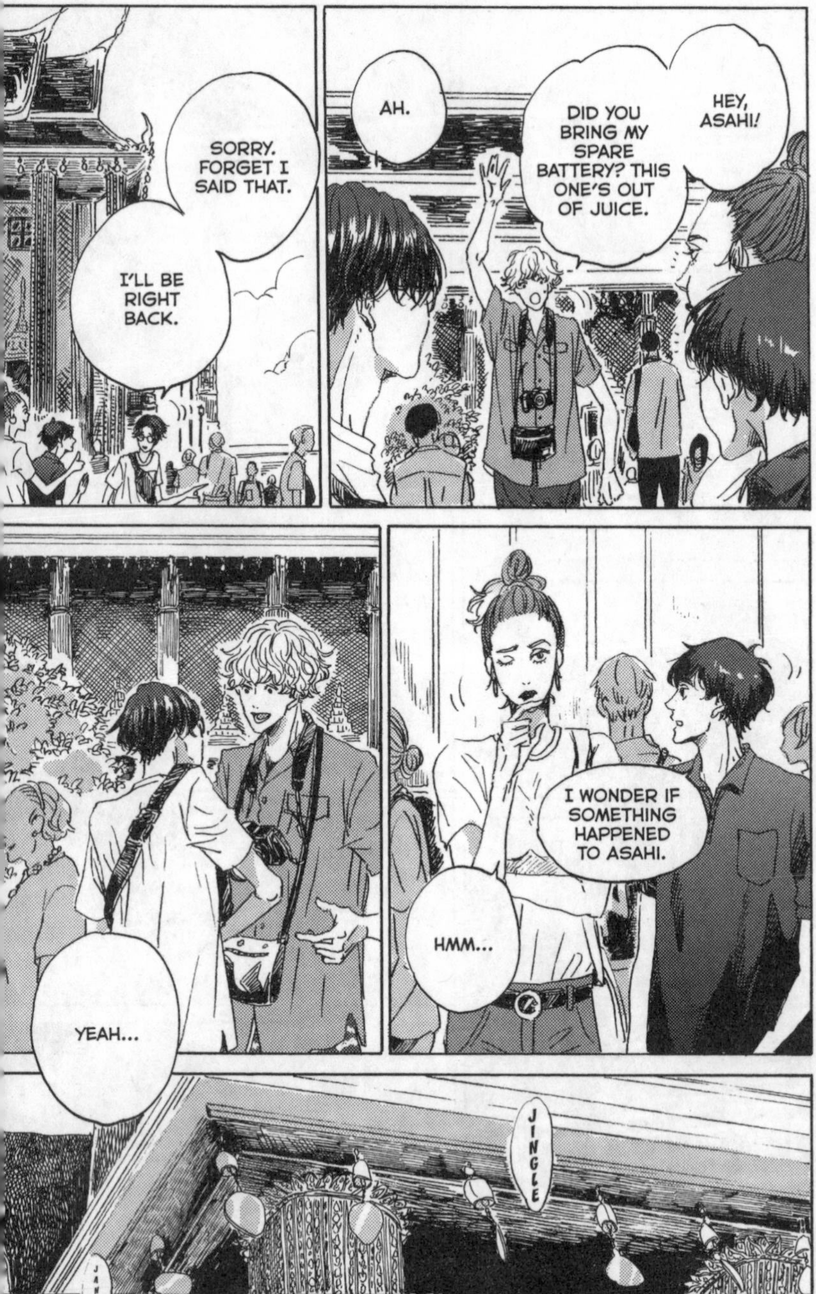
HEY, ASAHI!
DID YOU BRING MY SPARE BATTERY? THIS ONE'S OUT OF JUICE.
AH.
SORRY. FORGET I SAID THAT.
I'LL BE RIGHT BACK.
I WONDER IF SOMETHING HAPPENED TO ASAHI.
HMM...
YEAH...
JINGLE
JANGLE

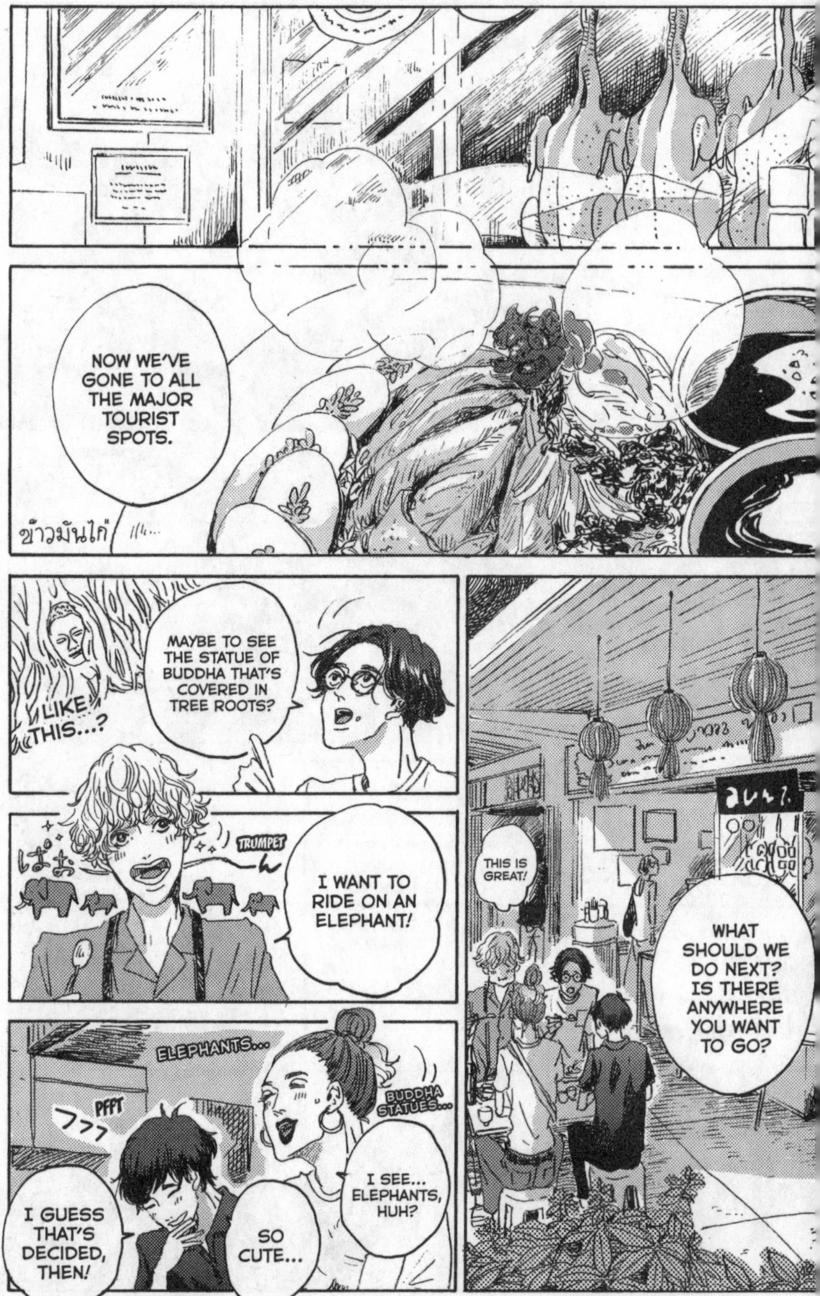

NOW WE'VE GONE TO ALL THE MAJOR TOURIST SPOTS.
ข้าวมันไก่
THIS IS GREAT!
WHAT SHOULD WE DO NEXT? IS THERE ANYWHERE YOU WANT TO GO?
MAYBE TO SEE THE STATUE OF BUDDHA THAT'S COVERED IN TREE ROOTS?
LIKE THIS...?
TRUMPET
ぱお
I WANT TO RIDE ON AN ELEPHANT!
ELEPHANTS...
BUDDHA STATUES...
I SEE... ELEPHANTS, HUH?
SO CUTE...
PFFT
I GUESS THAT'S DECIDED, THEN!

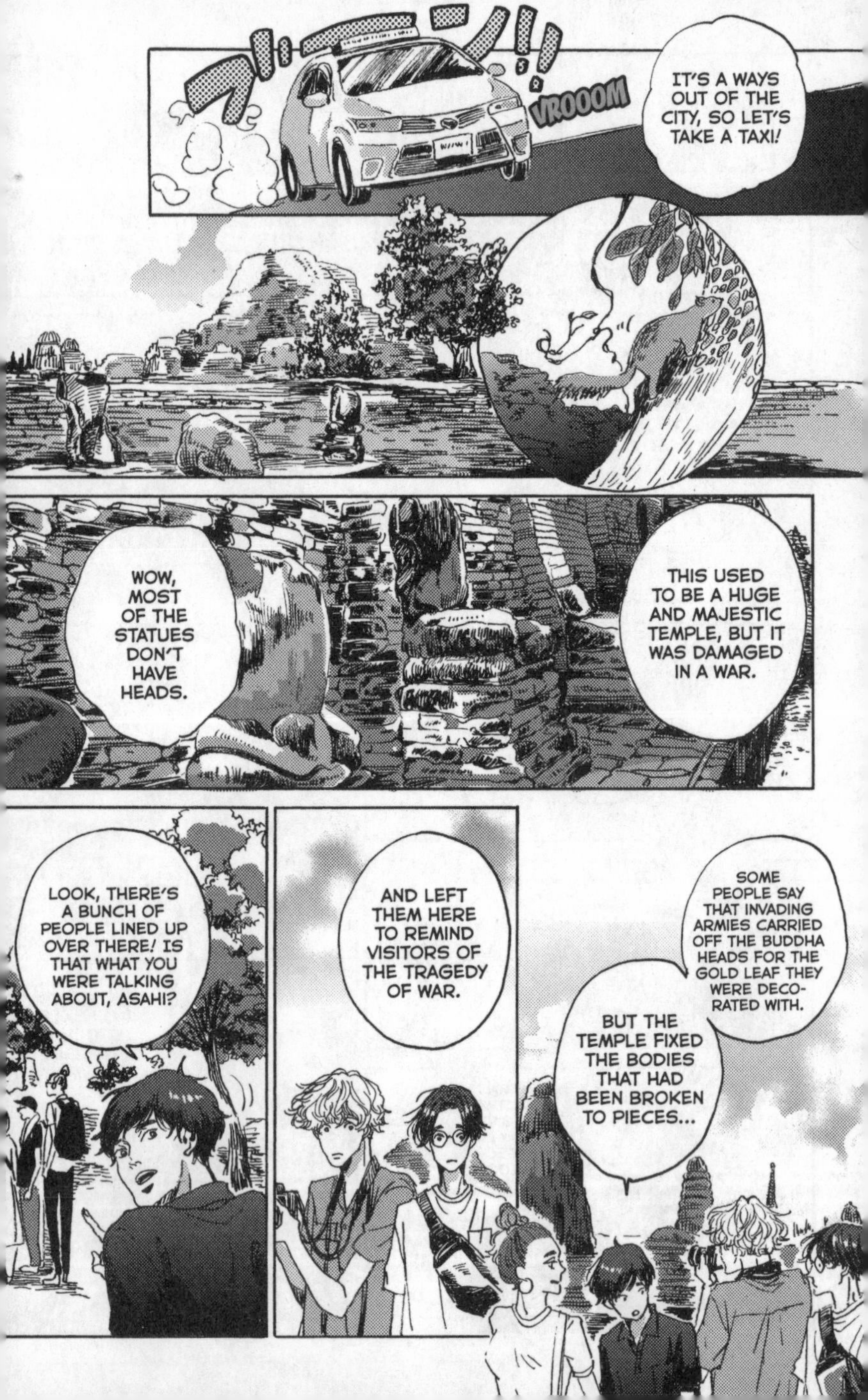
IT'S A WAYS OUT OF THE CITY, SO LET'S TAKE A TAXI!
VROOOM
THIS USED TO BE A HUGE AND MAJESTIC TEMPLE, BUT IT WAS DAMAGED IN A WAR.
WOW, MOST OF THE STATUES DON'T HAVE HEADS.
SOME PEOPLE SAY THAT INVADING ARMIES CARRIED OFF THE BUDDHA HEADS FOR THE GOLD LEAF THEY WERE DECO-RATED WITH.
BUT THE TEMPLE FIXED THE BODIES THAT HAD BEEN BROKEN TO PIECES...
AND LEFT THEM HERE TO REMIND VISITORS OF THE TRAGEDY OF WAR.
LOOK, THERE'S A BUNCH OF PEOPLE LINED UP OVER THERE! IS THAT WHAT YOU WERE TALKING ABOUT, ASAHI?

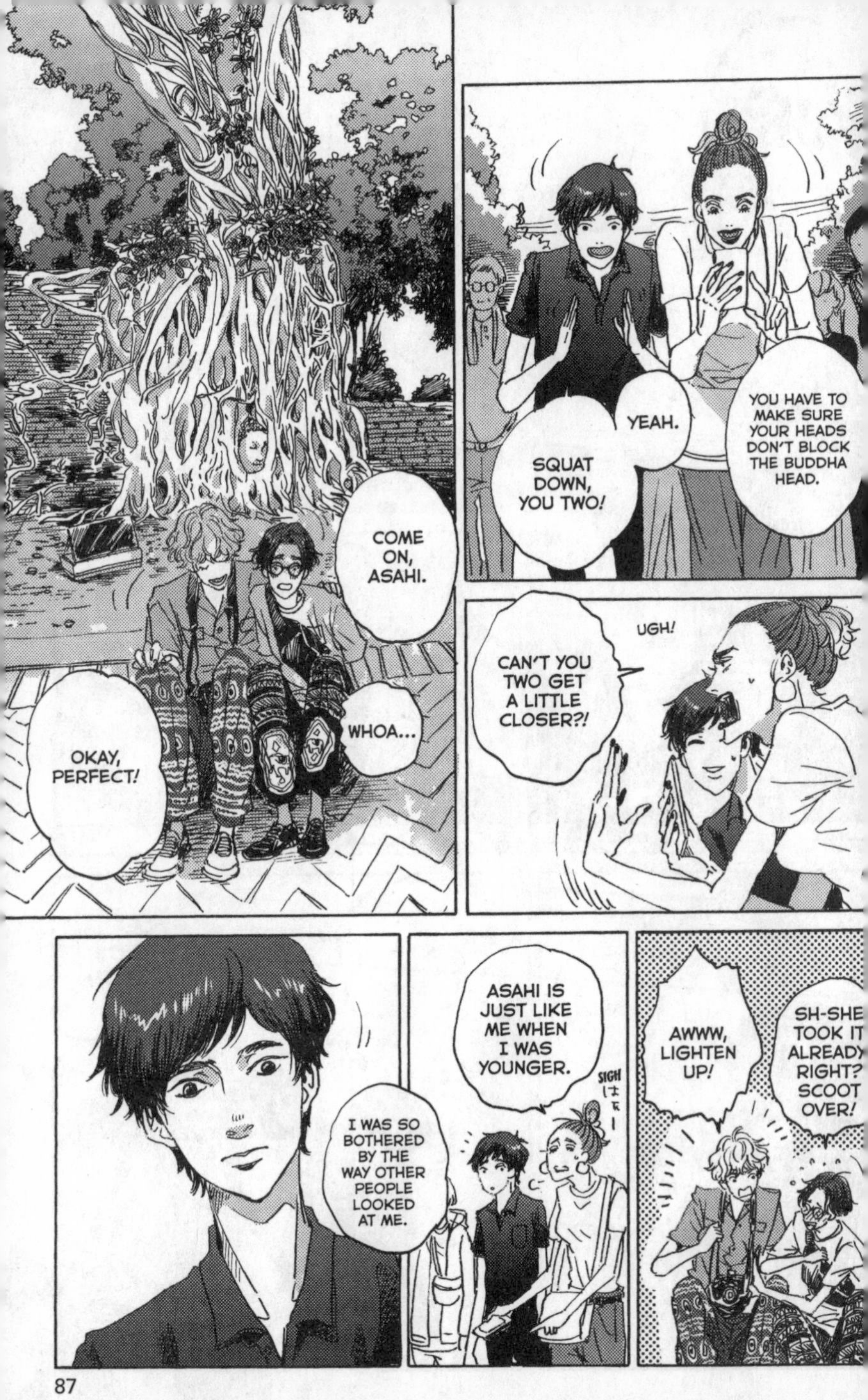
YOU HAVE TO MAKE SURE YOUR HEADS DON'T BLOCK THE BUDDHA HEAD.
YEAH.
SQUAT DOWN, YOU TWO!
UGH!
CAN'T YOU TWO GET A LITTLE CLOSER?!
COME ON, ASAHI.
WHOA...
OKAY, PERFECT!
SH-SHE TOOK IT ALREADY RIGHT? SCOOT OVER!
AWWW, LIGHTEN UP!
ASAHI IS JUST LIKE ME WHEN I WAS YOUNGER.
SIGH
I WAS SO BOTHERED BY THE WAY OTHER PEOPLE LOOKED AT ME.

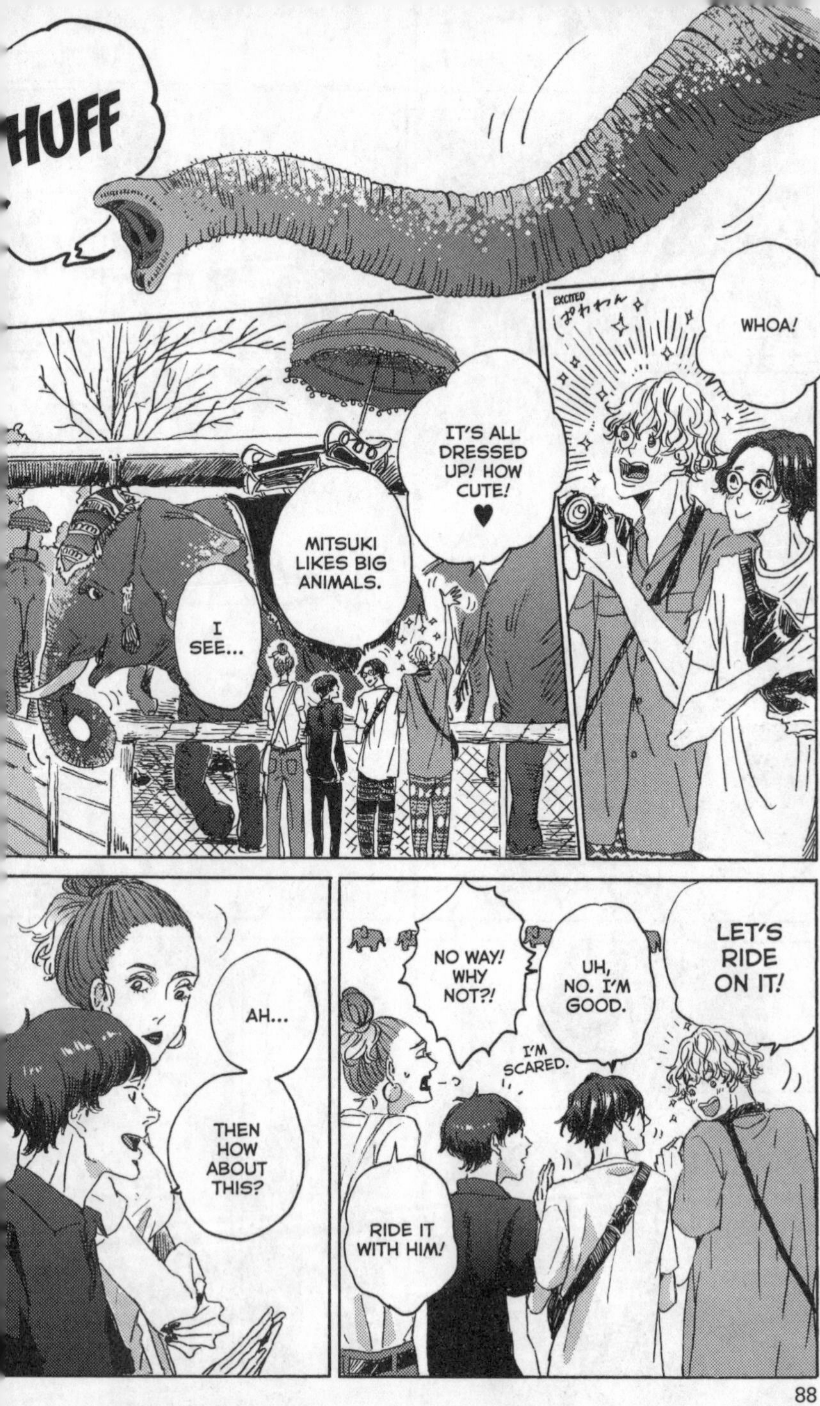
HUFF
WHOA!
EXCITED
IT'S ALL DRESSED UP! HOW CUTE! ♥
MITSUKI LIKES BIG ANIMALS.
I SEE...
LET'S RIDE ON IT!
UH, NO. I'M GOOD.
I'M SCARED.
NO WAY! WHY NOT?!
RIDE IT WITH HIM!
AH...
THEN HOW ABOUT THIS?

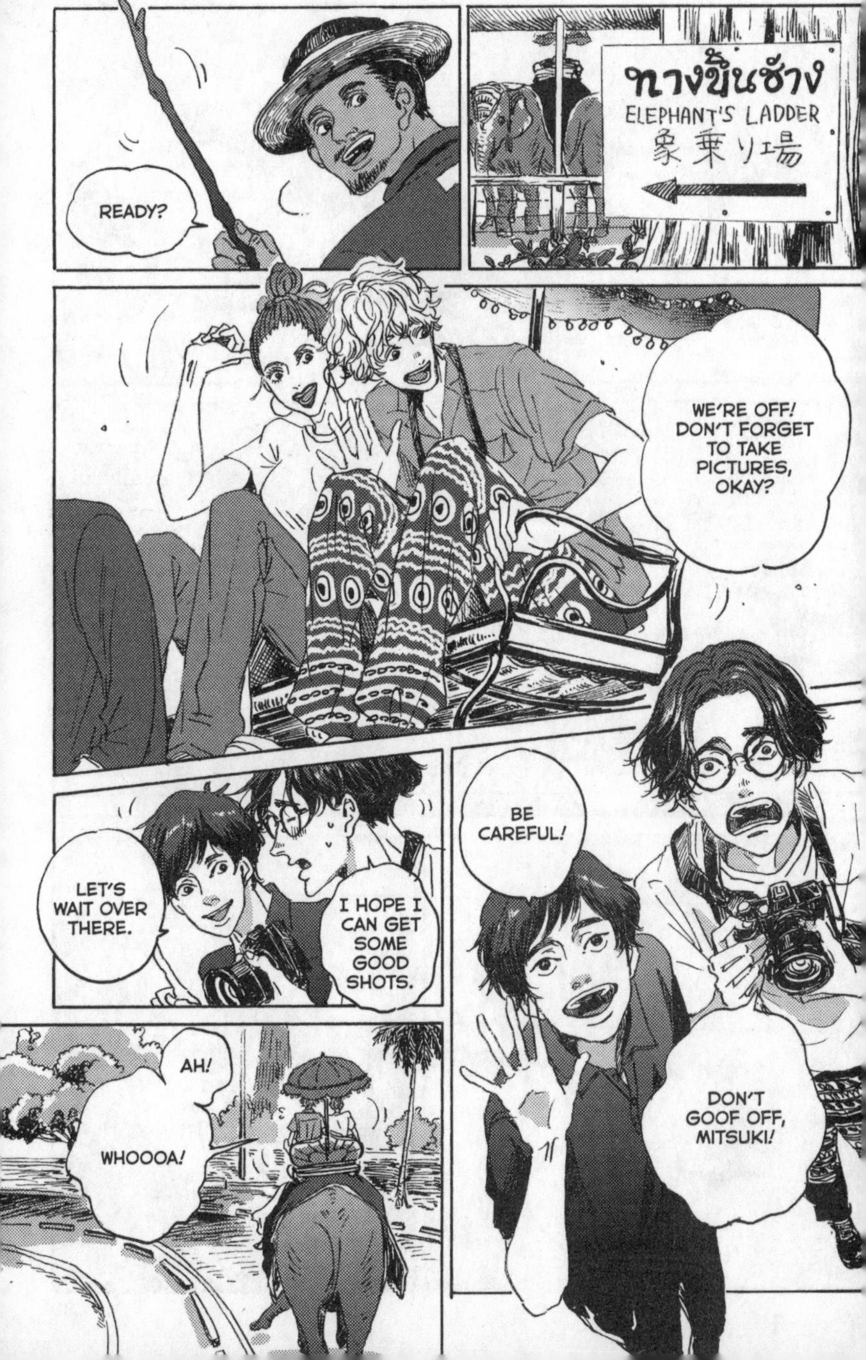
ทางขึ้นช้าง
ELEPHANT'S LADDER
象乗り場
READY?
WE'RE OFF! DON'T FORGET TO TAKE PICTURES, OKAY?
BE CAREFUL!
DON'T GOOF OFF, MITSUKI!
I HOPE I CAN GET SOME GOOD SHOTS.
LET'S WAIT OVER THERE.
AH!
WHOOOA!

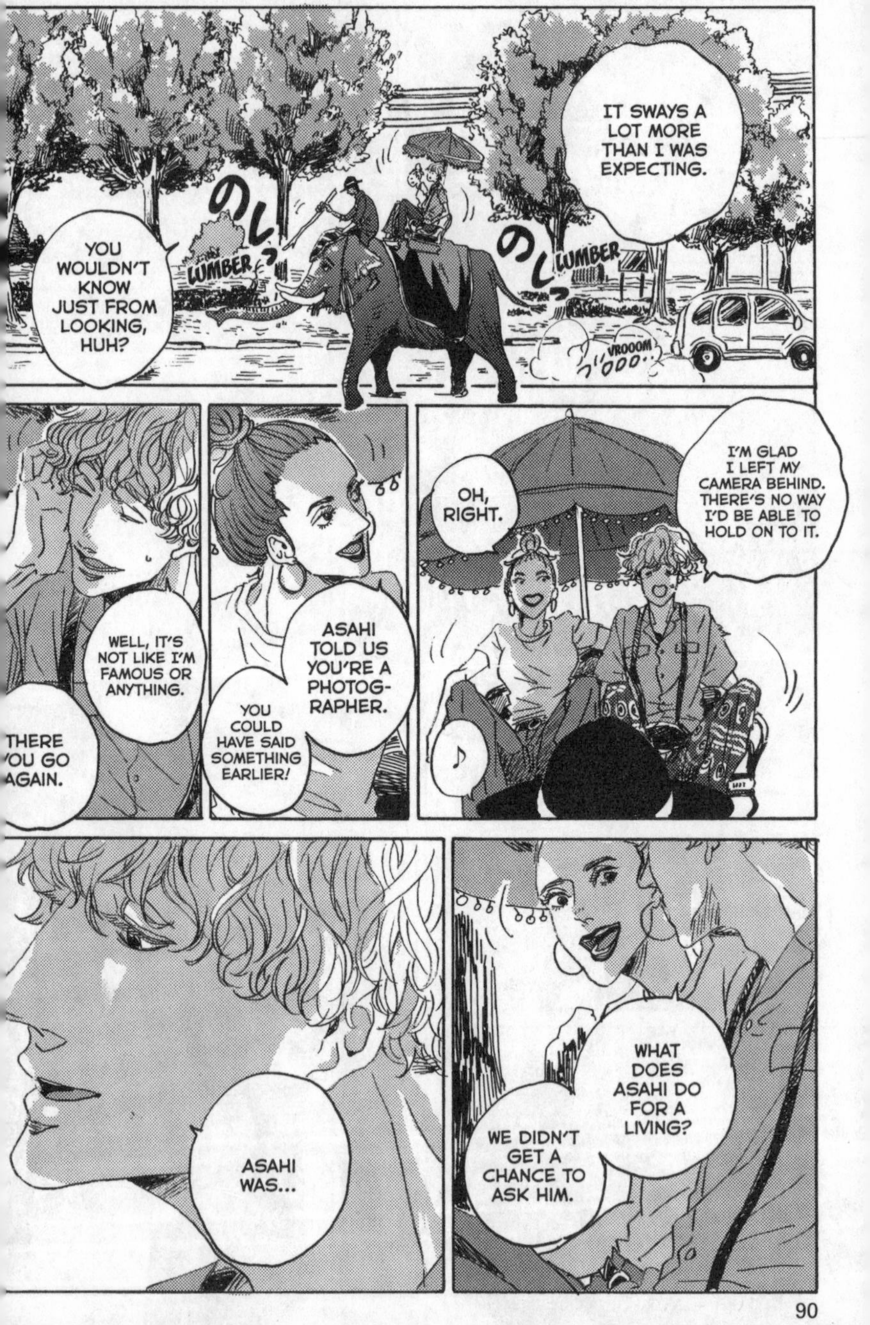
IT SWAYS A LOT MORE THAN I WAS EXPECTING.
のしっ LUMBER
のしっ LUMBER
VROOOM
YOU WOULDN'T KNOW JUST FROM LOOKING, HUH?
I'M GLAD I LEFT MY CAMERA BEHIND. THERE'S NO WAY I'D BE ABLE TO HOLD ON TO IT.
OH, RIGHT.
♪
ASAHI TOLD US YOU'RE A PHOTOG-RAPHER.
YOU COULD HAVE SAID SOMETHING EARLIER!
WELL, IT'S NOT LIKE I'M FAMOUS OR ANYTHING.
THERE 'OU GO AGAIN.
WHAT DOES ASAHI DO FOR A LIVING?
WE DIDN'T GET A CHANCE TO ASK HIM.
ASAHI WAS...

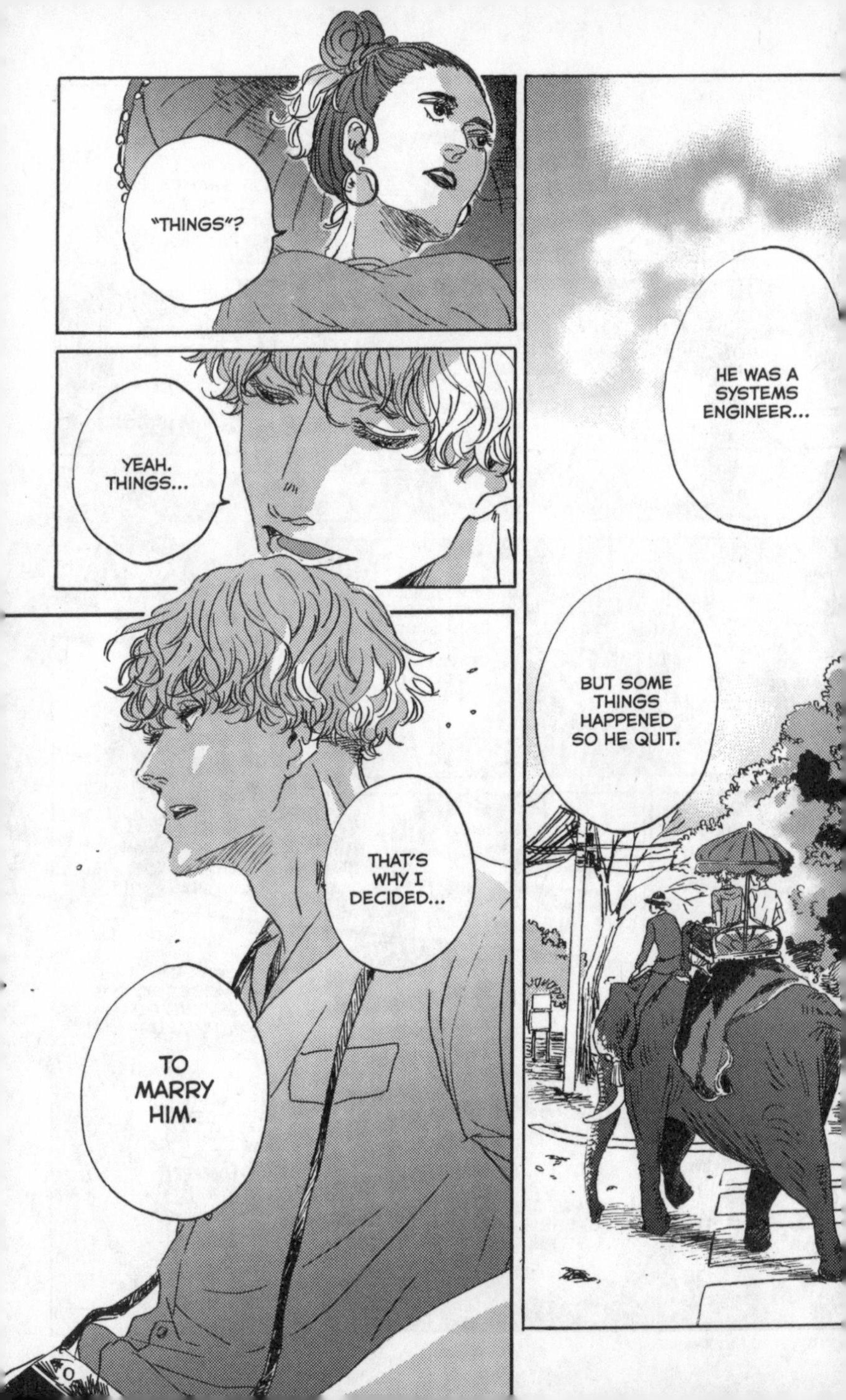
HE WAS A SYSTEMS ENGINEER...
BUT SOME THINGS HAPPENED SO HE QUIT.
"THINGS"?
YEAH. THINGS...
THAT'S WHY I DECIDED...
TO MARRY HIM.

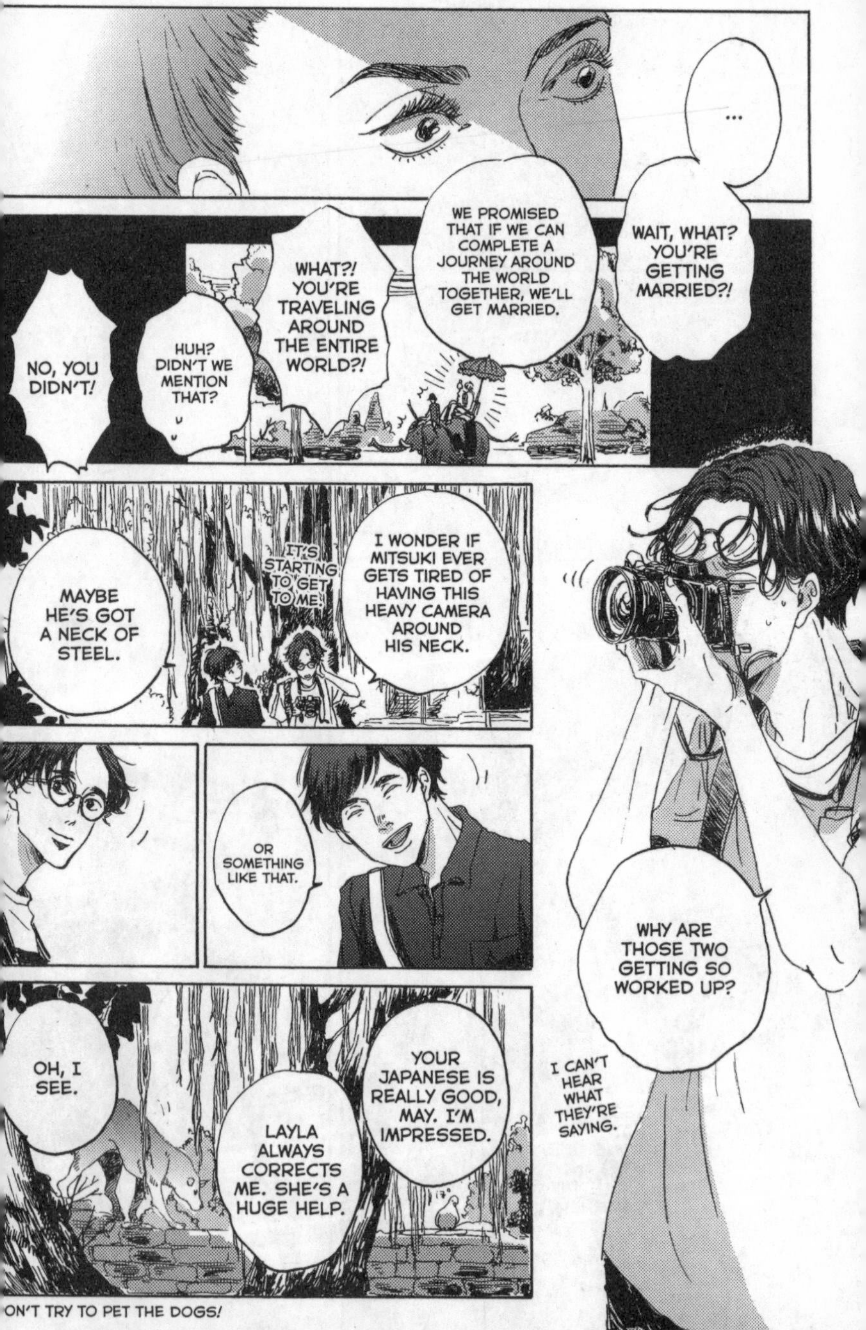
...
WAIT, WHAT? YOU'RE GETTING MARRIED?!
WE PROMISED THAT IF WE CAN COMPLETE A JOURNEY AROUND THE WORLD TOGETHER, WE'LL GET MARRIED.
WHAT?! YOU'RE TRAVELING AROUND THE ENTIRE WORLD?!
HUH? DIDN'T WE MENTION THAT?
NO, YOU DIDN'T!
WHY ARE THOSE TWO GETTING SO WORKED UP?
I CAN'T HEAR WHAT THEY'RE SAYING.
I WONDER IF MITSUKI EVER GETS TIRED OF HAVING THIS HEAVY CAMERA AROUND HIS NECK.
IT'S STARTING TO GET TO ME.
MAYBE HE'S GOT A NECK OF STEEL.
OR SOMETHING LIKE THAT.
YOUR JAPANESE IS REALLY GOOD, MAY. I'M IMPRESSED.
LAYLA ALWAYS CORRECTS ME. SHE'S A HUGE HELP.
OH, I SEE.

ON'T TRY TO PET THE DOGS!

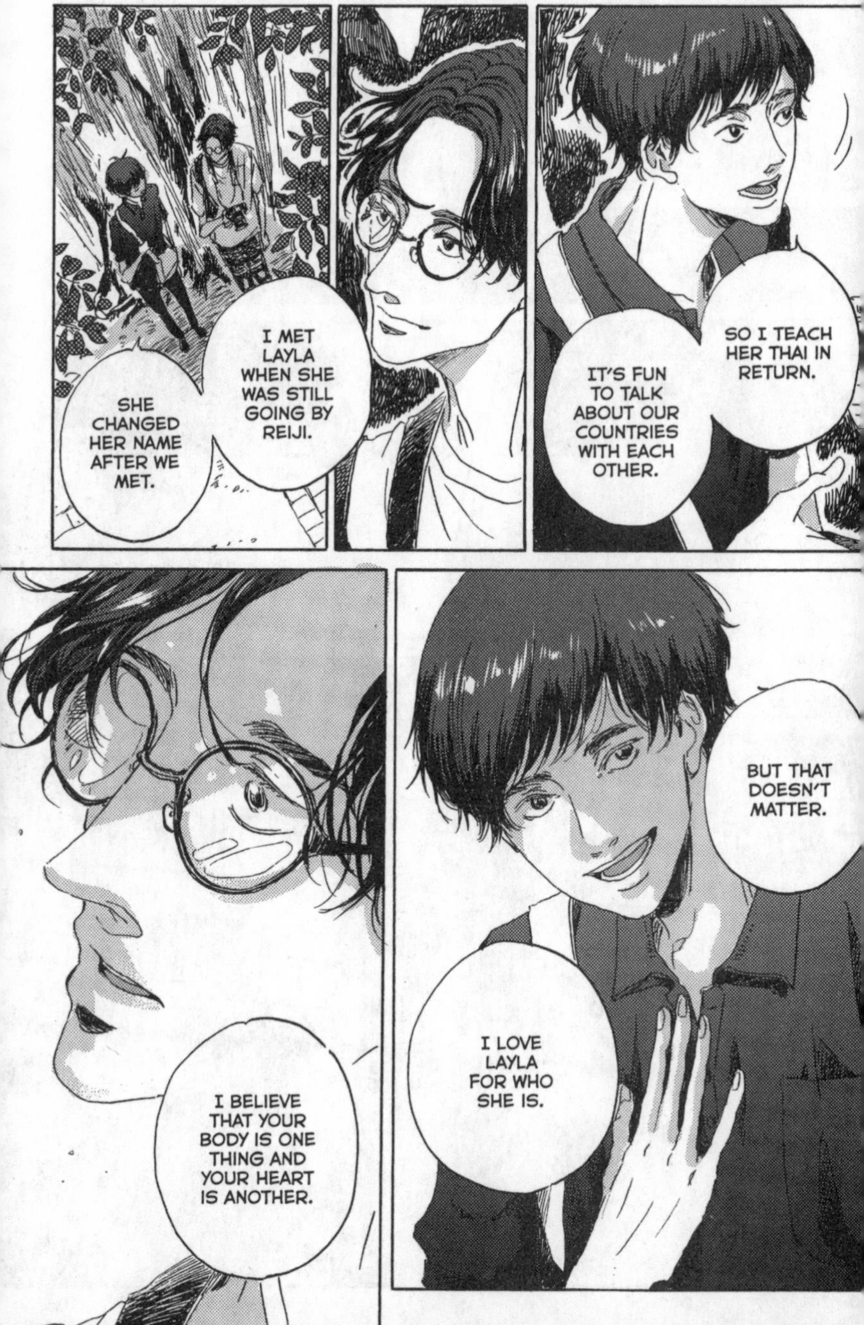
SO I TEACH HER THAI IN RETURN.
IT'S FUN TO TALK ABOUT OUR COUNTRIES WITH EACH OTHER.
I MET LAYLA WHEN SHE WAS STILL GOING BY REIJI.
SHE CHANGED HER NAME AFTER WE MET.
BUT THAT DOESN'T MATTER.
I LOVE LAYLA FOR WHO SHE IS.
I BELIEVE THAT YOUR BODY IS ONE THING AND YOUR HEART IS ANOTHER.

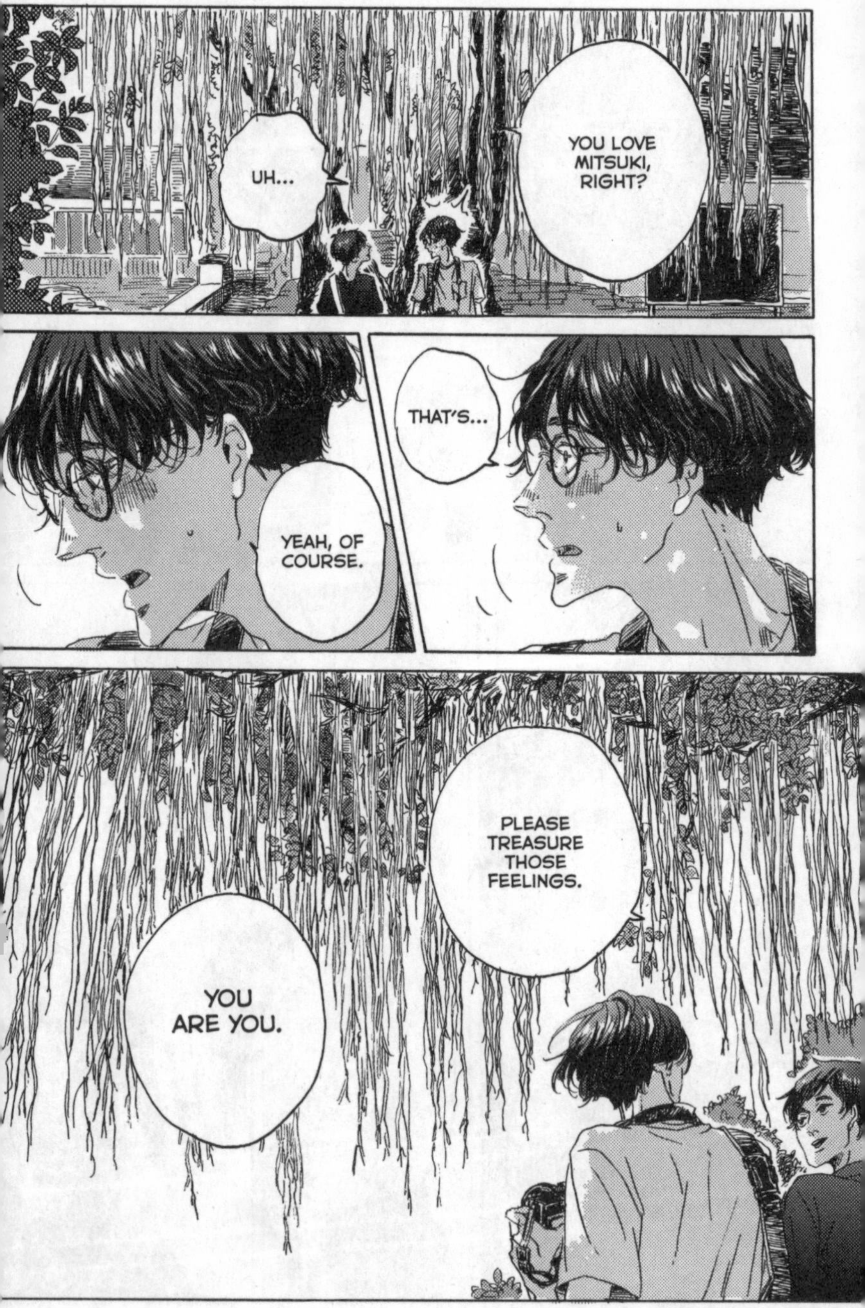
YOU LOVE MITSUKI, RIGHT?
UH...
THAT'S...
YEAH, OF COURSE.
PLEASE TREASURE THOSE FEELINGS.
YOU ARE YOU.

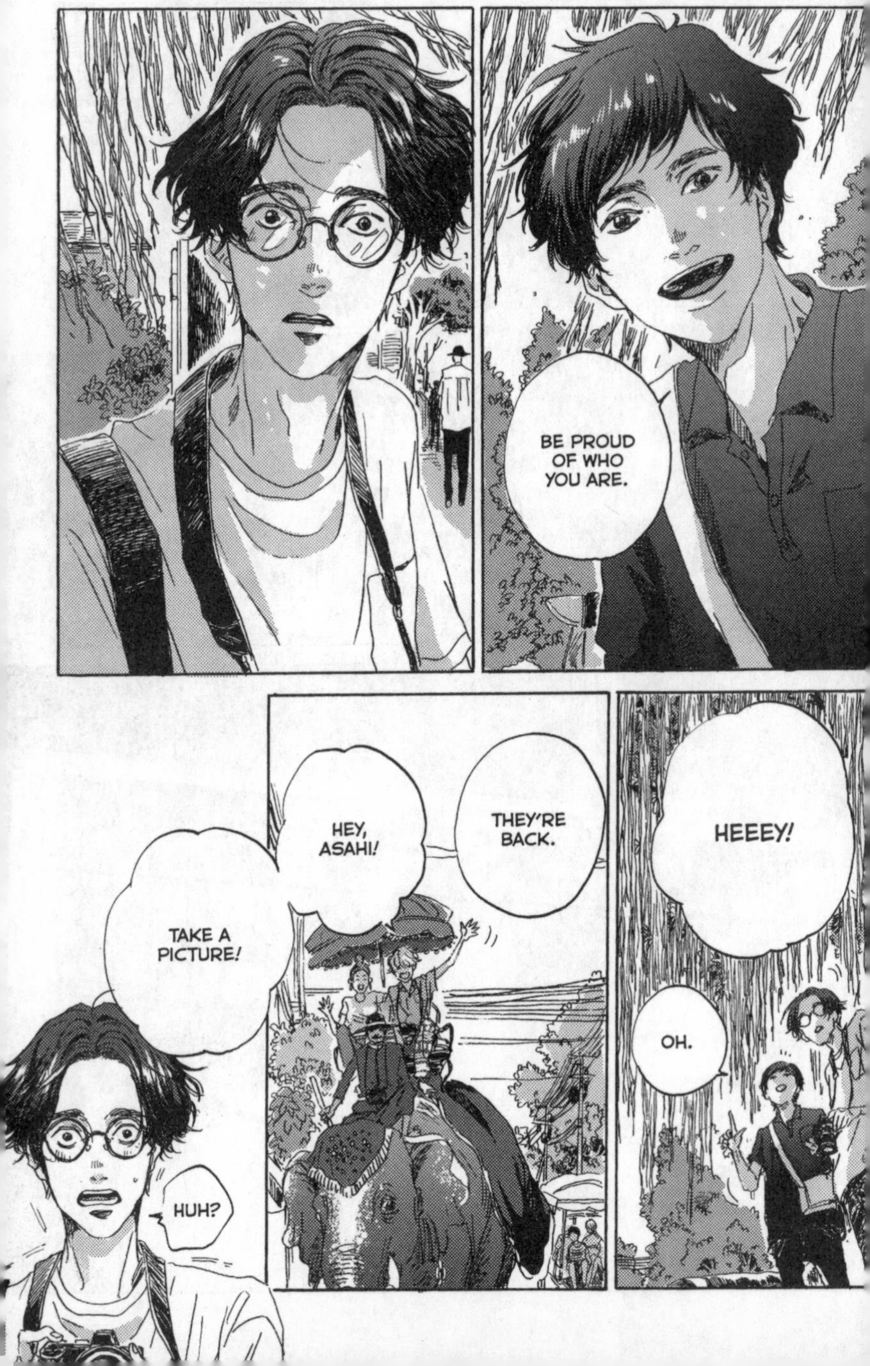
BE PROUD OF WHO YOU ARE.
HEEEY!
OH.
THEY'RE BACK.
HEY, ASAHI!
TAKE A PICTURE!
HUH?

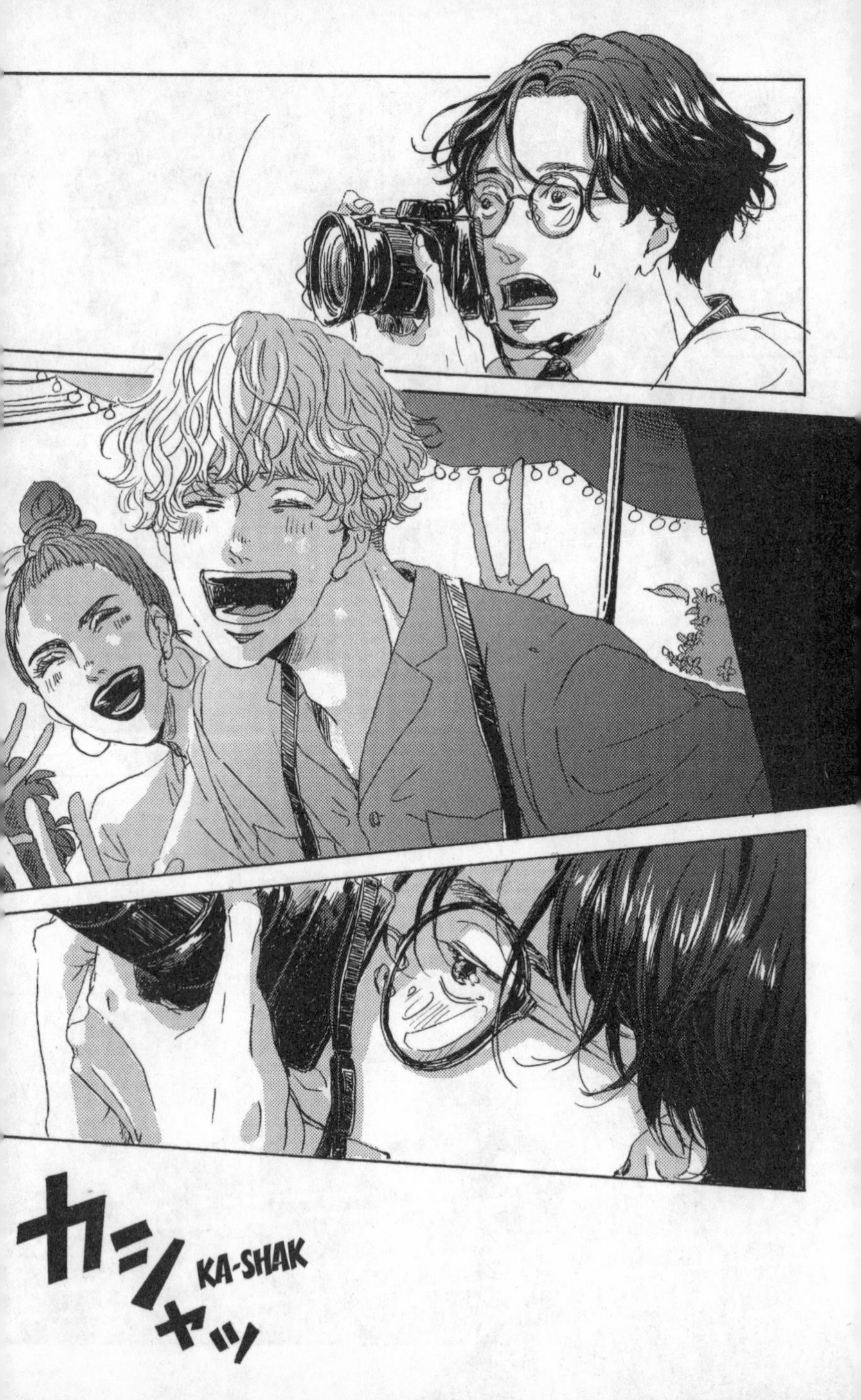
カシャッ
KA-SHAK

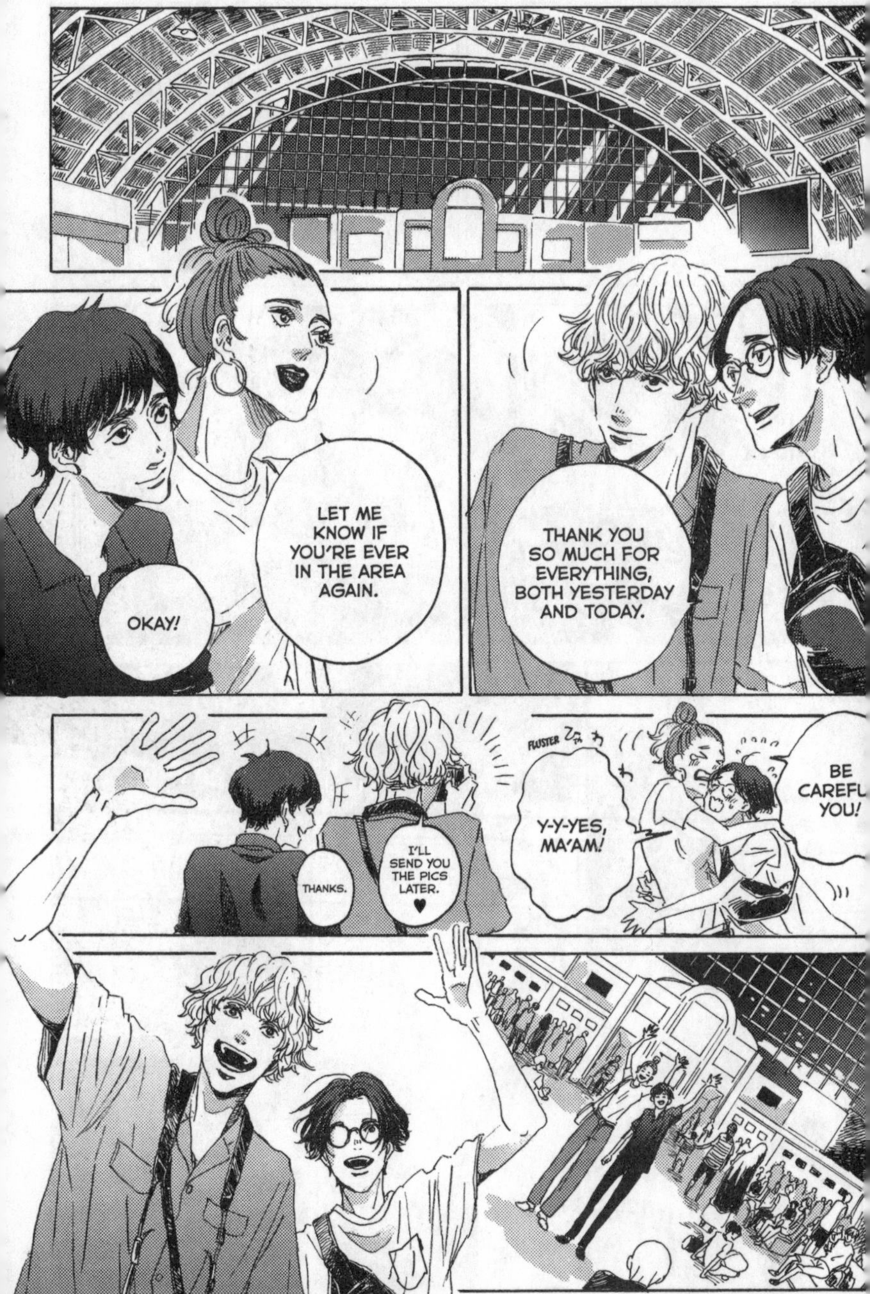
THANK YOU SO MUCH FOR EVERYTHING, BOTH YESTERDAY AND TODAY.
LET ME KNOW IF YOU'RE EVER IN THE AREA AGAIN.
OKAY!
BE CAREFU YOU!
FLUSTER
Y-Y-YES, MA'AM!
I'LL SEND YOU THE PICS LATER. ♥
THANKS.

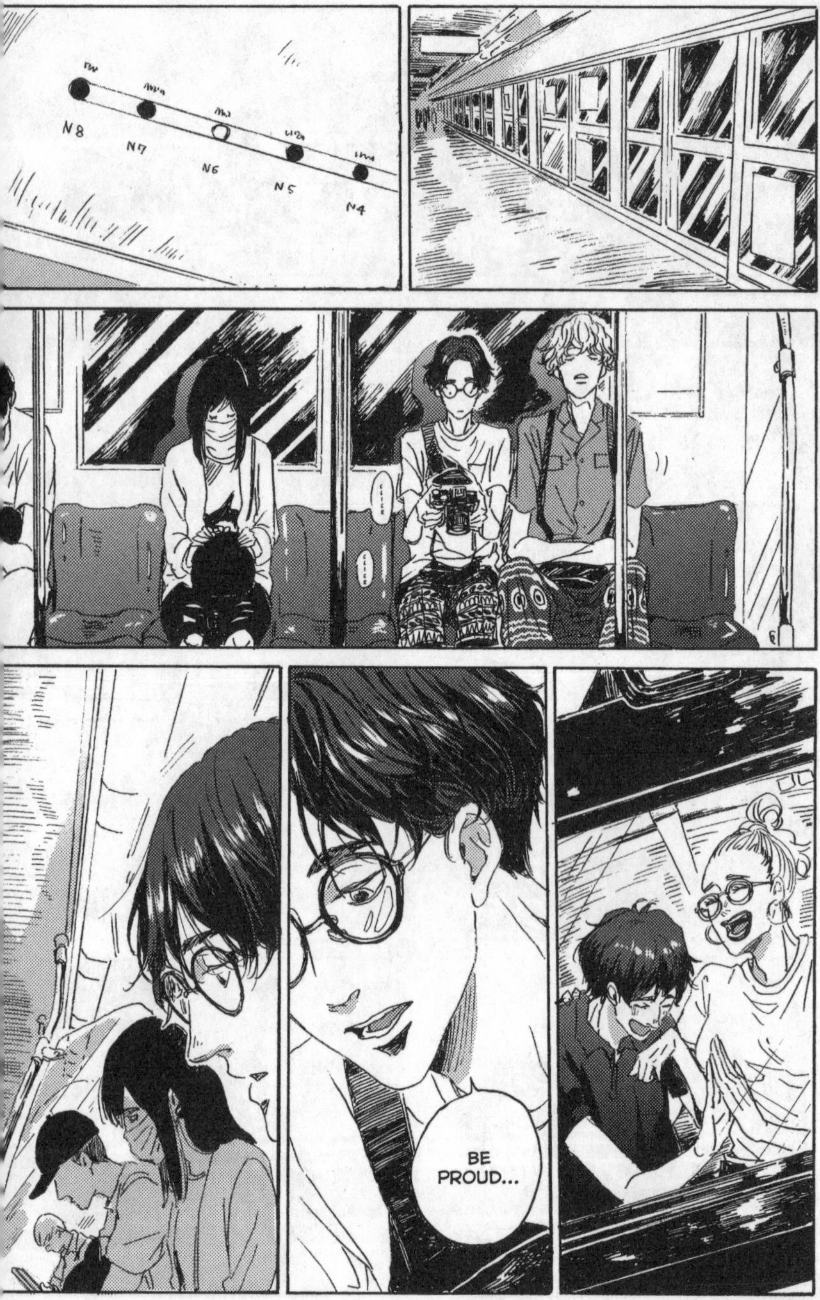
N8
N7
N6
N5
N4
CLICK
CLICK
BE PROUD...

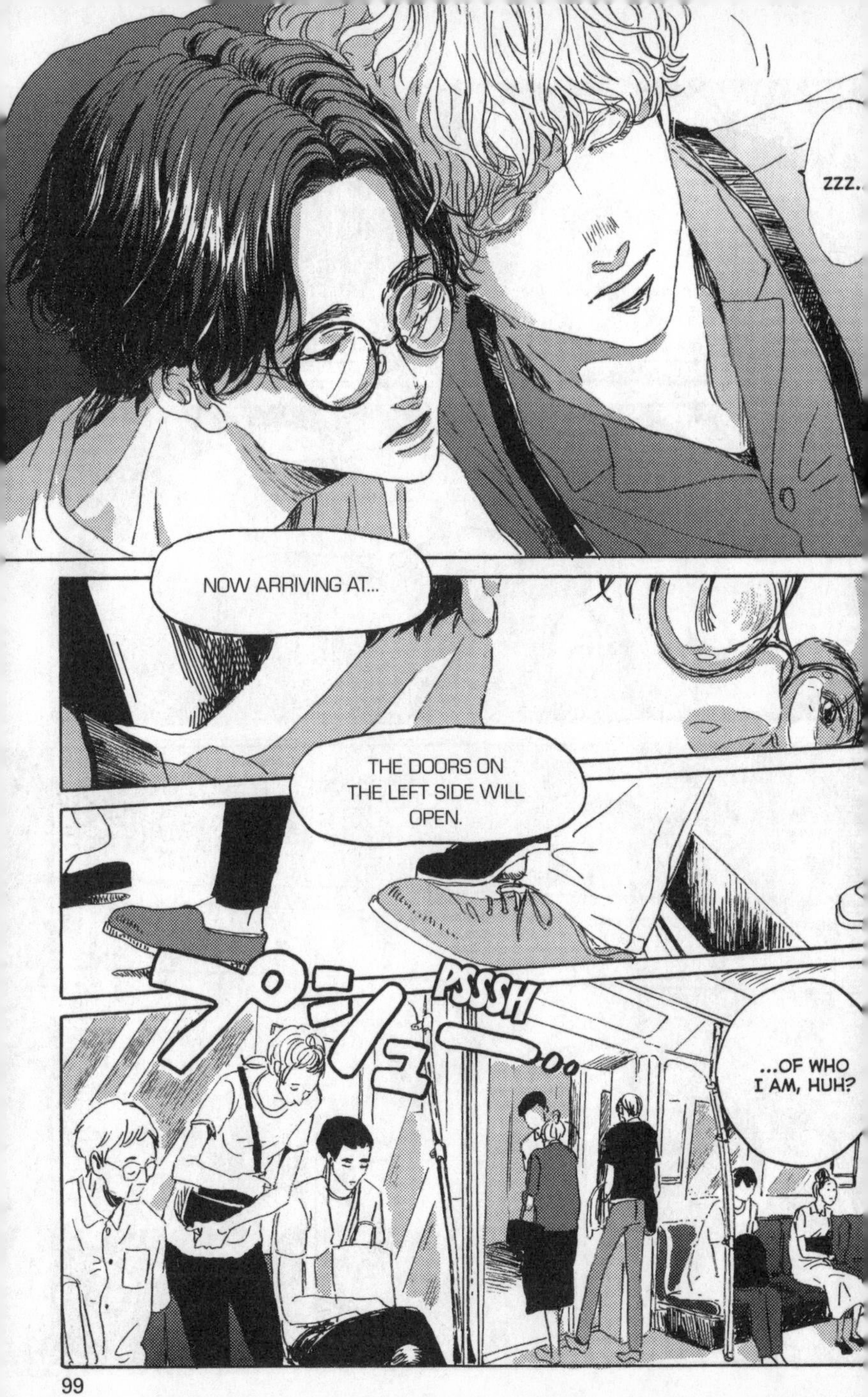
ZZZ..
NOW ARRIVING AT...
THE DOORS ON THE LEFT SIDE WILL OPEN.
PSSSH
...OF WHO I AM, HUH?

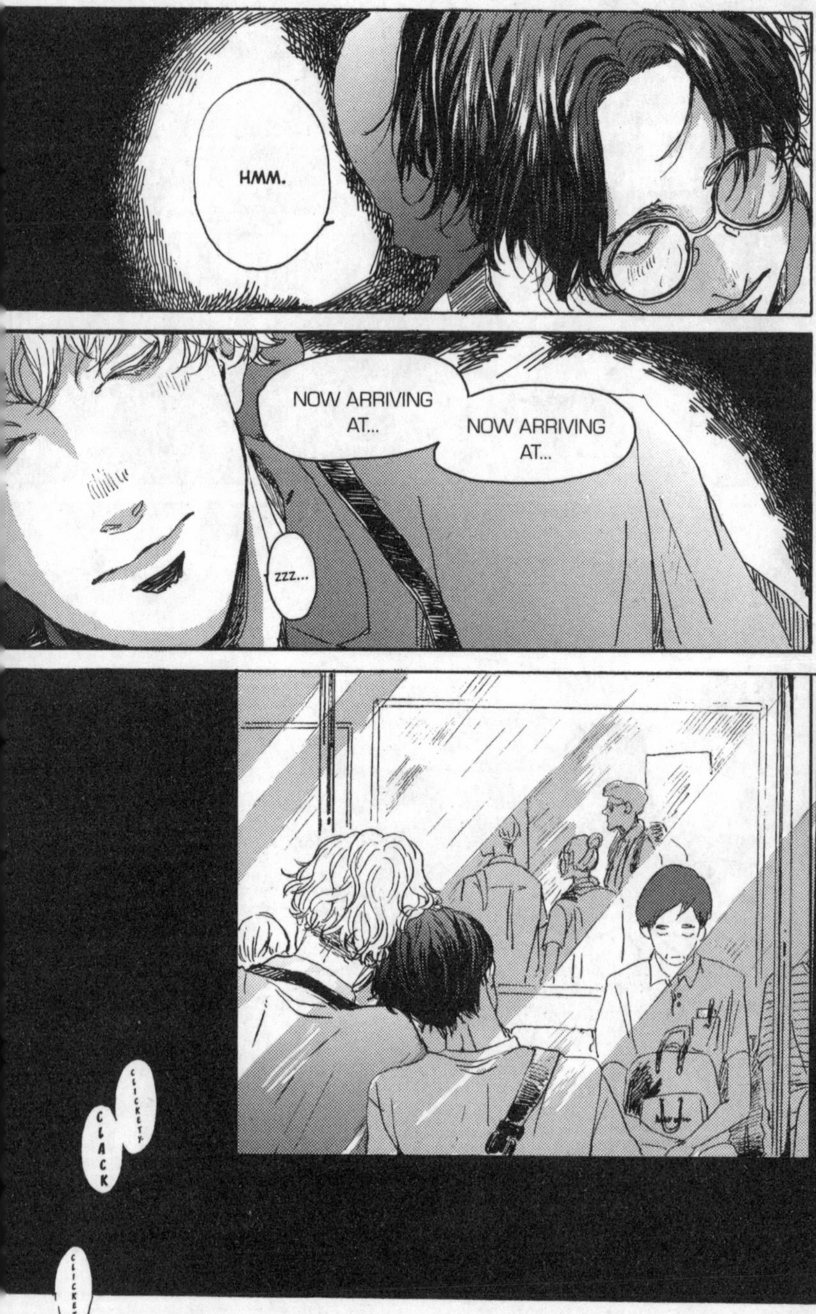
HMM.
NOW ARRIVING AT...
NOW ARRIVING AT...
ZZZ...
CLICKETY-
CLACK
CLICKETY-

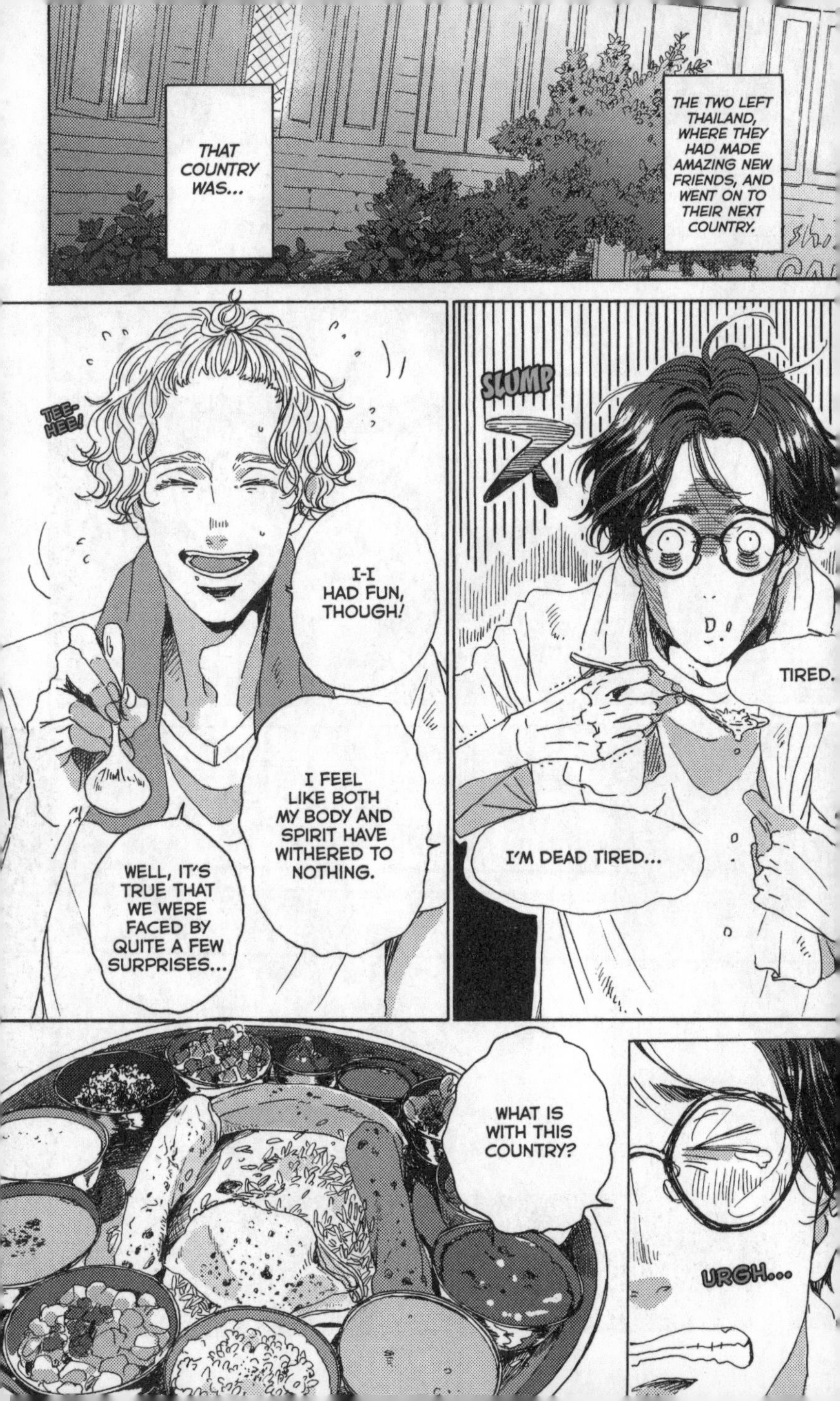
THE TWO LEFT THAILAND, WHERE THEY HAD MADE AMAZING NEW FRIENDS, AND WENT ON TO THEIR NEXT COUNTRY.
THAT COUNTRY WAS...
SLUMP
TIRED.
I'M DEAD TIRED...
I-I HAD FUN, THOUGH!
TEE-HEE!
I FEEL LIKE BOTH MY BODY AND SPIRIT HAVE WITHERED TO NOTHING.
WELL, IT'S TRUE THAT WE WERE FACED BY QUITE A FEW SURPRISES...
URGH...
WHAT IS WITH THIS COUNTRY?

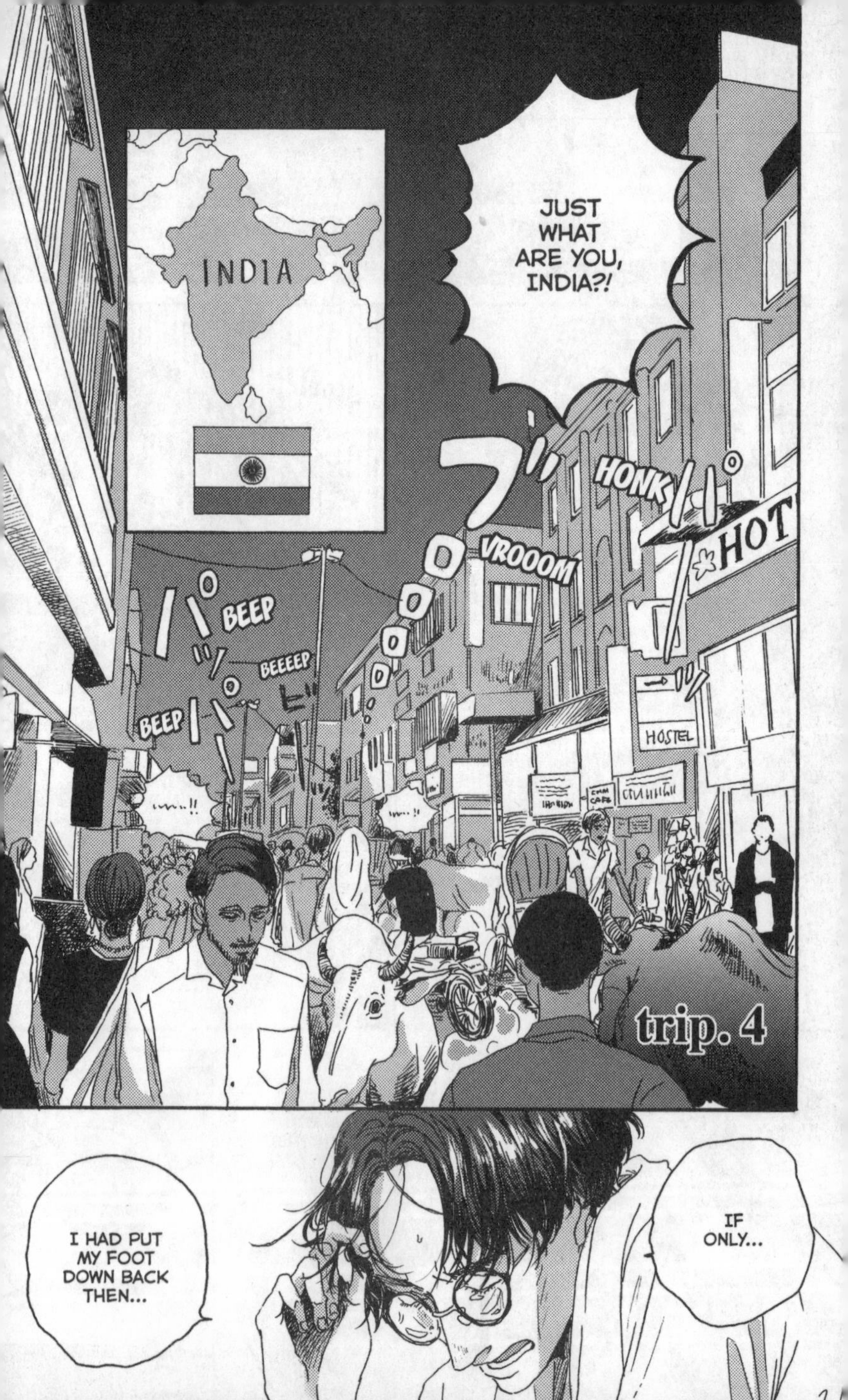
INDIA
JUST WHAT ARE YOU, INDIA?!
HONK
VROOOM
HOT
BEEP
BEEEEP
BEEP
HOSTEL
trip. 4
IF ONLY...
I HAD PUT MY FOOT DOWN BACK THEN...

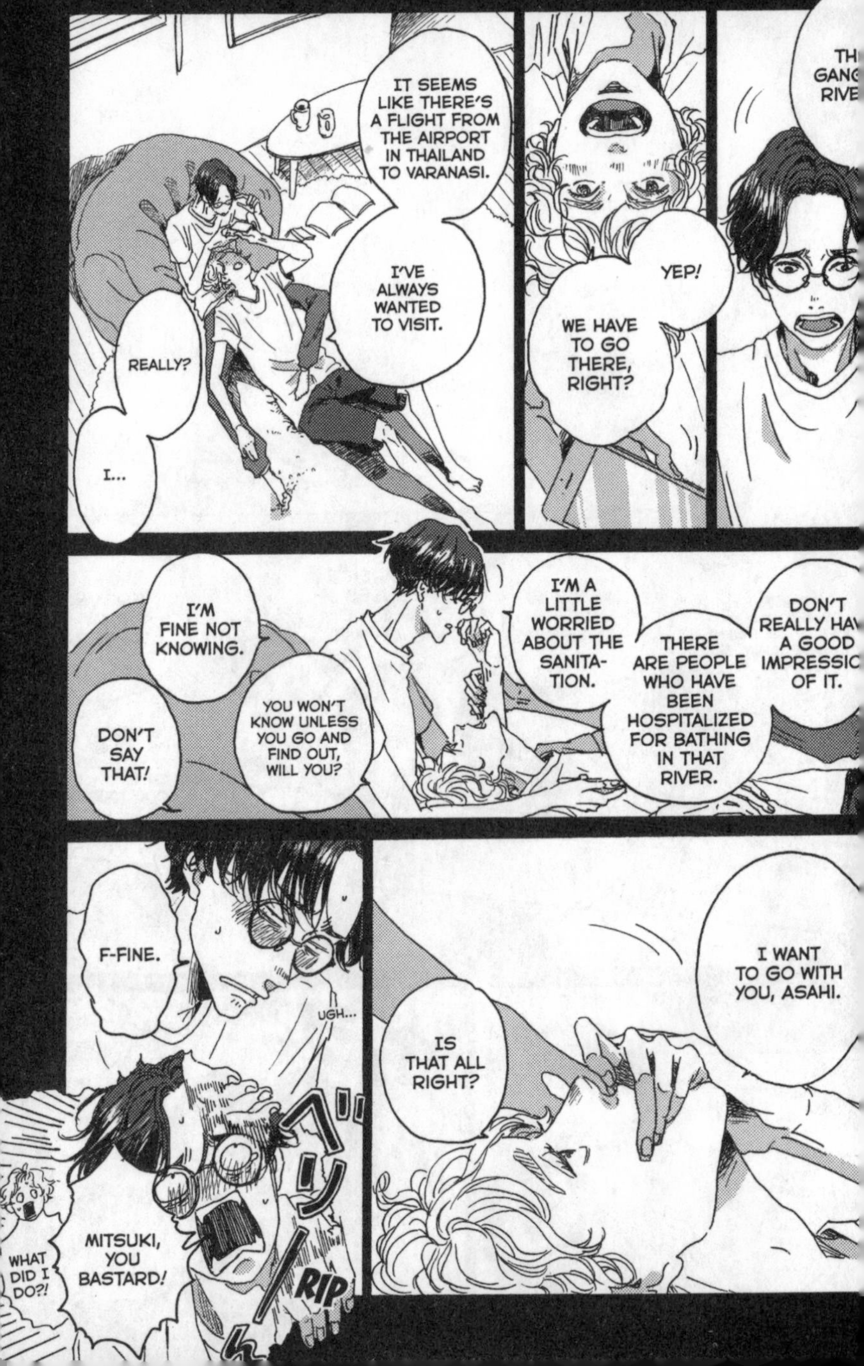
TH
GANG
RIVE
YEP!
WE HAVE TO GO THERE, RIGHT?
IT SEEMS LIKE THERE'S A FLIGHT FROM THE AIRPORT IN THAILAND TO VARANASI.
I'VE ALWAYS WANTED TO VISIT.
REALLY?
I...
DON'T REALLY HAV A GOOD IMPRESSIC OF IT.
THERE ARE PEOPLE WHO HAVE BEEN HOSPITALIZED FOR BATHING IN THAT RIVER.
I'M A LITTLE WORRIED ABOUT THE SANITATION.
I'M FINE NOT KNOWING.
YOU WON'T KNOW UNLESS YOU GO AND FIND OUT, WILL YOU?
DON'T SAY THAT!
I WANT TO GO WITH YOU, ASAHI.
IS THAT ALL RIGHT?
F-FINE.
UGH...
RIP
MITSUKI, YOU BASTARD!
WHAT DID I DO?!

*HE ISN'T DRINKING.

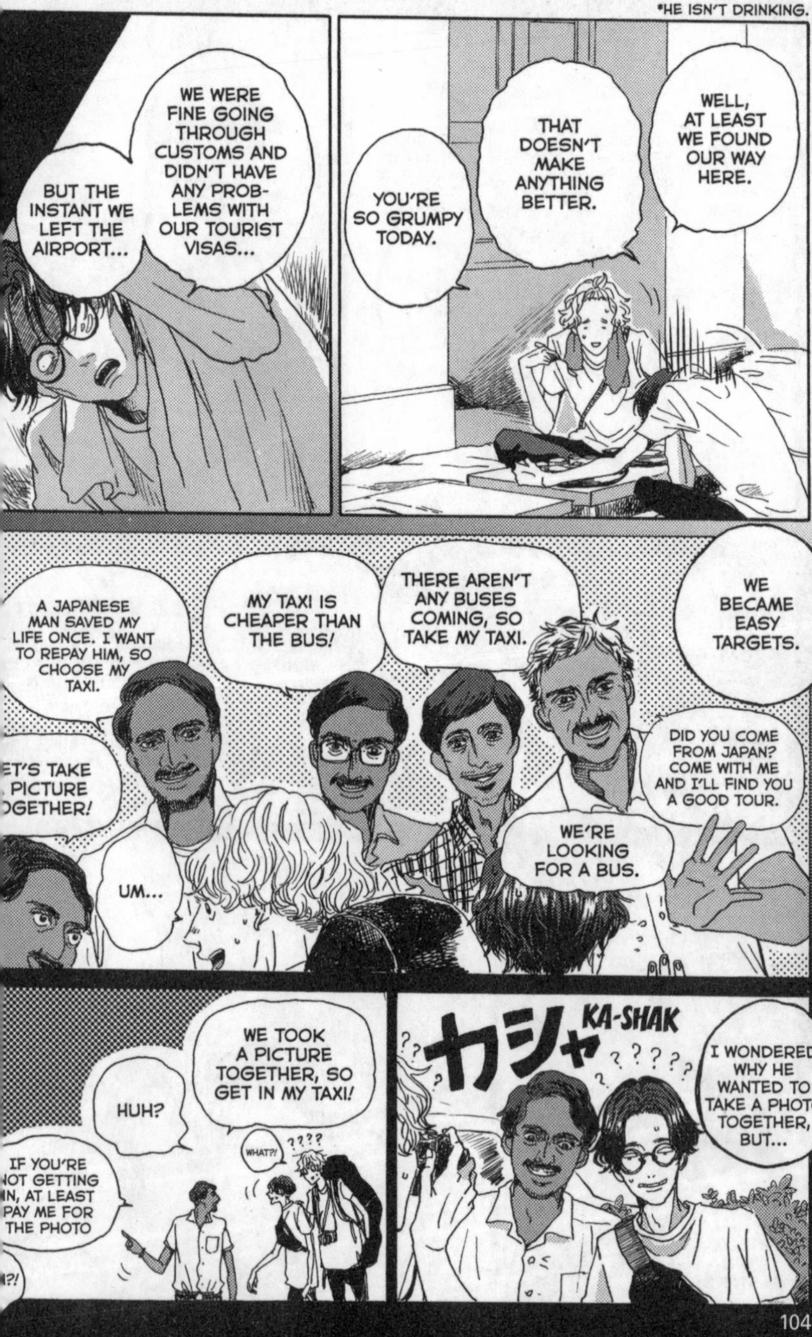
WELL, AT LEAST WE FOUND OUR WAY HERE.
THAT DOESN'T MAKE ANYTHING BETTER.
YOU'RE SO GRUMPY TODAY.
WE WERE FINE GOING THROUGH CUSTOMS AND DIDN'T HAVE ANY PROBLEMS WITH OUR TOURIST VISAS...
BUT THE INSTANT WE LEFT THE AIRPORT...
WE BECAME EASY TARGETS.
THERE AREN'T ANY BUSES COMING, SO TAKE MY TAXI.
MY TAXI IS CHEAPER THAN THE BUS!
A JAPANESE MAN SAVED MY LIFE ONCE. I WANT TO REPAY HIM, SO CHOOSE MY TAXI.
DID YOU COME FROM JAPAN? COME WITH ME AND I'LL FIND YOU A GOOD TOUR.
WE'RE LOOKING FOR A BUS.
ET'S TAKE PICTURE OGETHER!
UM...
カシャ KA-SHAK
? ? ? ? ?
I WONDERED WHY HE WANTED TO TAKE A PHOTO TOGETHER, BUT...
WE TOOK A PICTURE TOGETHER, SO GET IN MY TAXI!
HUH?
WHAT?!
????
IF YOU'RE OT GETTING N, AT LEAST PAY ME FOR THE PHOTO
?!

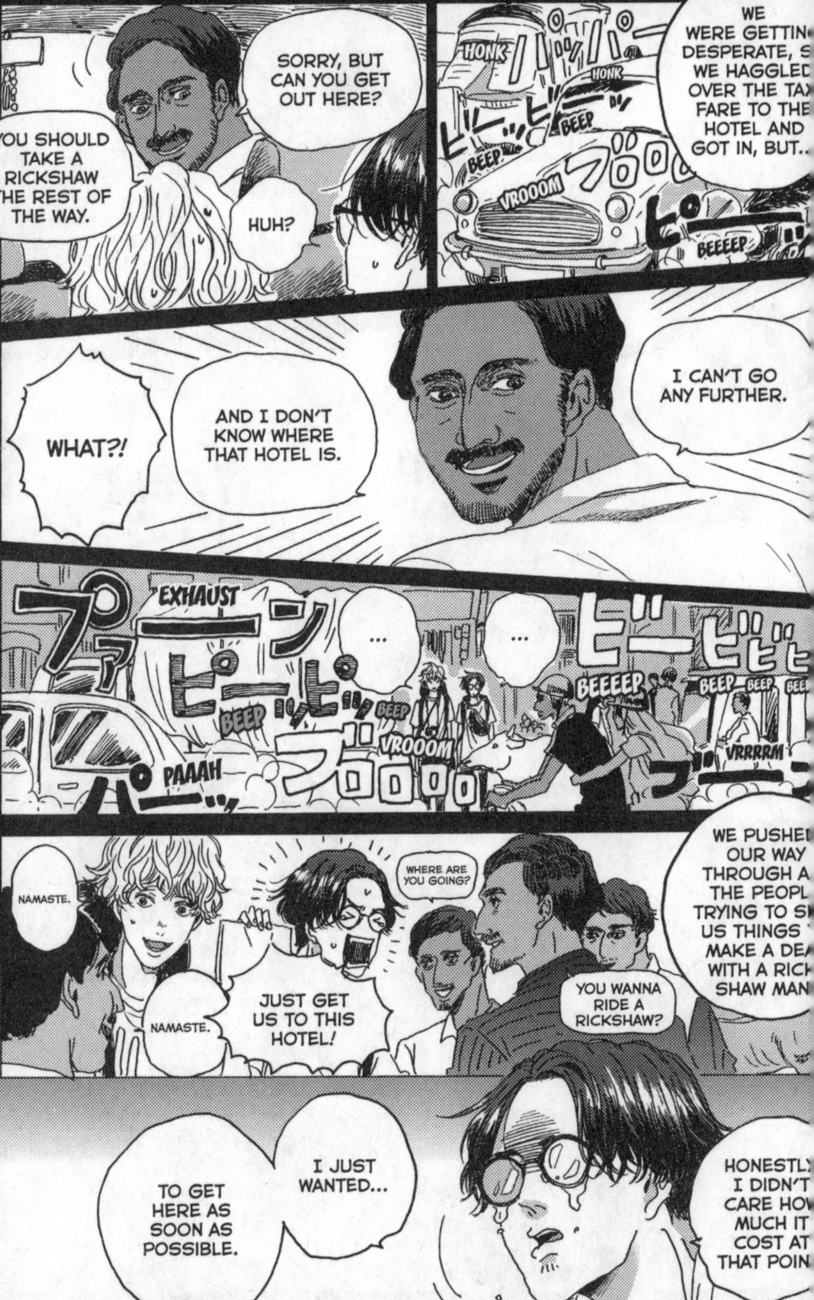
WE WERE GETTIN DESPERATE, S WE HAGGLED OVER THE TAX FARE TO THE HOTEL AND GOT IN, BUT...
HONK
HONK
BEEP
BEEP
VROOOM
BEEEEP
SORRY, BUT CAN YOU GET OUT HERE?
YOU SHOULD TAKE A RICKSHAW THE REST OF THE WAY.
HUH?
I CAN'T GO ANY FURTHER.
AND I DON'T KNOW WHERE THAT HOTEL IS.
WHAT?!
BEEEEP
BEEP
BEEP
VRRRRM
...
...
EXHAUST
BEEP
BEEP
VROOOM
PAAAH
WE PUSHE OUR WAY THROUGH A THE PEOPL TRYING TO S US THINGS MAKE A DEA WITH A RICK SHAW MAN
YOU WANNA RIDE A RICKSHAW?
WHERE ARE YOU GOING?
JUST GET US TO THIS HOTEL!
NAMASTE.
NAMASTE.
HONESTL I DIDN'T CARE HO MUCH IT COST AT THAT POIN
I JUST WANTED...
TO GET HERE AS SOON AS POSSIBLE.

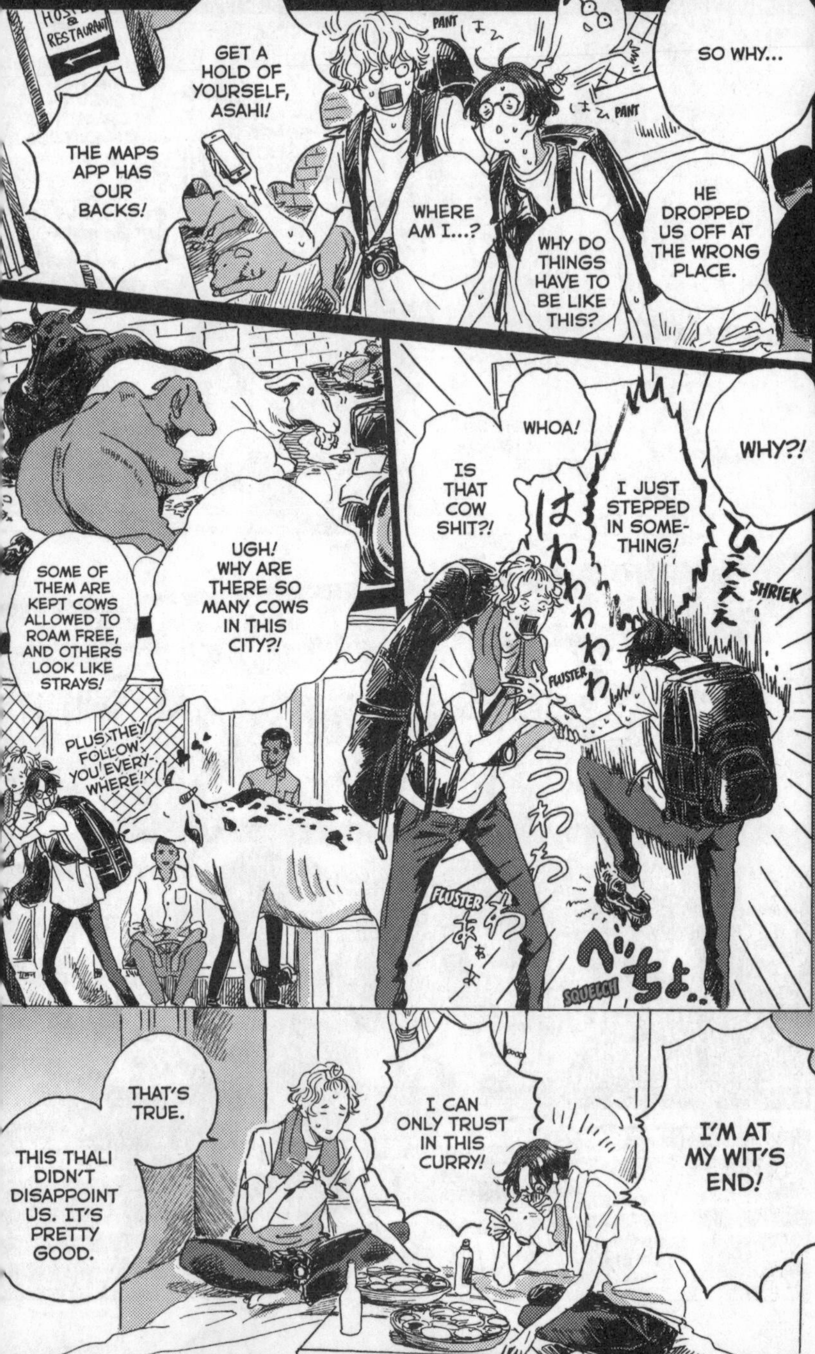
SO WHY...
HE DROPPED US OFF AT THE WRONG PLACE.
WHY DO THINGS HAVE TO BE LIKE THIS?
PANT はぁ
PANT はぁ
WHERE AM I...?
GET A HOLD OF YOURSELF, ASAHI!
THE MAPS APP HAS OUR BACKS!
RESTAURANT
WHY?!
SHRIEK
I JUST STEPPED IN SOME-THING!
WHOA!
IS THAT COW SHIT?!
FLUSTER
FLUSTER
SQUELCH
UGH! WHY ARE THERE SO MANY COWS IN THIS CITY?!
SOME OF THEM ARE KEPT COWS ALLOWED TO ROAM FREE, AND OTHERS LOOK LIKE STRAYS!
PLUS THEY FOLLOW YOU EVERY-WHERE!
I'M AT MY WIT'S END!
I CAN ONLY TRUST IN THIS CURRY!
THAT'S TRUE.
THIS THALI DIDN'T DISAPPOINT US. IT'S PRETTY GOOD.

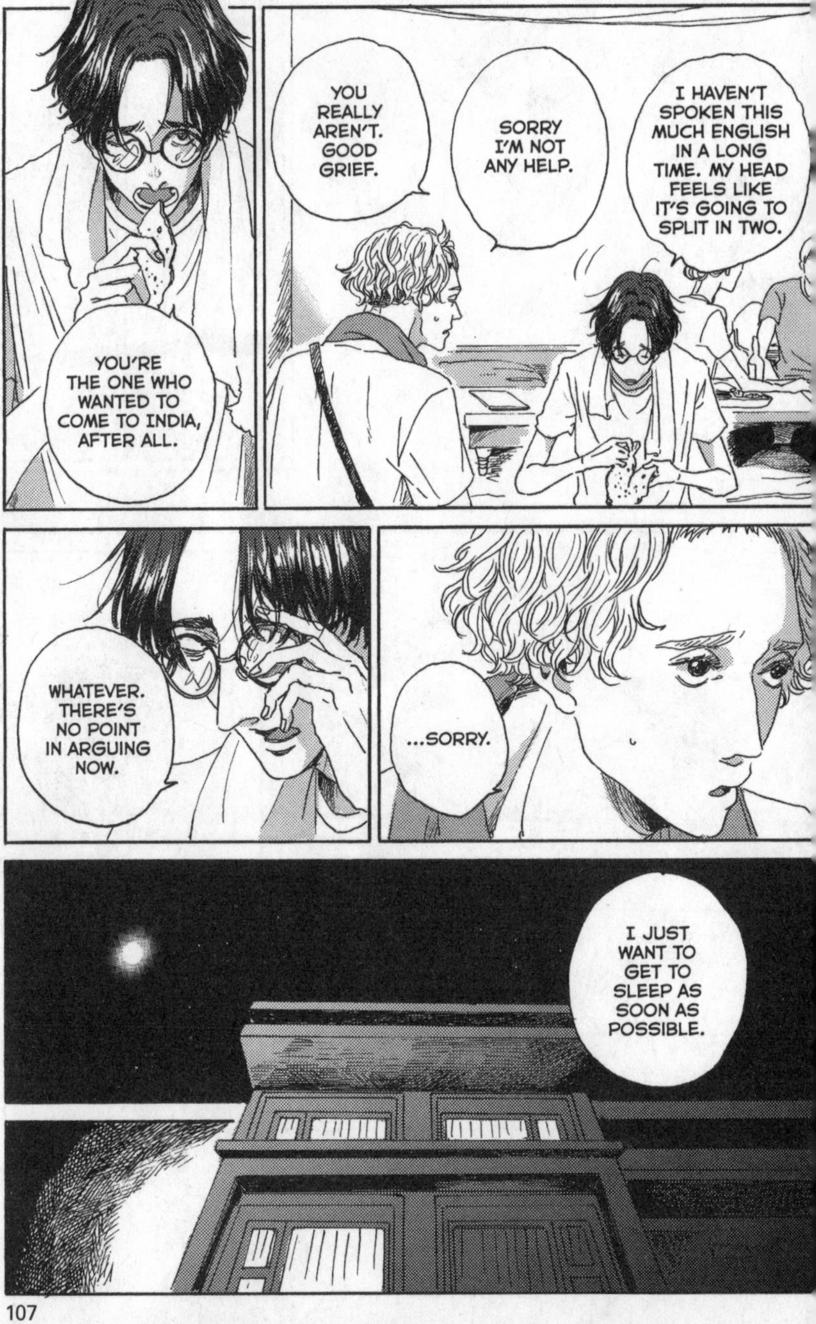
I HAVEN'T SPOKEN THIS MUCH ENGLISH IN A LONG TIME. MY HEAD FEELS LIKE IT'S GOING TO SPLIT IN TWO.
SORRY I'M NOT ANY HELP.
YOU REALLY AREN'T. GOOD GRIEF.
YOU'RE THE ONE WHO WANTED TO COME TO INDIA, AFTER ALL.
...SORRY.
WHATEVER. THERE'S NO POINT IN ARGUING NOW.
I JUST WANT TO GET TO SLEEP AS SOON AS POSSIBLE.

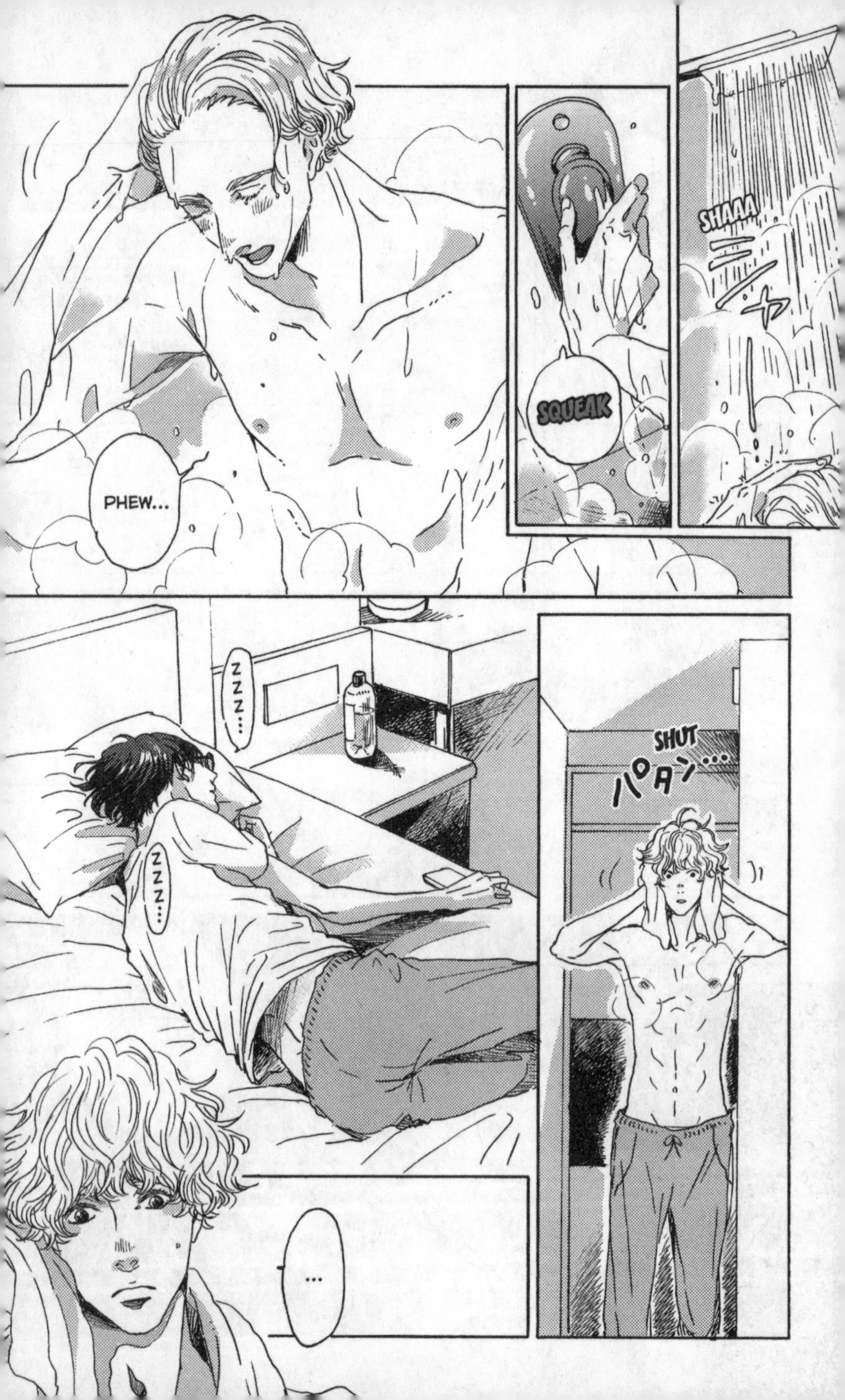
SHAAA
SQUEAK
PHEW...
SHUT
パタン…
Zzz...
Zzz...
—...

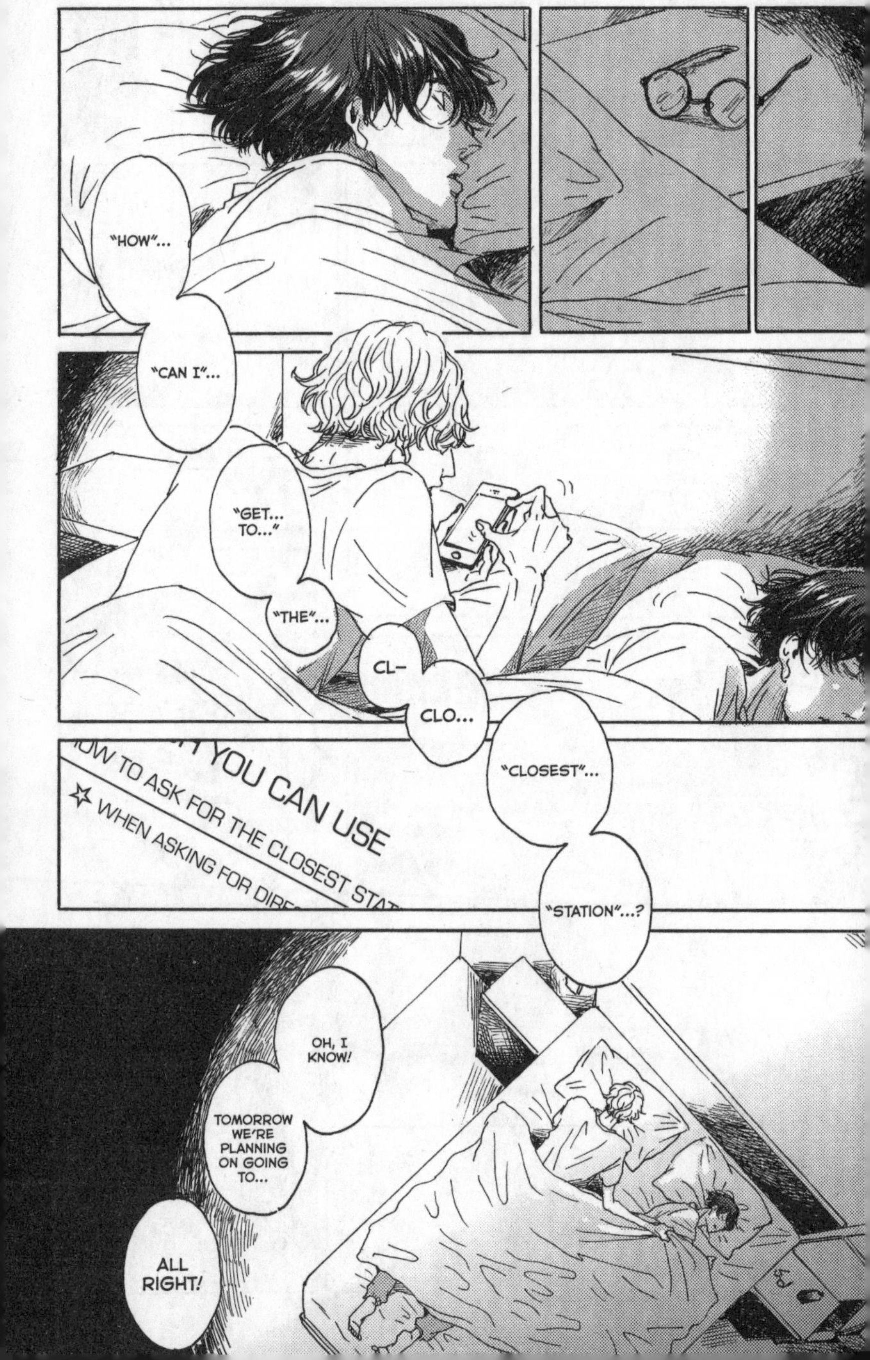
"HOW"...
"CAN I"...
"GET... TO..."
"THE"...
CL–
CLO...
"CLOSEST"...
YOU CAN USE
TO ASK FOR THE CLOSEST
☆ WHEN ASKING FOR
"STATION"...?
OH, I KNOW!
TOMORROW WE'RE PLANNING ON GOING TO...
ALL RIGHT!

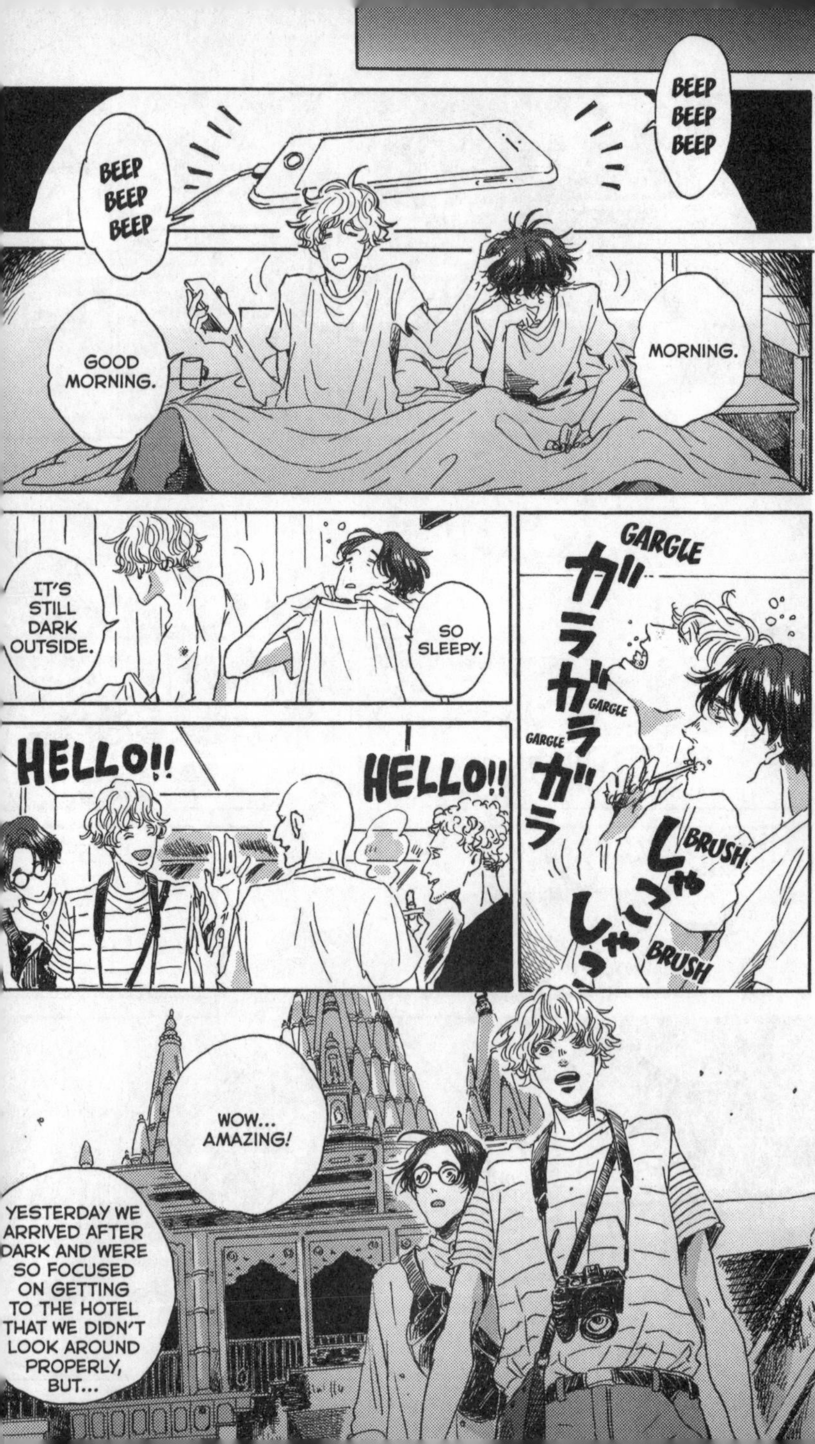
BEEP BEEP BEEP
BEEP BEEP BEEP
MORNING.
GOOD MORNING.
GARGLE
ガラガラ
GARGLE
GARGLE
ガラ
しゃこしゃっ
BRUSH
BRUSH
SO SLEEPY.
IT'S STILL DARK OUTSIDE.
HELLO!!
HELLO!!
WOW... AMAZING!
YESTERDAY WE ARRIVED AFTER DARK AND WERE SO FOCUSED ON GETTING TO THE HOTEL THAT WE DIDN'T LOOK AROUND PROPERLY, BUT...

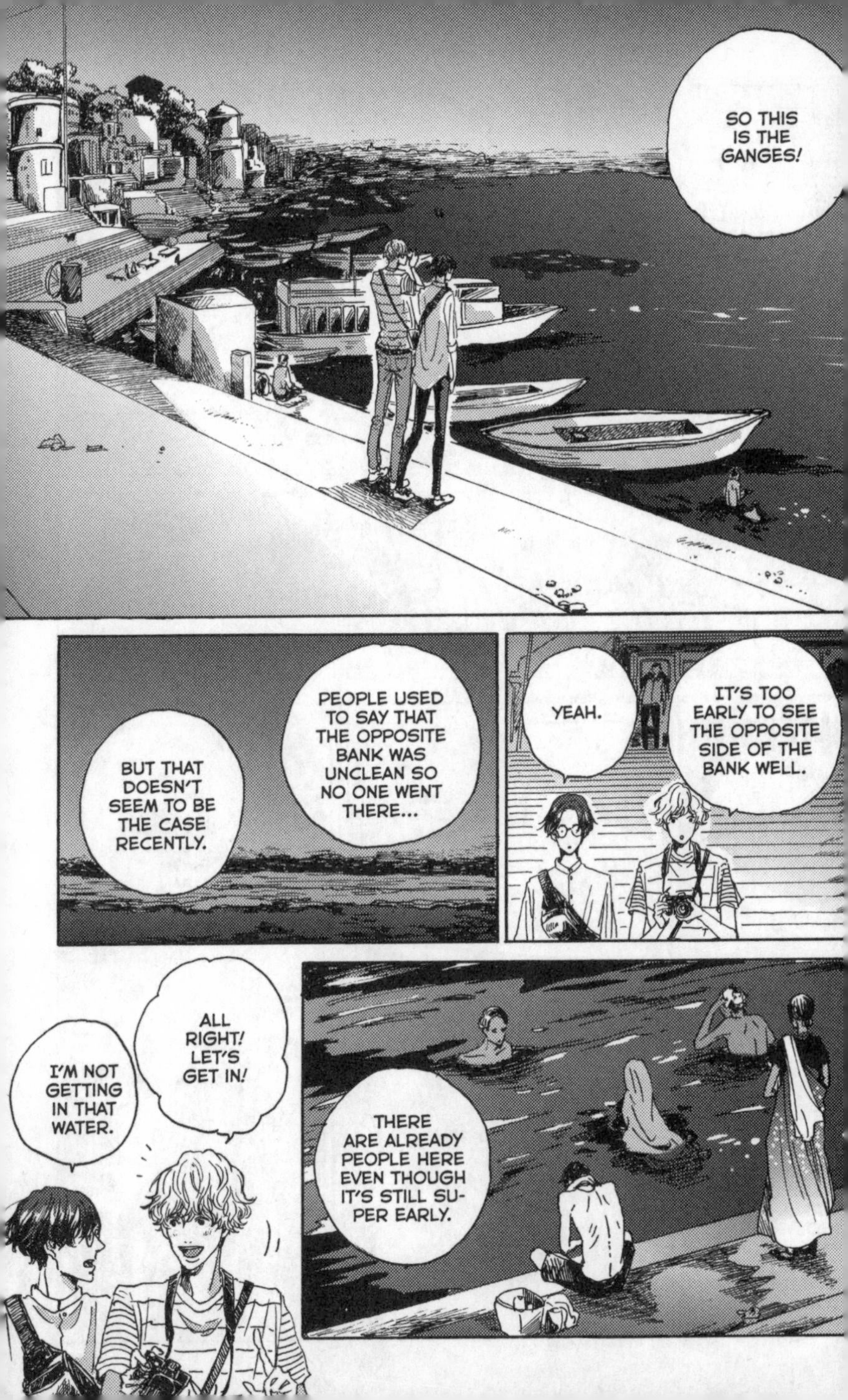
SO THIS IS THE GANGES!
IT'S TOO EARLY TO SEE THE OPPOSITE SIDE OF THE BANK WELL.
YEAH.
PEOPLE USED TO SAY THAT THE OPPOSITE BANK WAS UNCLEAN SO NO ONE WENT THERE...
BUT THAT DOESN'T SEEM TO BE THE CASE RECENTLY.
THERE ARE ALREADY PEOPLE HERE EVEN THOUGH IT'S STILL SU-PER EARLY.
ALL RIGHT! LET'S GET IN!
I'M NOT GETTING IN THAT WATER.

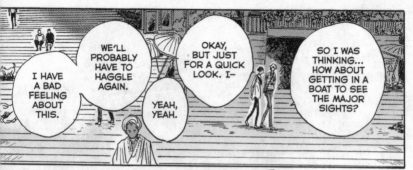

SO I WAS THINKING... HOW ABOUT GETTING IN A BOAT TO SEE THE MAJOR SIGHTS?
OKAY, BUT JUST FOR A QUICK LOOK. I–
YEAH, YEAH.
WE'LL PROBABLY HAVE TO HAGGLE AGAIN.
I HAVE A BAD FEELING ABOUT THIS.
GET IN...
T-TODAY I'LL BE THE ONE TO HAGGLE!
ばっ
FWAP
HUH?
MY BOAT!
HEY! YOU GUYS ARE FROM JAPAN, RIGHT?
HE'S SPEAKING JAPANESE?
I USED TO LIVE IN JAPAN.
I CAN GIVE YOU A TOUR IN JAPANESE!
I'LL EVEN GIVE YOU A SPECIAL DISCOUNT, SO COME ON!
HE'S KIND OF SUSPICIOUS...

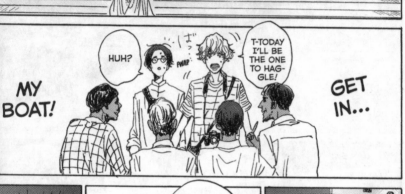

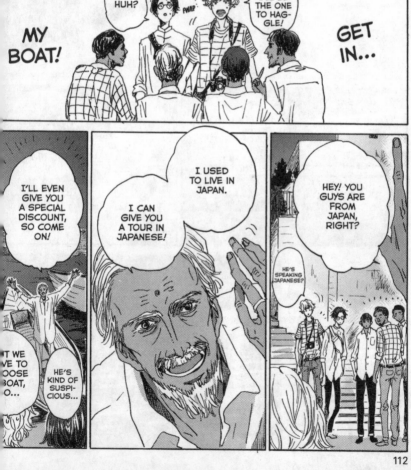

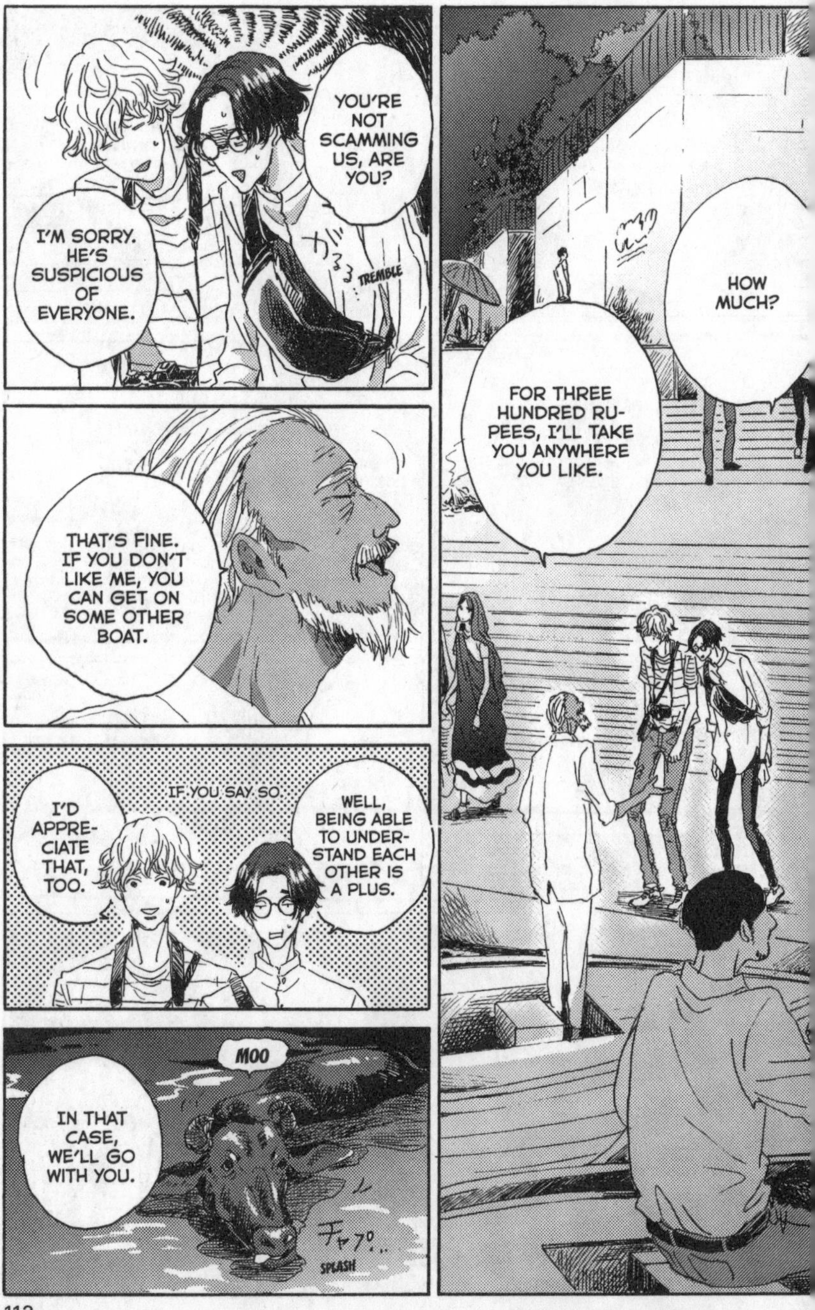
HOW MUCH?
FOR THREE HUNDRED RUPEES, I'LL TAKE YOU ANYWHERE YOU LIKE.
YOU'RE NOT SCAMMING US, ARE YOU?
TREMBLE
I'M SORRY. HE'S SUSPICIOUS OF EVERYONE.
THAT'S FINE. IF YOU DON'T LIKE ME, YOU CAN GET ON SOME OTHER BOAT.
WELL, BEING ABLE TO UNDERSTAND EACH OTHER IS A PLUS.
IF YOU SAY SO.
I'D APPRECIATE THAT, TOO.
MOO
IN THAT CASE, WE'LL GO WITH YOU.
SPLASH

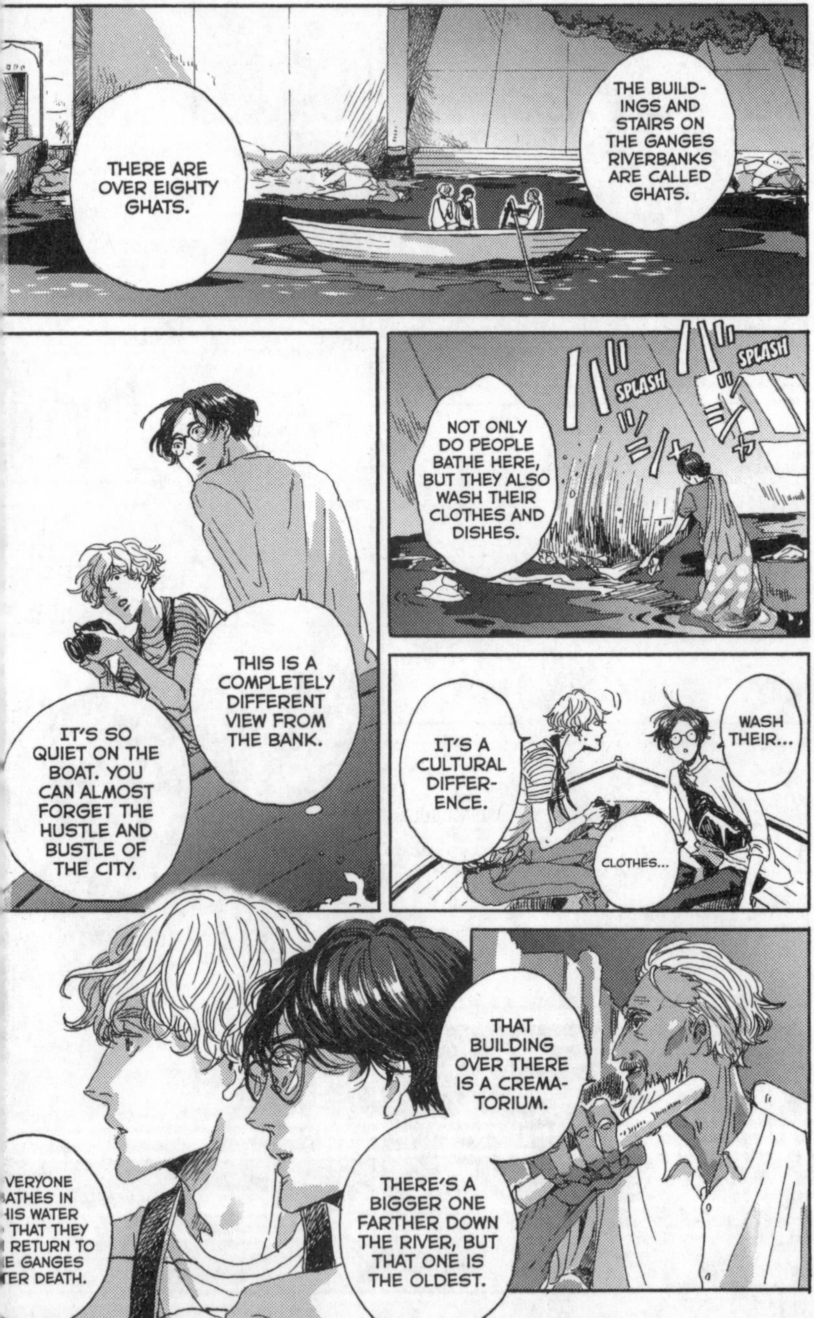
THE BUILDINGS AND STAIRS ON THE GANGES RIVERBANKS ARE CALLED GHATS.
THERE ARE OVER EIGHTY GHATS.
SPLASH
SPLASH
NOT ONLY DO PEOPLE BATHE HERE, BUT THEY ALSO WASH THEIR CLOTHES AND DISHES.
WASH THEIR...
CLOTHES...
IT'S A CULTURAL DIFFERENCE.
THIS IS A COMPLETELY DIFFERENT VIEW FROM THE BANK.
IT'S SO QUIET ON THE BOAT. YOU CAN ALMOST FORGET THE HUSTLE AND BUSTLE OF THE CITY.
THAT BUILDING OVER THERE IS A CREMATORIUM.
THERE'S A BIGGER ONE FARTHER DOWN THE RIVER, BUT THAT ONE IS THE OLDEST.
VERYONE
ATHES IN
IS WATER
THAT THEY
RETURN TO
E GANGES
TER DEATH.

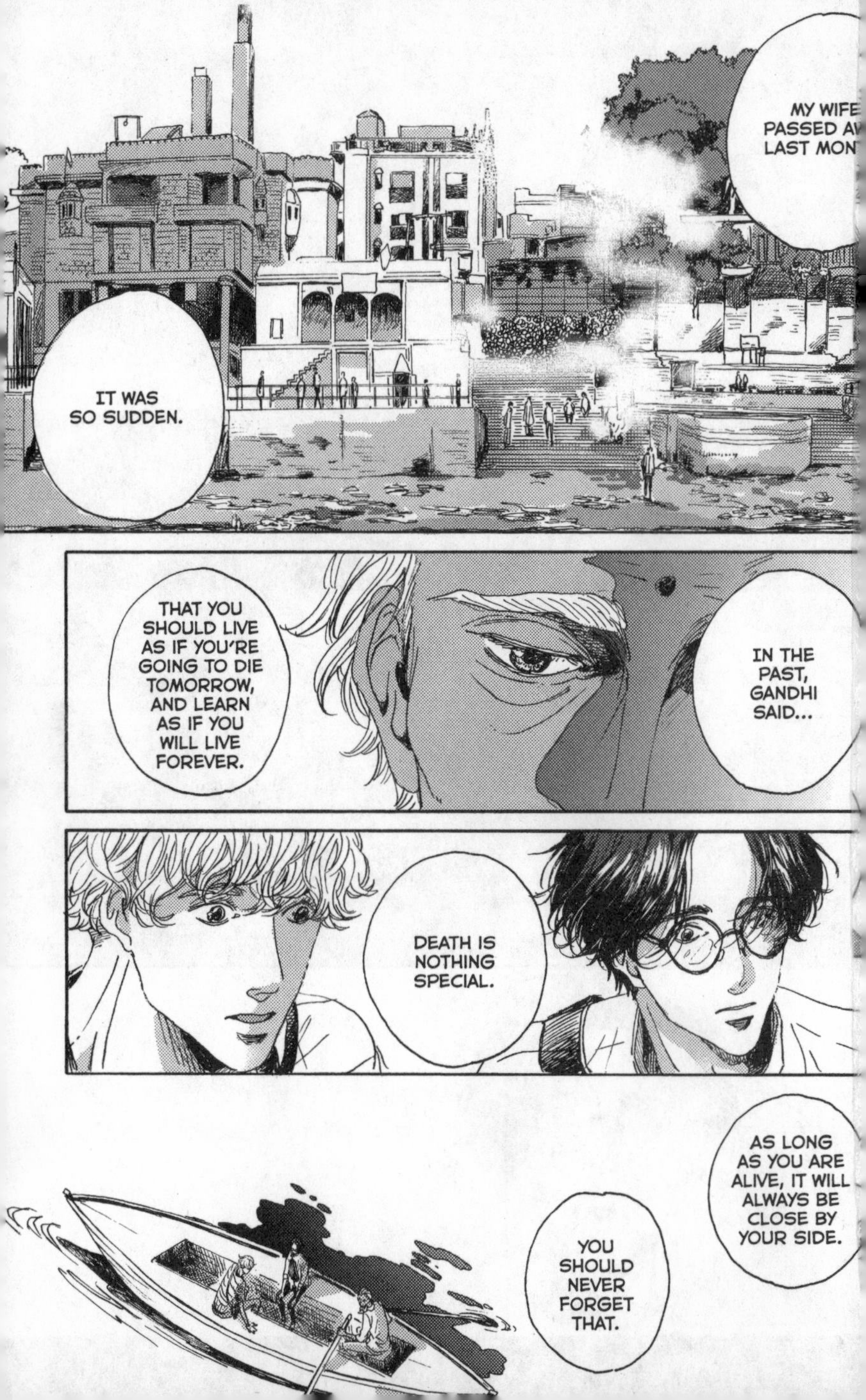
MY WIFE PASSED A LAST MON
IT WAS SO SUDDEN.
IN THE PAST, GANDHI SAID...
THAT YOU SHOULD LIVE AS IF YOU'RE GOING TO DIE TOMORROW, AND LEARN AS IF YOU WILL LIVE FOREVER.
DEATH IS NOTHING SPECIAL.
AS LONG AS YOU ARE ALIVE, IT WILL ALWAYS BE CLOSE BY YOUR SIDE.
YOU SHOULD NEVER FORGET THAT.

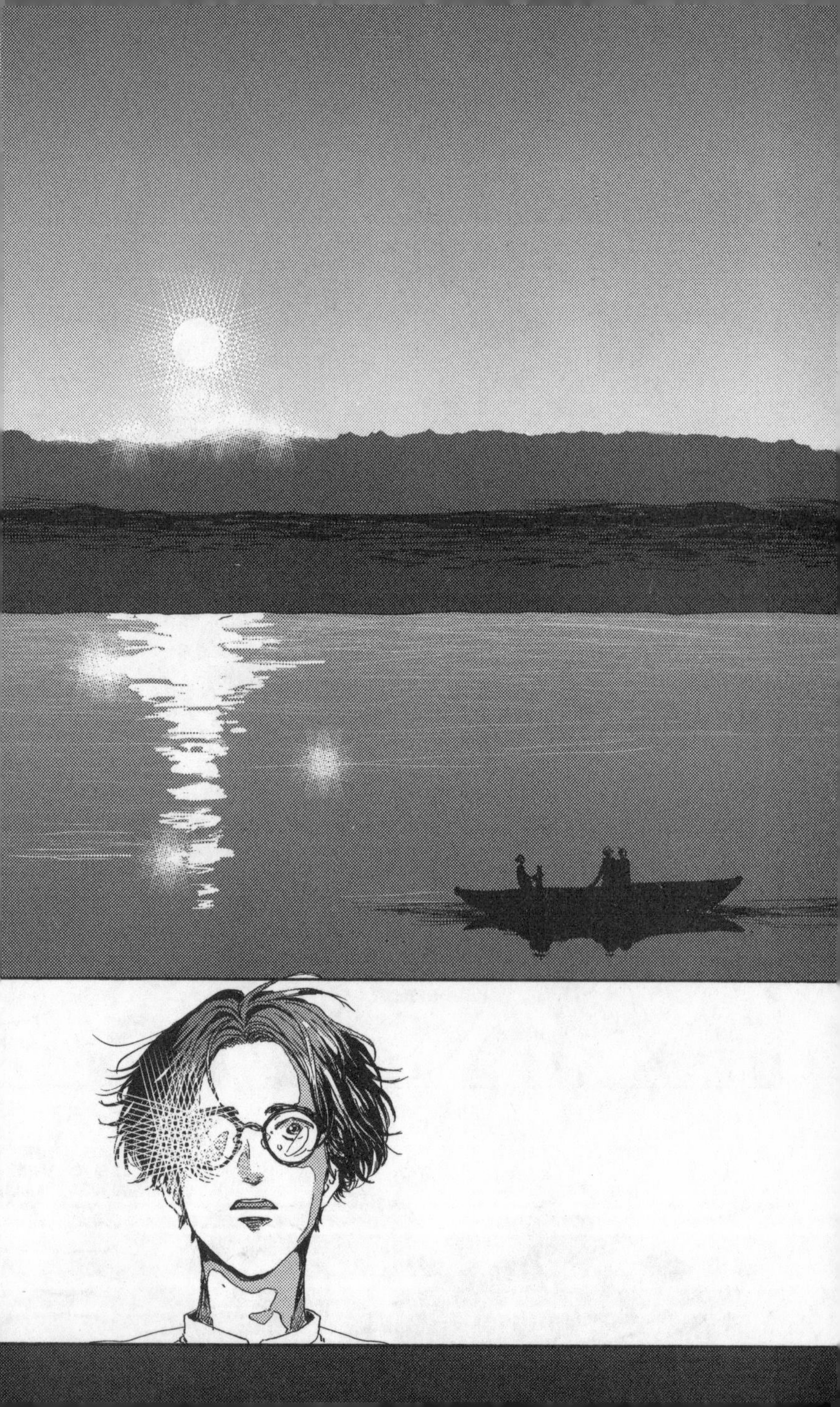

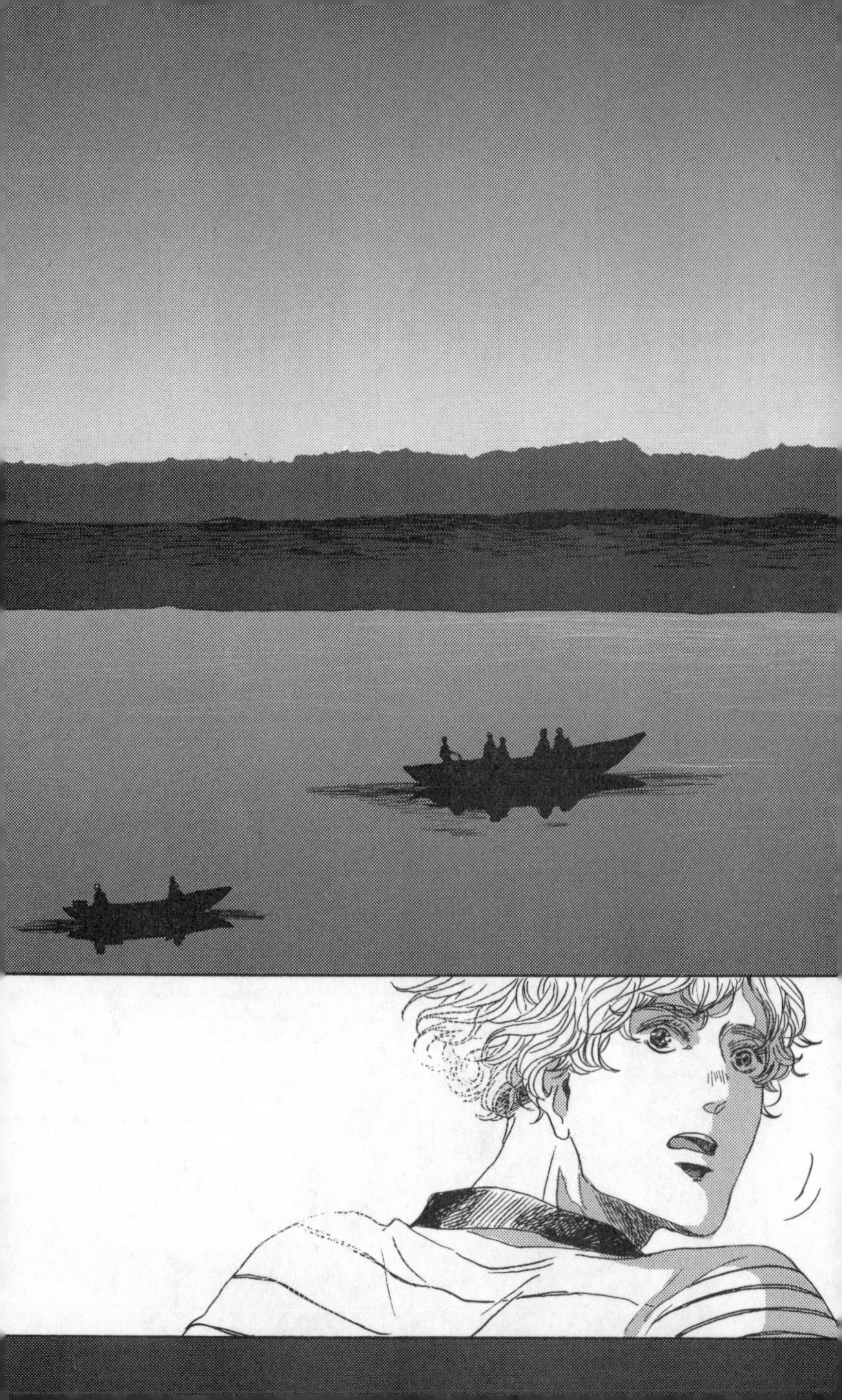

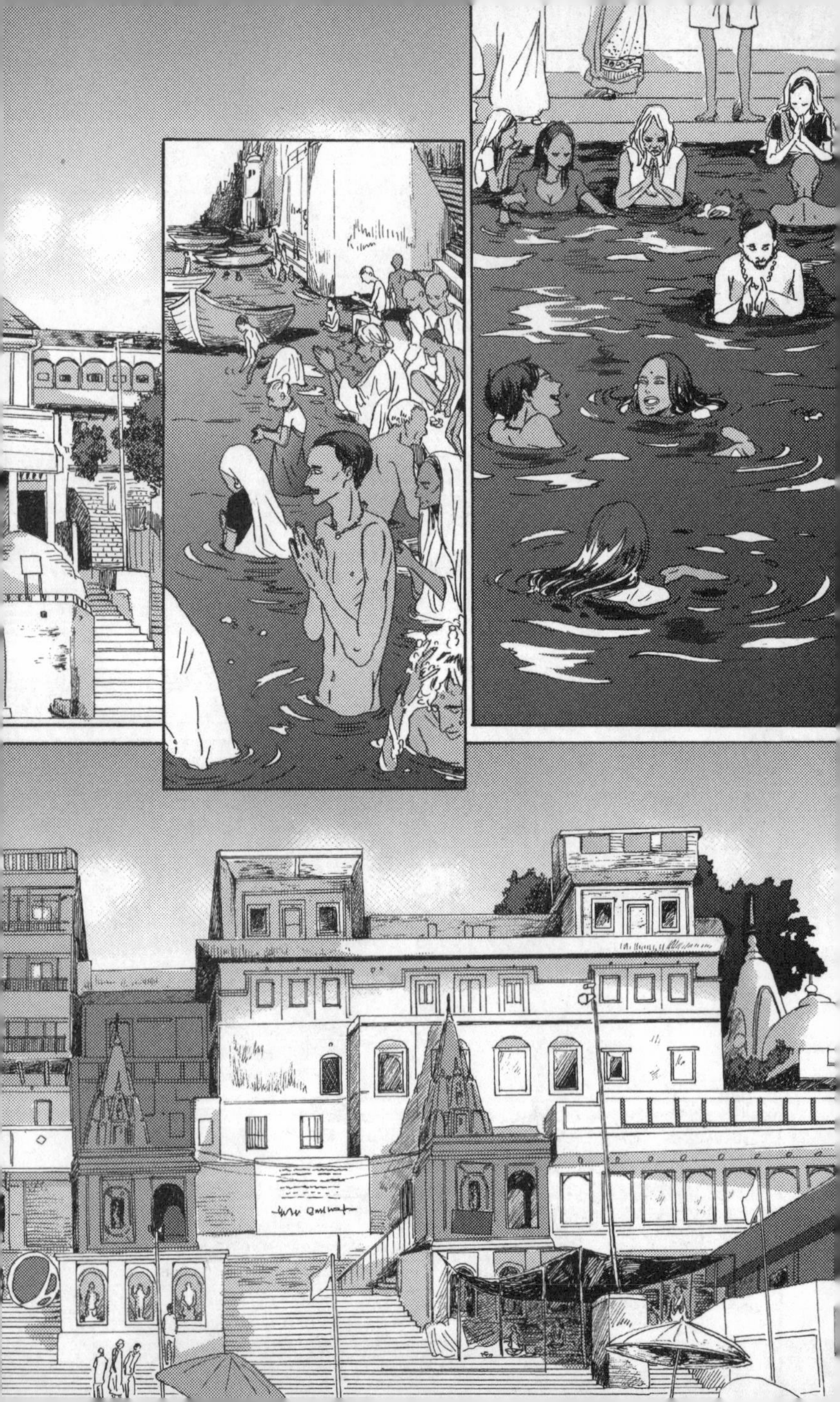

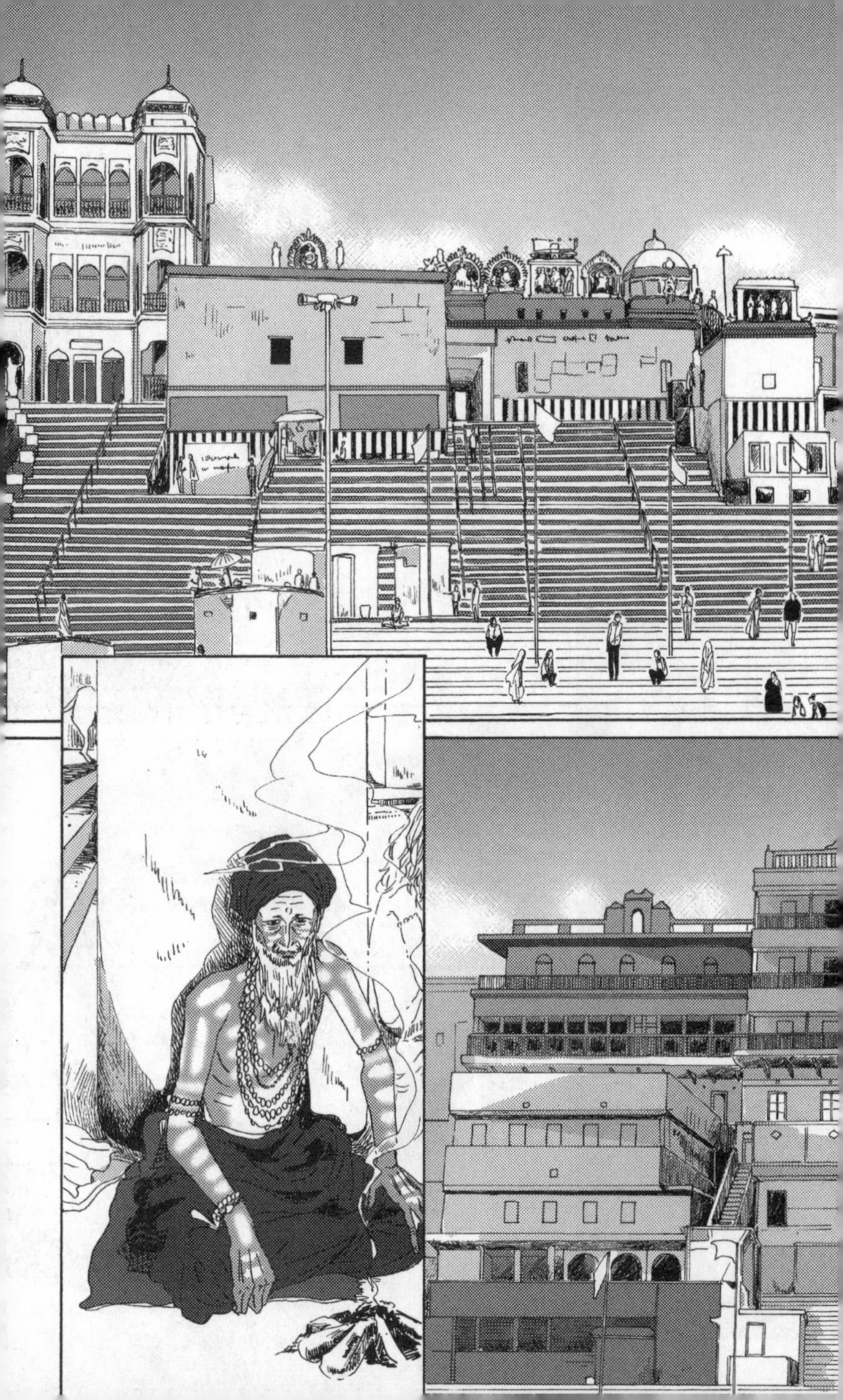

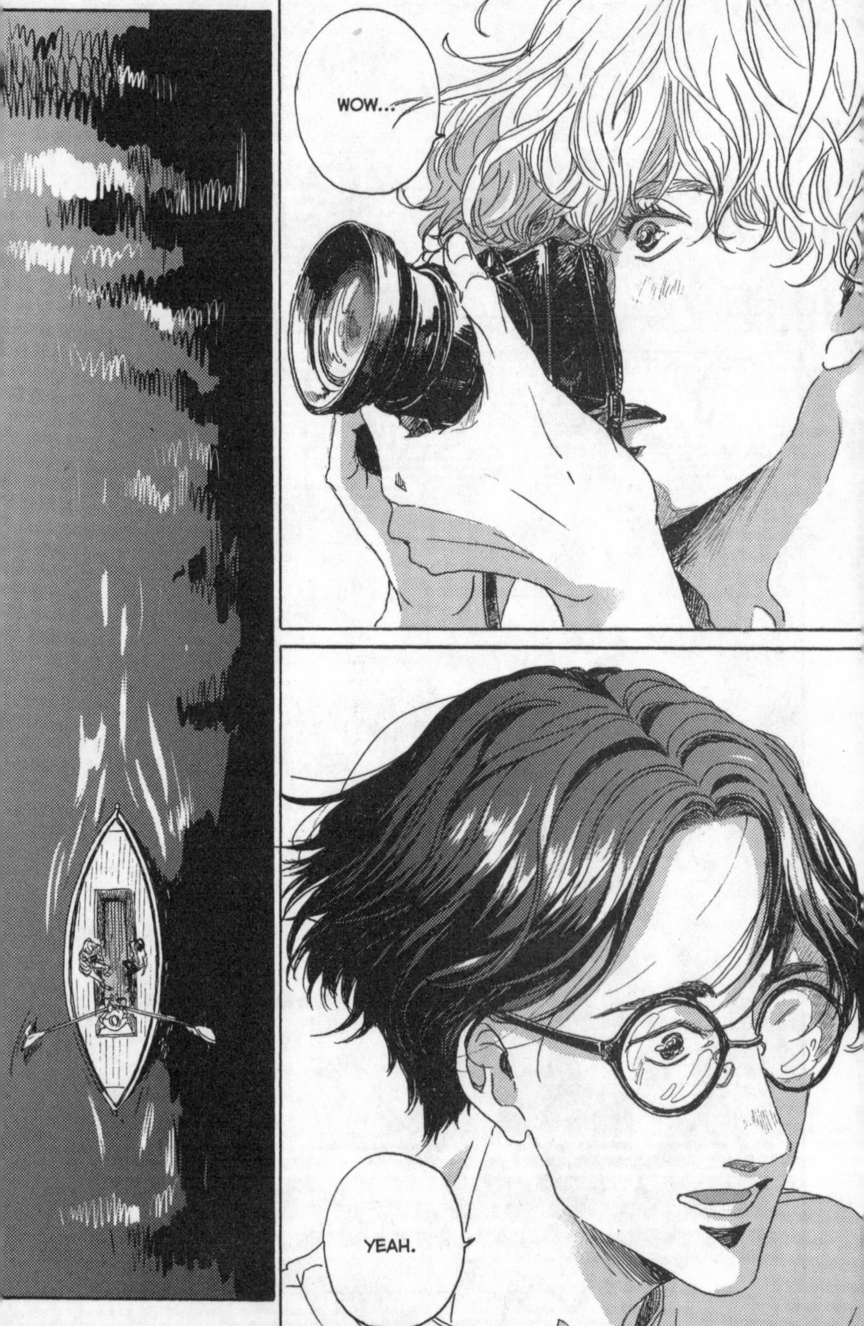
WOW...
YEAH.

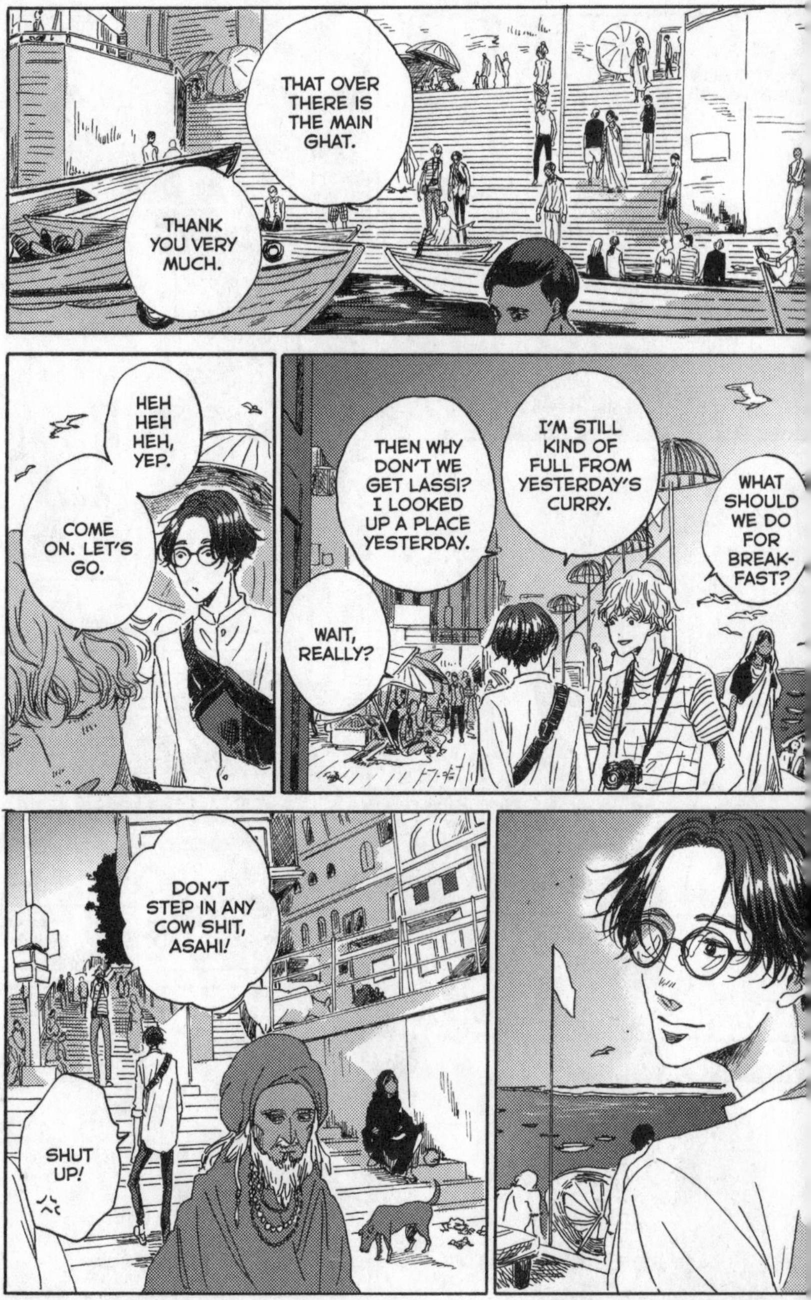
THAT OVER THERE IS THE MAIN GHAT.
THANK YOU VERY MUCH.
WHAT SHOULD WE DO FOR BREAKFAST?
I'M STILL KIND OF FULL FROM YESTERDAY'S CURRY.
THEN WHY DON'T WE GET LASSI? I LOOKED UP A PLACE YESTERDAY.
WAIT, REALLY?
HEH HEH HEH, YEP.
COME ON. LET'S GO.
DON'T STEP IN ANY COW SHIT, ASAHI!
SHUT UP!

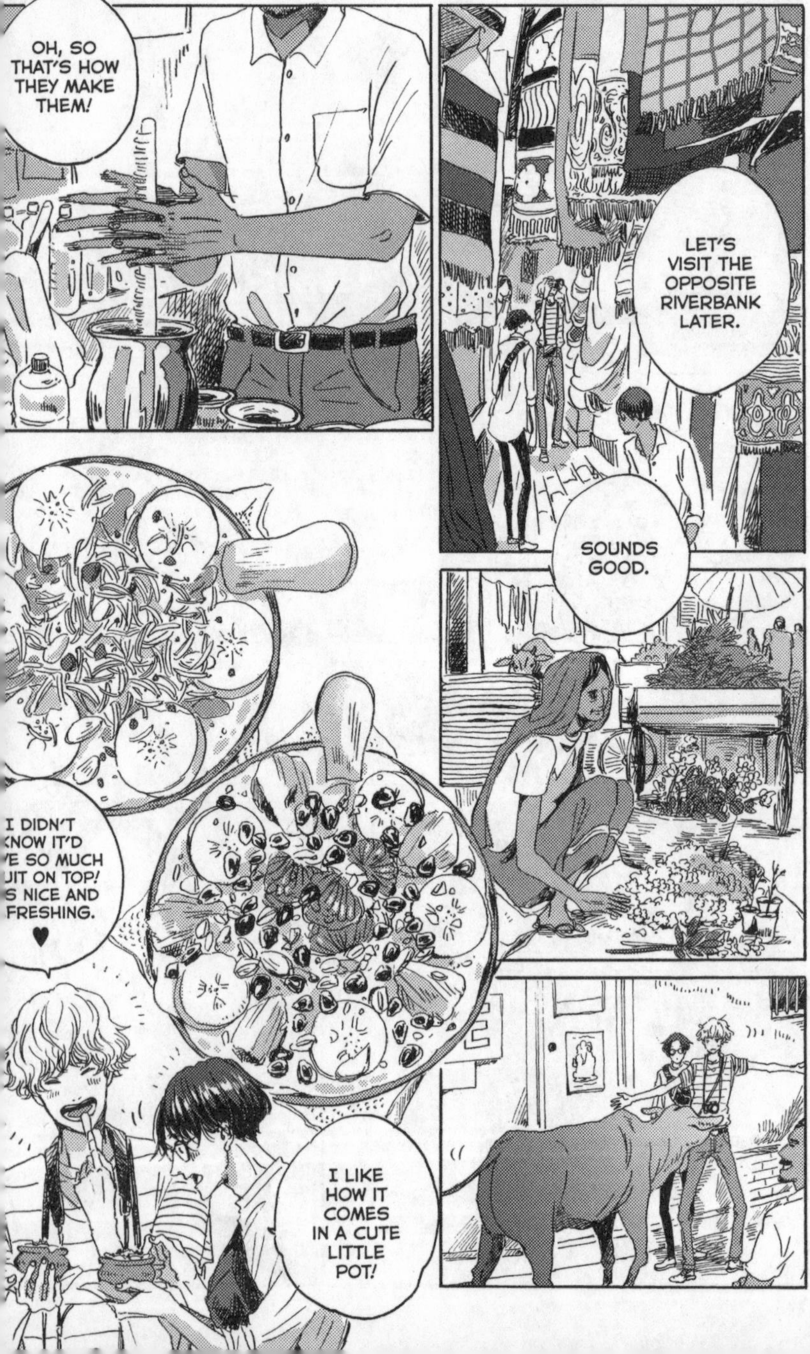
LET'S VISIT THE OPPOSITE RIVERBANK LATER.
SOUNDS GOOD.
OH, SO THAT'S HOW THEY MAKE THEM!
I DIDN'T KNOW IT'D VE SO MUCH UIT ON TOP! S NICE AND FRESHING. ♥
I LIKE HOW IT COMES IN A CUTE LITTLE POT!

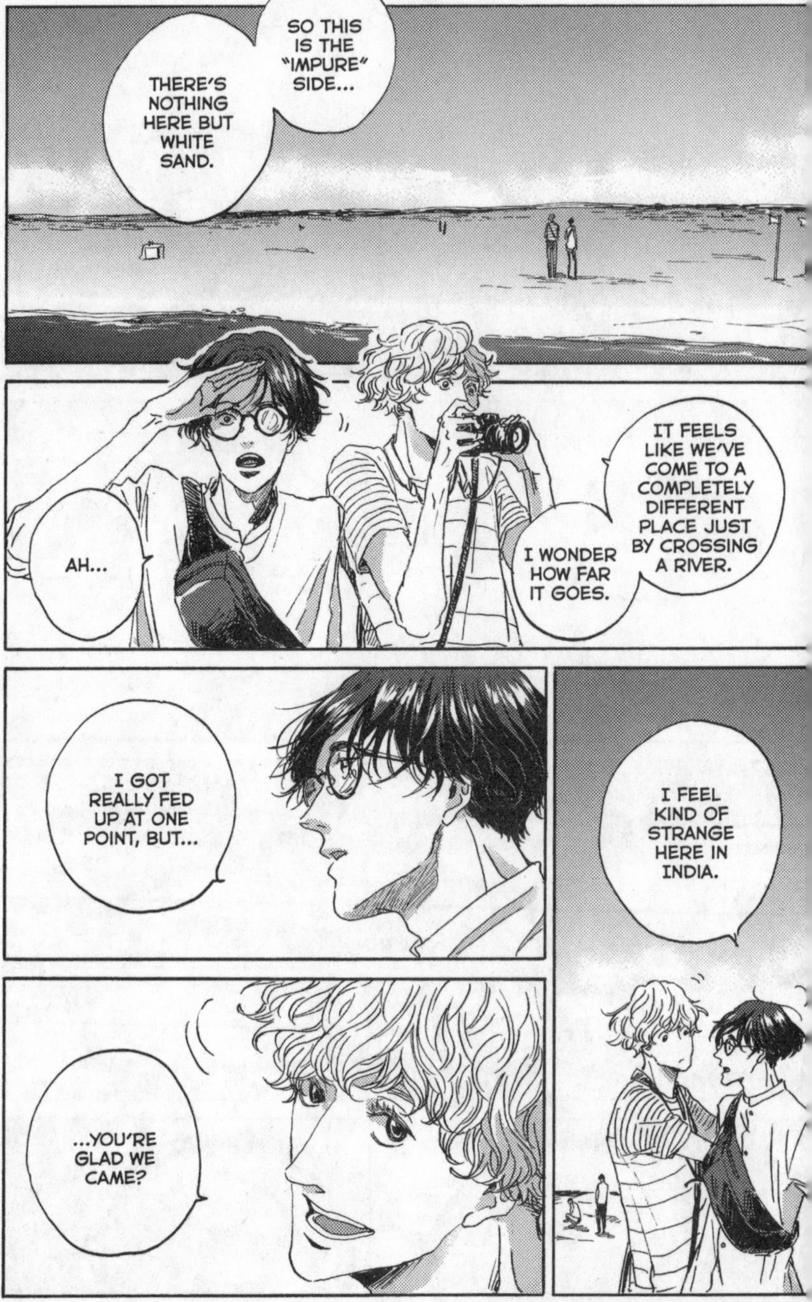
SO THIS IS THE "IMPURE" SIDE...
THERE'S NOTHING HERE BUT WHITE SAND.
IT FEELS LIKE WE'VE COME TO A COMPLETELY DIFFERENT PLACE JUST BY CROSSING A RIVER.
I WONDER HOW FAR IT GOES.
AH...
I FEEL KIND OF STRANGE HERE IN INDIA.
I GOT REALLY FED UP AT ONE POINT, BUT...
...YOU'RE GLAD WE CAME?

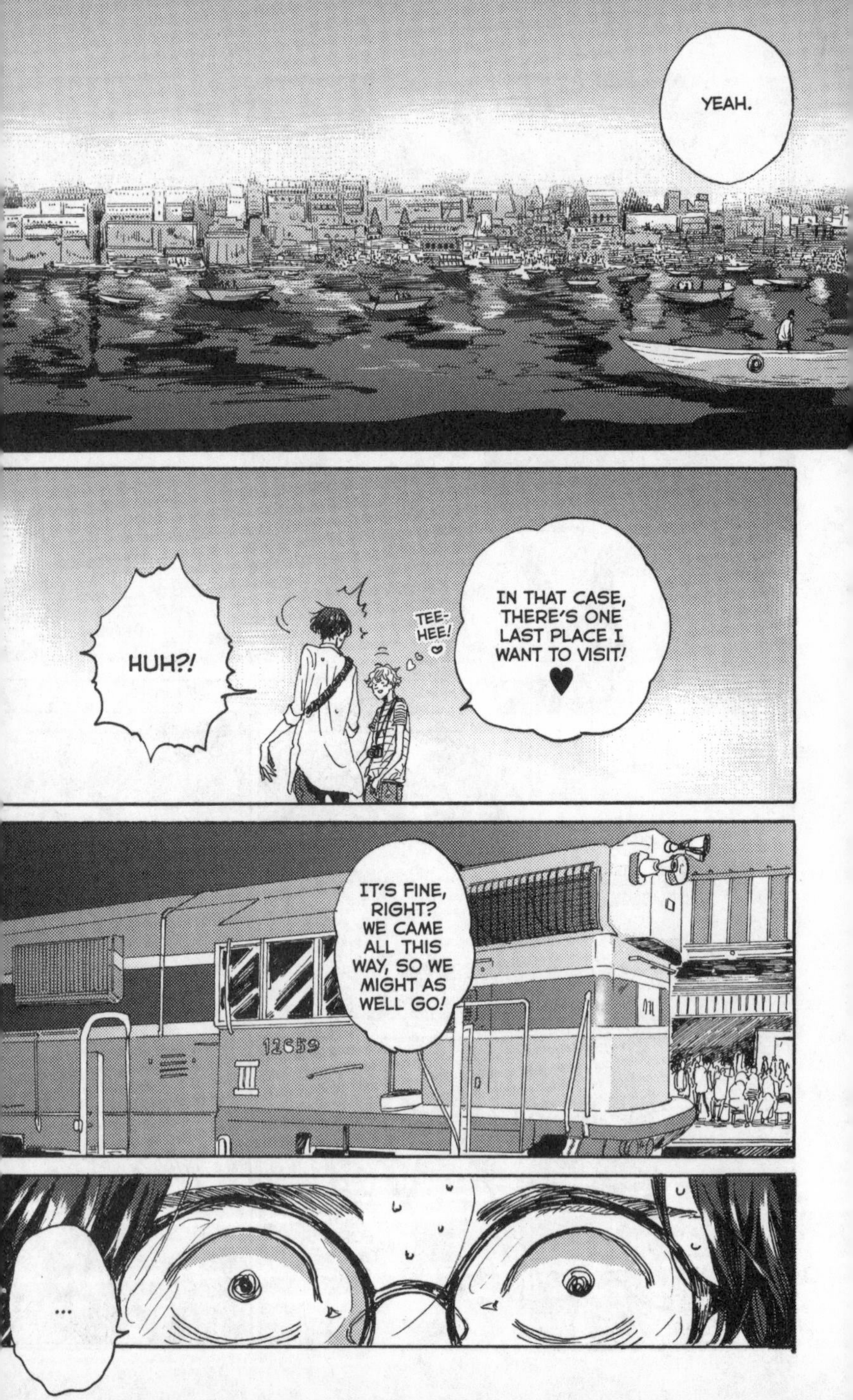
YEAH.
IN THAT CASE, THERE'S ONE LAST PLACE I WANT TO VISIT! ♥
TEE-HEE!
HUH?!
IT'S FINE, RIGHT? WE CAME ALL THIS WAY, SO WE MIGHT AS WELL GO!
...

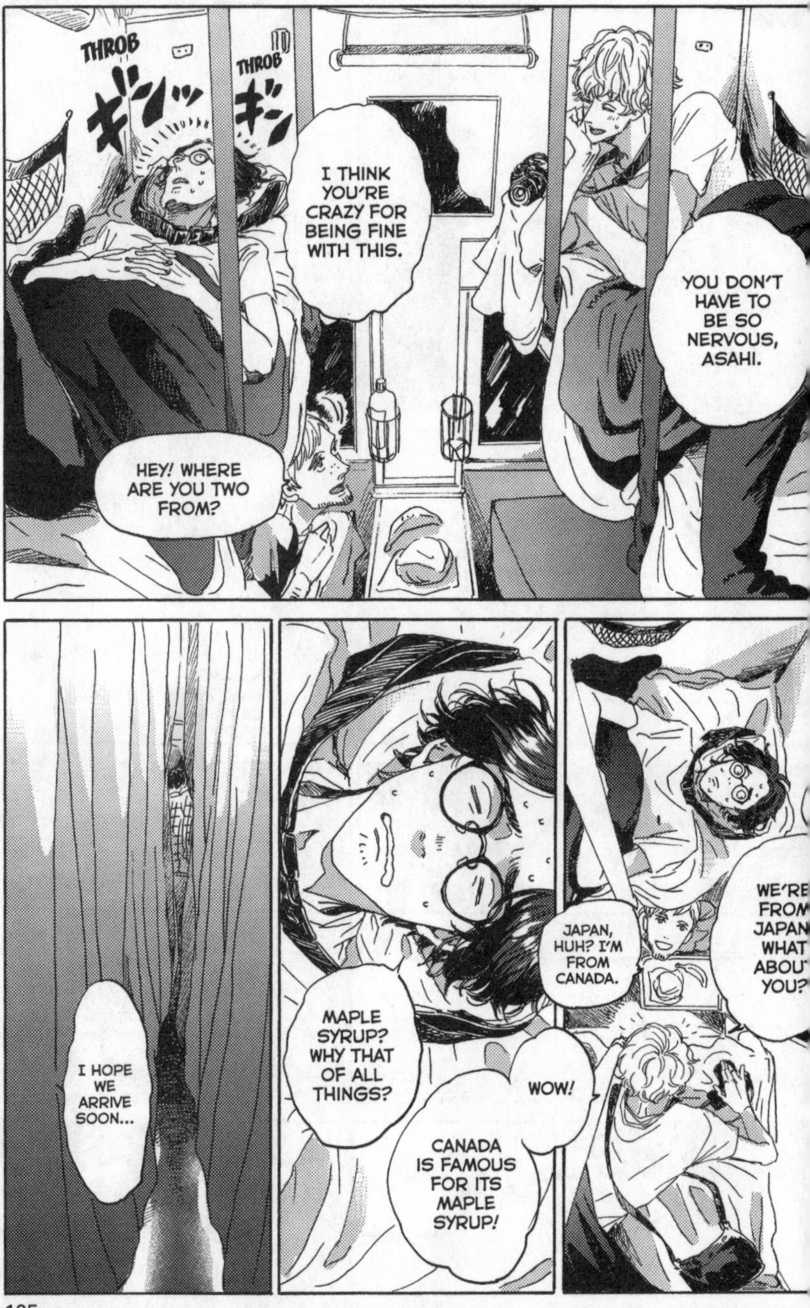
THROB
ギンッ
THROB
ギン
YOU DON'T HAVE TO BE SO NERVOUS, ASAHI.
I THINK YOU'RE CRAZY FOR BEING FINE WITH THIS.
HEY! WHERE ARE YOU TWO FROM?
WE'RE FROM JAPAN WHAT ABOUT YOU?
JAPAN, HUH? I'M FROM CANADA.
WOW!
CANADA IS FAMOUS FOR ITS MAPLE SYRUP!
MAPLE SYRUP? WHY THAT OF ALL THINGS?
I HOPE WE ARRIVE SOON...

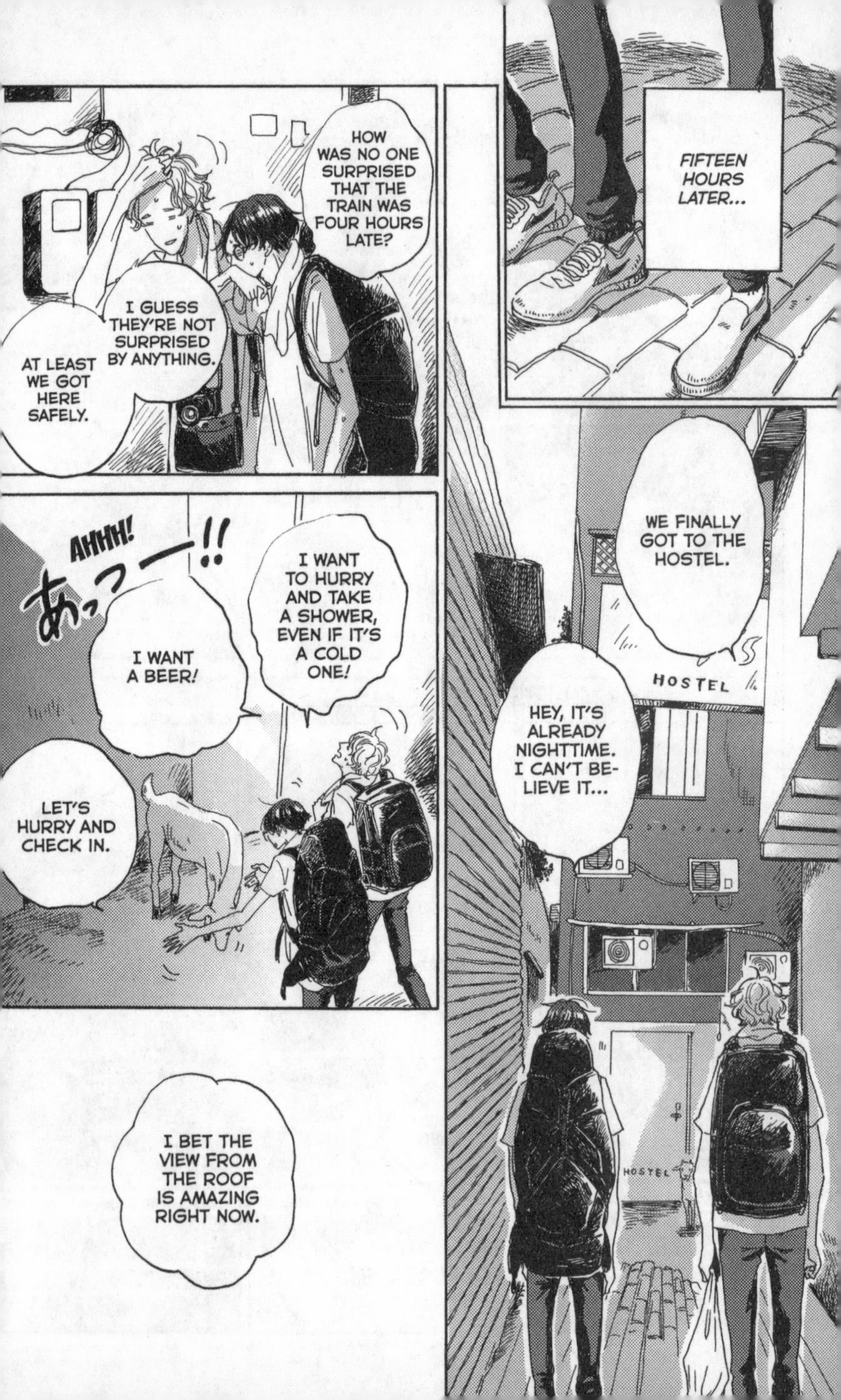
FIFTEEN HOURS LATER...
WE FINALLY GOT TO THE HOSTEL.
HOSTEL
HEY, IT'S ALREADY NIGHTTIME. I CAN'T BELIEVE IT...
HOSTEL
HOW WAS NO ONE SURPRISED THAT THE TRAIN WAS FOUR HOURS LATE?
I GUESS THEY'RE NOT SURPRISED BY ANYTHING.
AT LEAST WE GOT HERE SAFELY.
I WANT TO HURRY AND TAKE A SHOWER, EVEN IF IT'S A COLD ONE!
AHHH!
あっつー!!
I WANT A BEER!
LET'S HURRY AND CHECK IN.
I BET THE VIEW FROM THE ROOF IS AMAZING RIGHT NOW.

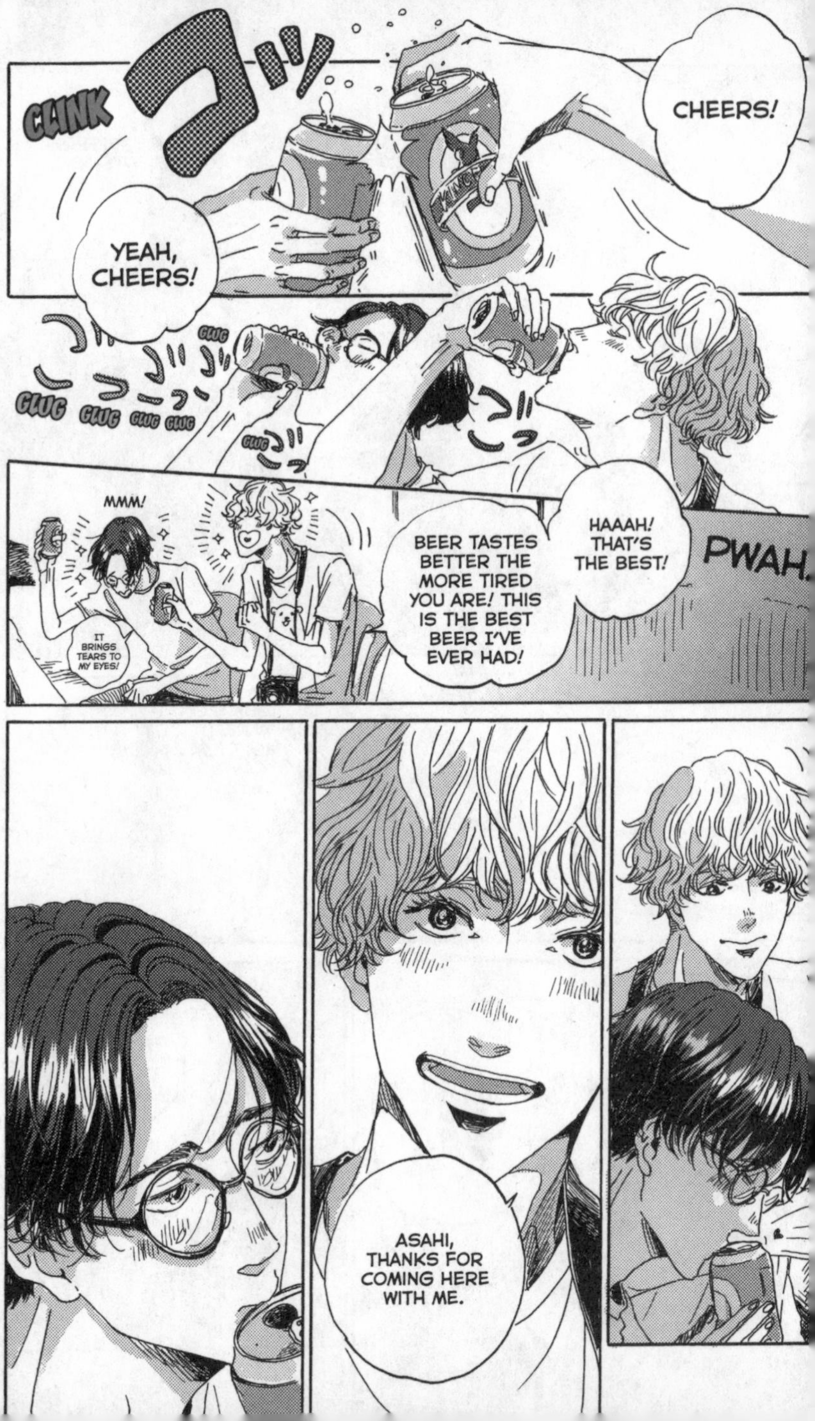
CHEERS!
YEAH, CHEERS!
CLINK
GLUG
GLUG
GLUG GLUG GLUG GLUG
GLUG
PWAH
HAAAH! THAT'S THE BEST!
BEER TASTES BETTER THE MORE TIRED YOU ARE! THIS IS THE BEST BEER I'VE EVER HAD!
MMM!
IT BRINGS TEARS TO MY EYES!
ASAHI, THANKS FOR COMING HERE WITH ME.

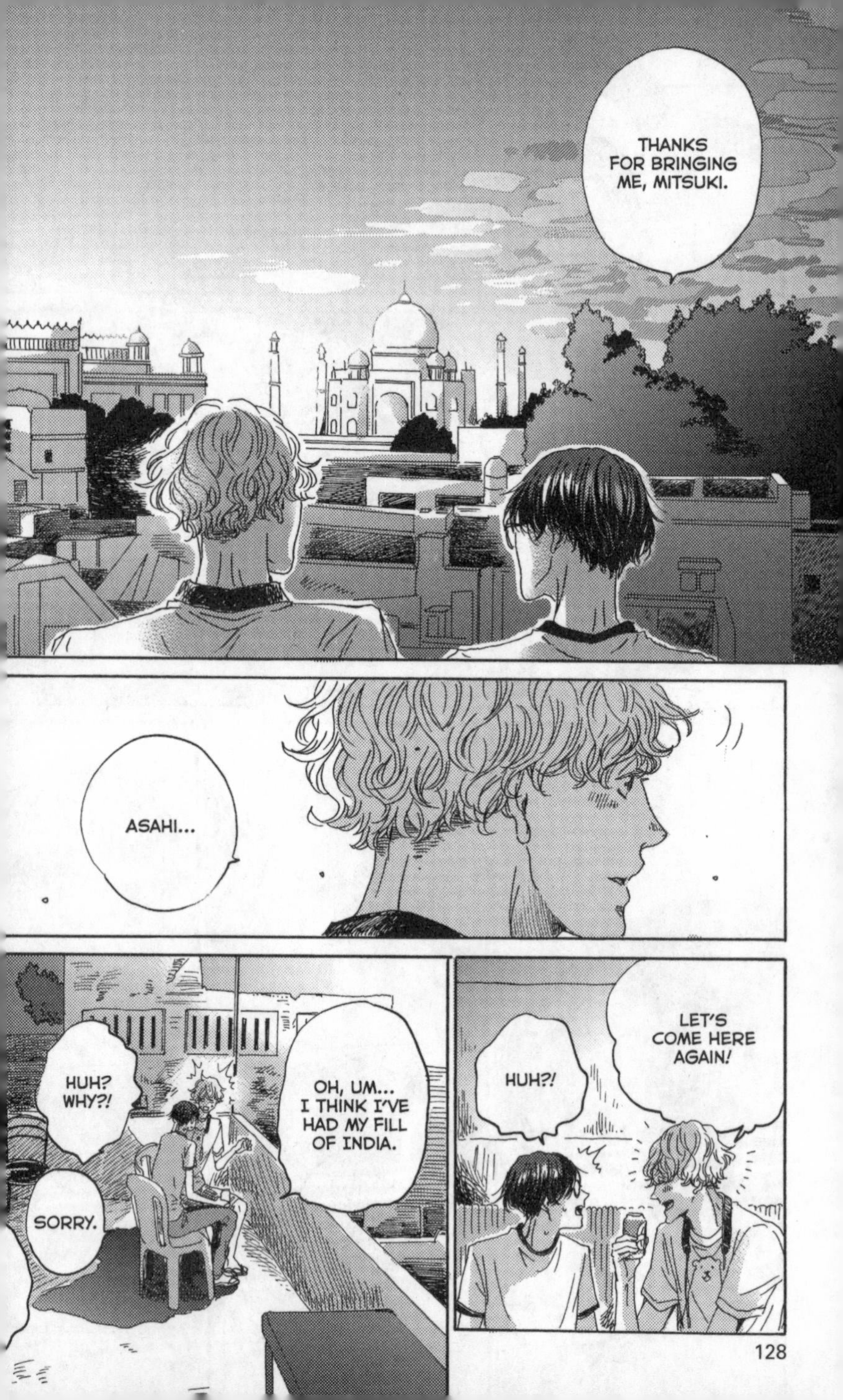
THANKS FOR BRINGING ME, MITSUKI.
ASAHI...
LET'S COME HERE AGAIN!
HUH?!
OH, UM... I THINK I'VE HAD MY FILL OF INDIA.
HUH? WHY?!
SORRY.

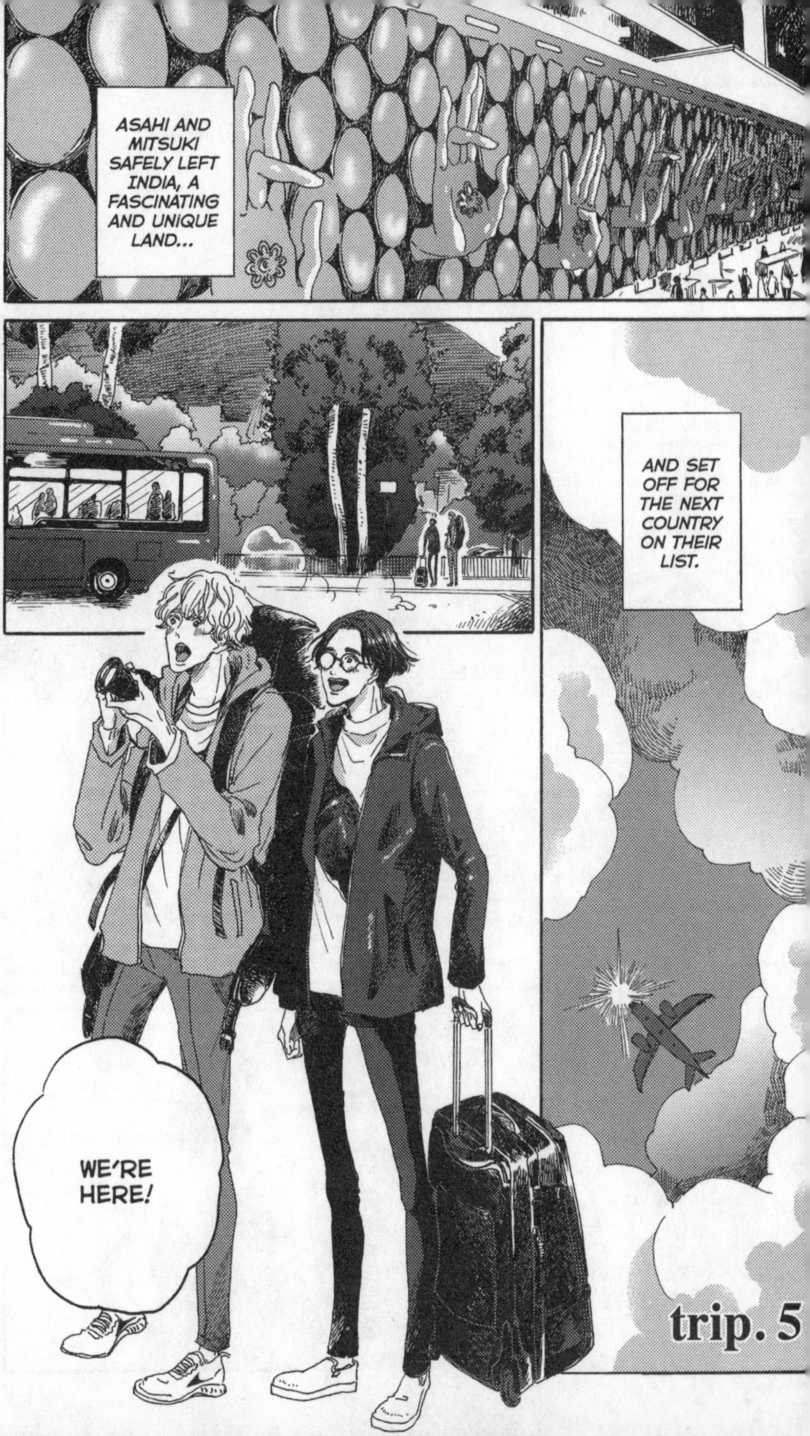
ASAHI AND MITSUKI SAFELY LEFT INDIA, A FASCINATING AND UNIQUE LAND...
AND SET OFF FOR THE NEXT COUNTRY ON THEIR LIST.
trip. 5
WE'RE HERE!

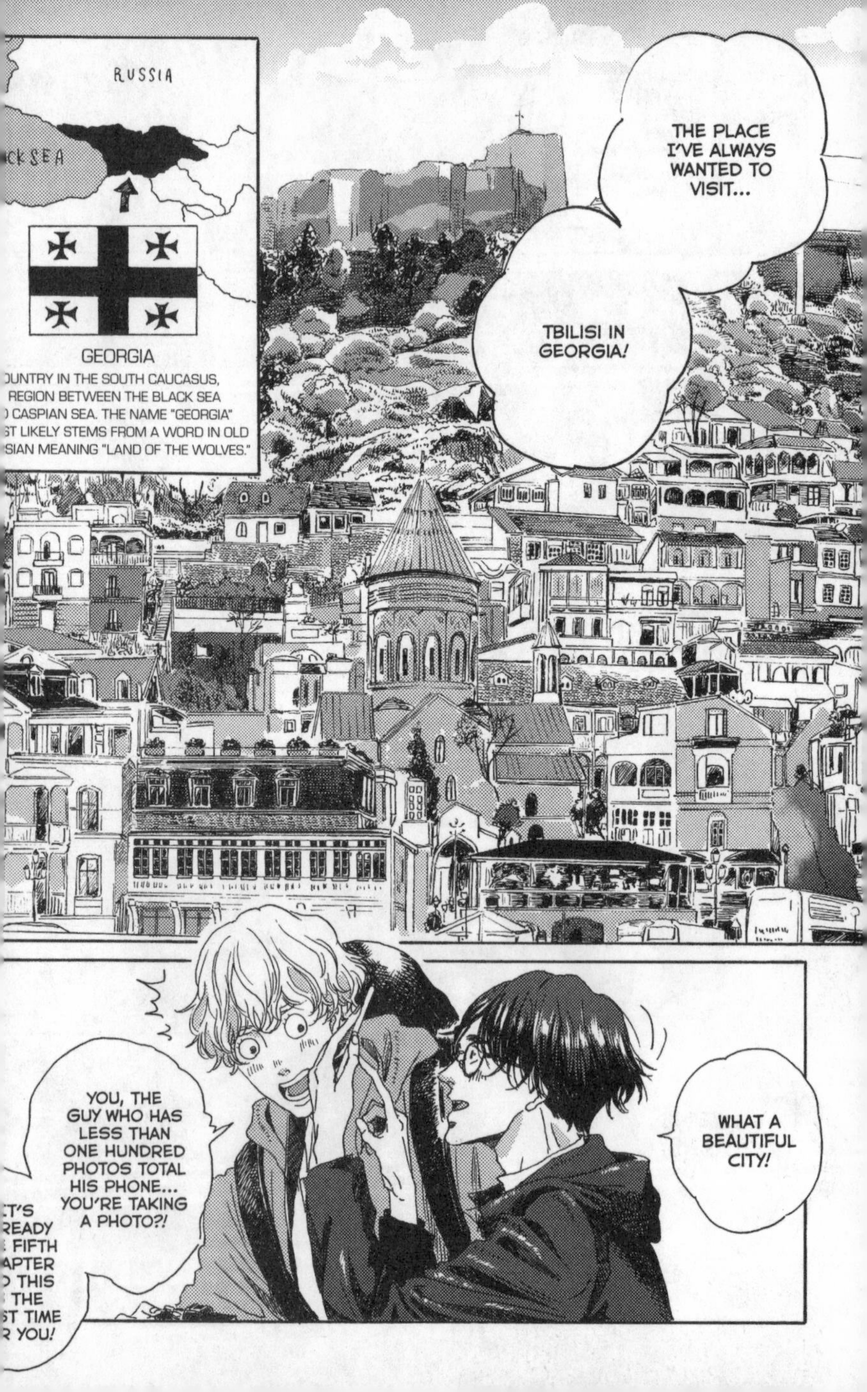
THE PLACE I'VE ALWAYS WANTED TO VISIT...
TBILISI IN GEORGIA!
RUSSIA
CK SEA
GEORGIA
OUNTRY IN THE SOUTH CAUCASUS,
REGION BETWEEN THE BLACK SEA
CASPIAN SEA. THE NAME "GEORGIA"
ST LIKELY STEMS FROM A WORD IN OLD
SIAN MEANING "LAND OF THE WOLVES."
WHAT A BEAUTIFUL CITY!
YOU, THE GUY WHO HAS LESS THAN ONE HUNDRED PHOTOS TOTAL HIS PHONE... YOU'RE TAKING A PHOTO?!
T'S READY FIFTH APTER THIS THE ST TIME YOU!

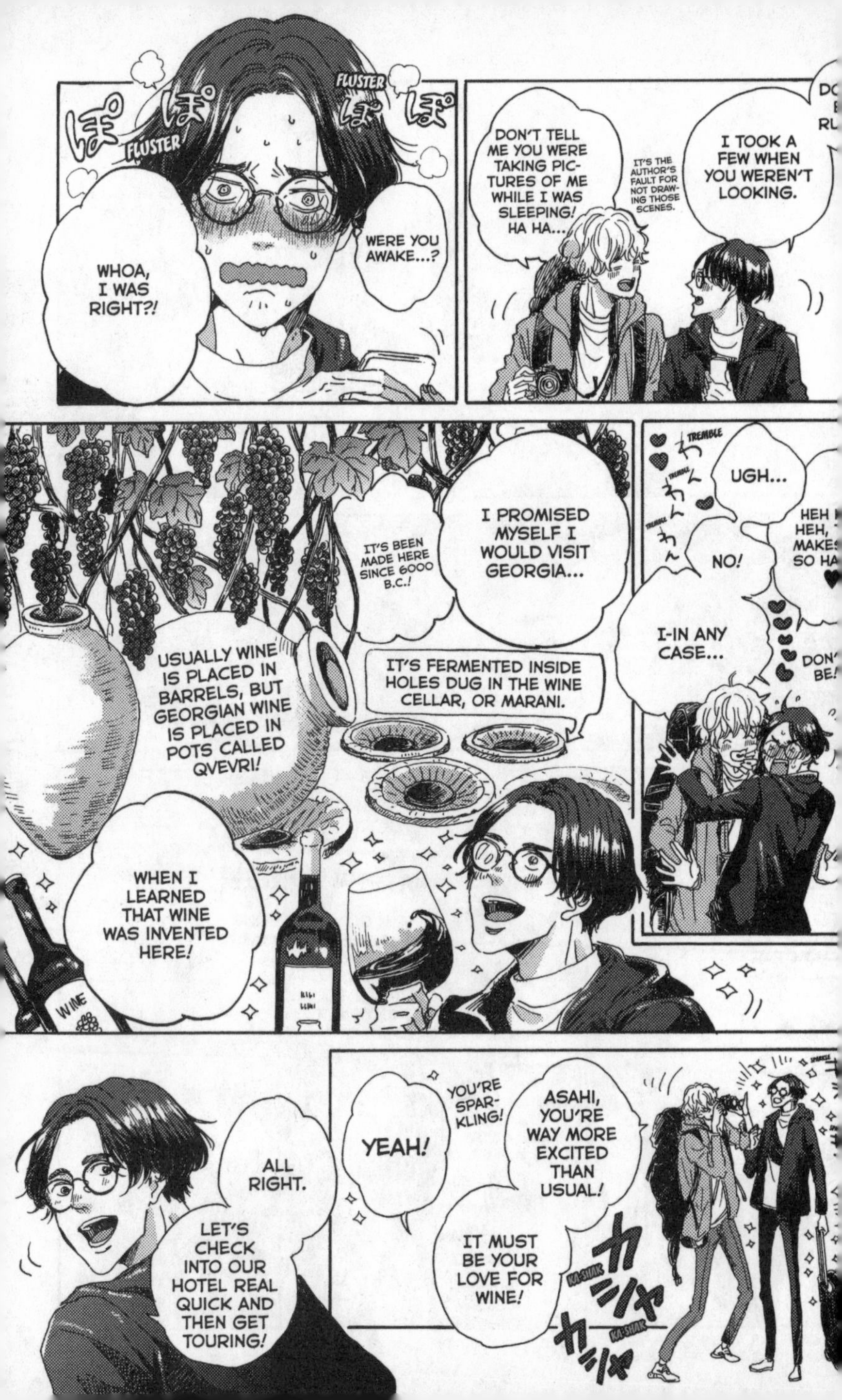
I TOOK A FEW WHEN YOU WEREN'T LOOKING.
IT'S THE AUTHOR'S FAULT FOR NOT DRAWING THOSE SCENES.
DON'T TELL ME YOU WERE TAKING PICTURES OF ME WHILE I WAS SLEEPING! HA HA...
FLUSTER
ぽ ぽ
WERE YOU AWAKE...?
ぽ ぽ
FLUSTER
WHOA, I WAS RIGHT?!
UGH...
TREMBLE
わん
TREMBLE
わん
TREMBLE
わん
NO!
I-IN ANY CASE...
I PROMISED MYSELF I WOULD VISIT GEORGIA...
IT'S BEEN MADE HERE SINCE 6000 B.C.!
IT'S FERMENTED INSIDE HOLES DUG IN THE WINE CELLAR, OR MARANI.
USUALLY WINE IS PLACED IN BARRELS, BUT GEORGIAN WINE IS PLACED IN POTS CALLED QVEVRI!
WHEN I LEARNED THAT WINE WAS INVENTED HERE!
WINE
SPARKLE
ASAHI, YOU'RE WAY MORE EXCITED THAN USUAL!
YOU'RE SPARKLING!
YEAH!
IT MUST BE YOUR LOVE FOR WINE!
KA-SHAK
カシャ
KA-SHAK
カシャ
ALL RIGHT.
LET'S CHECK INTO OUR HOTEL REAL QUICK AND THEN GET TOURING!

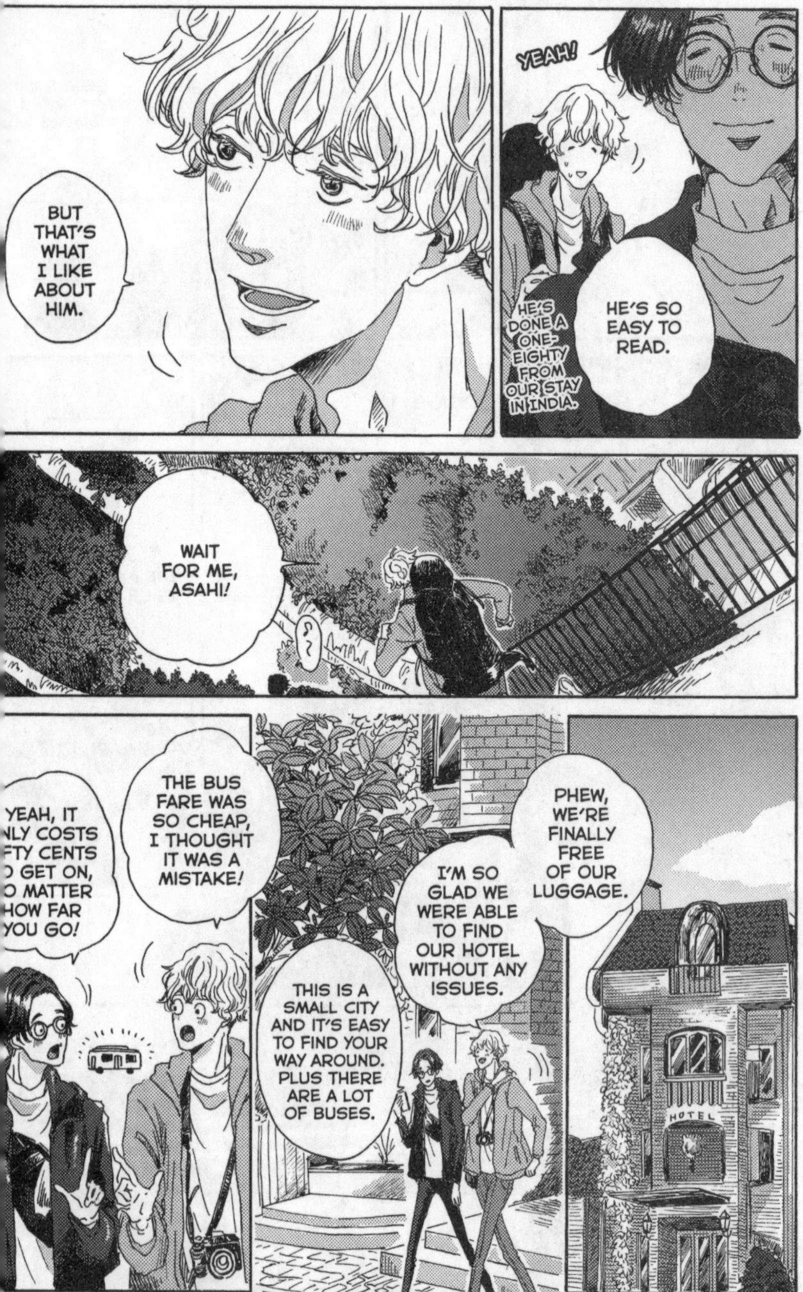
YEAH!
HE'S SO EASY TO READ.
HE'S DONE A ONE-EIGHTY FROM OUR STAY IN INDIA.
BUT THAT'S WHAT I LIKE ABOUT HIM.
WAIT FOR ME, ASAHI!
PHEW, WE'RE FINALLY FREE OF OUR LUGGAGE.
HOTEL
I'M SO GLAD WE WERE ABLE TO FIND OUR HOTEL WITHOUT ANY ISSUES.
THIS IS A SMALL CITY AND IT'S EASY TO FIND YOUR WAY AROUND. PLUS THERE ARE A LOT OF BUSES.
THE BUS FARE WAS SO CHEAP, I THOUGHT IT WAS A MISTAKE!
YEAH, IT NLY COSTS FTY CENTS GET ON, MATTER HOW FAR YOU GO!
CAN TAKE A BUS FROM THE ORT TO DOWNTOWN TBILISI.

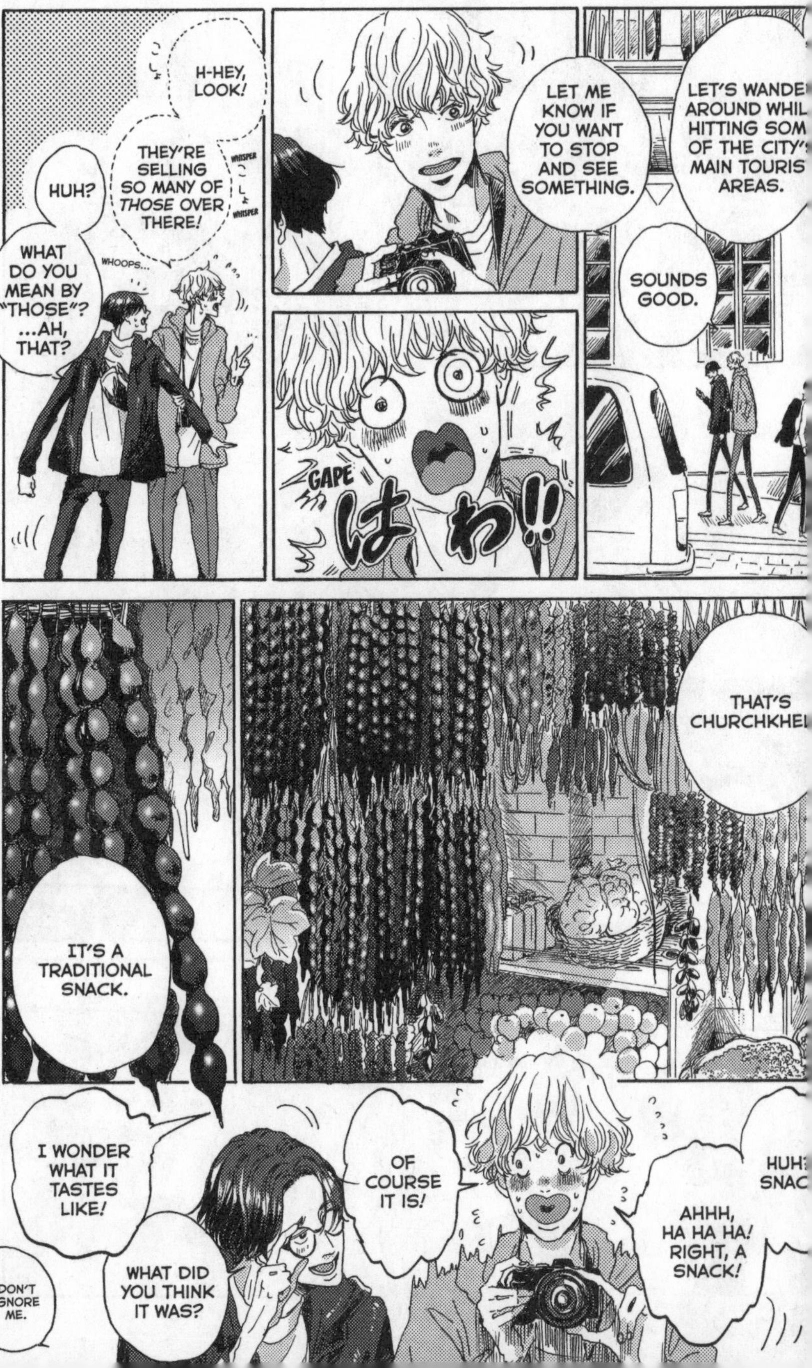
LET'S WANDE AROUND WHIL HITTING SOM OF THE CITY'S MAIN TOURIS AREAS.
SOUNDS GOOD.
LET ME KNOW IF YOU WANT TO STOP AND SEE SOMETHING.
GAPE
はわ!!
こしょ
H-HEY, LOOK!
THEY'RE SELLING SO MANY OF *THOSE* OVER THERE!
WHISPER こしょ WHISPER
HUH?
WHAT DO YOU MEAN BY "THOSE"? ...AH, THAT?
WHOOPS...
THAT'S CHURCHKHE
IT'S A TRADITIONAL SNACK.
HUH SNAC
AHHH, HA HA HA! RIGHT, A SNACK!
OF COURSE IT IS!
I WONDER WHAT IT TASTES LIKE!
WHAT DID YOU THINK IT WAS?
DON'T IGNORE ME.

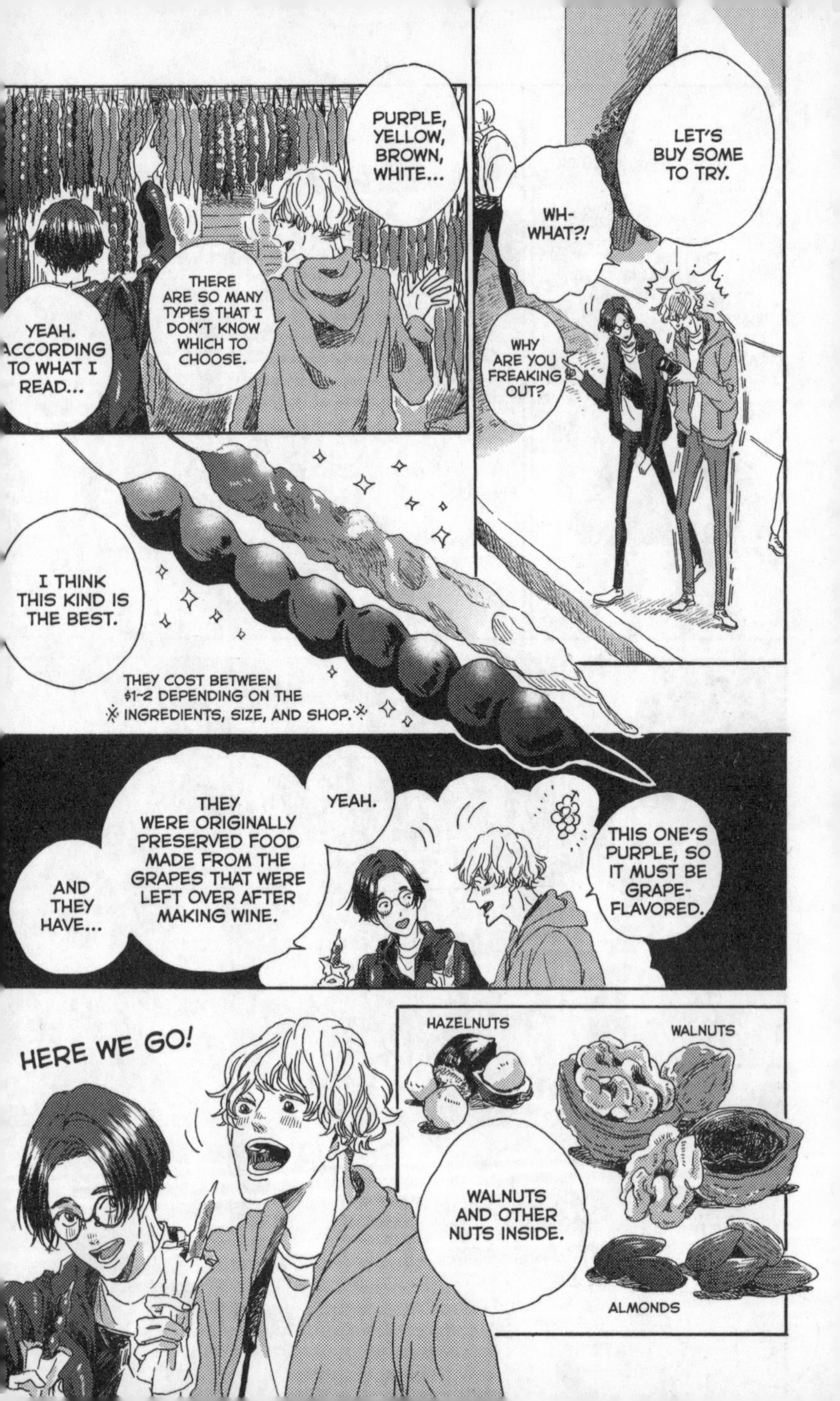

LET'S BUY SOME TO TRY.
WH- WHAT?!
WHY ARE YOU FREAKING OUT?
PURPLE, YELLOW, BROWN, WHITE...
THERE ARE SO MANY TYPES THAT I DON'T KNOW WHICH TO CHOOSE.
YEAH. ACCORDING TO WHAT I READ...
I THINK THIS KIND IS THE BEST.
※ THEY COST BETWEEN $1~2 DEPENDING ON THE INGREDIENTS, SIZE, AND SHOP. ※
THIS ONE'S PURPLE, SO IT MUST BE GRAPE-FLAVORED.
YEAH.
THEY WERE ORIGINALLY PRESERVED FOOD MADE FROM THE GRAPES THAT WERE LEFT OVER AFTER MAKING WINE.
AND THEY HAVE...
HAZELNUTS
WALNUTS
WALNUTS AND OTHER NUTS INSIDE.
ALMONDS
HERE WE GO!

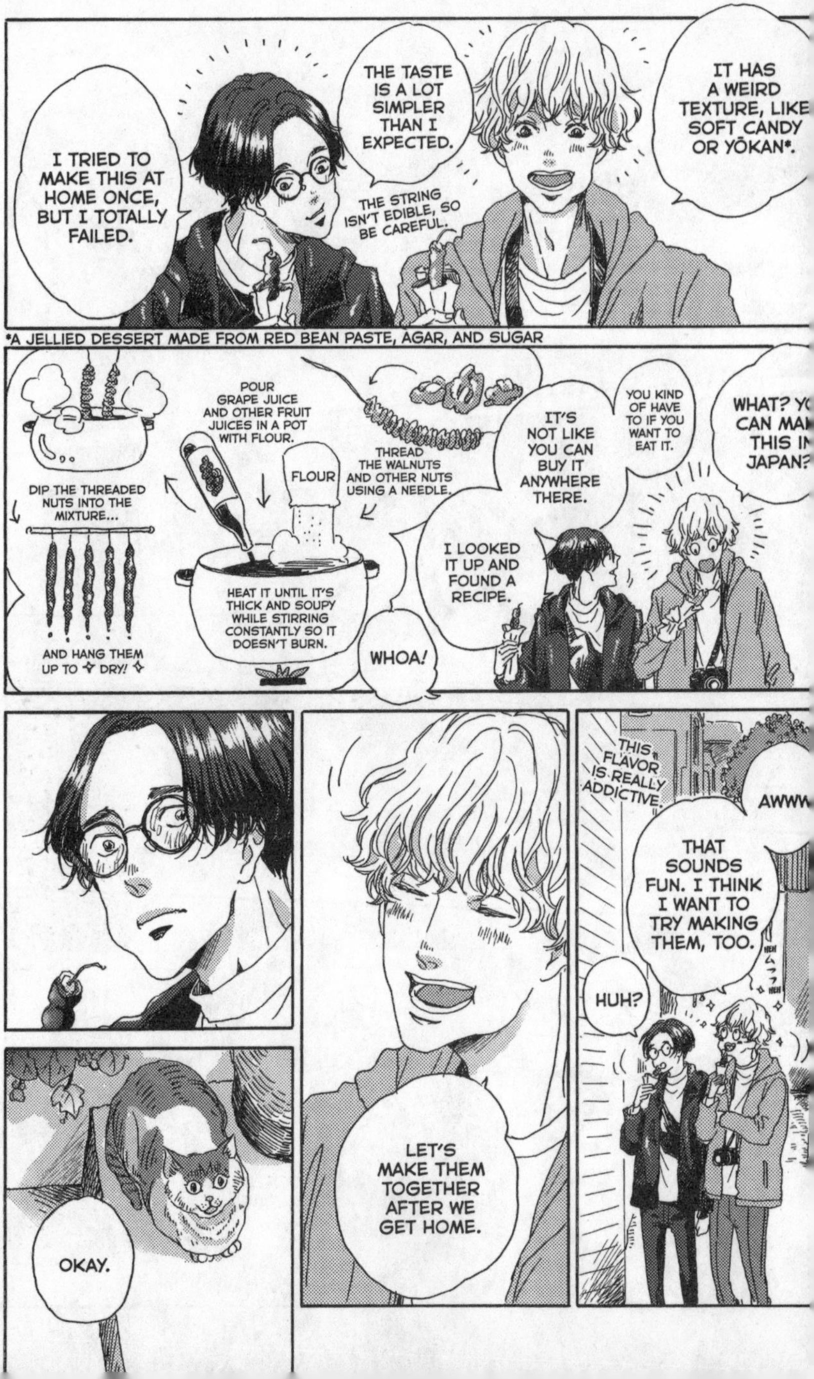
IT HAS A WEIRD TEXTURE, LIKE SOFT CANDY OR YŌKAN*.
THE TASTE IS A LOT SIMPLER THAN I EXPECTED.
THE STRING ISN'T EDIBLE, SO BE CAREFUL.
I TRIED TO MAKE THIS AT HOME ONCE, BUT I TOTALLY FAILED.
*A JELLIED DESSERT MADE FROM RED BEAN PASTE, AGAR, AND SUGAR
WHAT? YO CAN MA THIS I JAPAN?
YOU KIND OF HAVE TO IF YOU WANT TO EAT IT.
IT'S NOT LIKE YOU CAN BUY IT ANYWHERE THERE.
I LOOKED IT UP AND FOUND A RECIPE.
WHOA!
THREAD THE WALNUTS AND OTHER NUTS USING A NEEDLE.
POUR GRAPE JUICE AND OTHER FRUIT JUICES IN A POT WITH FLOUR.
FLOUR
HEAT IT UNTIL IT'S THICK AND SOUPY WHILE STIRRING CONSTANTLY SO IT DOESN'T BURN.
DIP THE THREADED NUTS INTO THE MIXTURE...
AND HANG THEM UP TO ✧ DRY! ✧
AWWW
THIS FLAVOR IS REALLY ADDICTIVE.
THAT SOUNDS FUN. I THINK I WANT TO TRY MAKING THEM, TOO.
HEH ムフフ HEH
HUH?
LET'S MAKE THEM TOGETHER AFTER WE GET HOME.
OKAY.

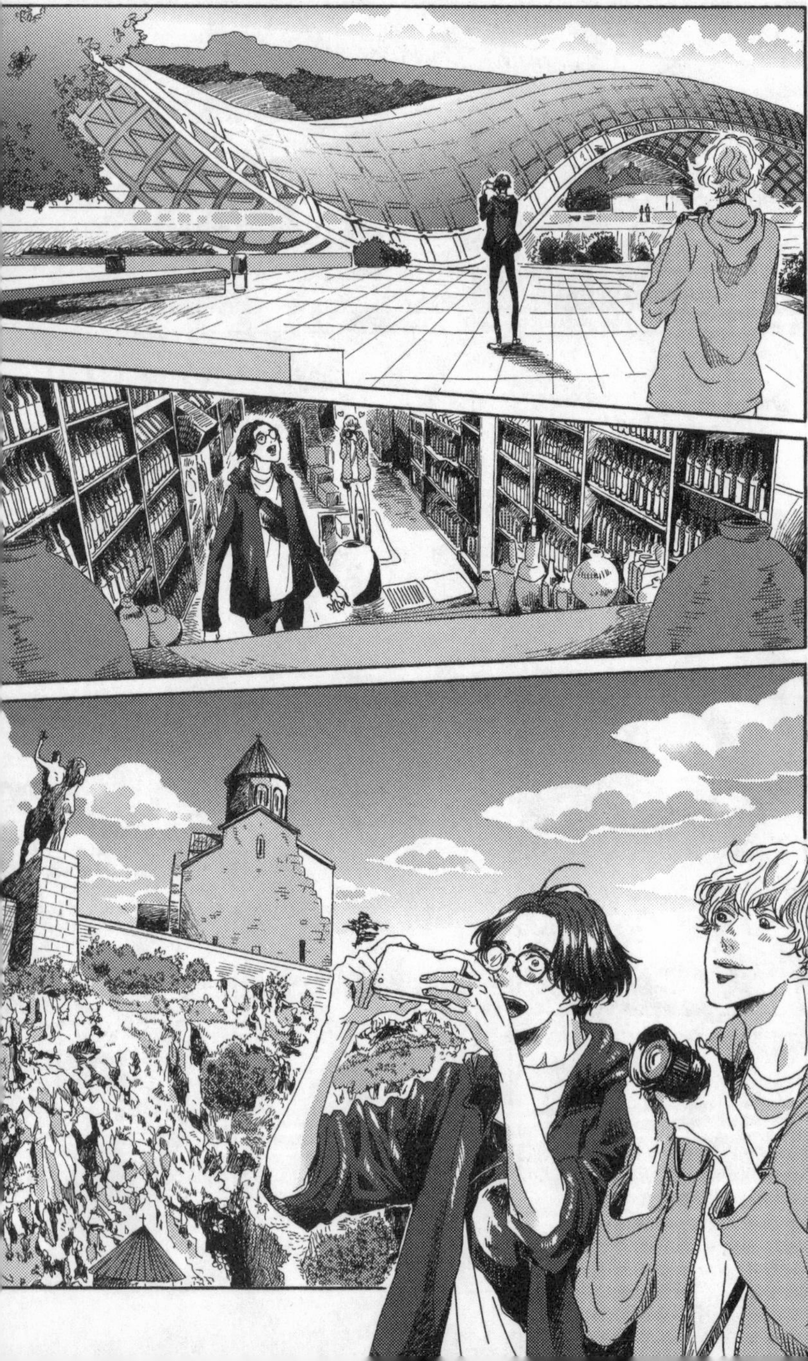

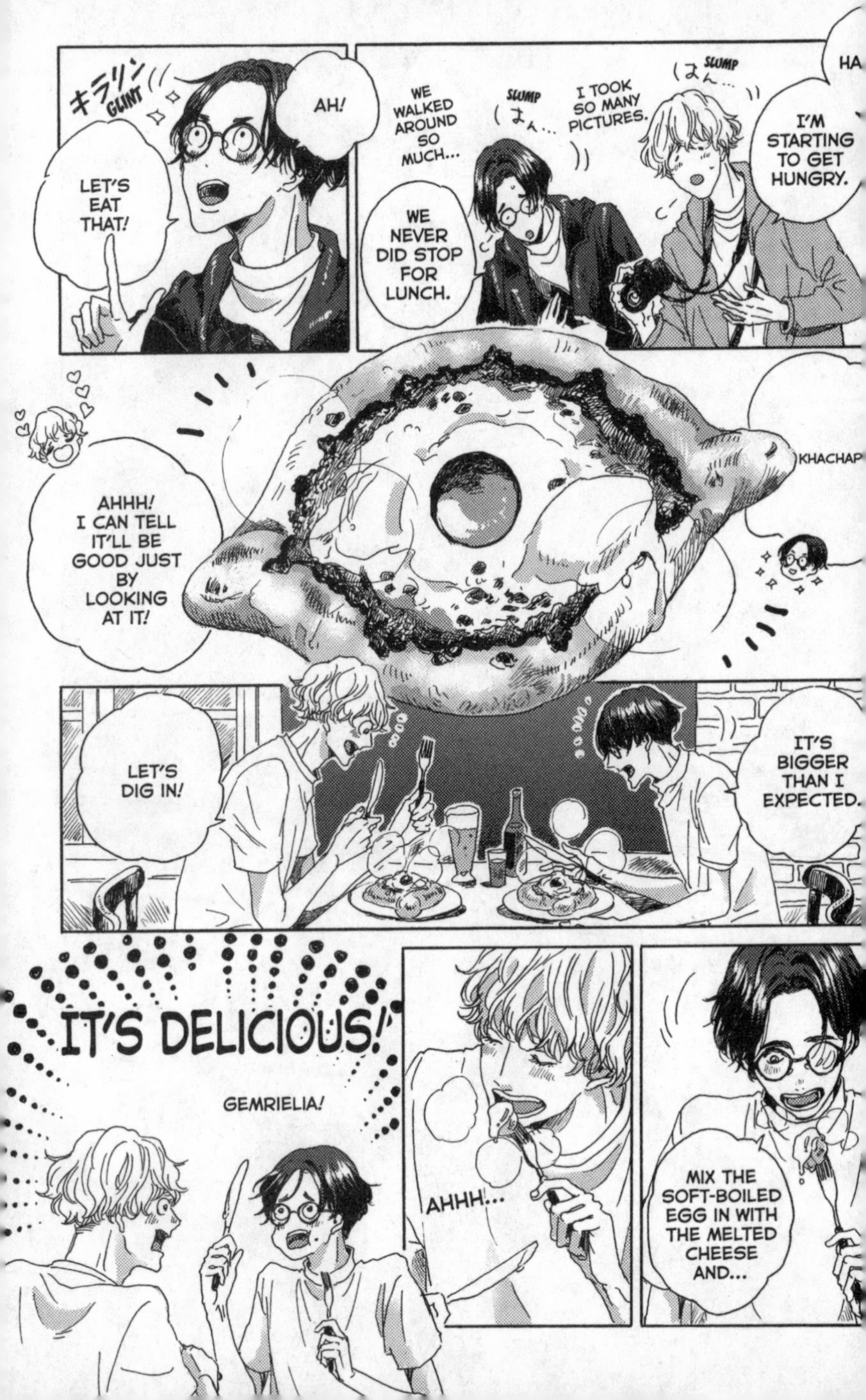
HA
I'M STARTING TO GET HUNGRY.
SLUMP
はん…
I TOOK SO MANY PICTURES.
SLUMP
はん…
WE WALKED AROUND SO MUCH...
WE NEVER DID STOP FOR LUNCH.
キラリン
GLINT
AH!
LET'S EAT THAT!
KHACHAP
AHHH! I CAN TELL IT'LL BE GOOD JUST BY LOOKING AT IT!
IT'S BIGGER THAN I EXPECTED.
LET'S DIG IN!
MIX THE SOFT-BOILED EGG IN WITH THE MELTED CHEESE AND...
AHHH...
IT'S DELICIOUS!
GEMRIELIA!

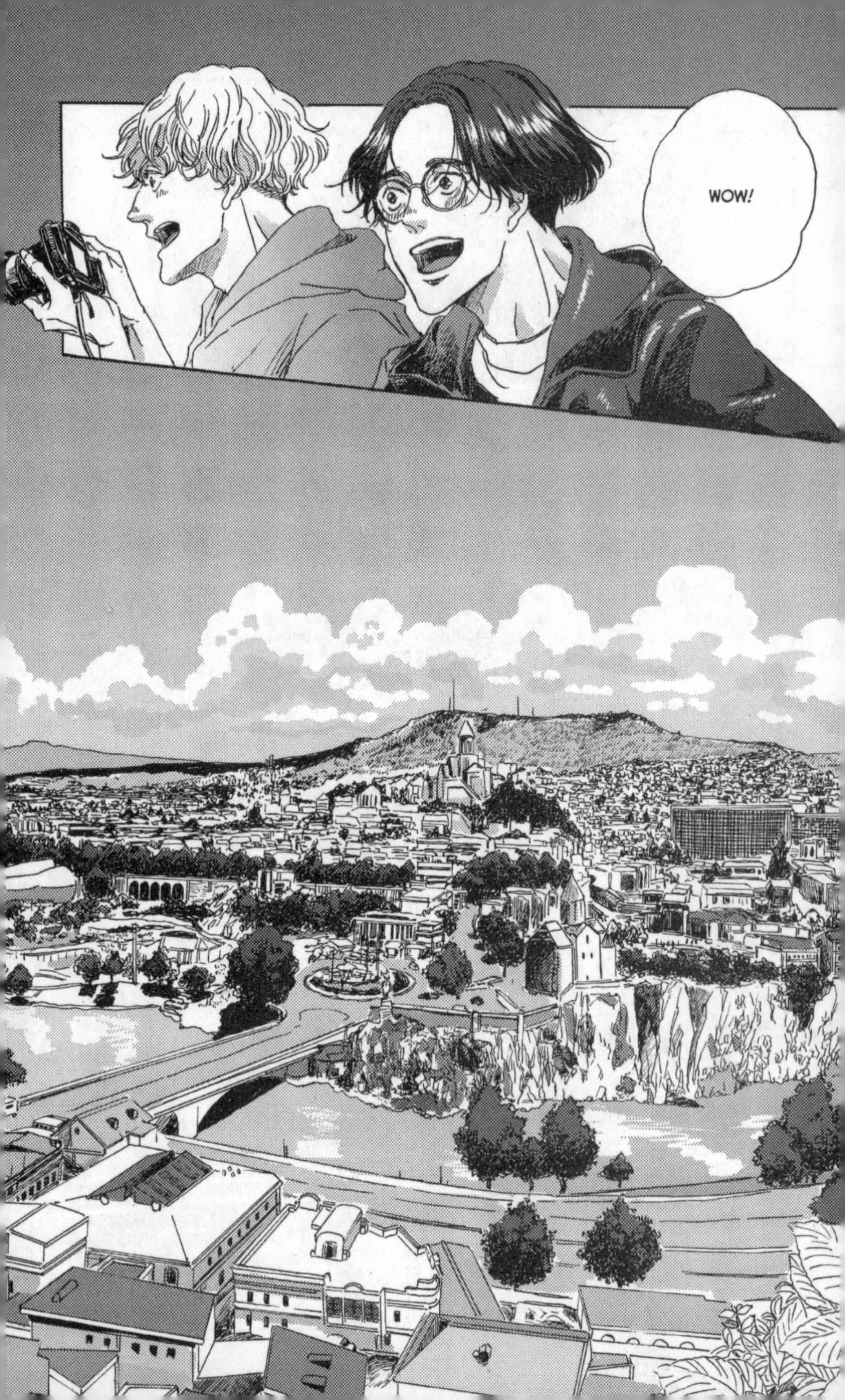
WOW!

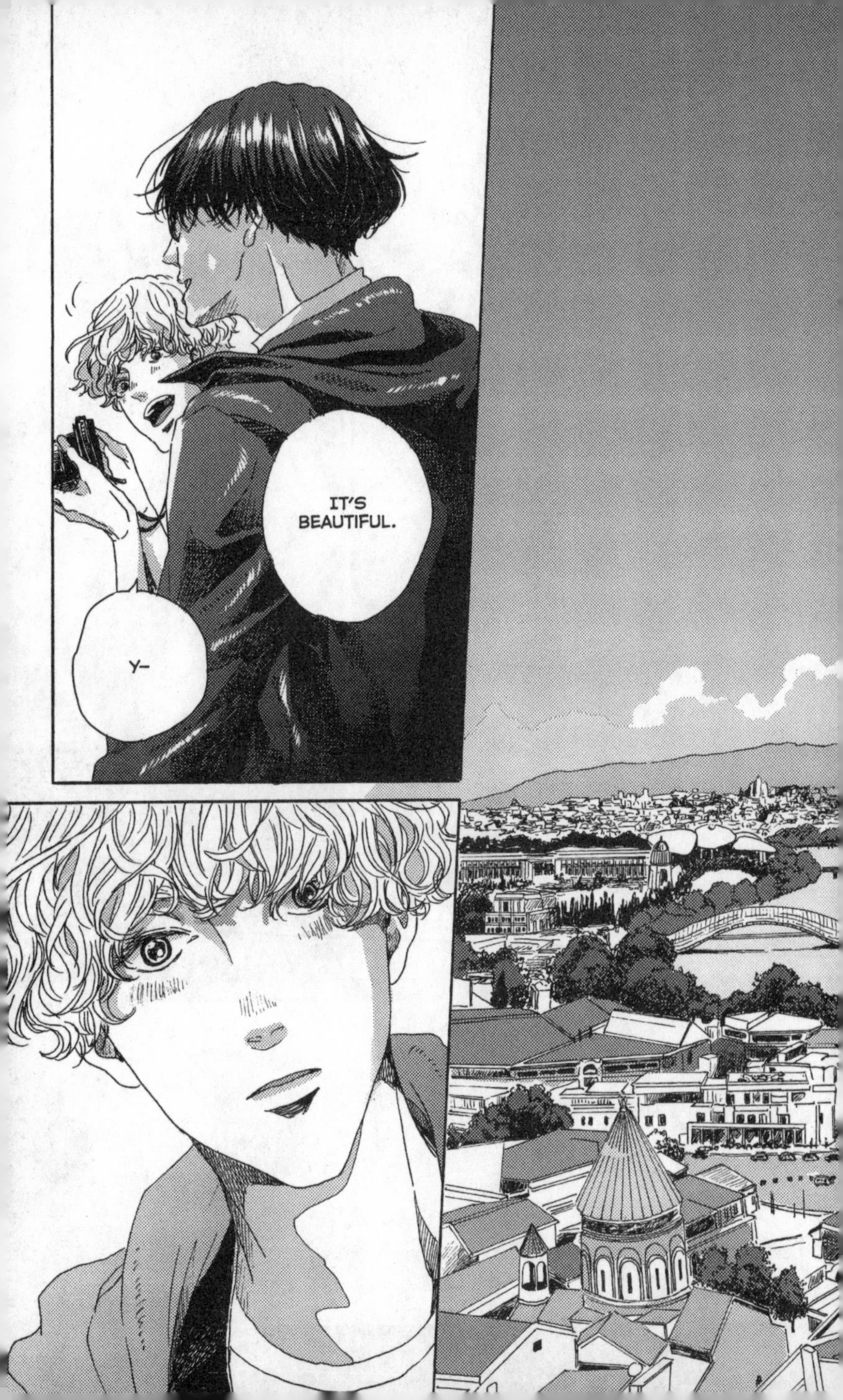
IT'S BEAUTIFUL.
Y–

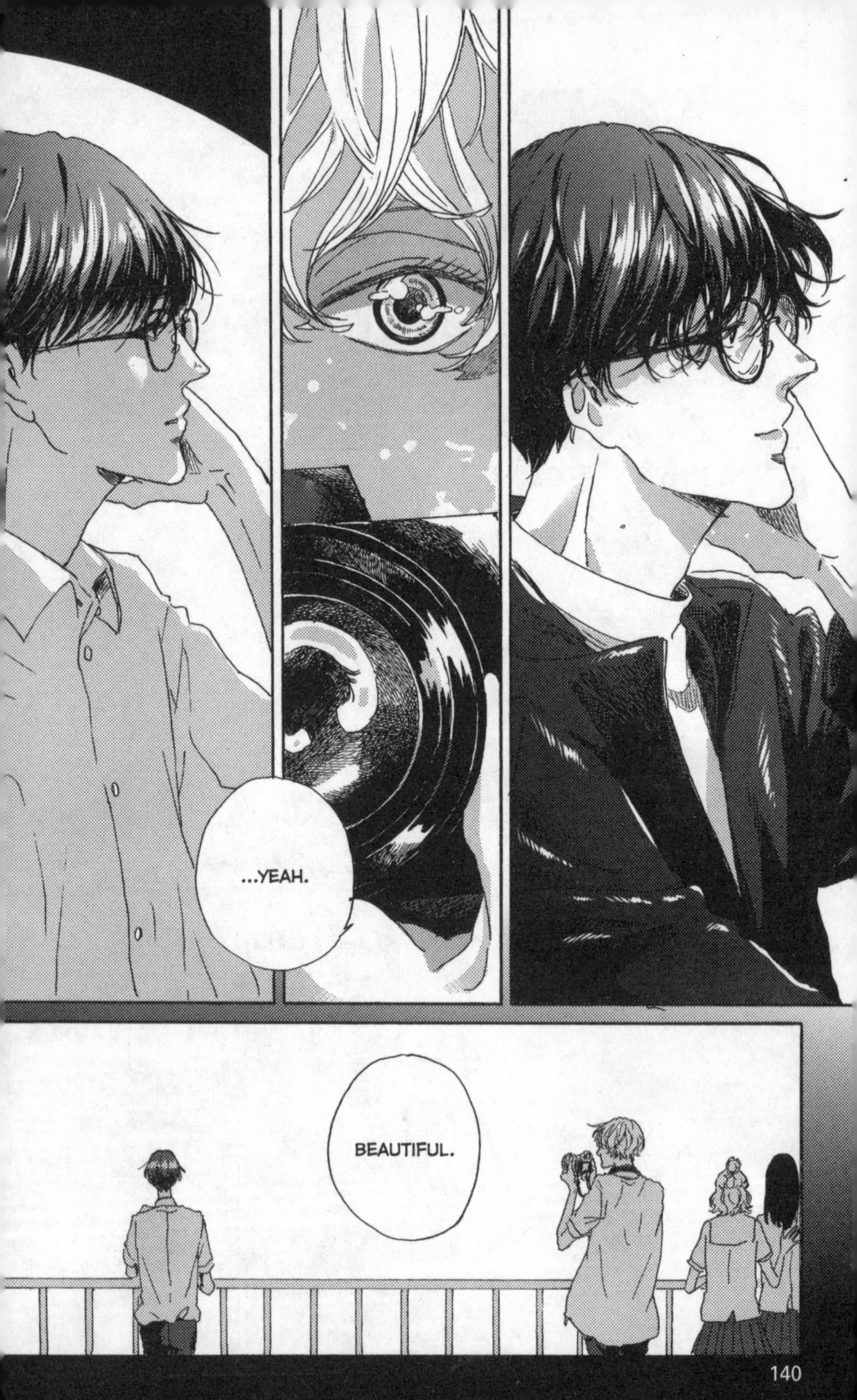
...YEAH.
BEAUTIFUL.

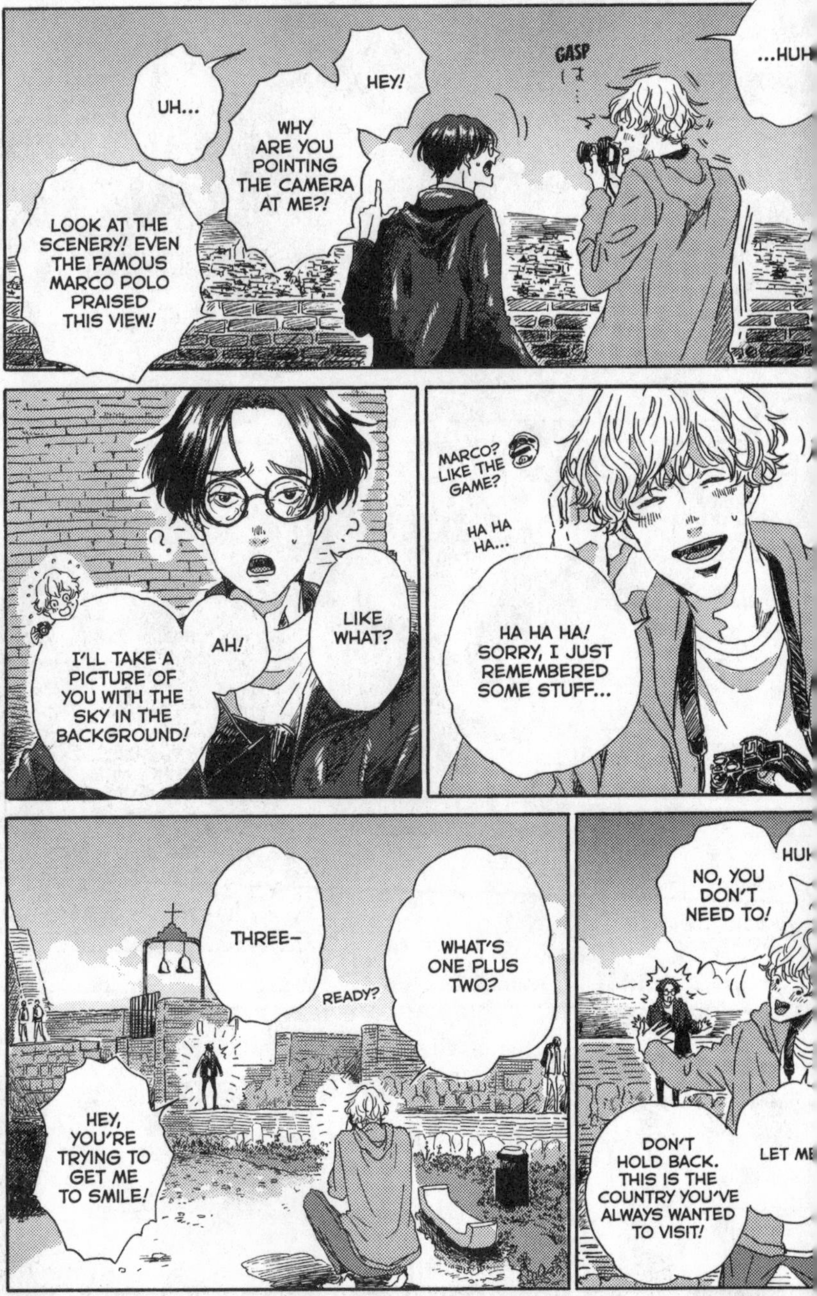
...HUH
GASP
HEY!
WHY ARE YOU POINTING THE CAMERA AT ME?!
UH...
LOOK AT THE SCENERY! EVEN THE FAMOUS MARCO POLO PRAISED THIS VIEW!
MARCO? LIKE THE GAME?
HA HA HA...
HA HA HA! SORRY, I JUST REMEMBERED SOME STUFF...
LIKE WHAT?
AH!
I'LL TAKE A PICTURE OF YOU WITH THE SKY IN THE BACKGROUND!
HU
NO, YOU DON'T NEED TO!
LET ME
DON'T HOLD BACK. THIS IS THE COUNTRY YOU'VE ALWAYS WANTED TO VISIT!
WHAT'S ONE PLUS TWO?
READY?
THREE–
HEY, YOU'RE TRYING TO GET ME TO SMILE!

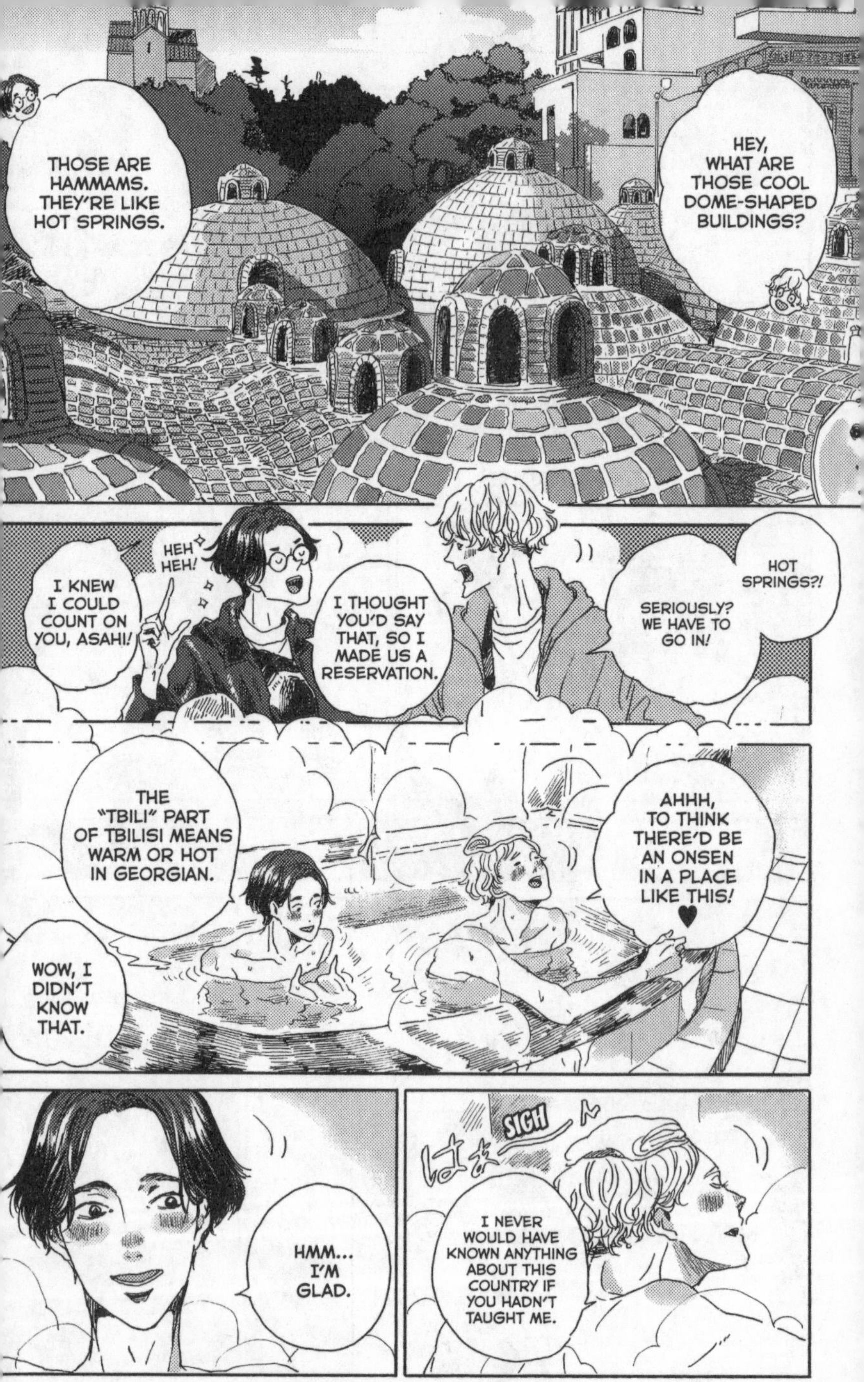
HEY, WHAT ARE THOSE COOL DOME-SHAPED BUILDINGS?
THOSE ARE HAMMAMS. THEY'RE LIKE HOT SPRINGS.
HOT SPRINGS?!
SERIOUSLY? WE HAVE TO GO IN!
I THOUGHT YOU'D SAY THAT, SO I MADE US A RESERVATION.
HEH HEH!
I KNEW I COULD COUNT ON YOU, ASAHI!
AHHH, TO THINK THERE'D BE AN ONSEN IN A PLACE LIKE THIS! ♥
THE "TBILI" PART OF TBILISI MEANS WARM OR HOT IN GEORGIAN.
WOW, I DIDN'T KNOW THAT.
はぁーん
SIGH
I NEVER WOULD HAVE KNOWN ANYTHING ABOUT THIS COUNTRY IF YOU HADN'T TAUGHT ME.
HMM... I'M GLAD.

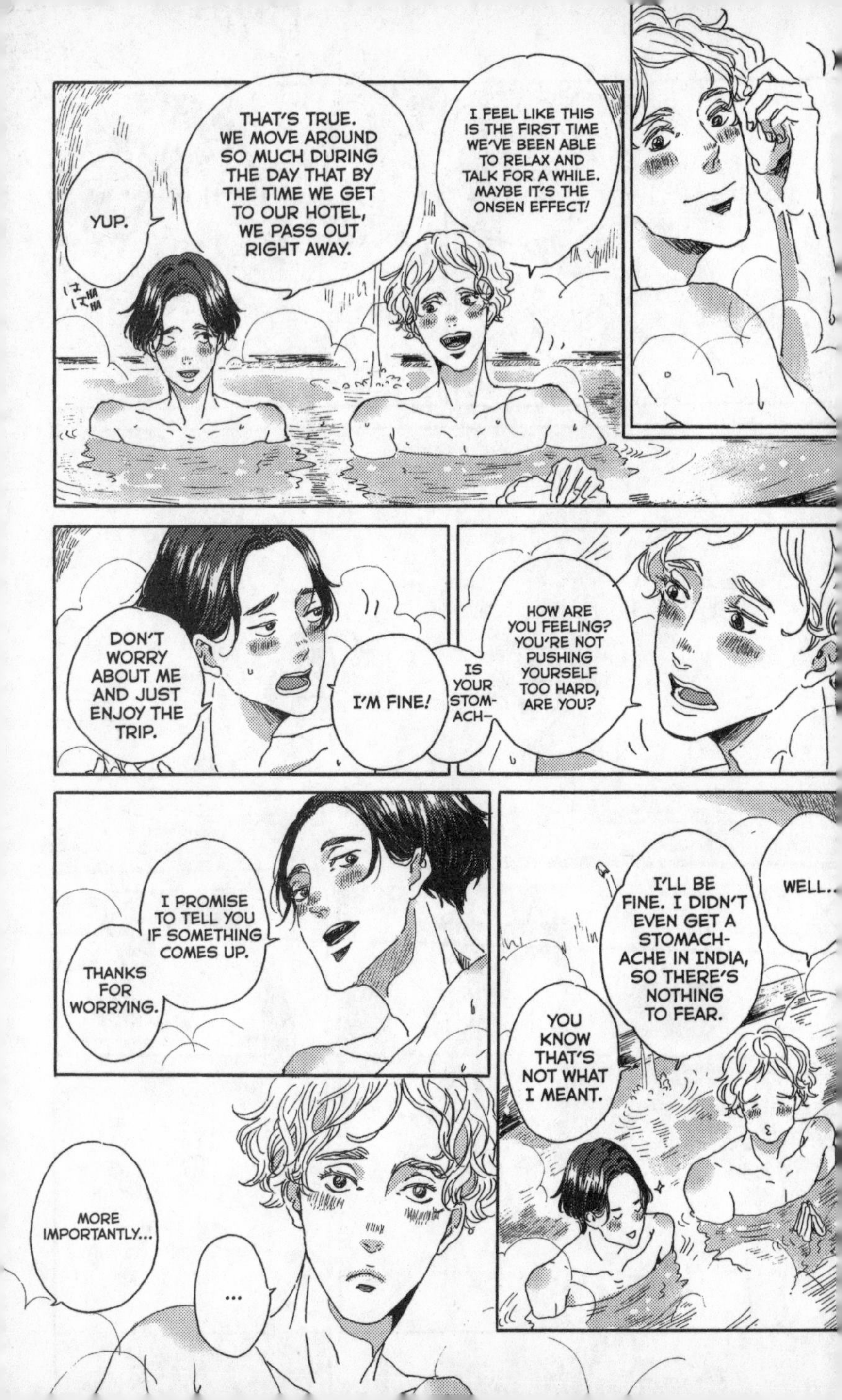
I FEEL LIKE THIS IS THE FIRST TIME WE'VE BEEN ABLE TO RELAX AND TALK FOR A WHILE. MAYBE IT'S THE ONSEN EFFECT!
THAT'S TRUE. WE MOVE AROUND SO MUCH DURING THE DAY THAT BY THE TIME WE GET TO OUR HOTEL, WE PASS OUT RIGHT AWAY.
YUP.
はは HA HA
HOW ARE YOU FEELING? YOU'RE NOT PUSHING YOURSELF TOO HARD, ARE YOU?
IS YOUR STOM-ACH-
I'M FINE!
DON'T WORRY ABOUT ME AND JUST ENJOY THE TRIP.
WELL...
I'LL BE FINE. I DIDN'T EVEN GET A STOMACH-ACHE IN INDIA, SO THERE'S NOTHING TO FEAR.
YOU KNOW THAT'S NOT WHAT I MEANT.
I PROMISE TO TELL YOU IF SOMETHING COMES UP.
THANKS FOR WORRYING.
...
MORE IMPORTANTLY...

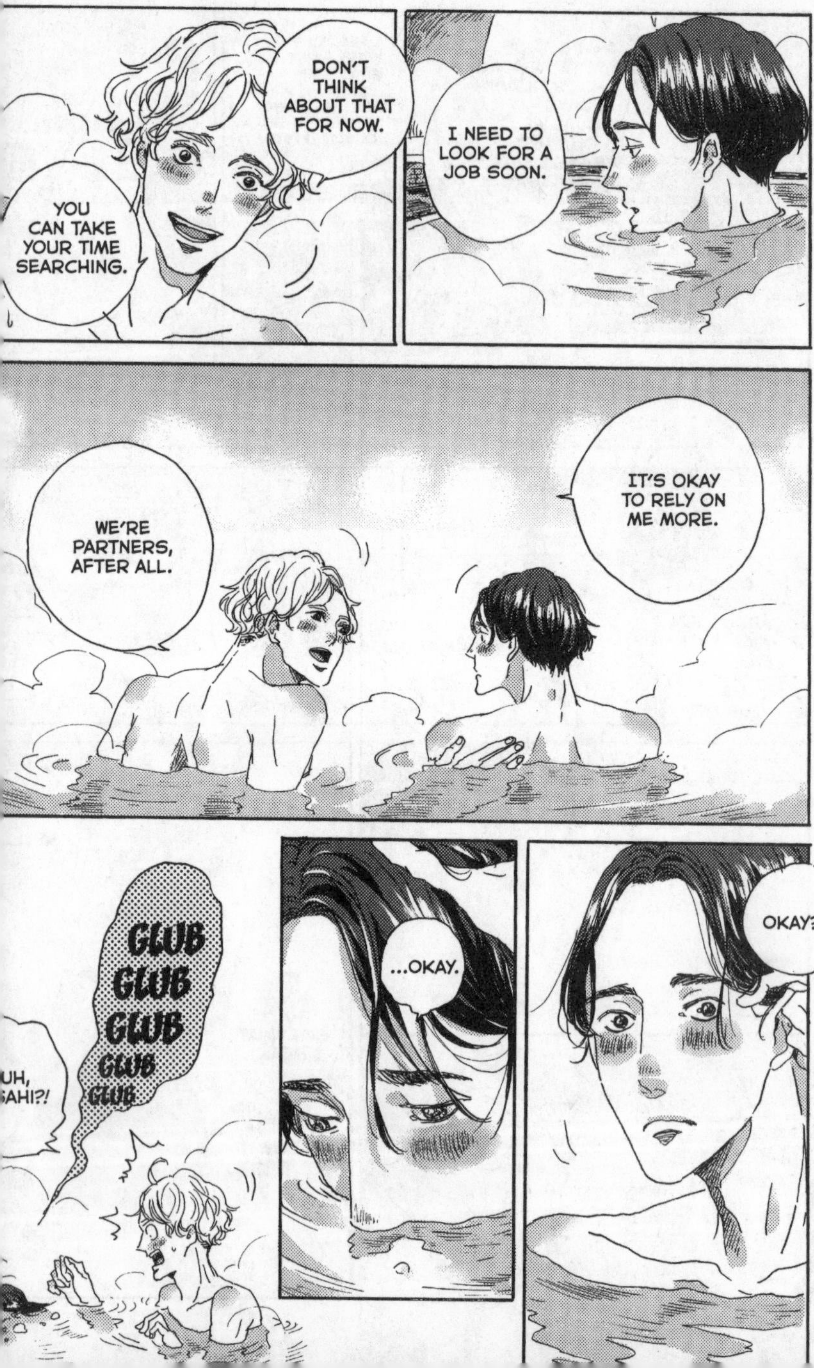
I NEED TO LOOK FOR A JOB SOON.
DON'T THINK ABOUT THAT FOR NOW.
YOU CAN TAKE YOUR TIME SEARCHING.
IT'S OKAY TO RELY ON ME MORE.
WE'RE PARTNERS, AFTER ALL.
OKAY?
...OKAY.
GLUB GLUB GLUB GLUB GLUB
UH, SAHI?!

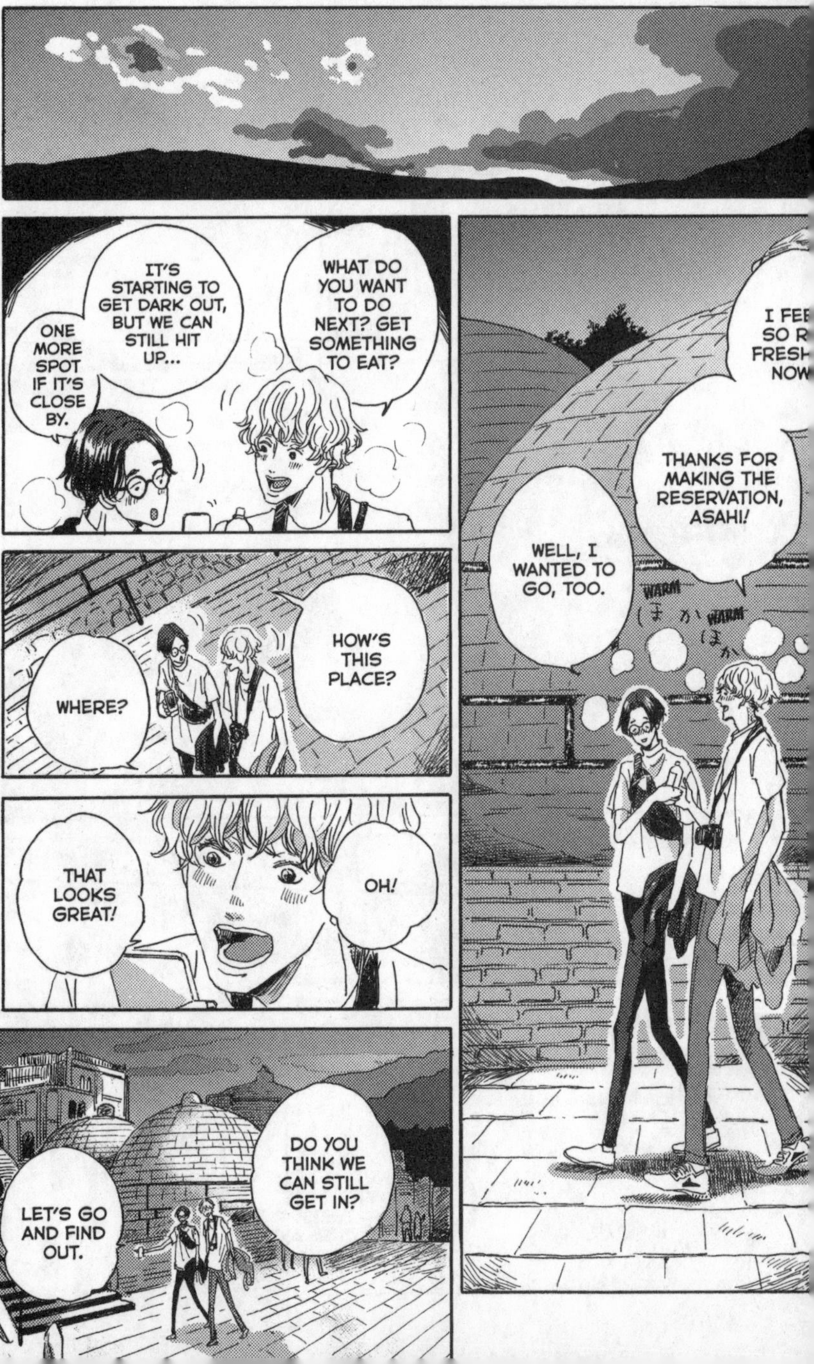
WHAT DO YOU WANT TO DO NEXT? GET SOMETHING TO EAT?
IT'S STARTING TO GET DARK OUT, BUT WE CAN STILL HIT UP...
ONE MORE SPOT IF IT'S CLOSE BY.
HOW'S THIS PLACE?
WHERE?
OH!
THAT LOOKS GREAT!
DO YOU THINK WE CAN STILL GET IN?
LET'S GO AND FIND OUT.
I FEE SO R FRESH NOW
THANKS FOR MAKING THE RESERVATION, ASAHI!
WELL, I WANTED TO GO, TOO.
WARM
WARM

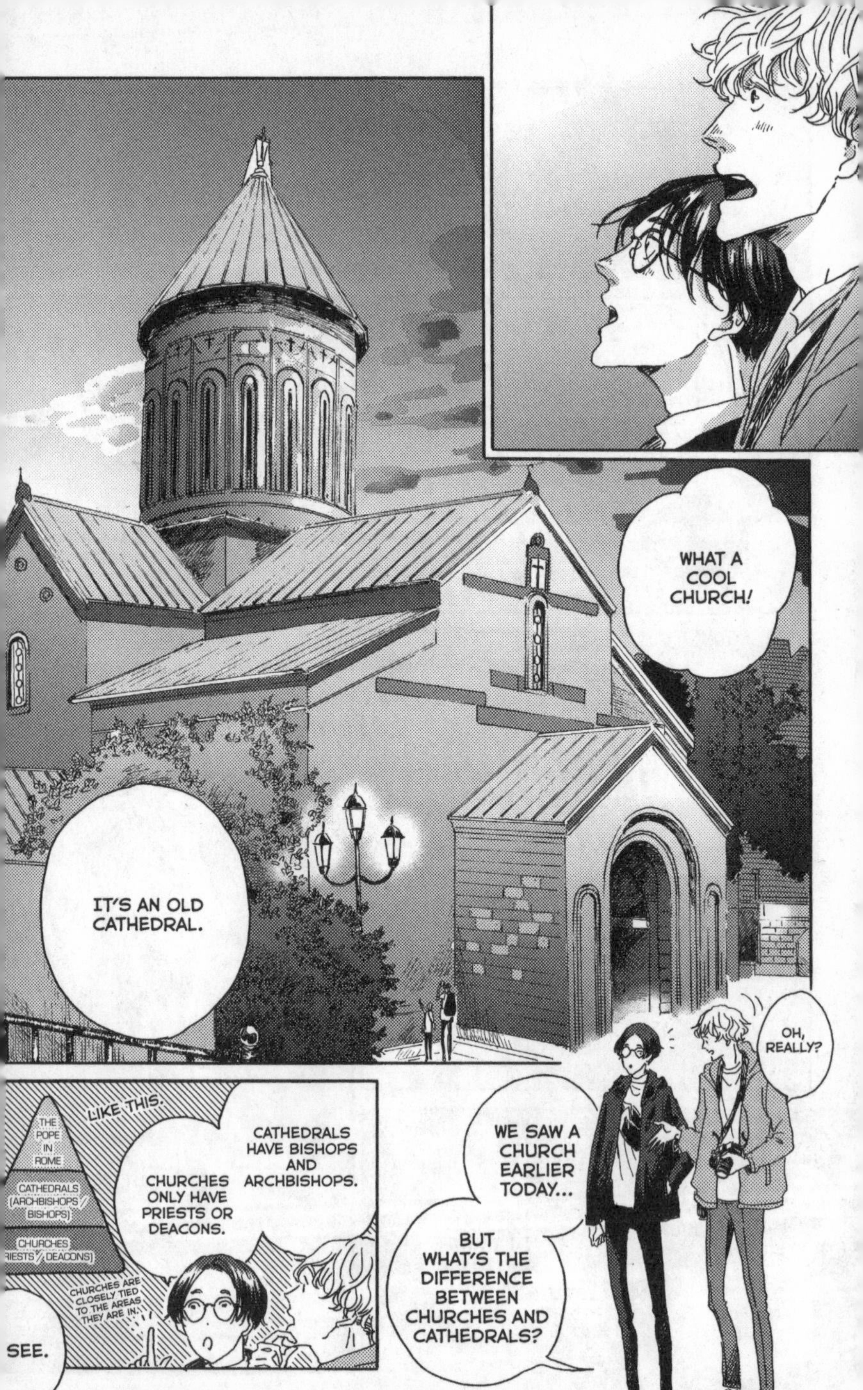
WHAT A COOL CHURCH!
IT'S AN OLD CATHEDRAL.
OH, REALLY?
WE SAW A CHURCH EARLIER TODAY...
BUT WHAT'S THE DIFFERENCE BETWEEN CHURCHES AND CATHEDRALS?
CATHEDRALS HAVE BISHOPS AND ARCHBISHOPS.
CHURCHES ONLY HAVE PRIESTS OR DEACONS.
LIKE THIS.
THE POPE IN ROME
CATHEDRALS (ARCHBISHOPS/BISHOPS)
CHURCHES
RIESTS/DEACONS)
CHURCHES ARE CLOSELY TIED TO THE AREAS THEY ARE IN.
SEE.

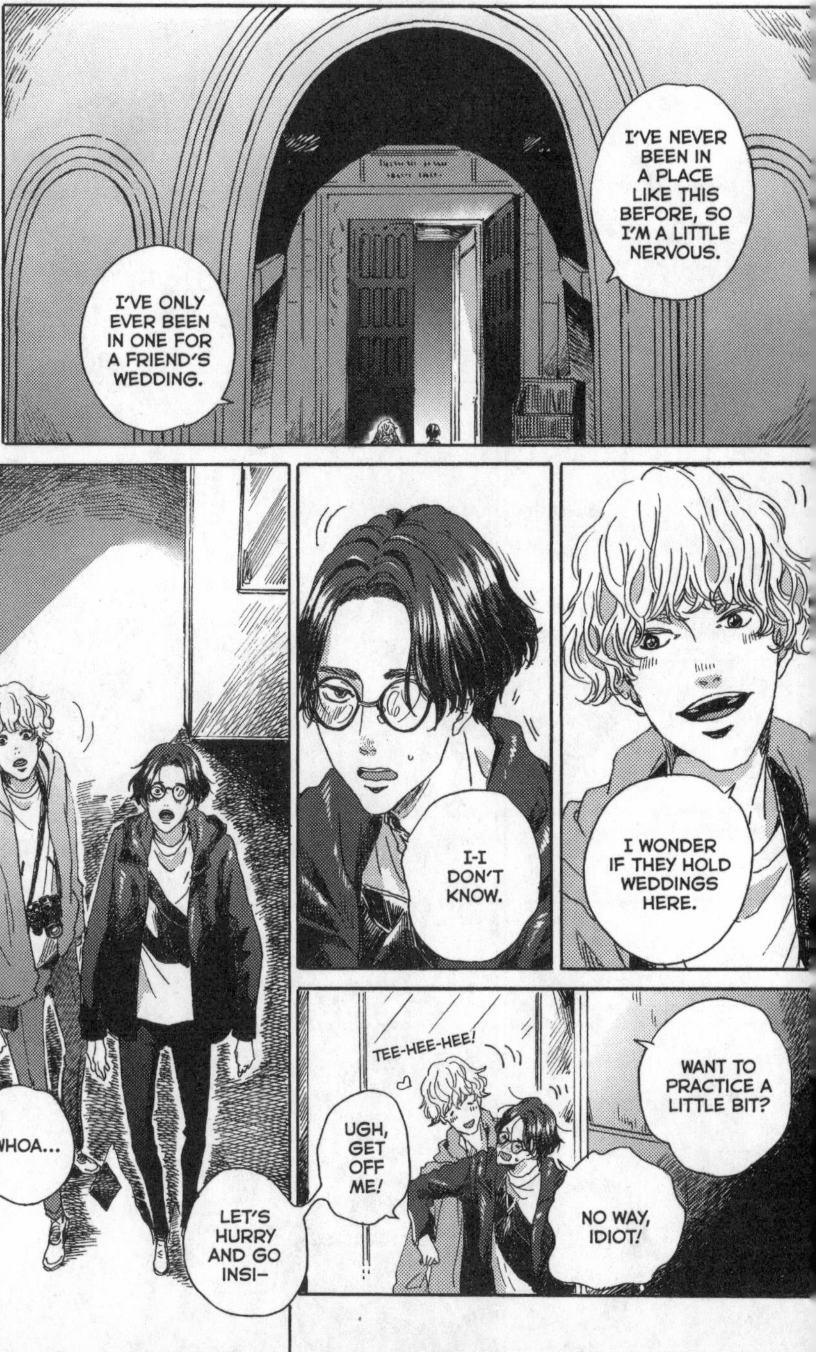
I'VE NEVER BEEN IN A PLACE LIKE THIS BEFORE, SO I'M A LITTLE NERVOUS.
I'VE ONLY EVER BEEN IN ONE FOR A FRIEND'S WEDDING.
I WONDER IF THEY HOLD WEDDINGS HERE.
I-I DON'T KNOW.
WANT TO PRACTICE A LITTLE BIT?
TEE-HEE-HEE!
NO WAY, IDIOT!
UGH, GET OFF ME!
WHOA...
LET'S HURRY AND GO INSI–

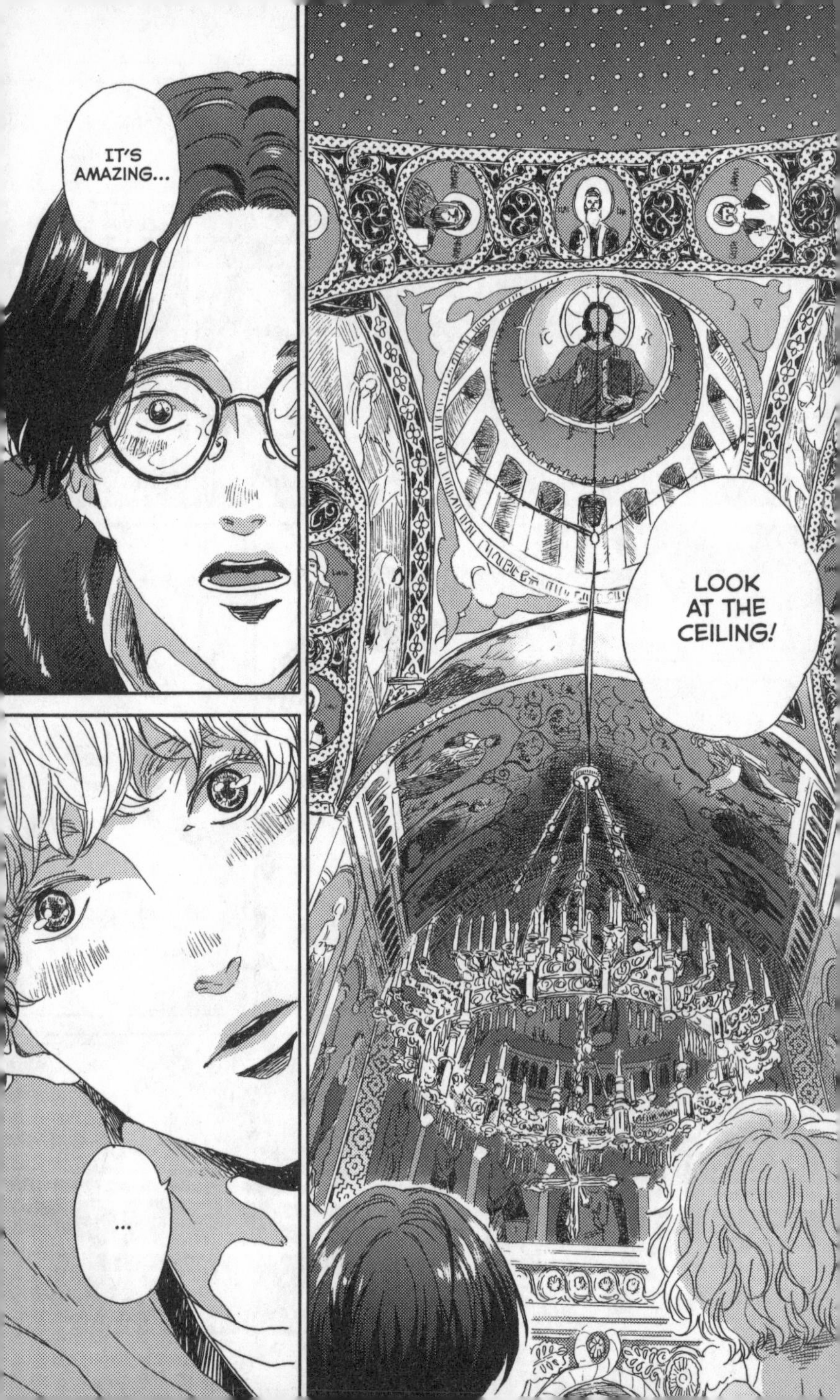
LOOK AT THE CEILING!
IT'S AMAZING...
...

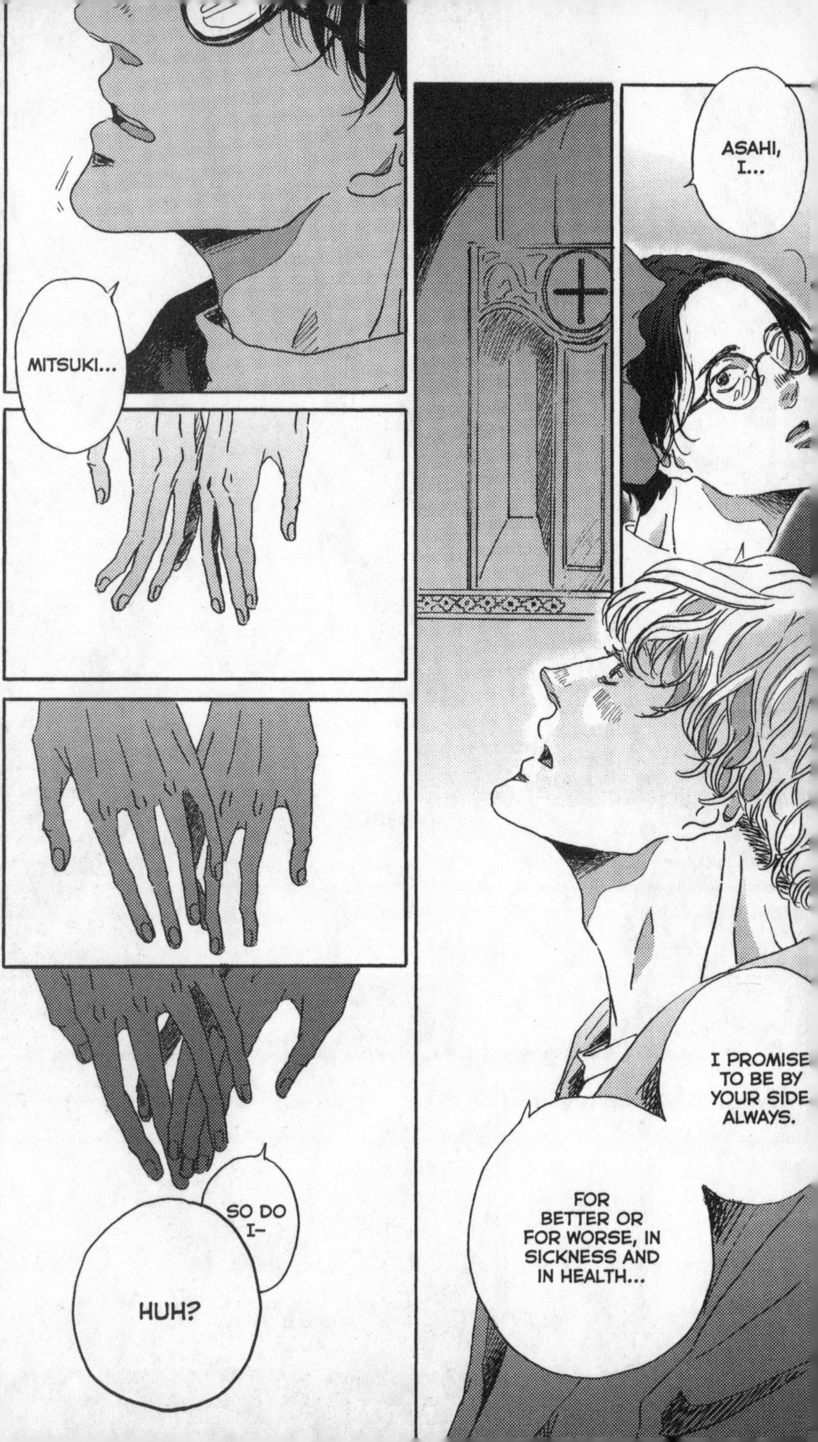
ASAHI, I...
I PROMISE TO BE BY YOUR SIDE ALWAYS.
FOR BETTER OR FOR WORSE, IN SICKNESS AND IN HEALTH...
MITSUKI...
SO DO I–
HUH?

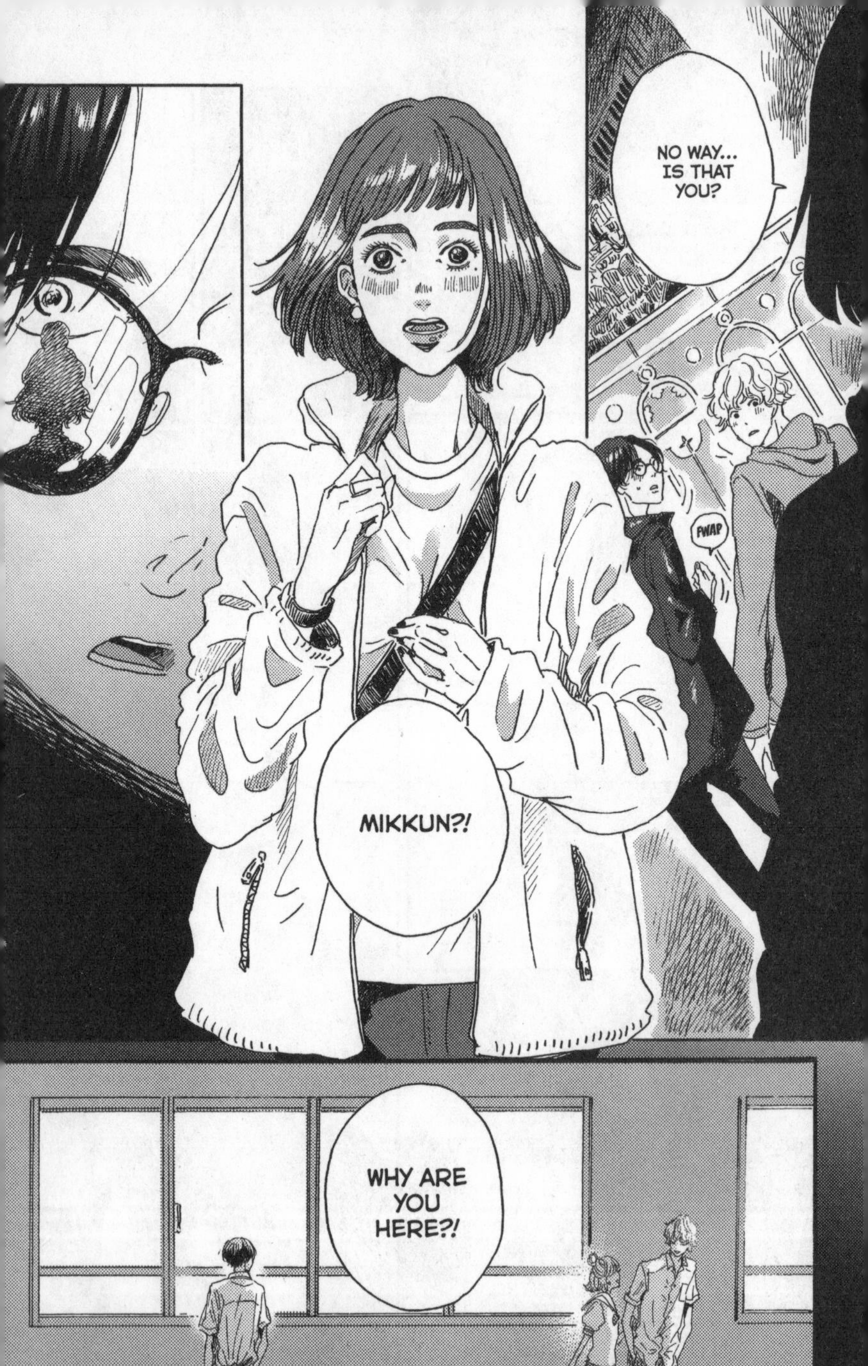
NO WAY... IS THAT YOU?
FWAP
MIKKUN?!
WHY ARE YOU HERE?!

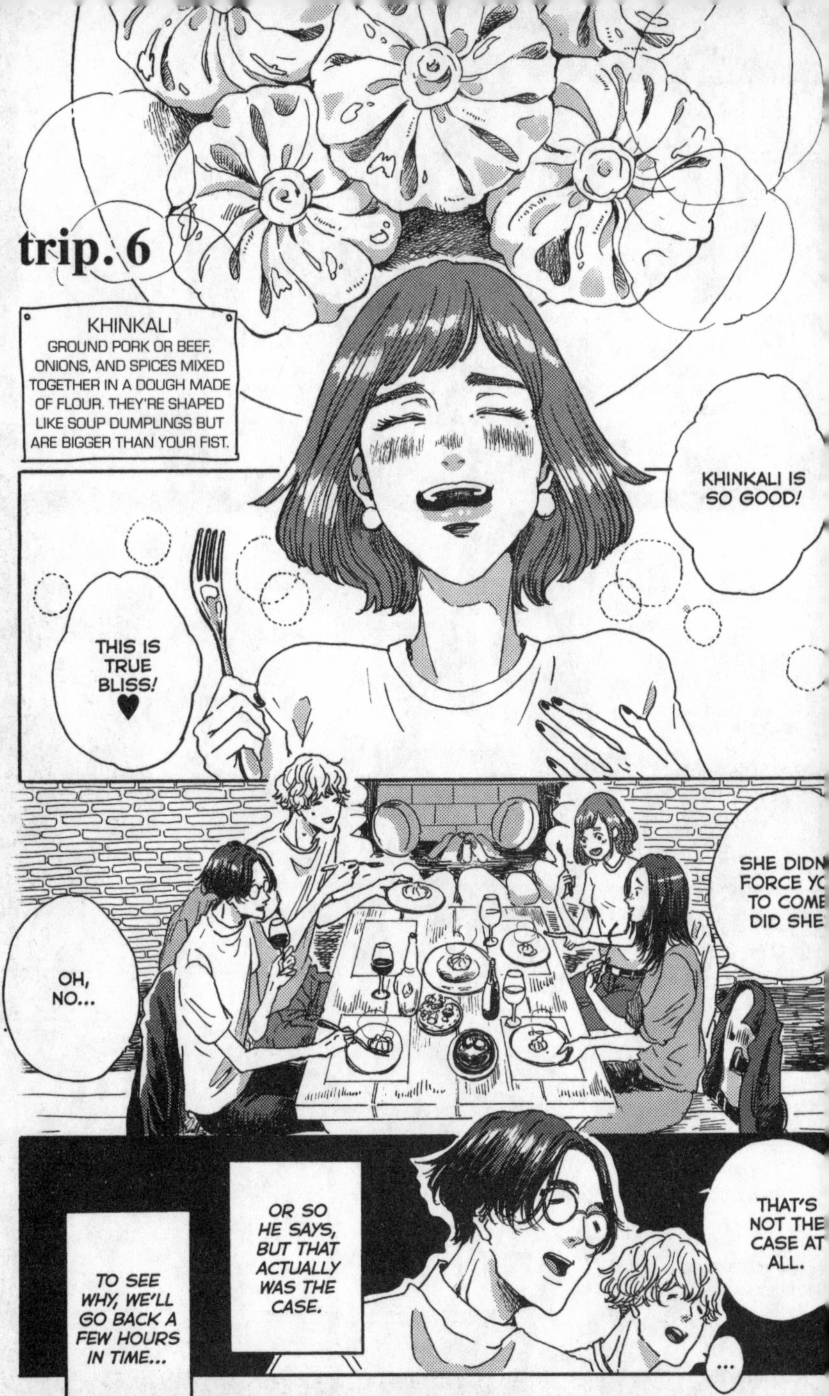
trip. 6
KHINKALI GROUND PORK OR BEEF, ONIONS, AND SPICES MIXED TOGETHER IN A DOUGH MADE OF FLOUR. THEY'RE SHAPED LIKE SOUP DUMPLINGS BUT ARE BIGGER THAN YOUR FIST.
KHINKALI IS SO GOOD!
THIS IS TRUE BLISS! ♥
SHE DIDN FORCE YO TO COME DID SHE
OH, NO...
THAT'S NOT THE CASE AT ALL.
...
OR SO HE SAYS, BUT THAT ACTUALLY WAS THE CASE.
TO SEE WHY, WE'LL GO BACK A FEW HOURS IN TIME...

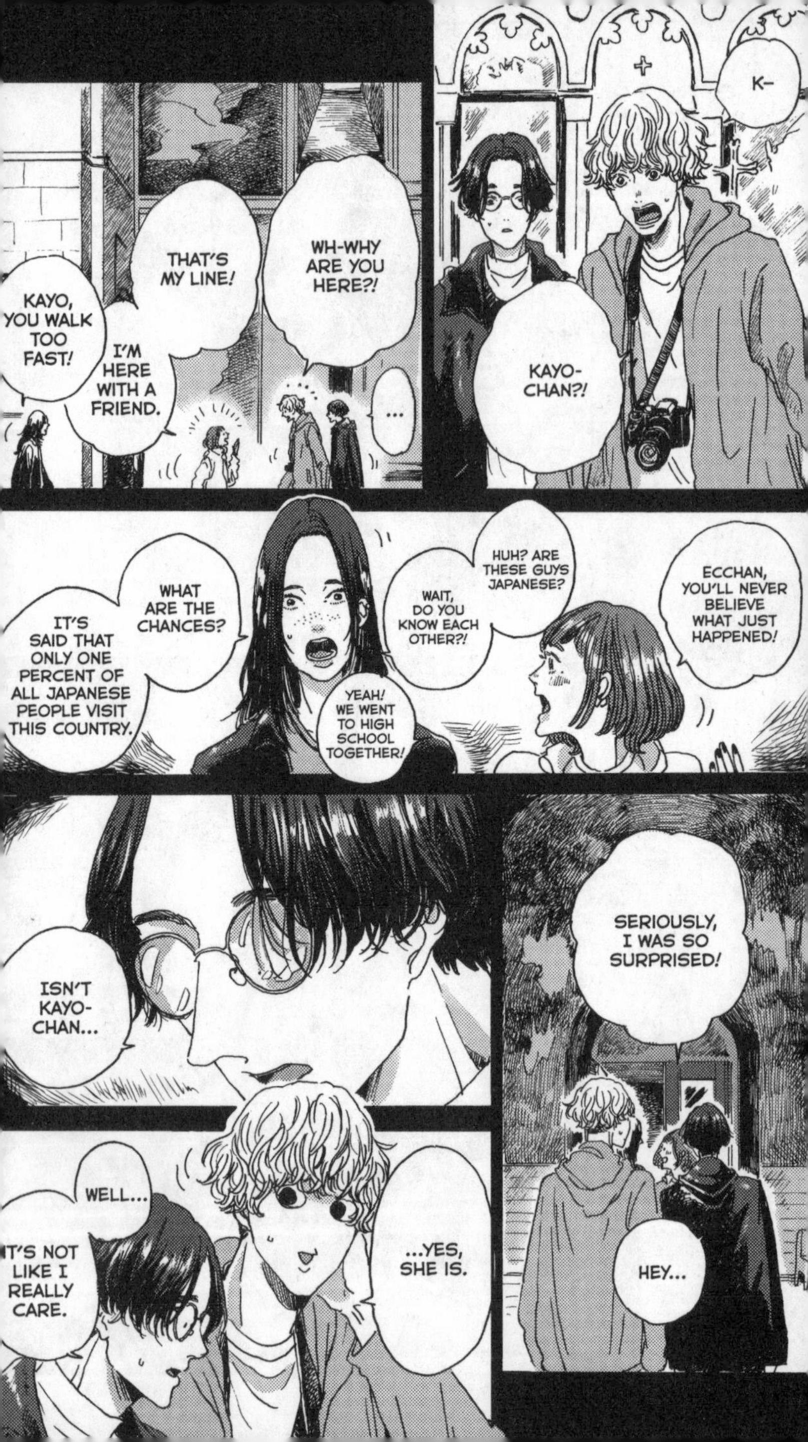
K–
KAYO-CHAN?!
WH-WHY ARE YOU HERE?!
THAT'S MY LINE!
...
I'M HERE WITH A FRIEND.
KAYO, YOU WALK TOO FAST!
ECCHAN, YOU'LL NEVER BELIEVE WHAT JUST HAPPENED!
HUH? ARE THESE GUYS JAPANESE?
WAIT, DO YOU KNOW EACH OTHER?!
YEAH! WE WENT TO HIGH SCHOOL TOGETHER!
WHAT ARE THE CHANCES?
IT'S SAID THAT ONLY ONE PERCENT OF ALL JAPANESE PEOPLE VISIT THIS COUNTRY.
SERIOUSLY, I WAS SO SURPRISED!
HEY...
ISN'T KAYO-CHAN...
...YES, SHE IS.
WELL...
IT'S NOT LIKE I REALLY CARE.

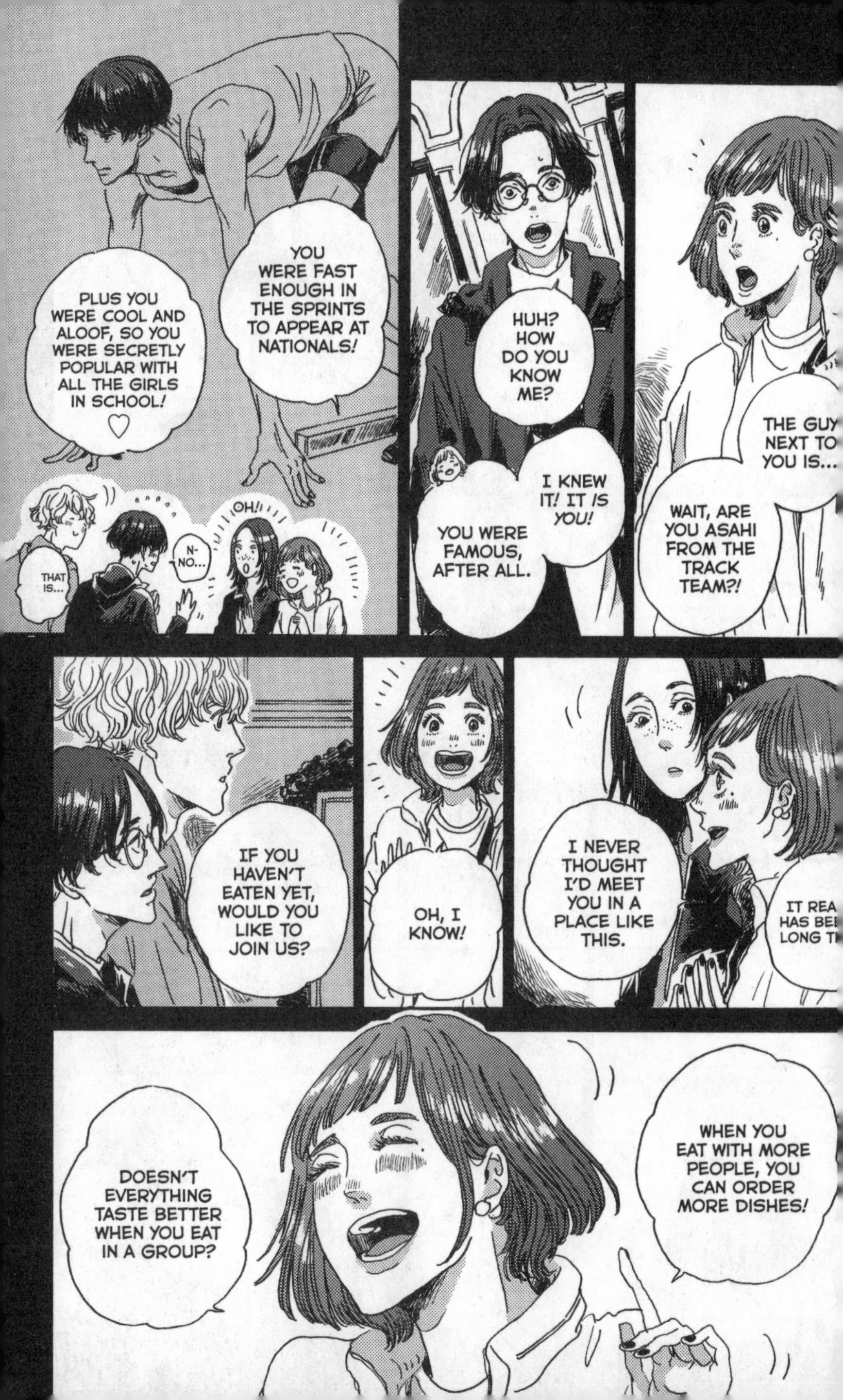
THE GUY NEXT TO YOU IS...
WAIT, ARE YOU ASAHI FROM THE TRACK TEAM?!
HUH? HOW DO YOU KNOW ME?
I KNEW IT! IT *IS* YOU!
YOU WERE FAMOUS, AFTER ALL.
YOU WERE FAST ENOUGH IN THE SPRINTS TO APPEAR AT NATIONALS!
PLUS YOU WERE COOL AND ALOOF, SO YOU WERE SECRETLY POPULAR WITH ALL THE GIRLS IN SCHOOL! ♡
OH!
N-NO...
THAT IS...
I NEVER THOUGHT I'D MEET YOU IN A PLACE LIKE THIS.
OH, I KNOW!
IF YOU HAVEN'T EATEN YET, WOULD YOU LIKE TO JOIN US?
WHEN YOU EAT WITH MORE PEOPLE, YOU CAN ORDER MORE DISHES!
DOESN'T EVERYTHING TASTE BETTER WHEN YOU EAT IN A GROUP?

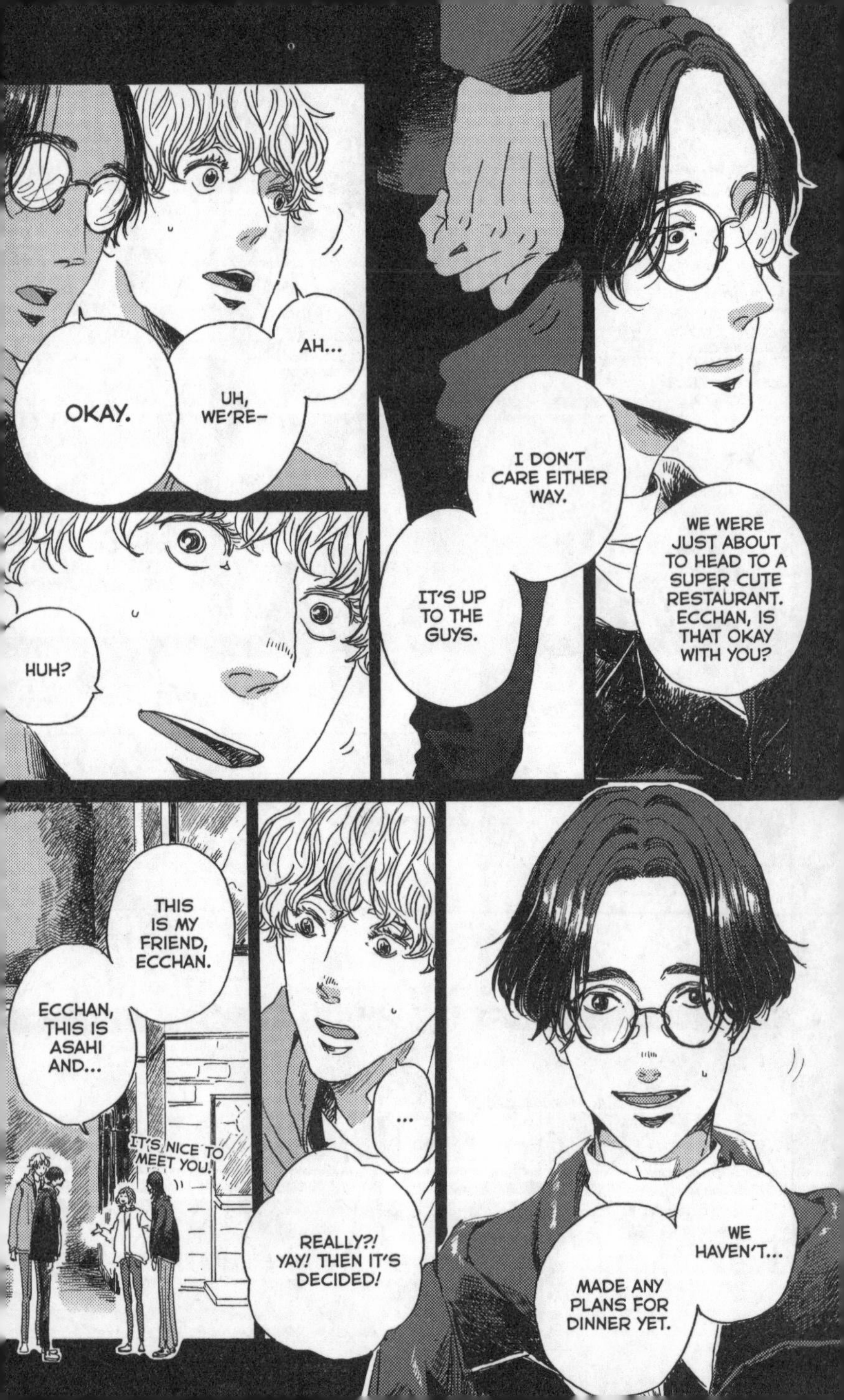
WE WERE JUST ABOUT TO HEAD TO A SUPER CUTE RESTAURANT. ECCHAN, IS THAT OKAY WITH YOU?
I DON'T CARE EITHER WAY.
IT'S UP TO THE GUYS.
AH...
UH, WE'RE–
OKAY.
HUH?
WE HAVEN'T...
MADE ANY PLANS FOR DINNER YET.
...
REALLY?! YAY! THEN IT'S DECIDED!
THIS IS MY FRIEND, ECCHAN.
ECCHAN, THIS IS ASAHI AND...
IT'S NICE TO MEET YOU!

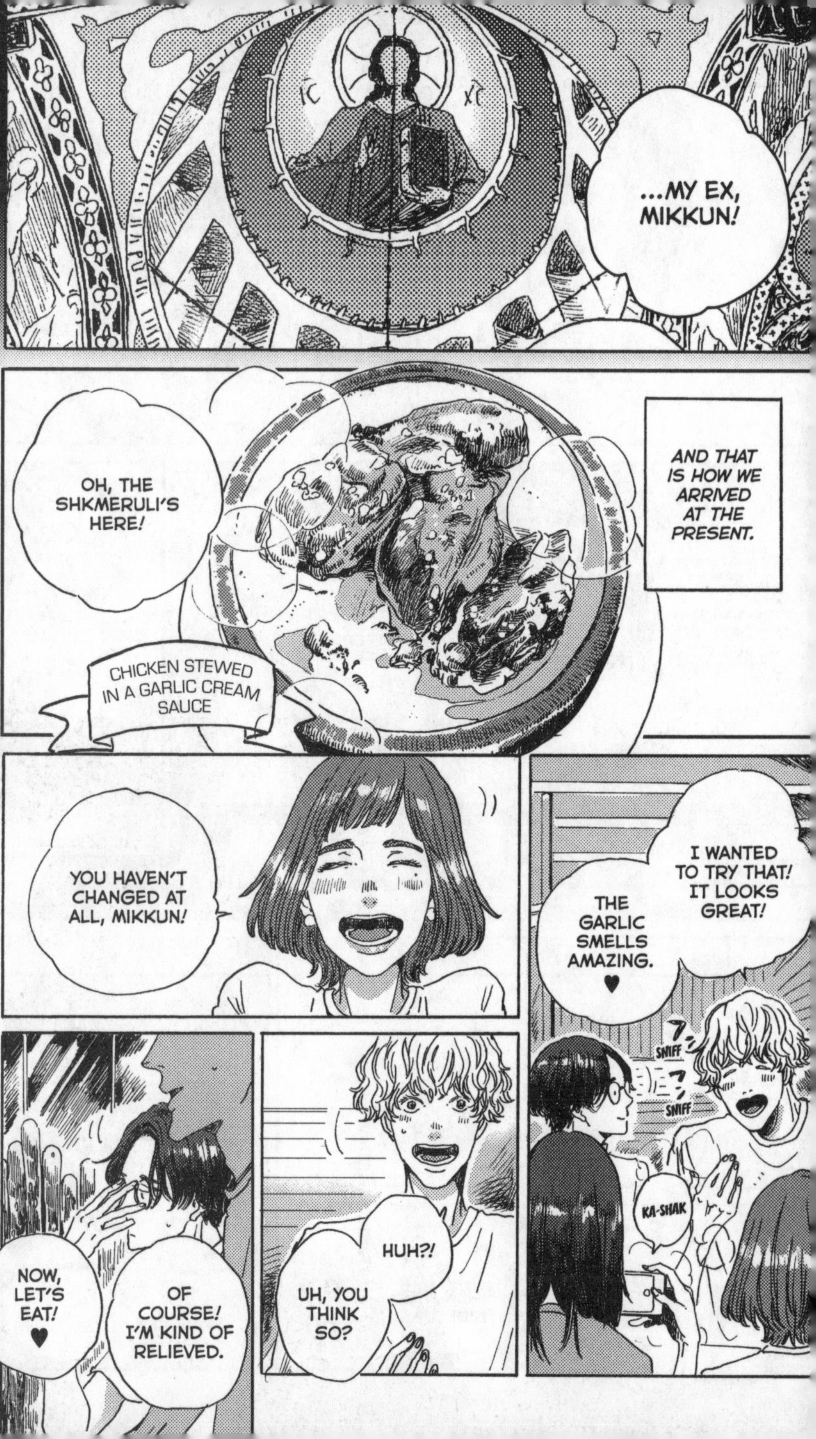
...MY EX, MIKKUN!
AND THAT IS HOW WE ARRIVED AT THE PRESENT.
OH, THE SHKMERULI'S HERE!
CHICKEN STEWED IN A GARLIC CREAM SAUCE
I WANTED TO TRY THAT! IT LOOKS GREAT!
THE GARLIC SMELLS AMAZING. ♥
SNIFF
SNIFF
KA-SHAK
YOU HAVEN'T CHANGED AT ALL, MIKKUN!
HUH?!
UH, YOU THINK SO?
OF COURSE! I'M KIND OF RELIEVED.
NOW, LET'S EAT! ♥

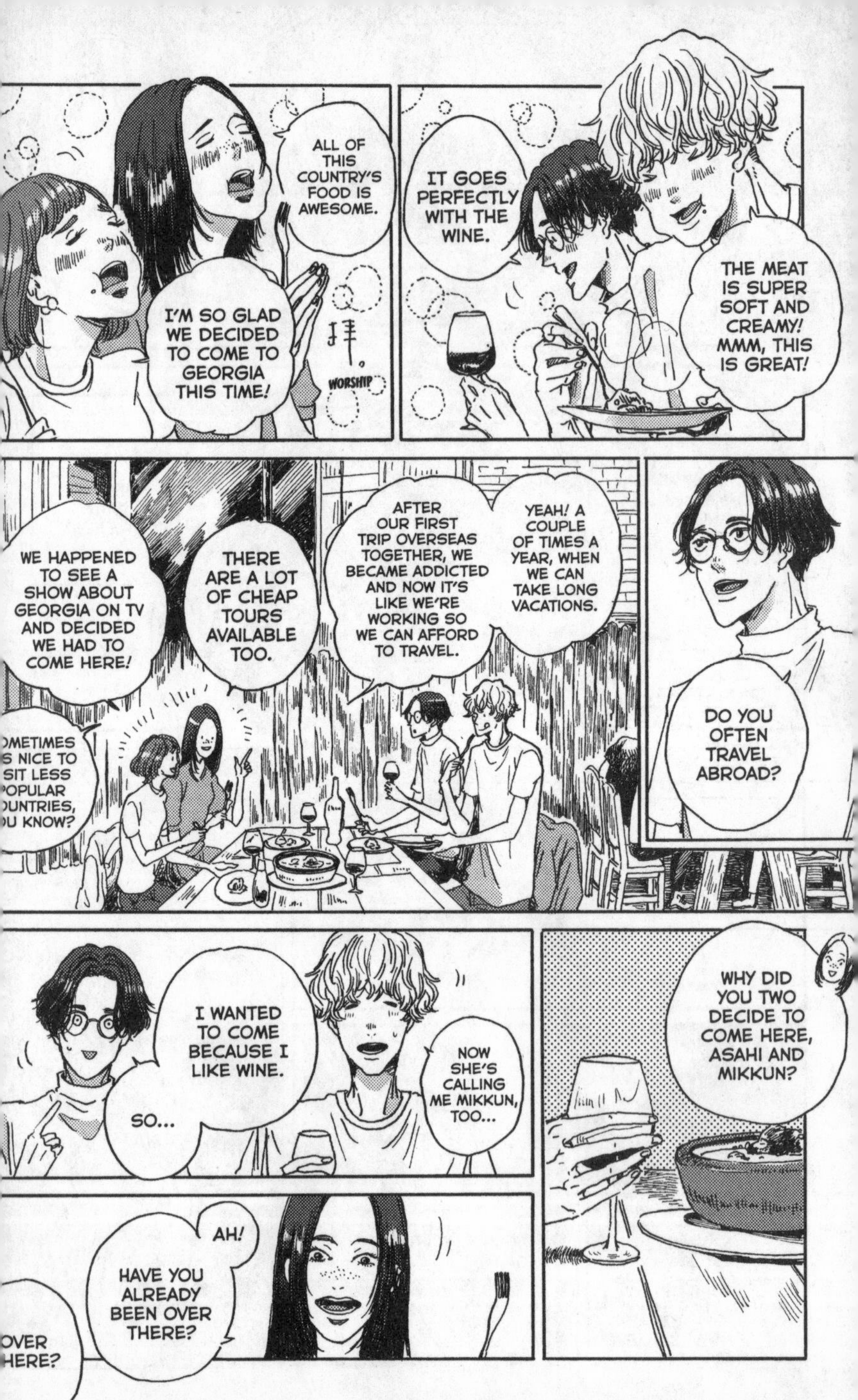
THE MEAT IS SUPER SOFT AND CREAMY! MMM, THIS IS GREAT!
IT GOES PERFECTLY WITH THE WINE.
ALL OF THIS COUNTRY'S FOOD IS AWESOME.
I'M SO GLAD WE DECIDED TO COME TO GEORGIA THIS TIME!
拝
WORSHIP
DO YOU OFTEN TRAVEL ABROAD?
YEAH! A COUPLE OF TIMES A YEAR, WHEN WE CAN TAKE LONG VACATIONS.
AFTER OUR FIRST TRIP OVERSEAS TOGETHER, WE BECAME ADDICTED AND NOW IT'S LIKE WE'RE WORKING SO WE CAN AFFORD TO TRAVEL.
THERE ARE A LOT OF CHEAP TOURS AVAILABLE TOO.
WE HAPPENED TO SEE A SHOW ABOUT GEORGIA ON TV AND DECIDED WE HAD TO COME HERE!
OMETIMES S NICE TO SIT LESS POPULAR OUNTRIES, OU KNOW?
WHY DID YOU TWO DECIDE TO COME HERE, ASAHI AND MIKKUN?
NOW SHE'S CALLING ME MIKKUN, TOO...
I WANTED TO COME BECAUSE I LIKE WINE.
SO...
AH!
HAVE YOU ALREADY BEEN OVER THERE?
OVER HERE?

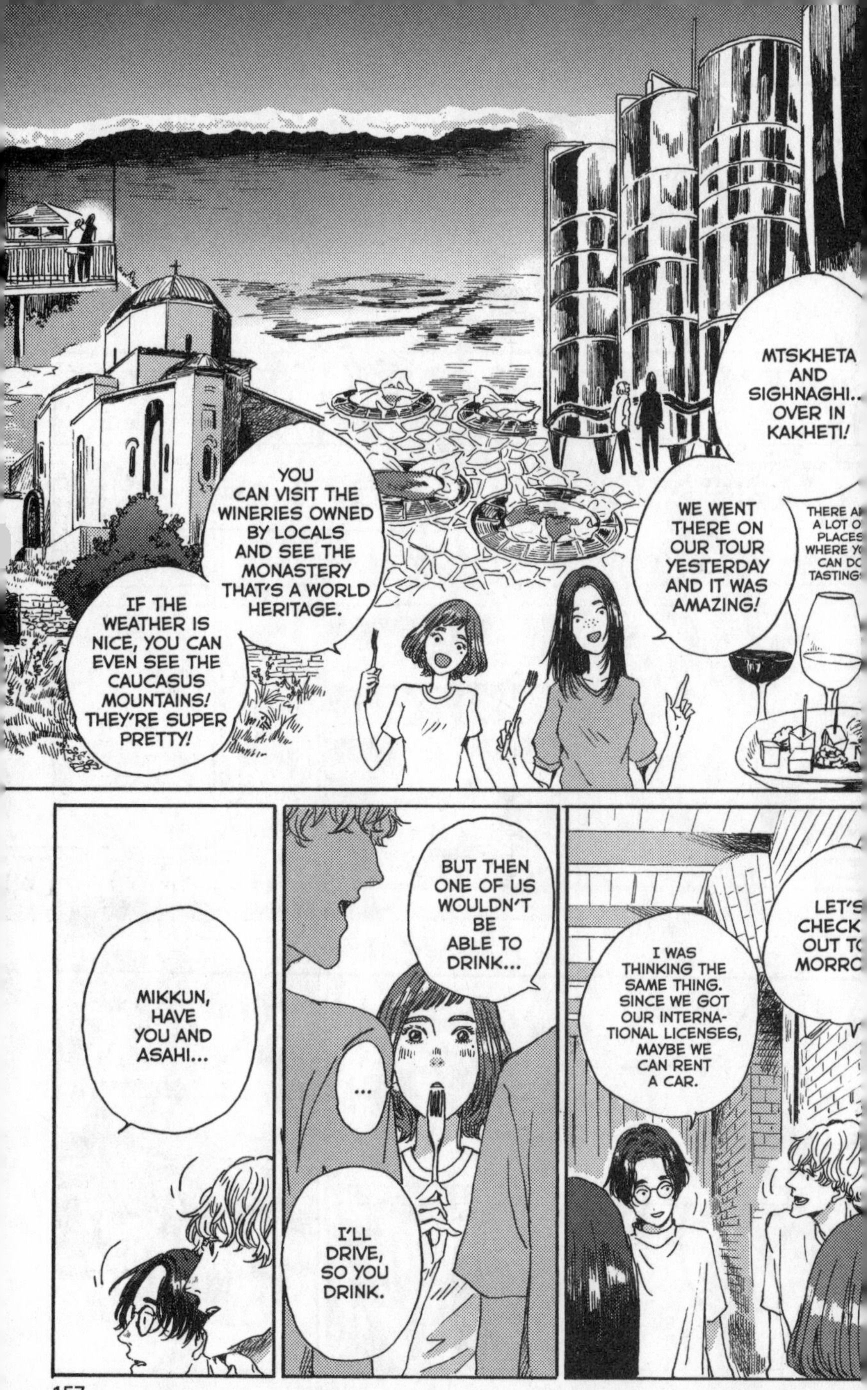
MTSKHETA AND SIGHNAGHI.. OVER IN KAKHETI!
THERE A A LOT O PLACES WHERE Y CAN DO TASTING
WE WENT THERE ON OUR TOUR YESTERDAY AND IT WAS AMAZING!
YOU CAN VISIT THE WINERIES OWNED BY LOCALS AND SEE THE MONASTERY THAT'S A WORLD HERITAGE.
IF THE WEATHER IS NICE, YOU CAN EVEN SEE THE CAUCASUS MOUNTAINS! THEY'RE SUPER PRETTY!
LET'S CHECK OUT T MORRO
I WAS THINKING THE SAME THING. SINCE WE GOT OUR INTERNA-TIONAL LICENSES, MAYBE WE CAN RENT A CAR.
BUT THEN ONE OF US WOULDN'T BE ABLE TO DRINK...
...
I'LL DRIVE, SO YOU DRINK.
MIKKUN, HAVE YOU AND ASAHI...

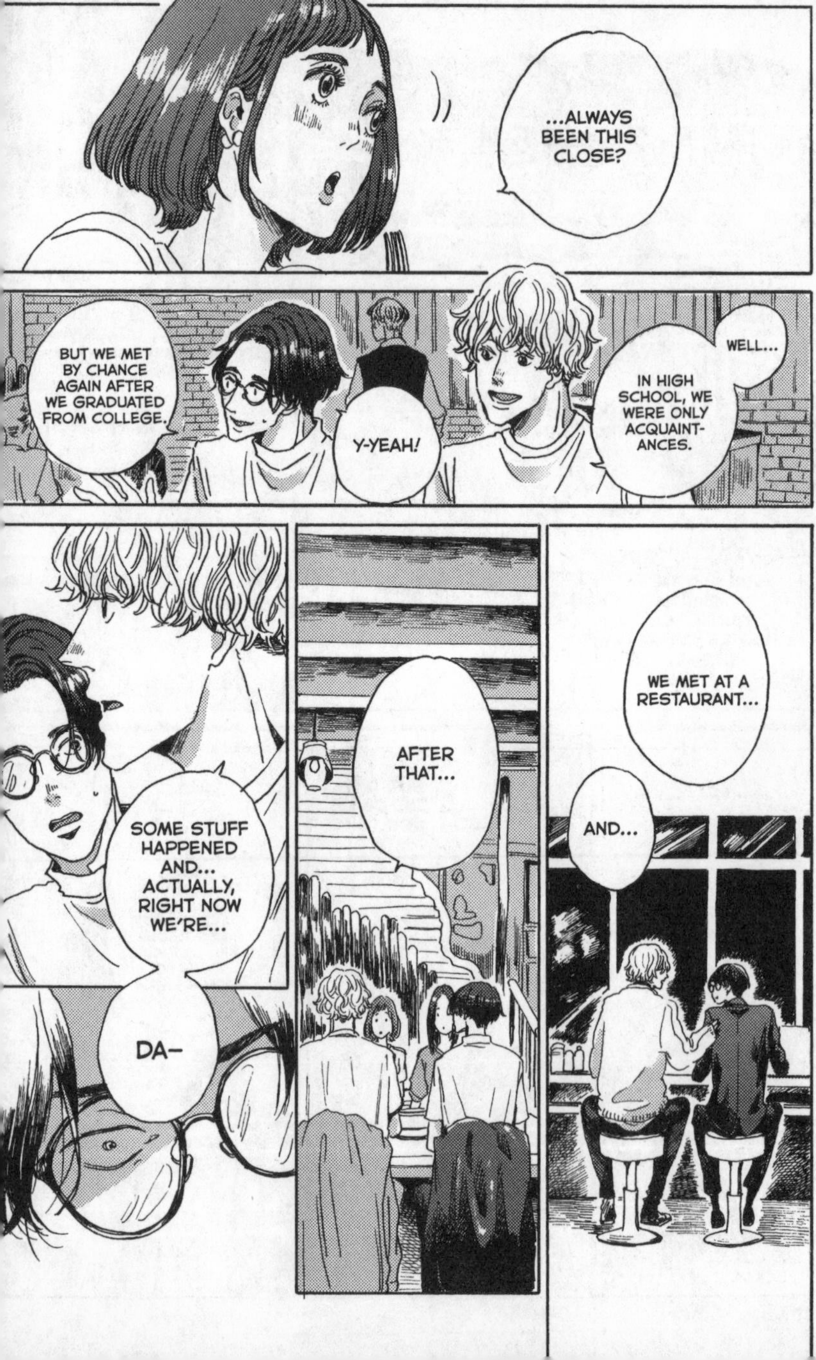
...ALWAYS BEEN THIS CLOSE?
WELL...
IN HIGH SCHOOL, WE WERE ONLY ACQUAINT-ANCES.
Y-YEAH!
BUT WE MET BY CHANCE AGAIN AFTER WE GRADUATED FROM COLLEGE.
WE MET AT A RESTAURANT...
AND...
AFTER THAT...
SOME STUFF HAPPENED AND... ACTUALLY, RIGHT NOW WE'RE...
DA–

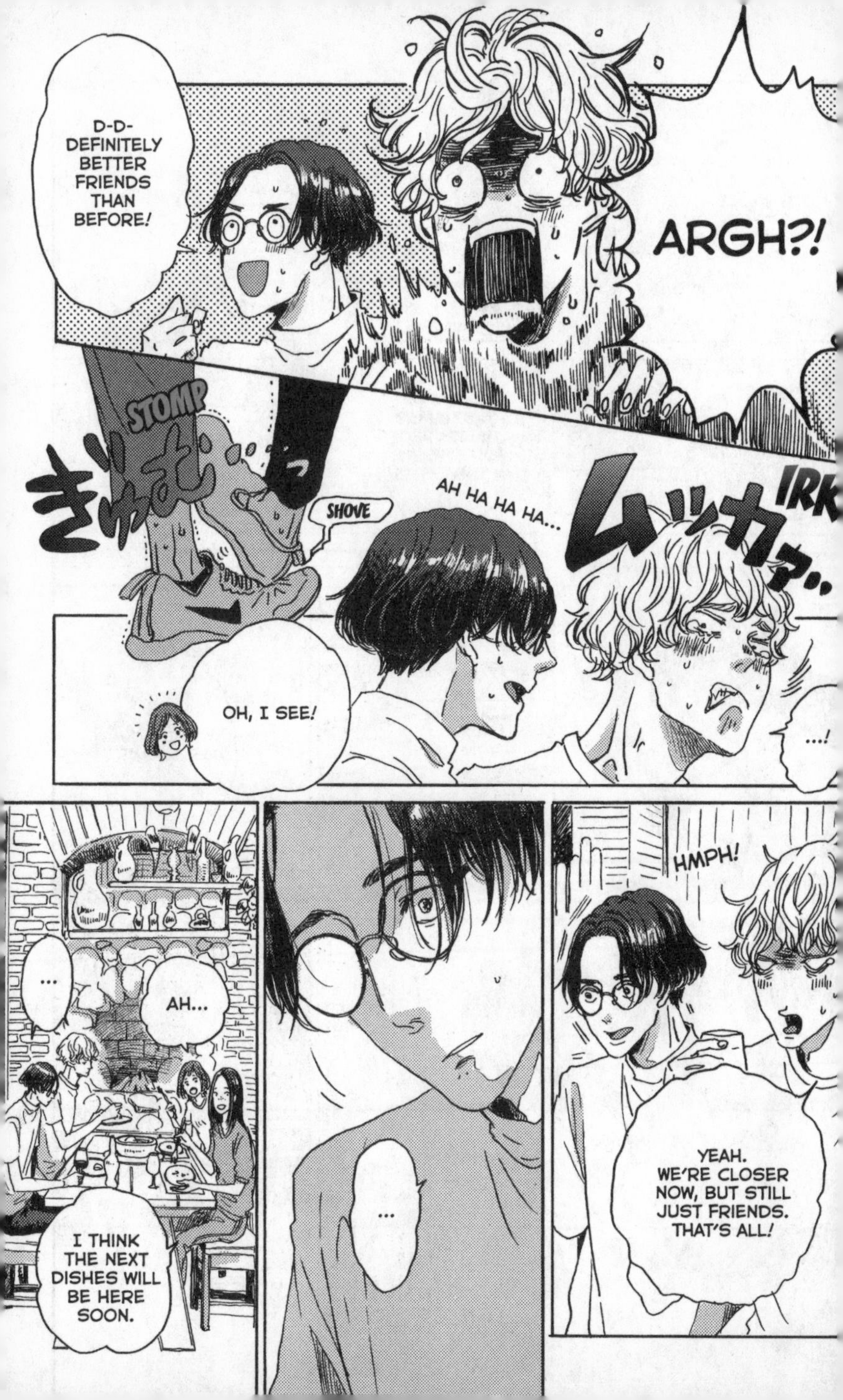

D-D-DEFINITELY BETTER FRIENDS THAN BEFORE!
ARGH?!
ムッカァ..
IRK
...!
AH HA HA HA...
OH, I SEE!
SHOVE
STOMP
ぎゅむっ
HMPH!
YEAH. WE'RE CLOSER NOW, BUT STILL JUST FRIENDS. THAT'S ALL!
...
AH...
...
I THINK THE NEXT DISHES WILL BE HERE SOON.

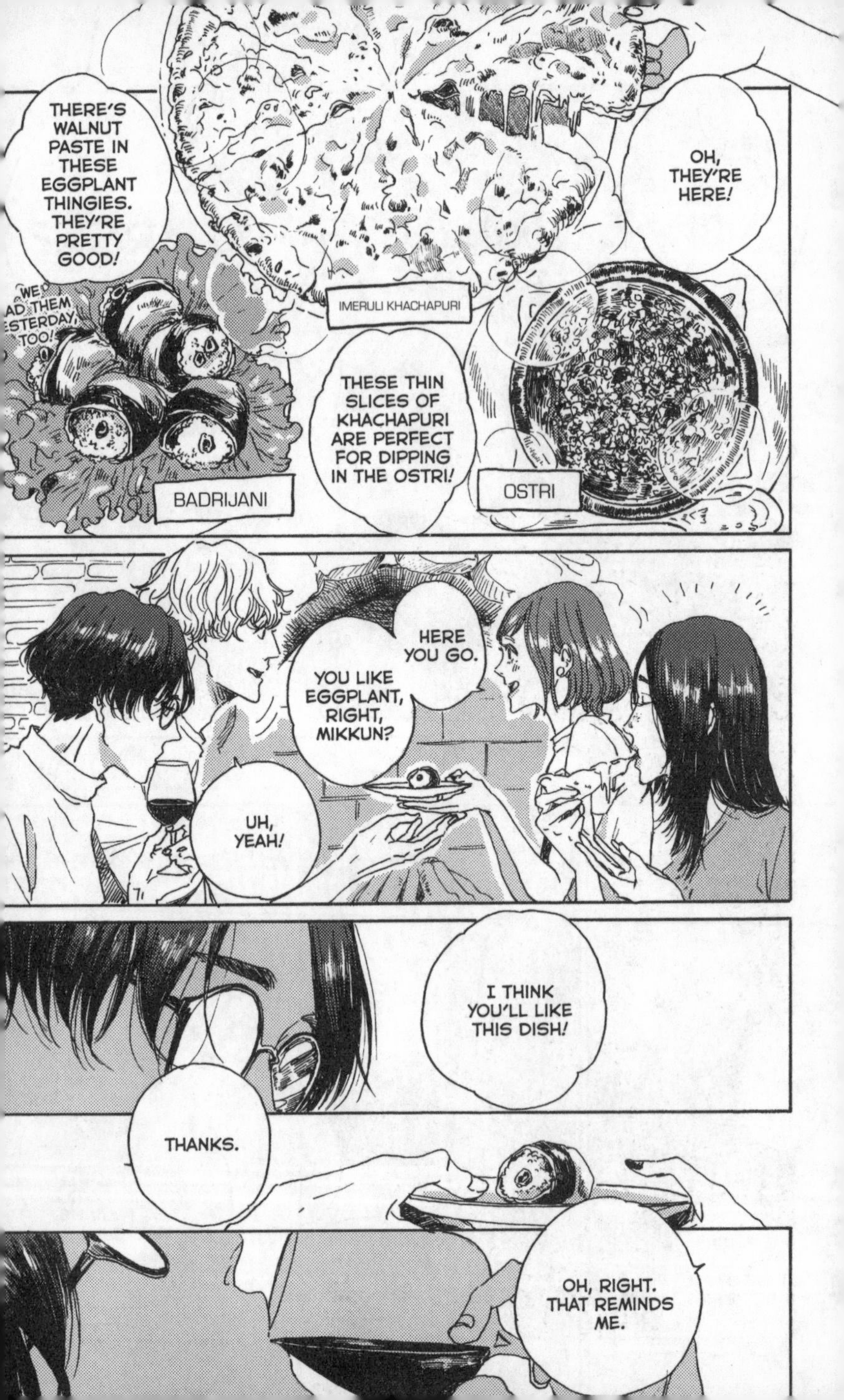
OH, THEY'RE HERE!
IMERULI KHACHAPURI
THERE'S WALNUT PASTE IN THESE EGGPLANT THINGIES. THEY'RE PRETTY GOOD!
WE AD THEM ESTERDAY, TOO!
THESE THIN SLICES OF KHACHAPURI ARE PERFECT FOR DIPPING IN THE OSTRI!
OSTRI
BADRIJANI
HERE YOU GO.
YOU LIKE EGGPLANT, RIGHT, MIKKUN?
UH, YEAH!
I THINK YOU'LL LIKE THIS DISH!
THANKS.
OH, RIGHT. THAT REMINDS ME.

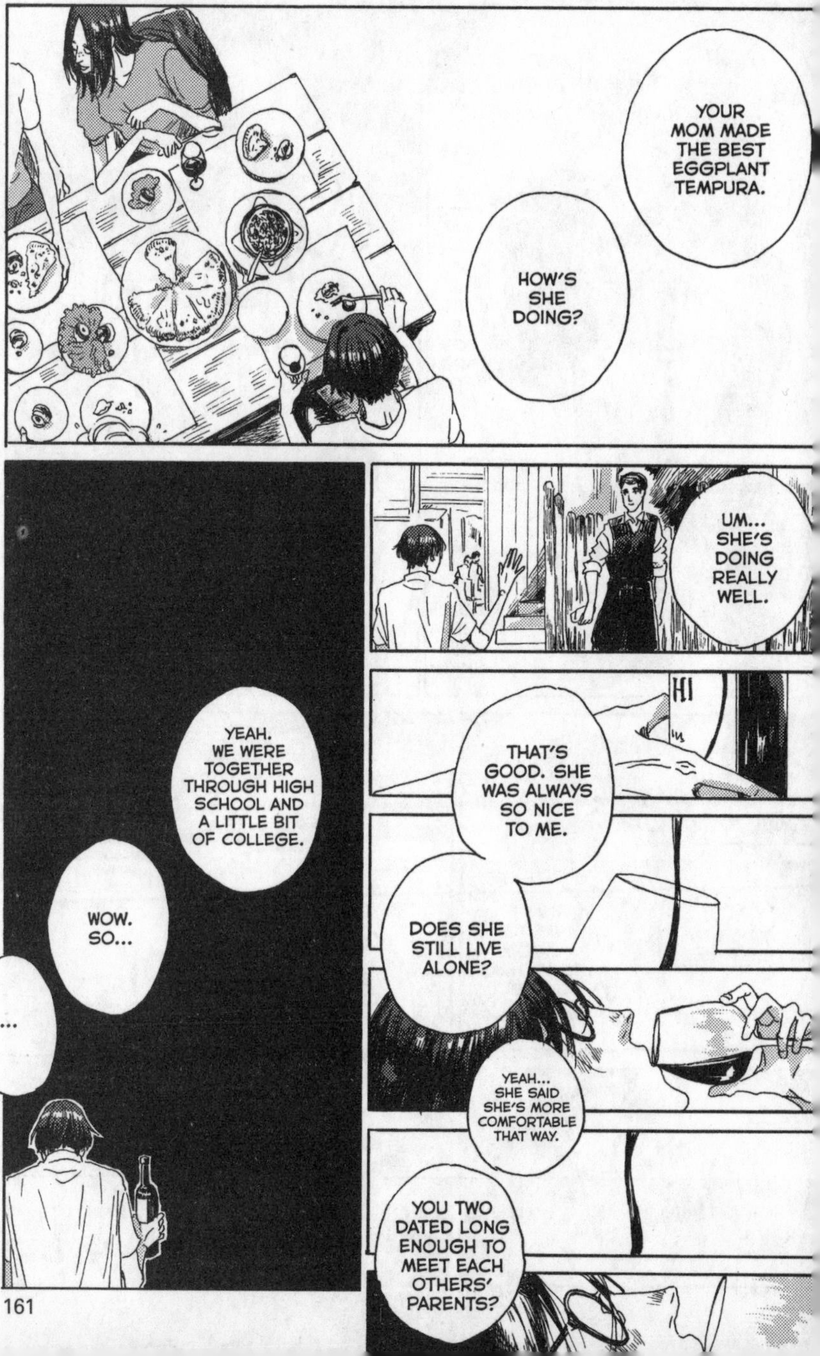
YOUR MOM MADE THE BEST EGGPLANT TEMPURA.
HOW'S SHE DOING?
UM... SHE'S DOING REALLY WELL.
HI
THAT'S GOOD. SHE WAS ALWAYS SO NICE TO ME.
DOES SHE STILL LIVE ALONE?
YEAH... SHE SAID SHE'S MORE COMFORTABLE THAT WAY.
YOU TWO DATED LONG ENOUGH TO MEET EACH OTHERS' PARENTS?
YEAH. WE WERE TOGETHER THROUGH HIGH SCHOOL AND A LITTLE BIT OF COLLEGE.
WOW. SO...
...

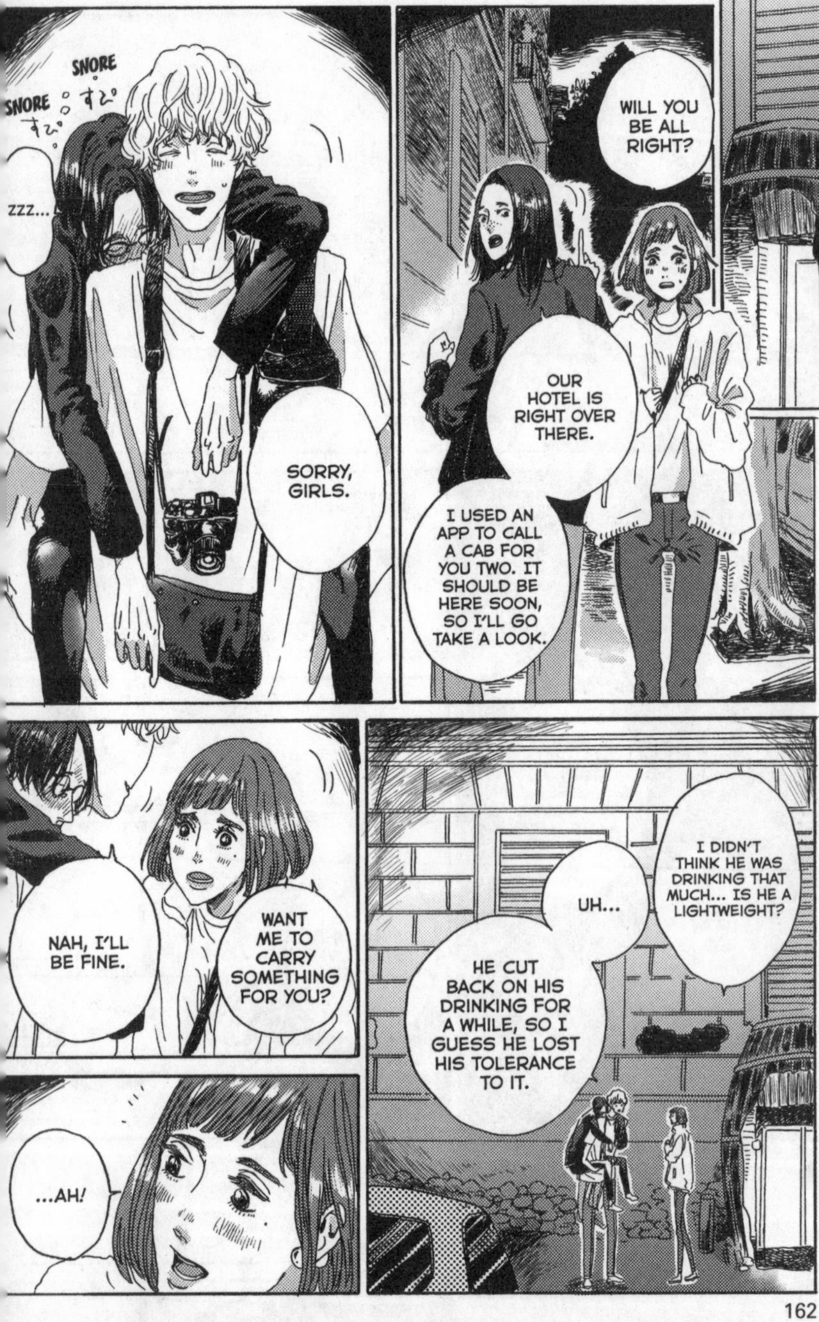
WILL YOU BE ALL RIGHT?
OUR HOTEL IS RIGHT OVER THERE.
I USED AN APP TO CALL A CAB FOR YOU TWO. IT SHOULD BE HERE SOON, SO I'LL GO TAKE A LOOK.
SNORE すぴ
SNORE すぴ
ZZZ...
SORRY, GIRLS.
I DIDN'T THINK HE WAS DRINKING THAT MUCH... IS HE A LIGHTWEIGHT?
UH...
HE CUT BACK ON HIS DRINKING FOR A WHILE, SO I GUESS HE LOST HIS TOLERANCE TO IT.
WANT ME TO CARRY SOMETHING FOR YOU?
NAH, I'LL BE FINE.
...AH!

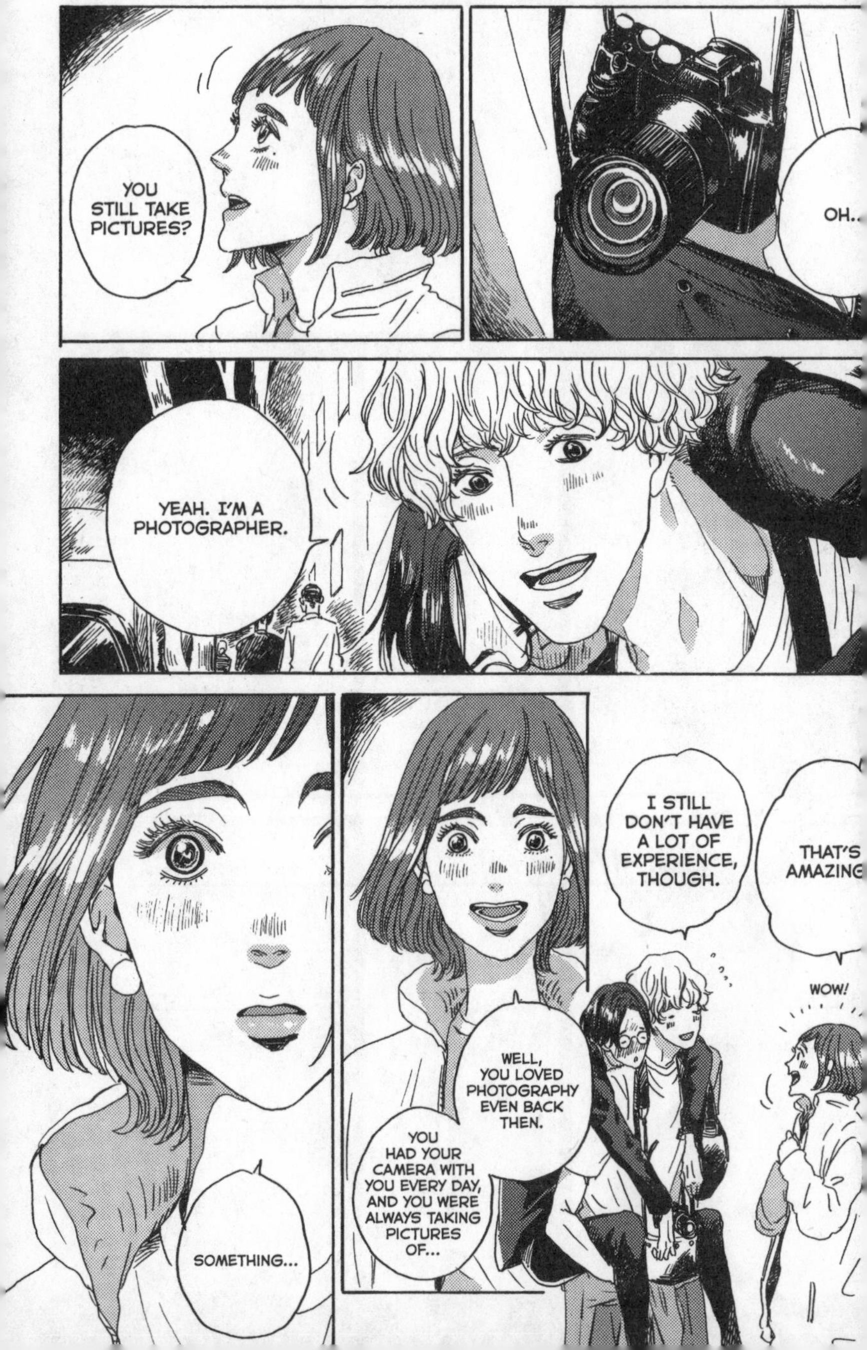
OH..
YOU STILL TAKE PICTURES?
YEAH. I'M A PHOTOGRAPHER.
THAT'S AMAZING
I STILL DON'T HAVE A LOT OF EXPERIENCE, THOUGH.
WOW!
WELL, YOU LOVED PHOTOGRAPHY EVEN BACK THEN.
YOU HAD YOUR CAMERA WITH YOU EVERY DAY, AND YOU WERE ALWAYS TAKING PICTURES OF...
SOMETHING...

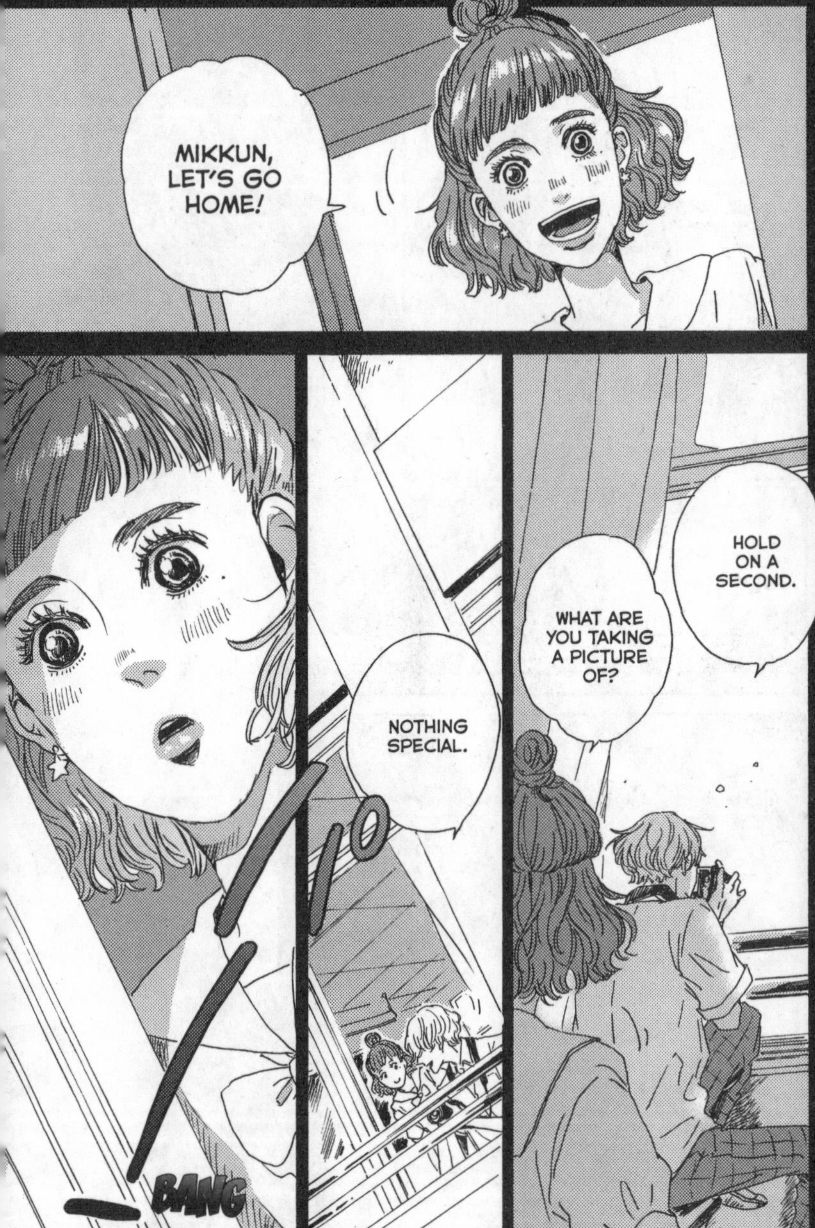
MIKKUN, LET'S GO HOME!
HOLD ON A SECOND.
WHAT ARE YOU TAKING A PICTURE OF?
NOTHING SPECIAL.
BANG

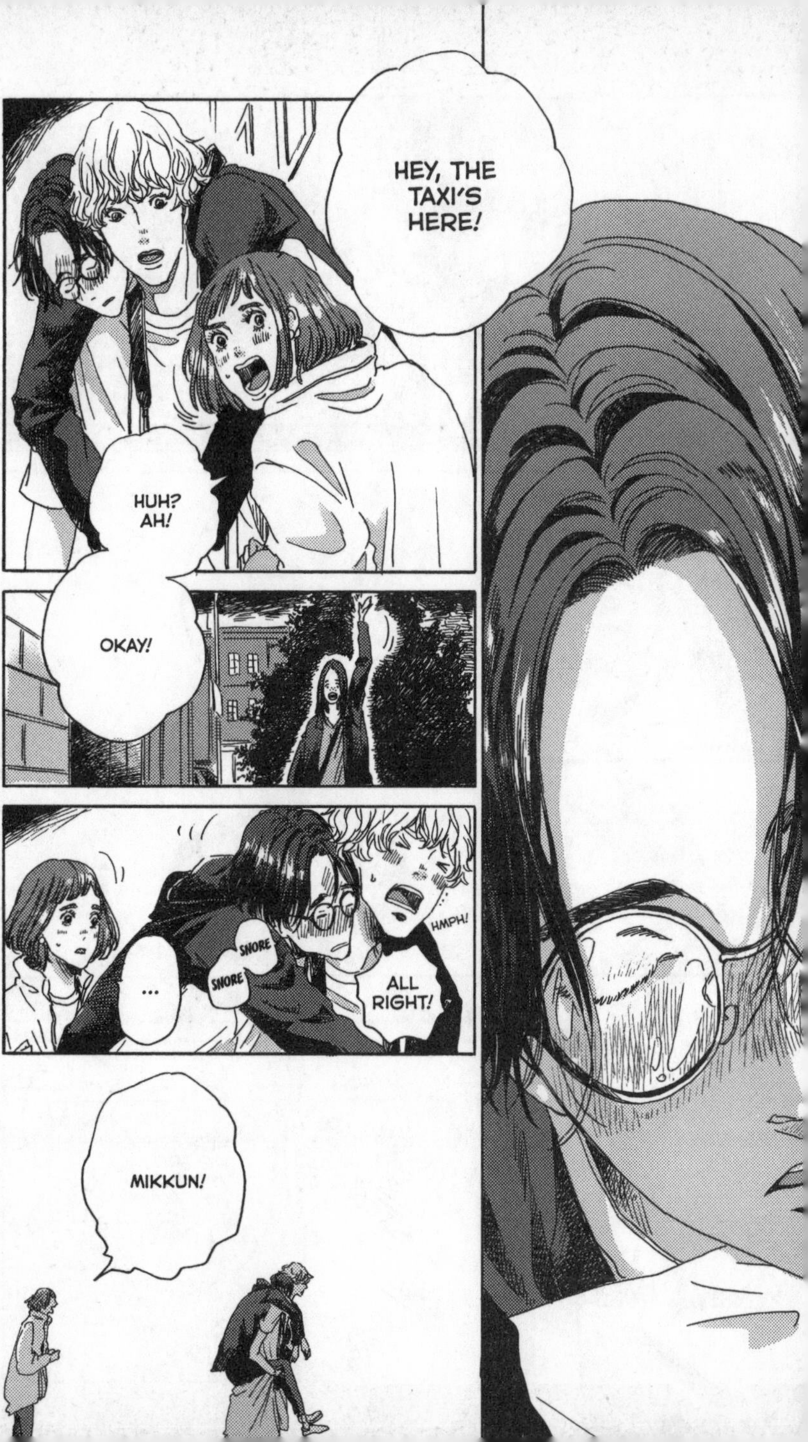
HEY, THE TAXI'S HERE!
HUH? AH!
OKAY!
HMPH!
ALL RIGHT!
SNORE
SNORE
...
MIKKUN!

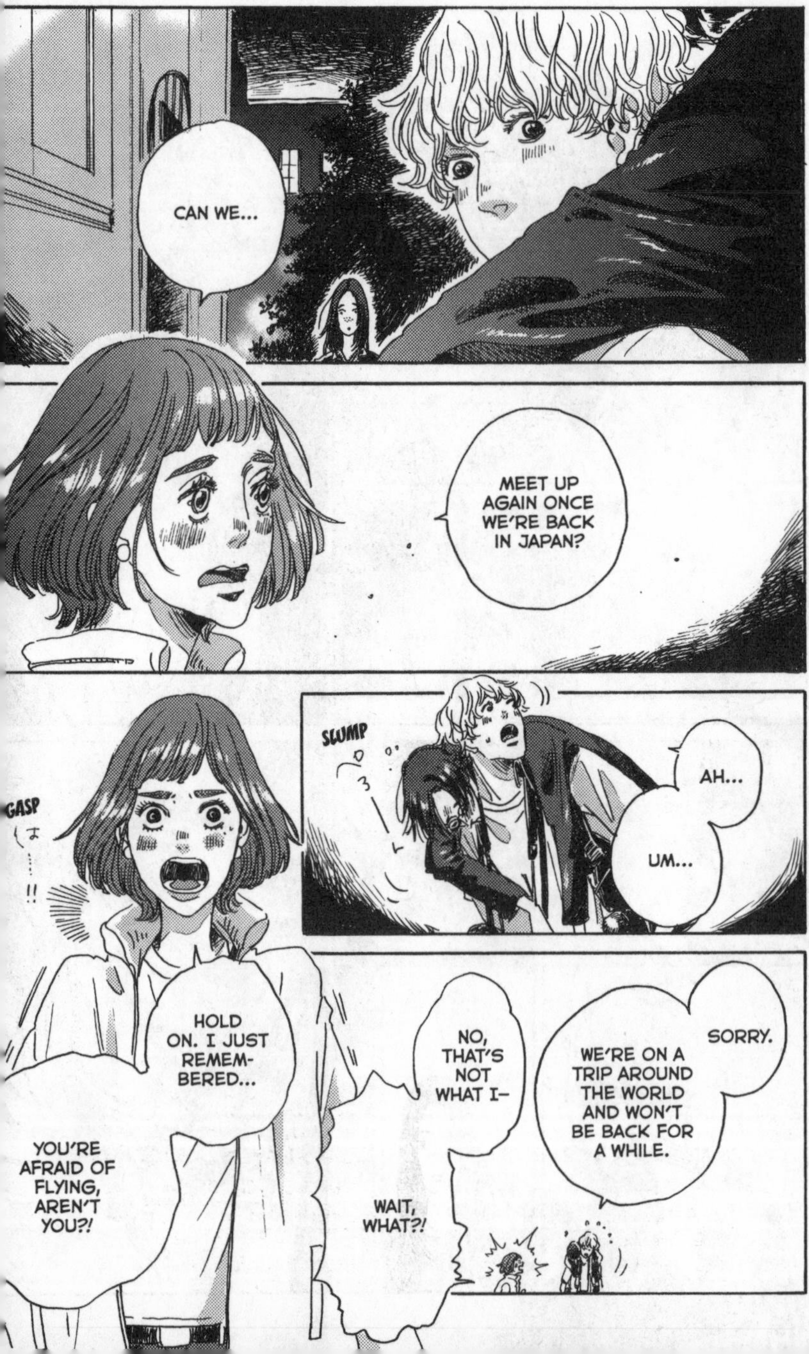
CAN WE...
MEET UP AGAIN ONCE WE'RE BACK IN JAPAN?
SLUMP
AH...
UM...
SORRY.
WE'RE ON A TRIP AROUND THE WORLD AND WON'T BE BACK FOR A WHILE.
NO, THAT'S NOT WHAT I-
GASP
は......!!
HOLD ON. I JUST REMEMBERED...
YOU'RE AFRAID OF FLYING, AREN'T YOU?!
WAIT, WHAT?!

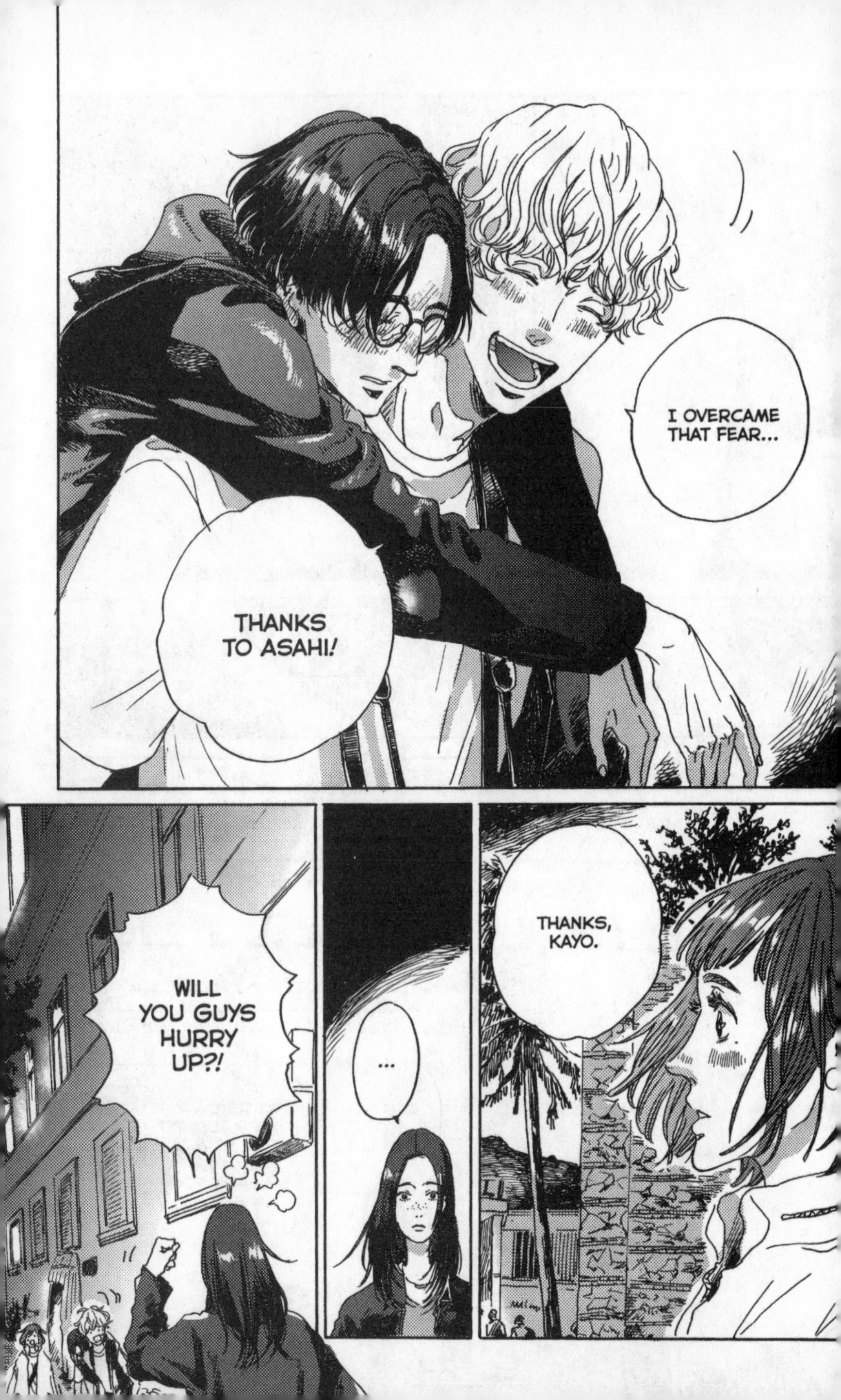
I OVERCAME THAT FEAR...
THANKS TO ASAHI!
THANKS, KAYO.
...
WILL YOU GUYS HURRY UP?!

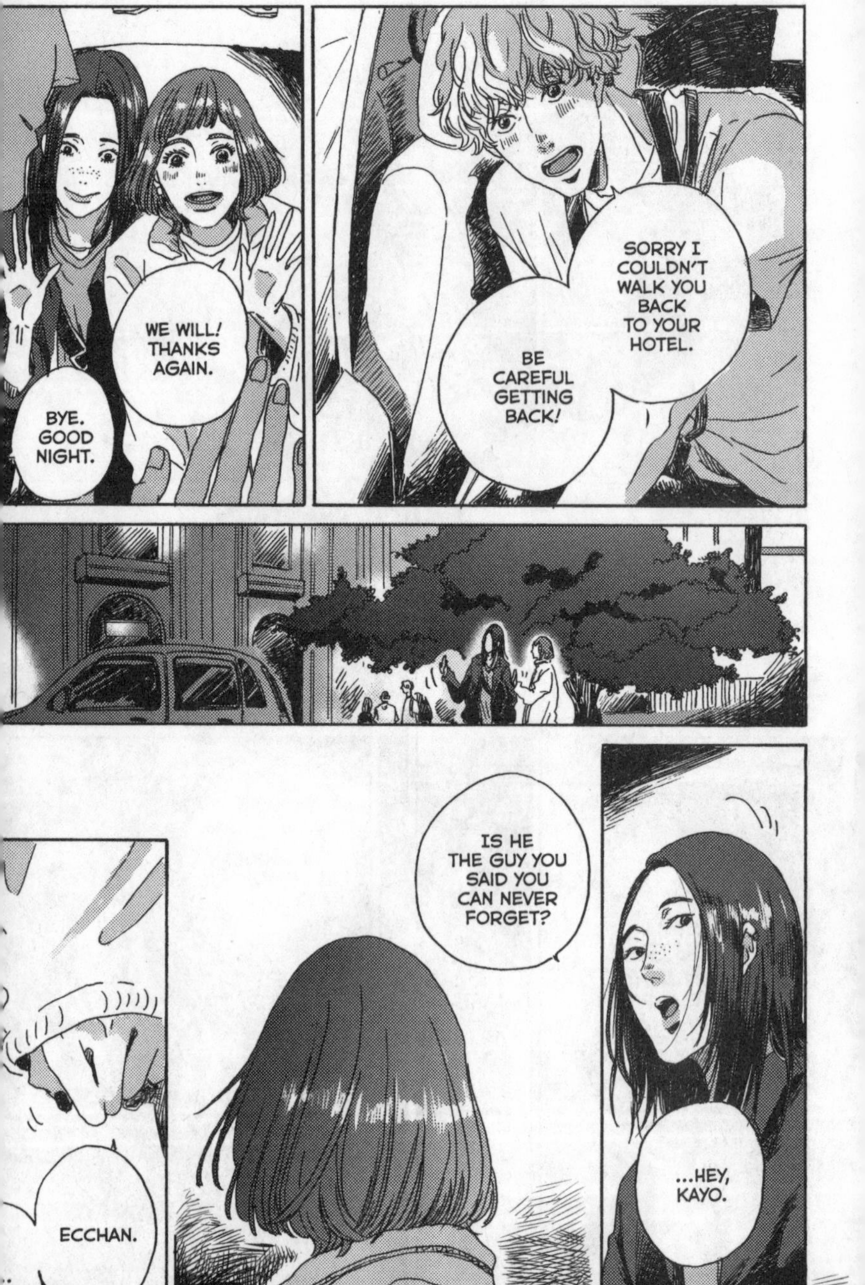
SORRY I COULDN'T WALK YOU BACK TO YOUR HOTEL.
BE CAREFUL GETTING BACK!
WE WILL! THANKS AGAIN.
BYE. GOOD NIGHT.
...HEY, KAYO.
IS HE THE GUY YOU SAID YOU CAN NEVER FORGET?
ECCHAN.

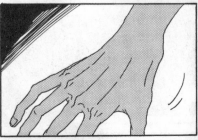

...I TAKE THAT BACK.

SORRY, ASAHI.

STUPID ASAHI.

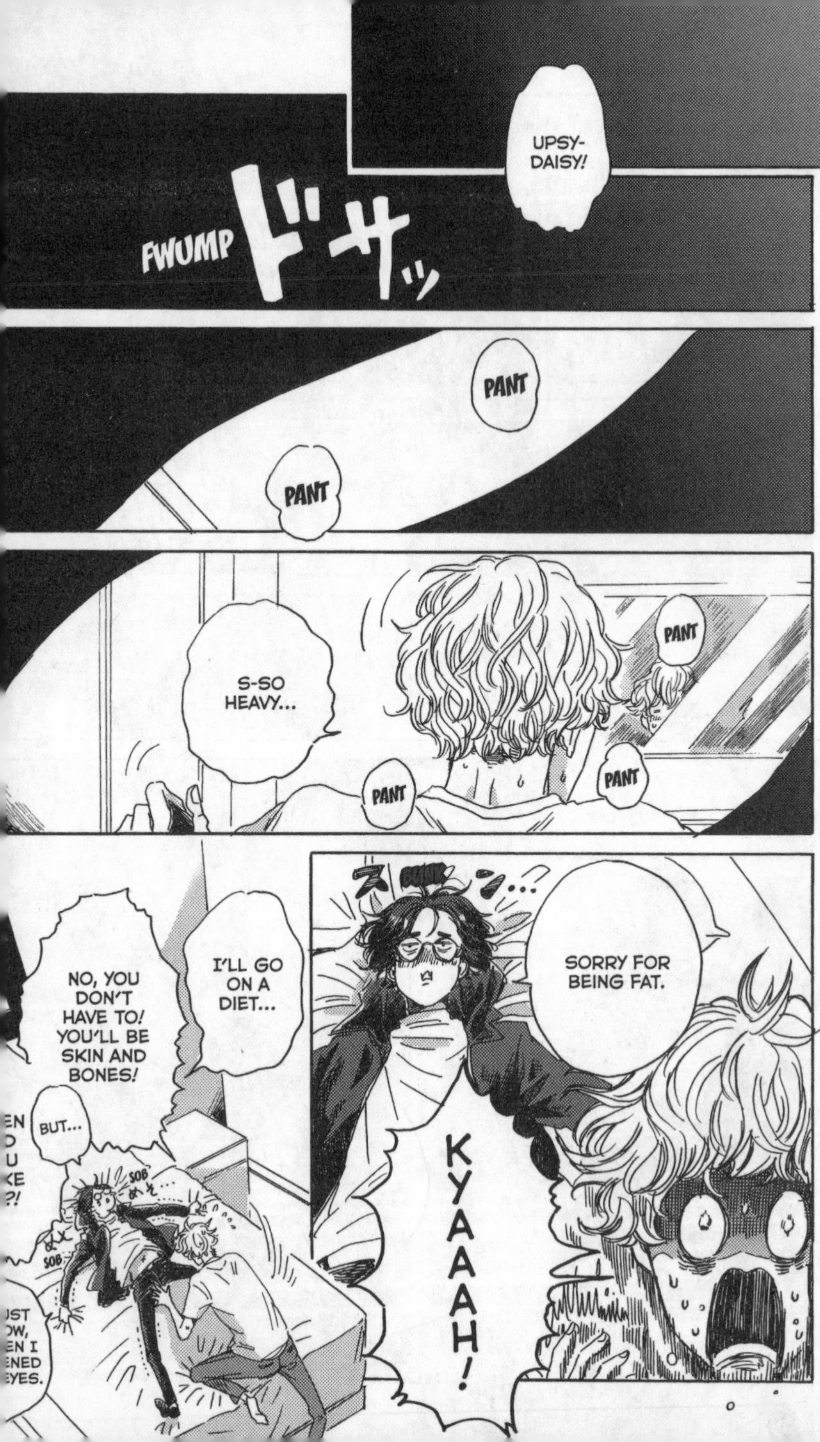
UPSY-DAISY!
FWUMP
ドサッ
PANT
PANT
PANT
S-SO HEAVY...
PANT
PANT
SORRY FOR BEING FAT.
KYAAAH!
I'LL GO ON A DIET...
NO, YOU DON'T HAVE TO! YOU'LL BE SKIN AND BONES!
BUT...
SOB
SOB

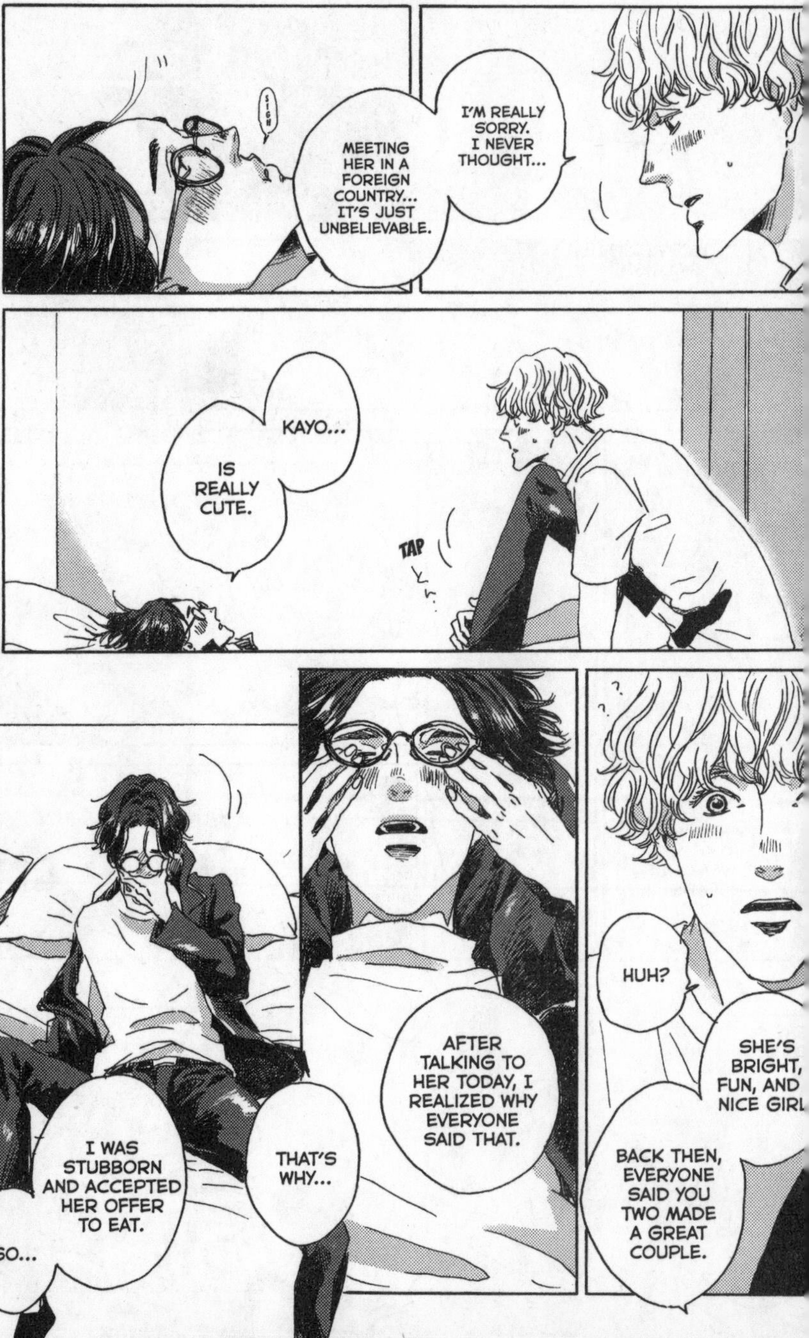
I'M REALLY SORRY. I NEVER THOUGHT...
SIGH
MEETING HER IN A FOREIGN COUNTRY... IT'S JUST UNBELIEVABLE.
KAYO...
IS REALLY CUTE.
TAP
HUH?
SHE'S BRIGHT, FUN, AND NICE GIRL
BACK THEN, EVERYONE SAID YOU TWO MADE A GREAT COUPLE.
AFTER TALKING TO HER TODAY, I REALIZED WHY EVERYONE SAID THAT.
THAT'S WHY...
I WAS STUBBORN AND ACCEPTED HER OFFER TO EAT.
SO...

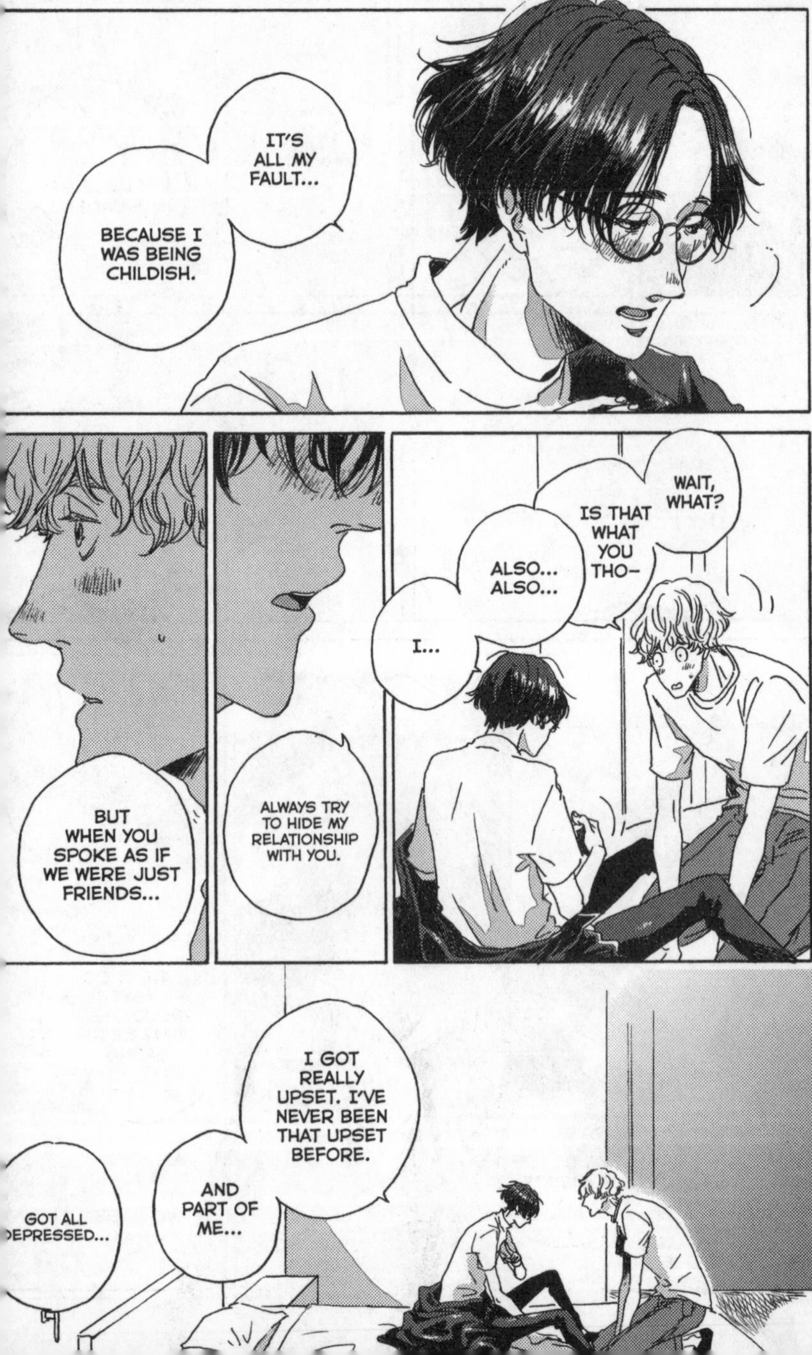
IT'S ALL MY FAULT...
BECAUSE I WAS BEING CHILDISH.
WAIT, WHAT?
IS THAT WHAT YOU THO–
ALSO... ALSO...
I...
ALWAYS TRY TO HIDE MY RELATIONSHIP WITH YOU.
BUT WHEN YOU SPOKE AS IF WE WERE JUST FRIENDS...
I GOT REALLY UPSET. I'VE NEVER BEEN THAT UPSET BEFORE.
AND PART OF ME...
GOT ALL DEPRESSED...

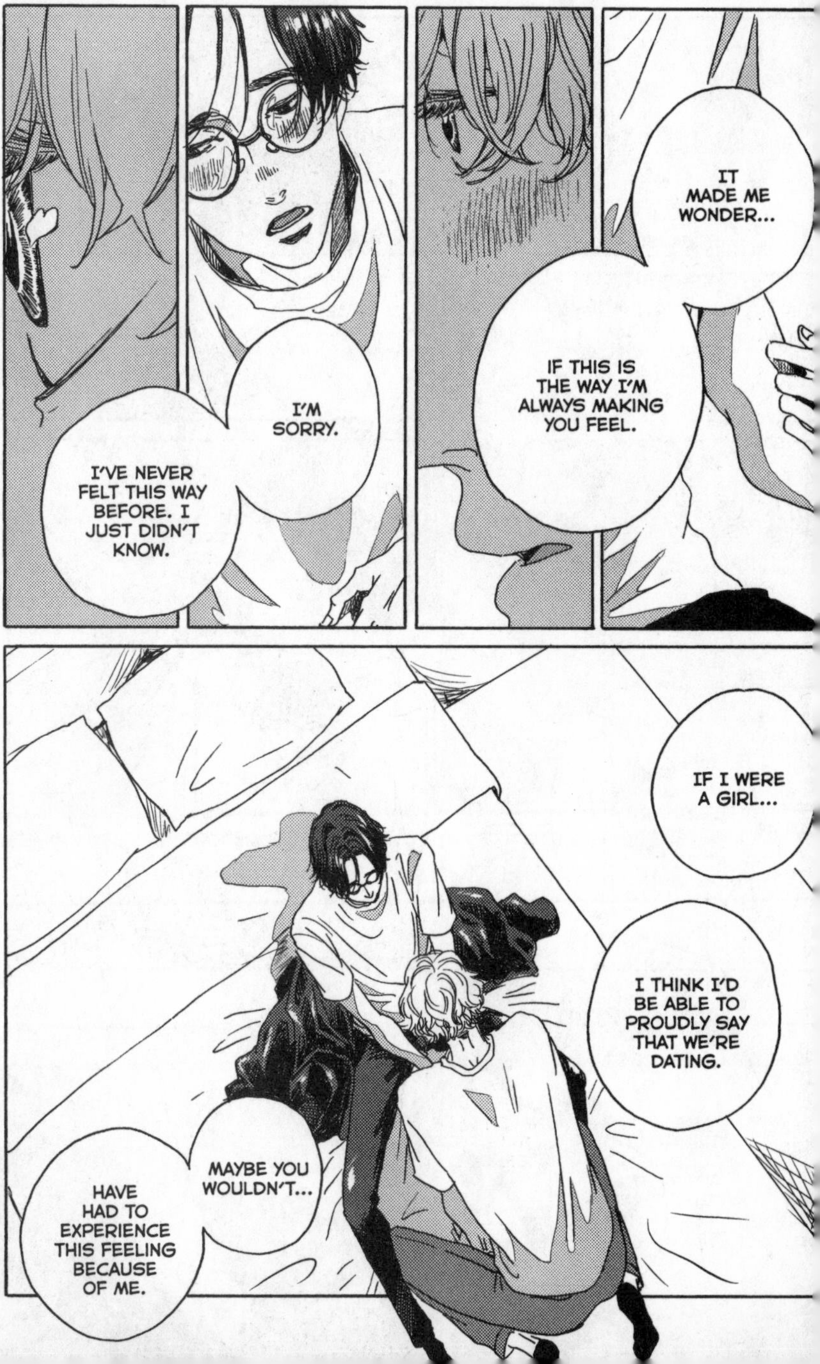
IT MADE ME WONDER...
IF THIS IS THE WAY I'M ALWAYS MAKING YOU FEEL.
I'M SORRY.
I'VE NEVER FELT THIS WAY BEFORE. I JUST DIDN'T KNOW.
IF I WERE A GIRL...
I THINK I'D BE ABLE TO PROUDLY SAY THAT WE'RE DATING.
MAYBE YOU WOULDN'T...
HAVE HAD TO EXPERIENCE THIS FEELING BECAUSE OF ME.

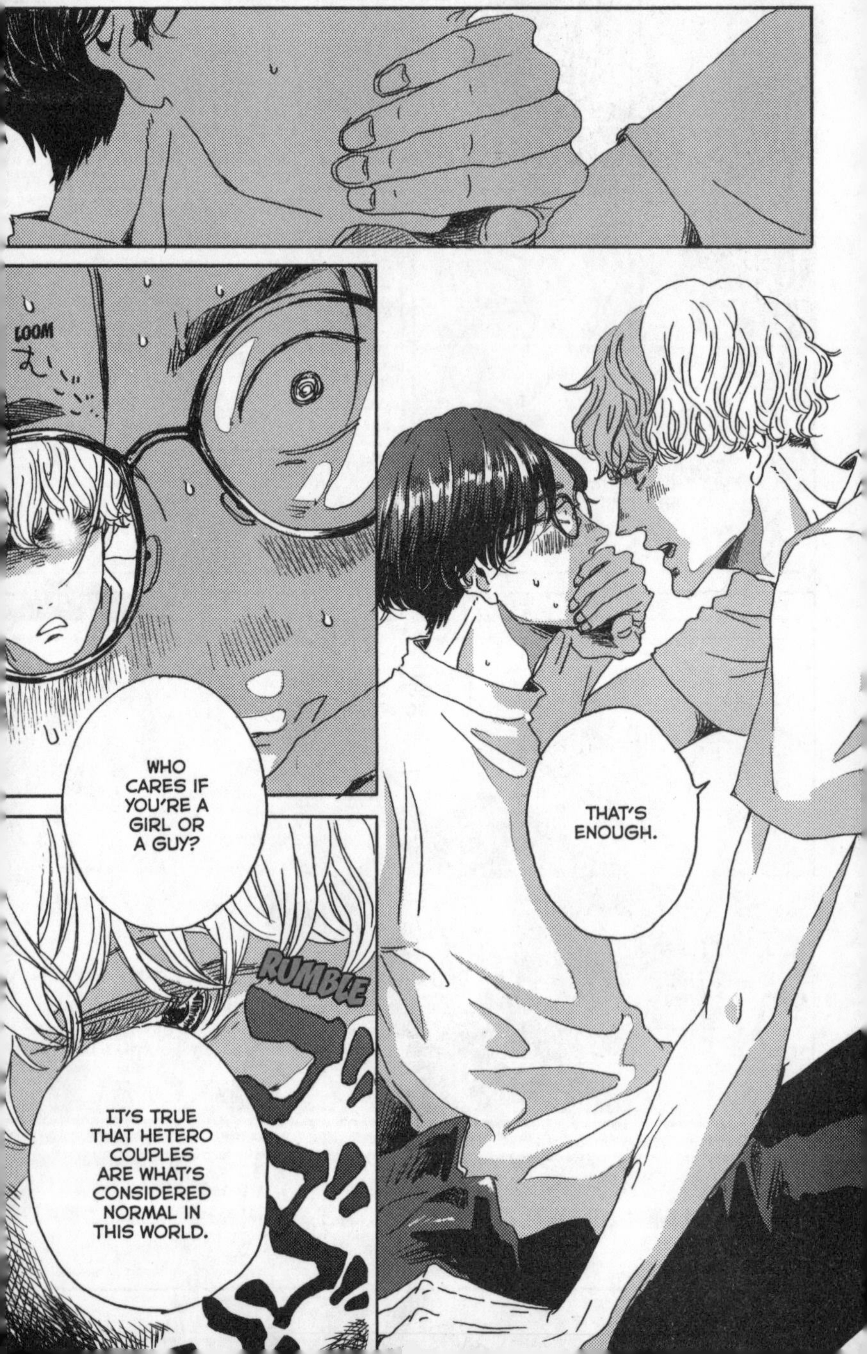
THAT'S ENOUGH.
LOOM
WHO CARES IF YOU'RE A GIRL OR A GUY?
RUMBLE
IT'S TRUE THAT HETERO COUPLES ARE WHAT'S CONSIDERED NORMAL IN THIS WORLD.

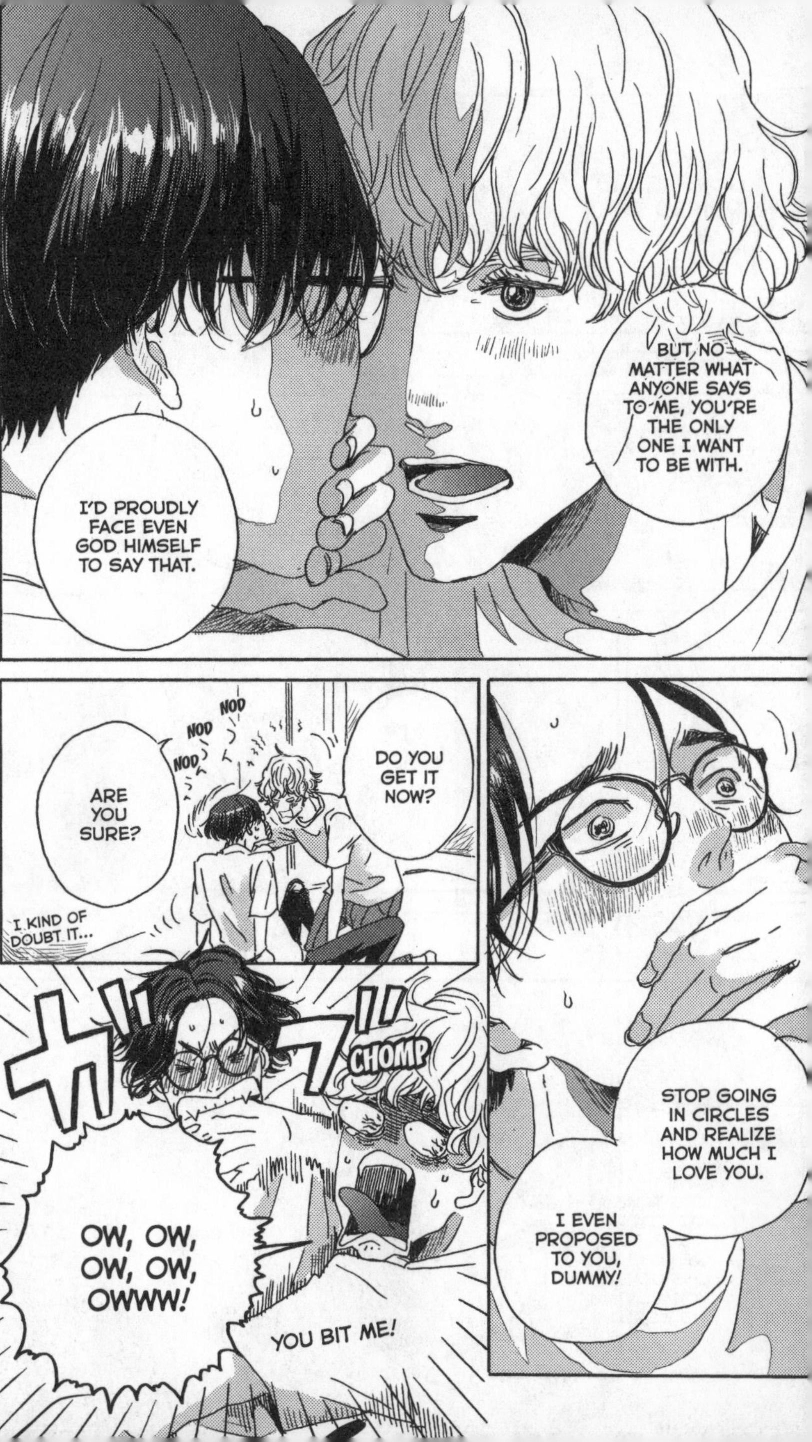
BUT, NO MATTER WHAT ANYONE SAYS TO ME, YOU'RE THE ONLY ONE I WANT TO BE WITH.
I'D PROUDLY FACE EVEN GOD HIMSELF TO SAY THAT.
STOP GOING IN CIRCLES AND REALIZE HOW MUCH I LOVE YOU.
I EVEN PROPOSED TO YOU, DUMMY!
DO YOU GET IT NOW?
NOD
NOD
NOD
ARE YOU SURE?
I KIND OF DOUBT IT...
ガブ
CHOMP
OW, OW, OW, OW, OWWW!
YOU BIT ME!

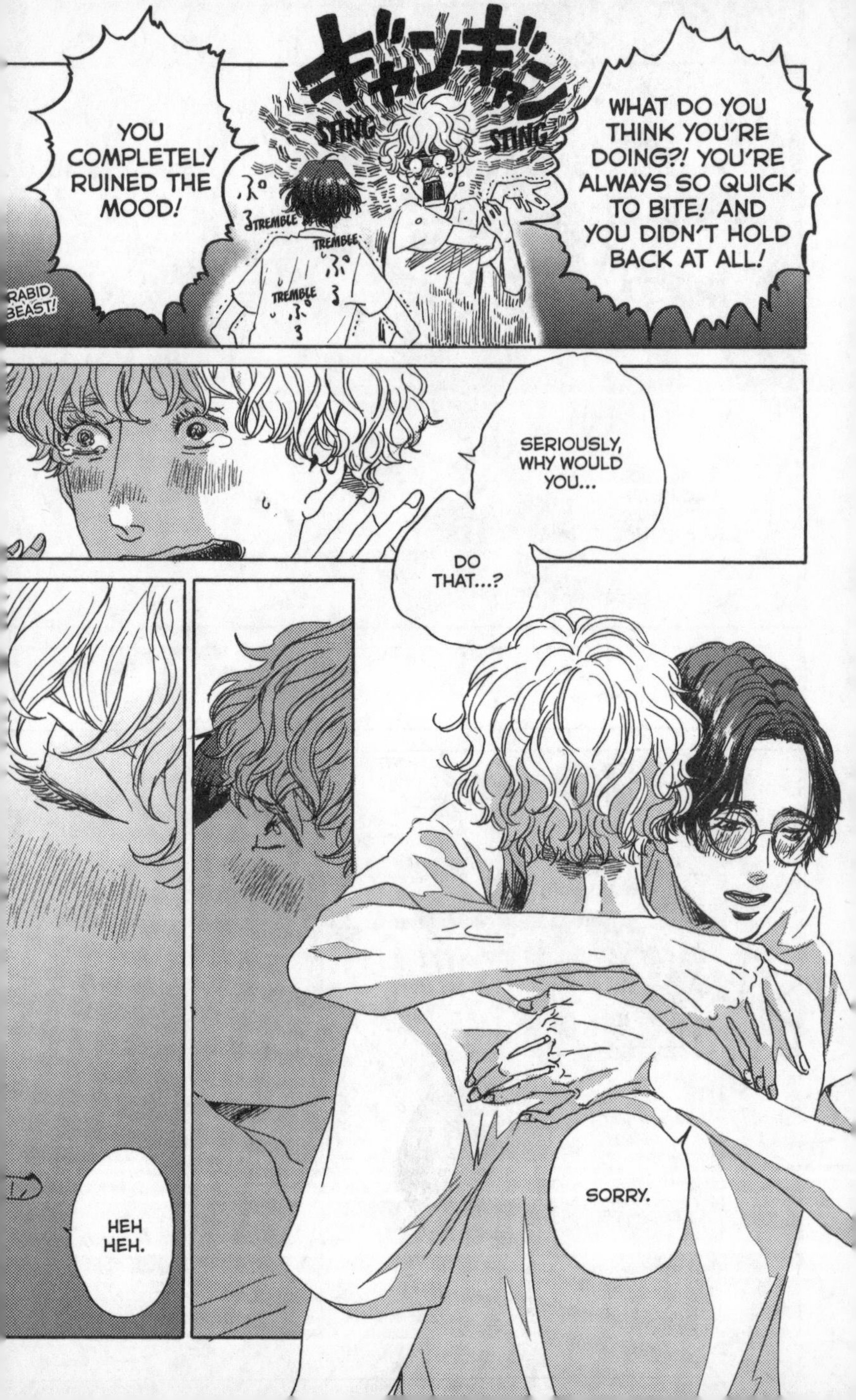

WHAT DO YOU THINK YOU'RE DOING?! YOU'RE ALWAYS SO QUICK TO BITE! AND YOU DIDN'T HOLD BACK AT ALL!
ギャンギャン
STING
STING
YOU COMPLETELY RUINED THE MOOD!
TREMBLE
TREMBLE
TREMBLE
RABID BEAST!
SERIOUSLY, WHY WOULD YOU...
DO THAT...?
SORRY.
HEH HEH.

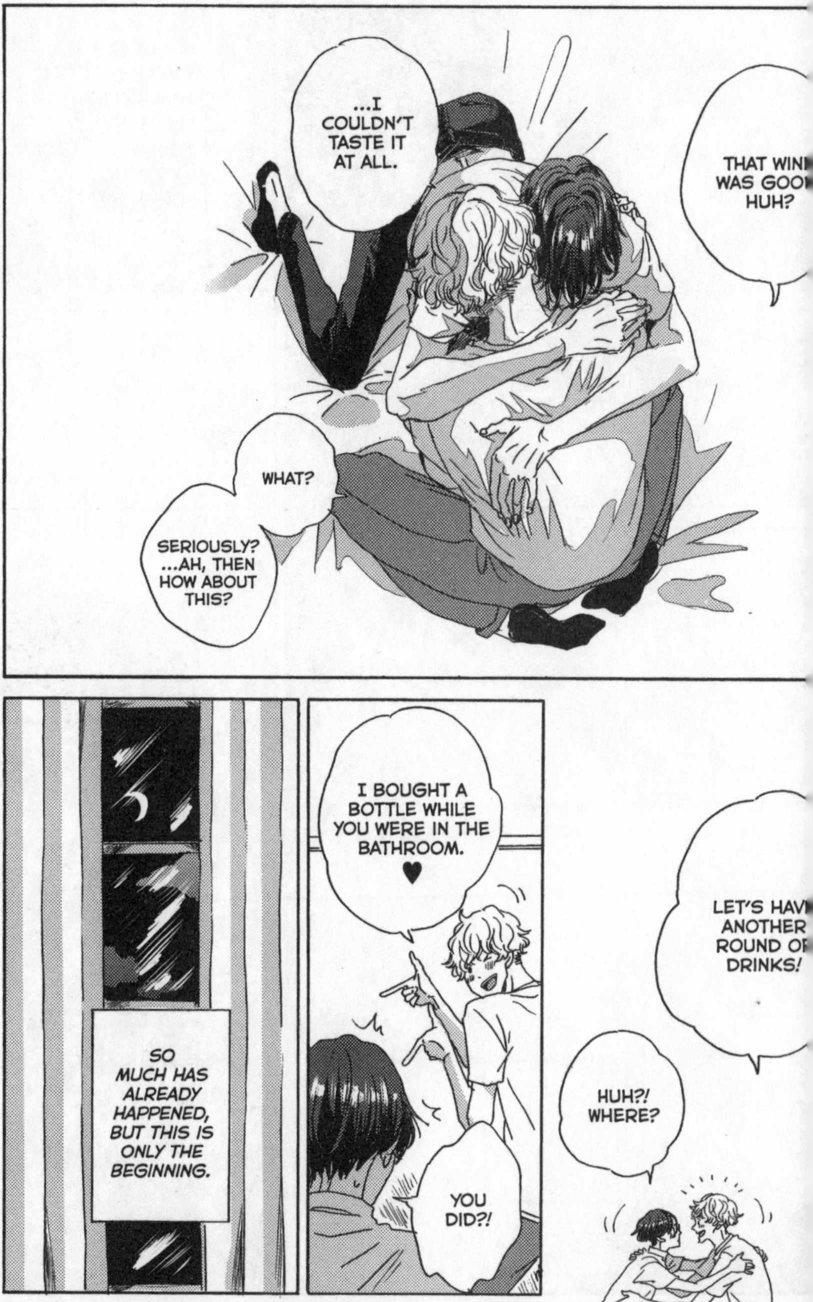
THAT WIN WAS GOO HUH?
...I COULDN'T TASTE IT AT ALL.
WHAT?
SERIOUSLY? ...AH, THEN HOW ABOUT THIS?
LET'S HAV ANOTHER ROUND O DRINKS!
HUH?! WHERE?
I BOUGHT A BOTTLE WHILE YOU WERE IN THE BATHROOM. ♥
YOU DID?!
SO MUCH HAS ALREADY HAPPENED, BUT THIS IS ONLY THE BEGINNING.

ASAHI AND
MITSUKI'S
JOURNEY...

CONTINUES...

Our Not-So-Lonely Planet Travel Guide, Vol. 1 - The End

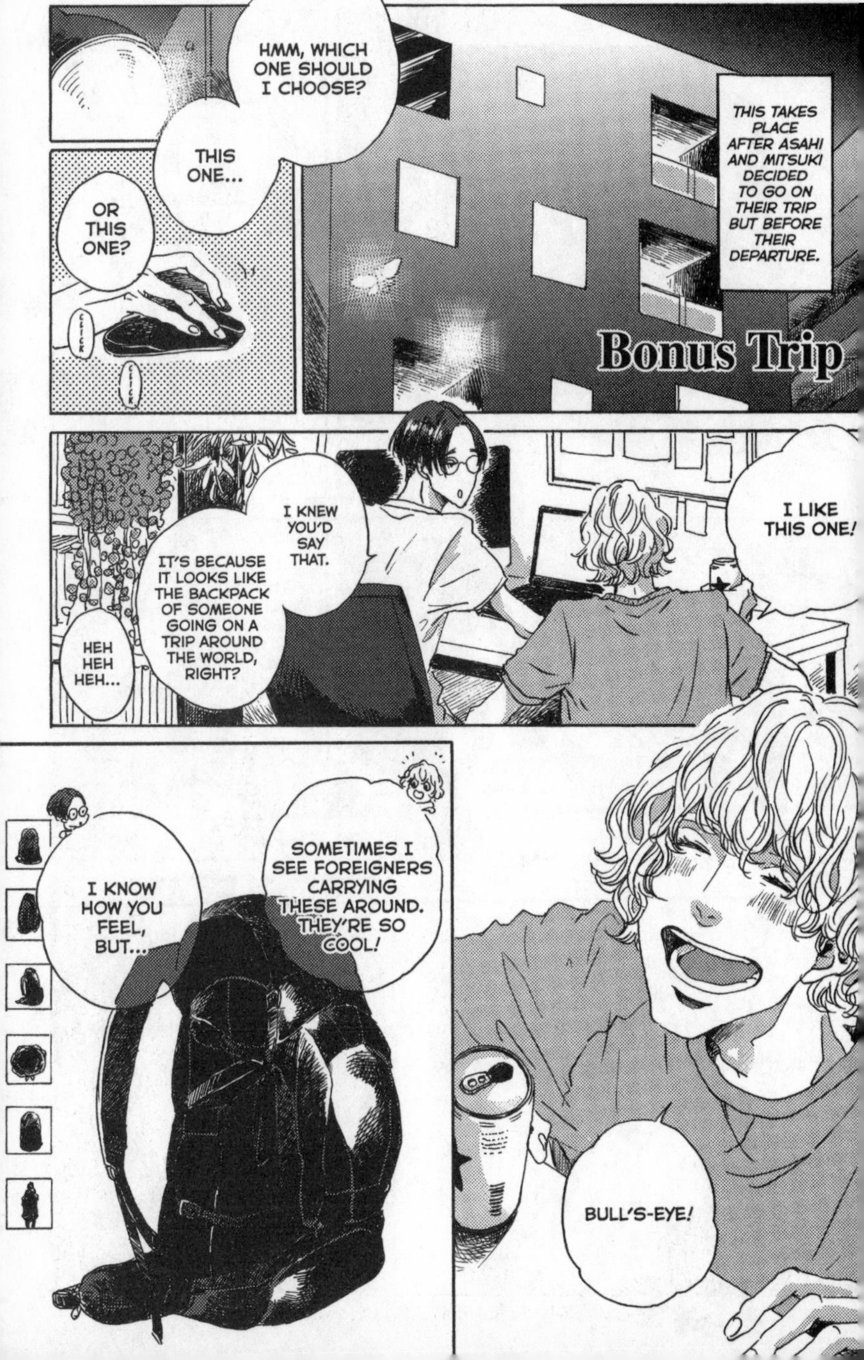
THIS TAKES PLACE AFTER ASAHI AND MITSUKI DECIDED TO GO ON THEIR TRIP BUT BEFORE THEIR DEPARTURE.
Bonus Trip
HMM, WHICH ONE SHOULD I CHOOSE?
THIS ONE...
OR THIS ONE?
CLICK
CLICK
I LIKE THIS ONE!
I KNEW YOU'D SAY THAT.
IT'S BECAUSE IT LOOKS LIKE THE BACKPACK OF SOMEONE GOING ON A TRIP AROUND THE WORLD, RIGHT?
HEH HEH HEH...
BULL'S-EYE!
SOMETIMES I SEE FOREIGNERS CARRYING THESE AROUND. THEY'RE SO COOL!
I KNOW HOW YOU FEEL, BUT...

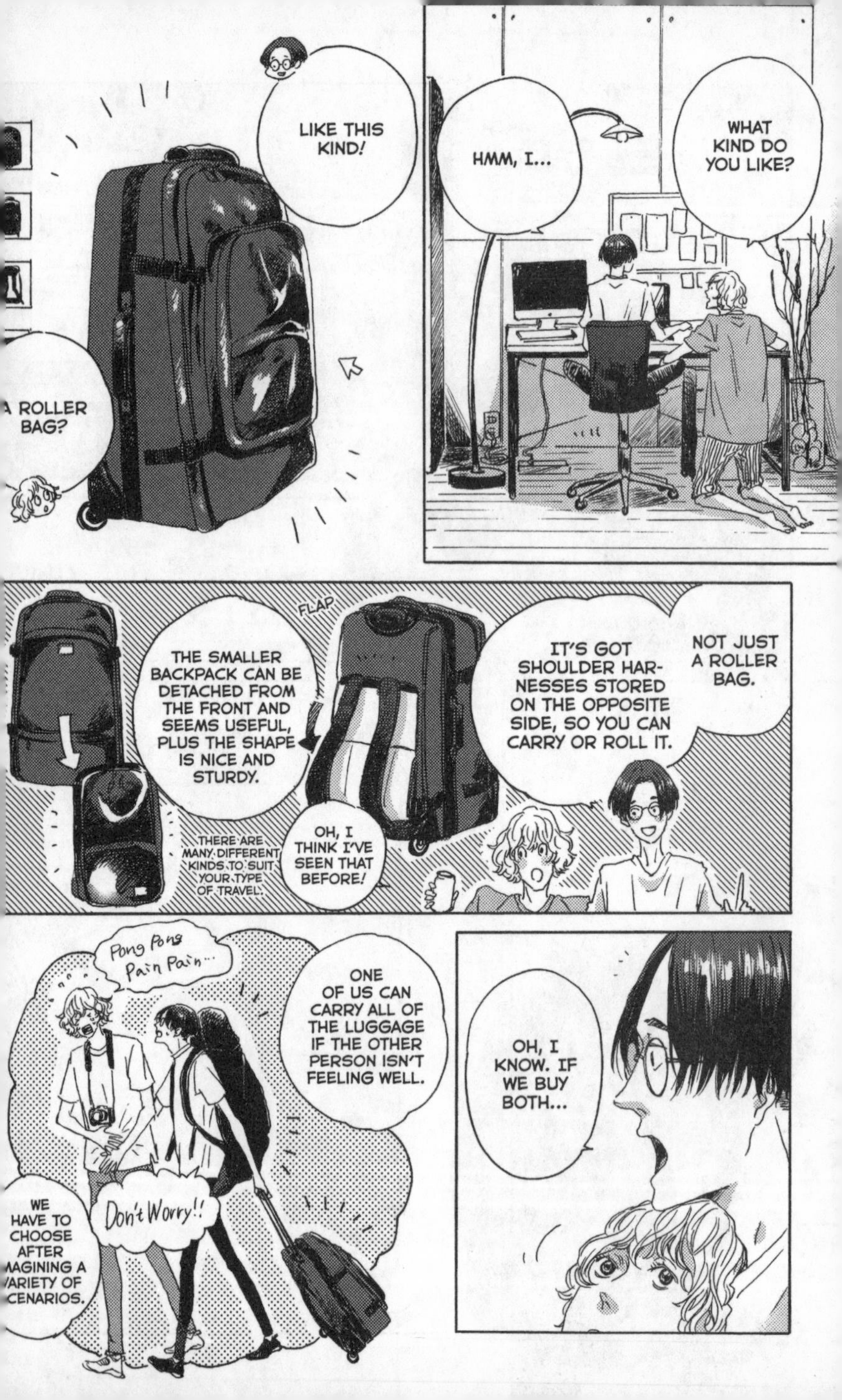

WHAT KIND DO YOU LIKE?
HMM, I...
LIKE THIS KIND!
A ROLLER BAG?
NOT JUST A ROLLER BAG.
IT'S GOT SHOULDER HAR-NESSES STORED ON THE OPPOSITE SIDE, SO YOU CAN CARRY OR ROLL IT.
FLAP
THE SMALLER BACKPACK CAN BE DETACHED FROM THE FRONT AND SEEMS USEFUL, PLUS THE SHAPE IS NICE AND STURDY.
OH, I THINK I'VE SEEN THAT BEFORE!
THERE ARE MANY DIFFERENT KINDS TO SUIT YOUR TYPE OF TRAVEL.
OH, I KNOW. IF WE BUY BOTH...
ONE OF US CAN CARRY ALL OF THE LUGGAGE IF THE OTHER PERSON ISN'T FEELING WELL.
Pong Pong Pain Pain...
Don't Worry!!
WE HAVE TO CHOOSE AFTER MAGINING A ARIETY OF CENARIOS.

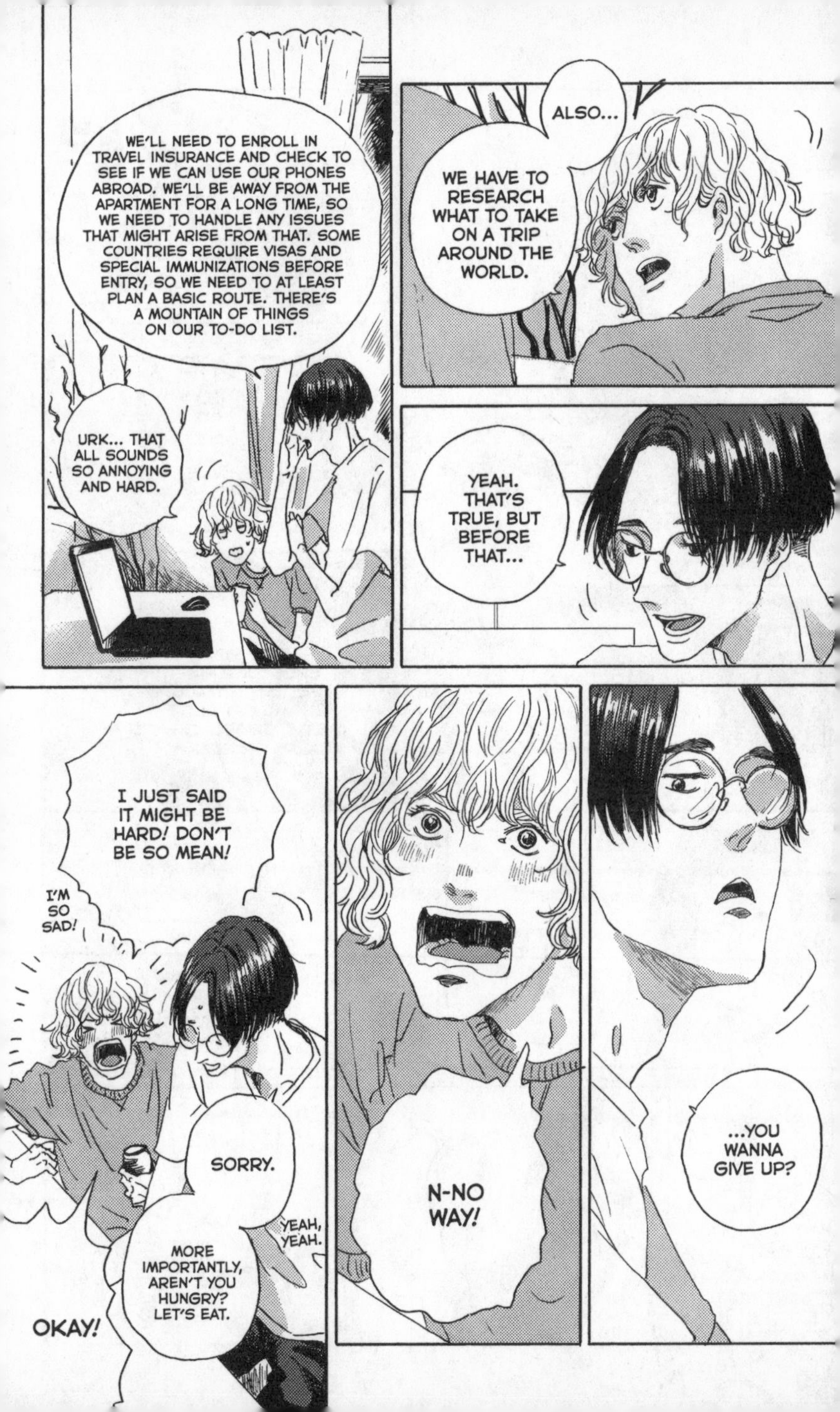
ALSO...
WE HAVE TO RESEARCH WHAT TO TAKE ON A TRIP AROUND THE WORLD.
YEAH. THAT'S TRUE, BUT BEFORE THAT...
WE'LL NEED TO ENROLL IN TRAVEL INSURANCE AND CHECK TO SEE IF WE CAN USE OUR PHONES ABROAD. WE'LL BE AWAY FROM THE APARTMENT FOR A LONG TIME, SO WE NEED TO HANDLE ANY ISSUES THAT MIGHT ARISE FROM THAT. SOME COUNTRIES REQUIRE VISAS AND SPECIAL IMMUNIZATIONS BEFORE ENTRY, SO WE NEED TO AT LEAST PLAN A BASIC ROUTE. THERE'S A MOUNTAIN OF THINGS ON OUR TO-DO LIST.
URK... THAT ALL SOUNDS SO ANNOYING AND HARD.
...YOU WANNA GIVE UP?
N-NO WAY!
I JUST SAID IT MIGHT BE HARD! DON'T BE SO MEAN!
I'M SO SAD!
SORRY.
YEAH, YEAH.
MORE IMPORTANTLY, AREN'T YOU HUNGRY? LET'S EAT.
OKAY!

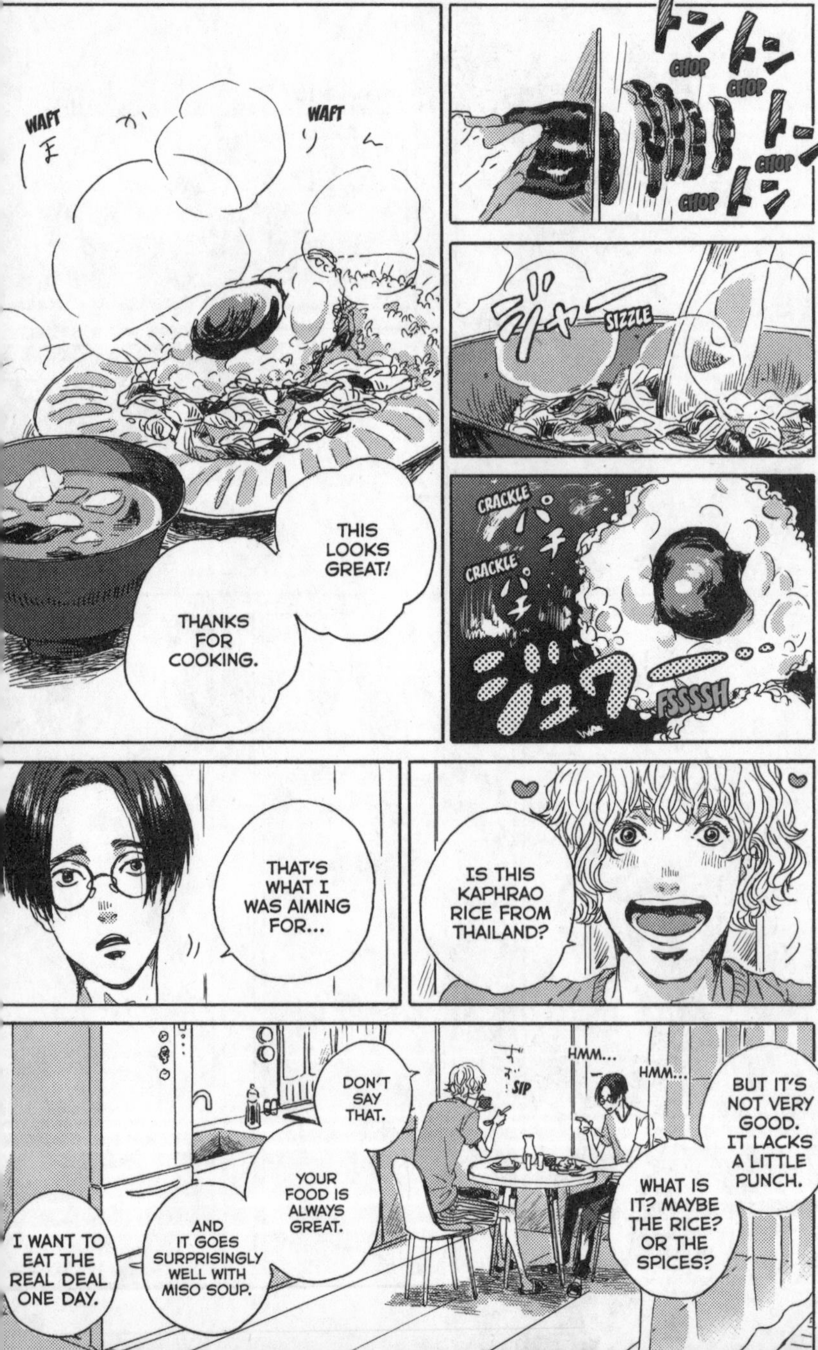
トントン
CHOP
CHOP
トントン
CHOP
CHOP
ジャー
SIZZLE
パチ
CRACKLE
パチ
CRACKLE
ジュワ～
FSSSSH
WAFT
WAFT
THIS LOOKS GREAT!
THANKS FOR COOKING.
IS THIS KAPHRAO RICE FROM THAILAND?
THAT'S WHAT I WAS AIMING FOR...
HMM...
HMM...
BUT IT'S NOT VERY GOOD. IT LACKS A LITTLE PUNCH.
WHAT IS IT? MAYBE THE RICE? OR THE SPICES?
SIP
DON'T SAY THAT.
YOUR FOOD IS ALWAYS GREAT.
AND IT GOES SURPRISINGLY WELL WITH MISO SOUP.
I WANT TO EAT THE REAL DEAL ONE DAY.

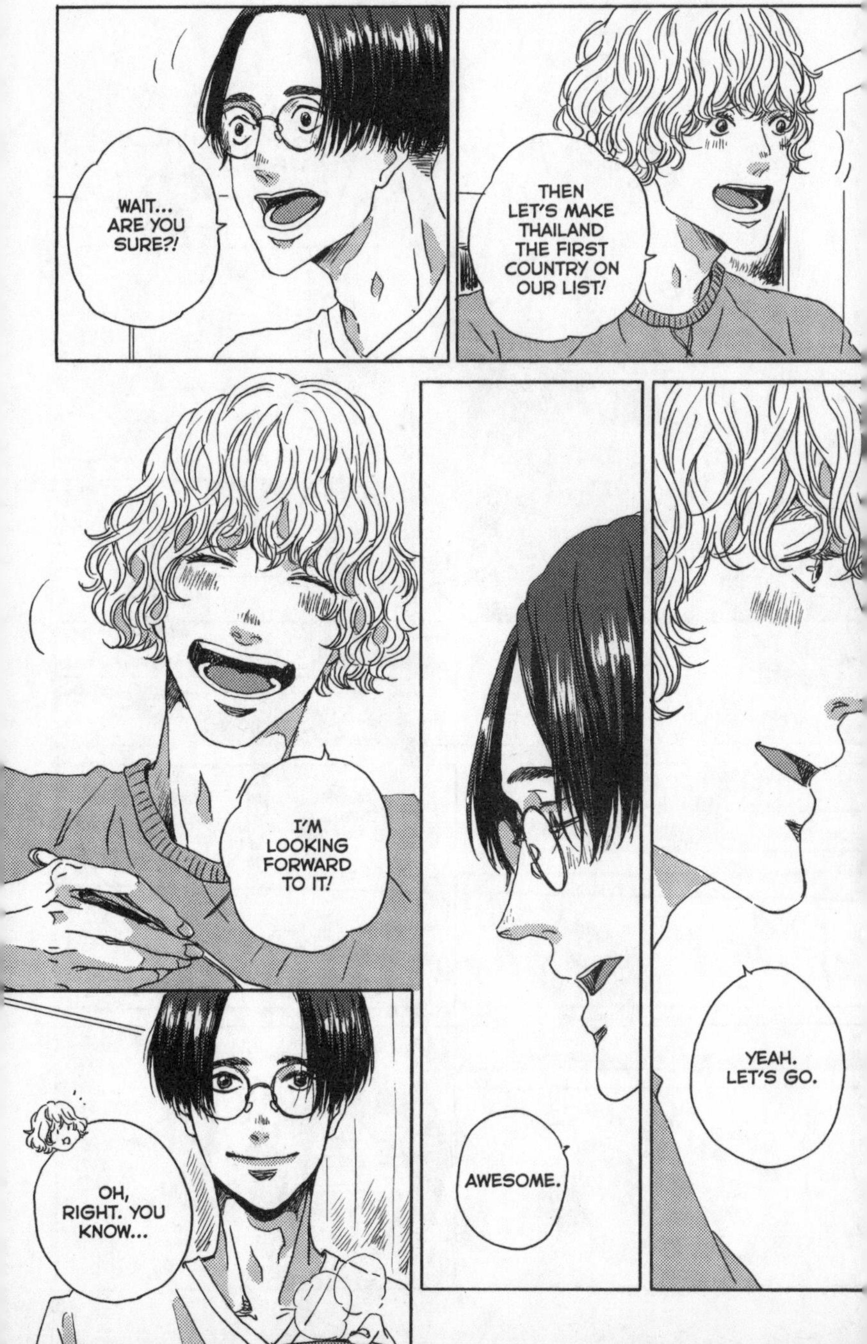
THEN LET'S MAKE THAILAND THE FIRST COUNTRY ON OUR LIST!
WAIT... ARE YOU SURE?!
YEAH. LET'S GO.
AWESOME.
I'M LOOKING FORWARD TO IT!
OH, RIGHT. YOU KNOW...

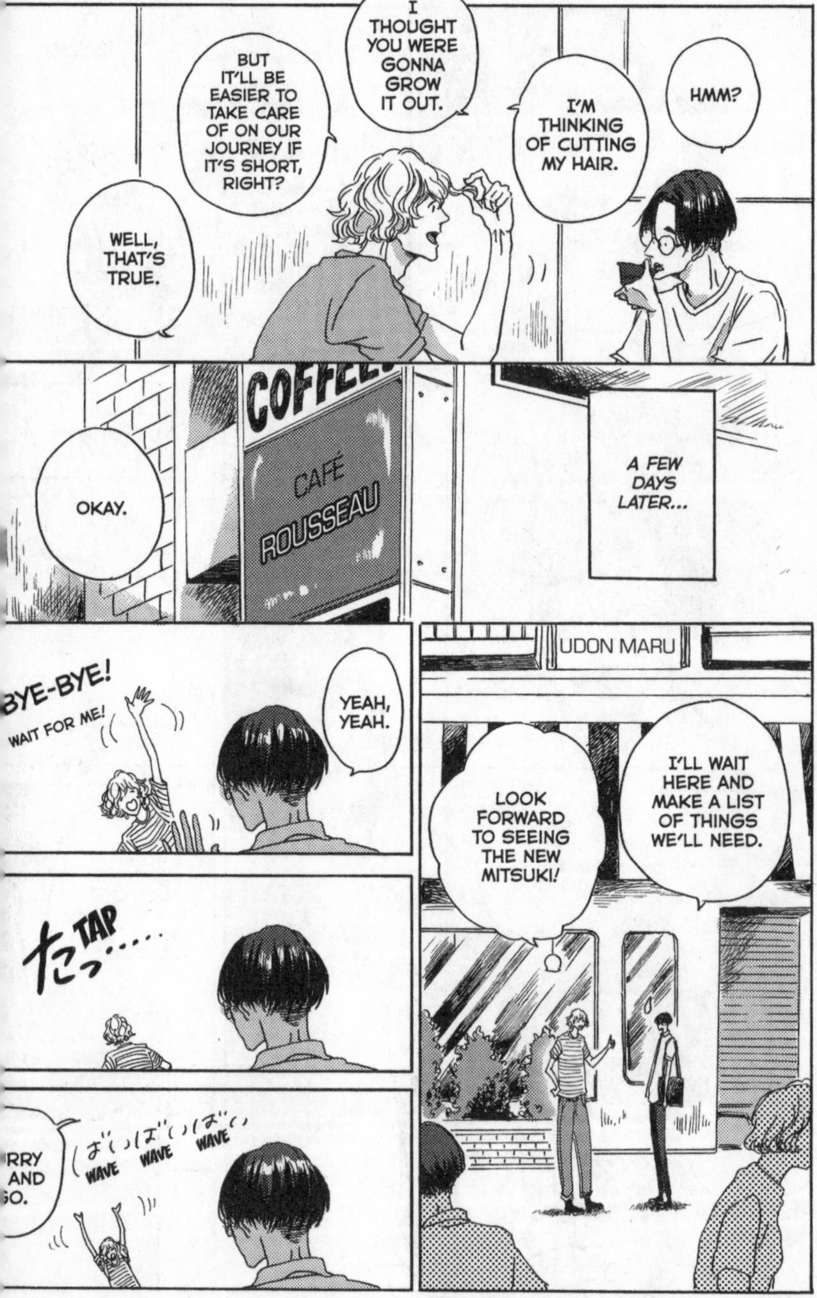
HMM?
I'M THINKING OF CUTTING MY HAIR.
I THOUGHT YOU WERE GONNA GROW IT OUT.
BUT IT'LL BE EASIER TO TAKE CARE OF ON OUR JOURNEY IF IT'S SHORT, RIGHT?
WELL, THAT'S TRUE.
A FEW DAYS LATER...
CAFÉ ROUSSEAU
OKAY.
UDON MARU
I'LL WAIT HERE AND MAKE A LIST OF THINGS WE'LL NEED.
LOOK FORWARD TO SEEING THE NEW MITSUKI!
YEAH, YEAH.
BYE-BYE!
WAIT FOR ME!
たっ TAP
ばいばいばい WAVE WAVE WAVE

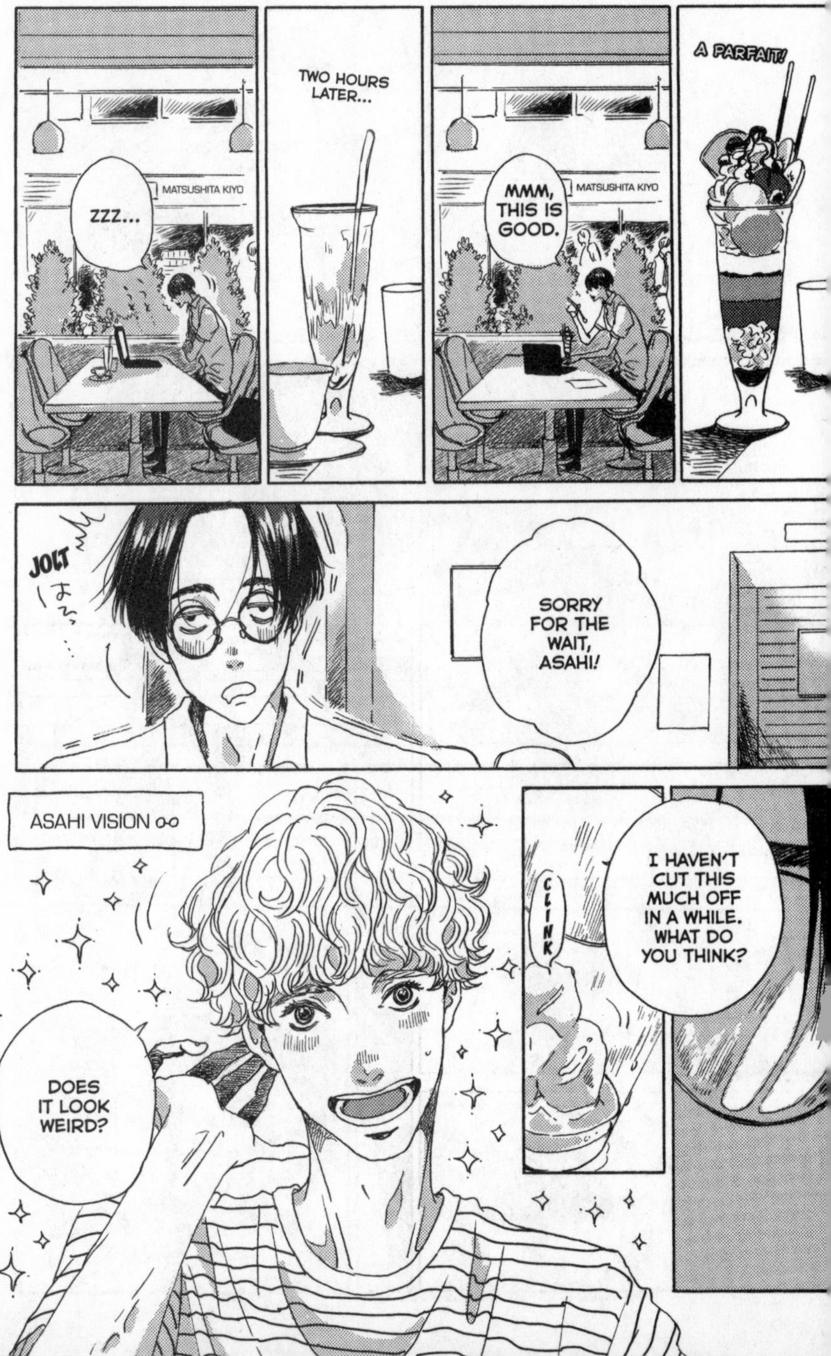
A PARFAIT!
MATSUSHITA KIYO
MMM, THIS IS GOOD.
TWO HOURS LATER...
MATSUSHITA KIYO
ZZZ...
SORRY FOR THE WAIT, ASAHI!
JOLT
はっ…
I HAVEN'T CUT THIS MUCH OFF IN A WHILE. WHAT DO YOU THINK?
CLINK
ASAHI VISION oo
DOES IT LOOK WEIRD?

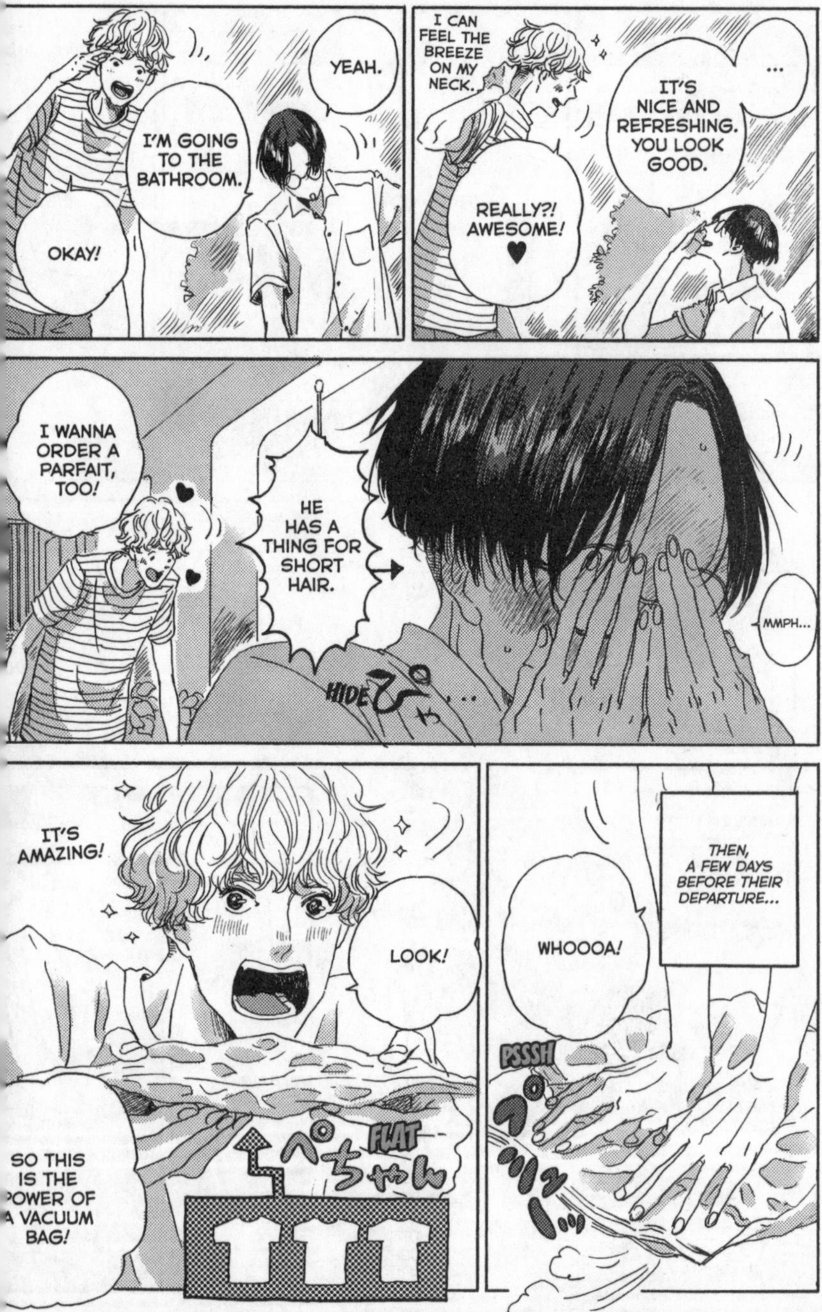
...
I CAN FEEL THE BREEZE ON MY NECK.
IT'S NICE AND REFRESHING. YOU LOOK GOOD.
REALLY?! AWESOME! ♥
YEAH.
I'M GOING TO THE BATHROOM.
OKAY!
MMPH...
HE HAS A THING FOR SHORT HAIR.
I WANNA ORDER A PARFAIT, TOO!
HIDE
THEN, A FEW DAYS BEFORE THEIR DEPARTURE...
WHOOOA!
PSSSH
IT'S AMAZING!
LOOK!
FLAT
ぺちゃん
SO THIS IS THE POWER OF A VACUUM BAG!

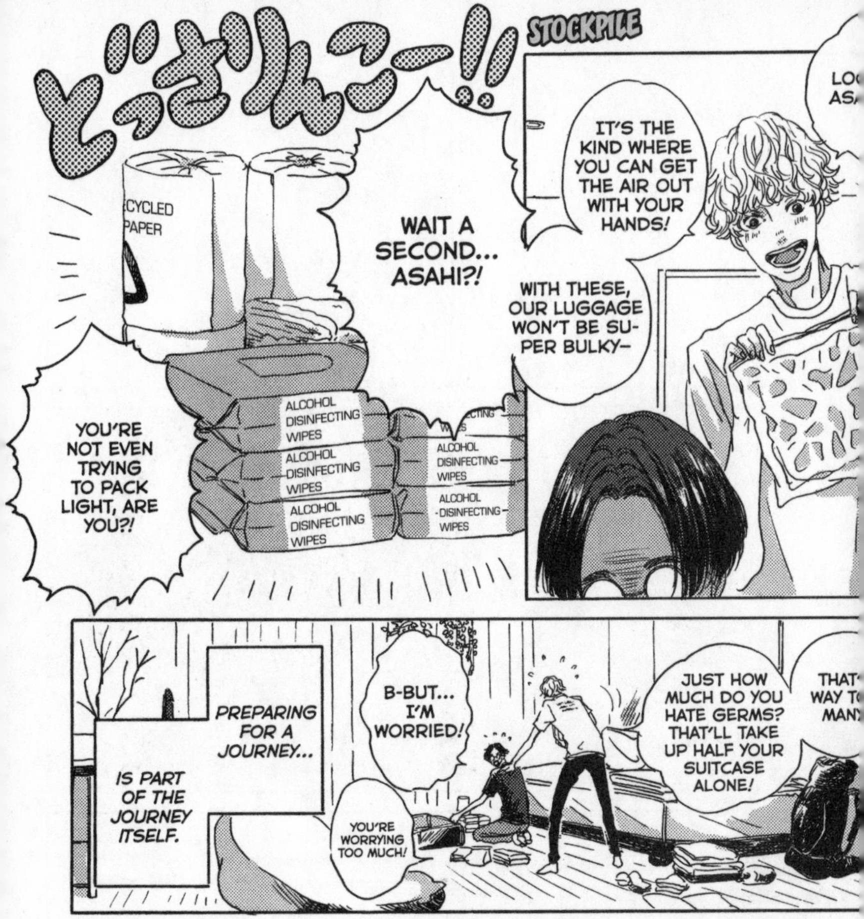

LO
AS
IT'S THE KIND WHERE YOU CAN GET THE AIR OUT WITH YOUR HANDS!
WITH THESE, OUR LUGGAGE WON'T BE SU-PER BULKY–
STOCKPILE
どっさりんこー!!
WAIT A SECOND... ASAHI?!
YOU'RE NOT EVEN TRYING TO PACK LIGHT, ARE YOU?!
ECYCLED PAPER
ALCOHOL DISINFECTING WIPES
ALCOHOL DISINFECTING WIPES
ALCOHOL DISINFECTING WIPES
ALCOHOL DISINFECTING WIPES
ALCOHOL DISINFECTING WIPES
THAT
WAY T
MANY
JUST HOW MUCH DO YOU HATE GERMS? THAT'LL TAKE UP HALF YOUR SUITCASE ALONE!
B-BUT... I'M WORRIED!
YOU'RE WORRYING TOO MUCH!
PREPARING FOR A JOURNEY...
IS PART OF THE JOURNEY ITSELF.

THINGS YOU SHOULD TAKE WITH YOU ON YOUR TRAVELS

CREDIT CARDS SOME EVEN COME WITH TRAVEL INSURANCE.

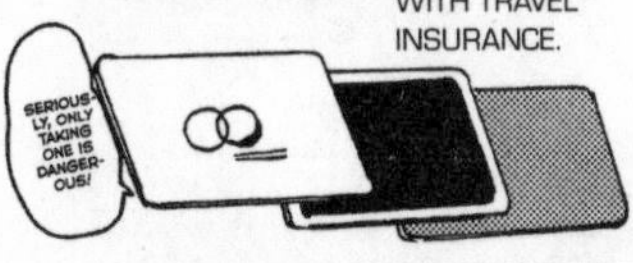

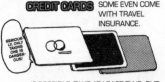

SERIOUSLY, ONLY TAKING ONE IS DANGEROUS!

IF POSSIBLE, TAKE AT LEAST TWO. PUT ONE IN YOUR WALLET AND THE REST IN A SAFER PLACE.

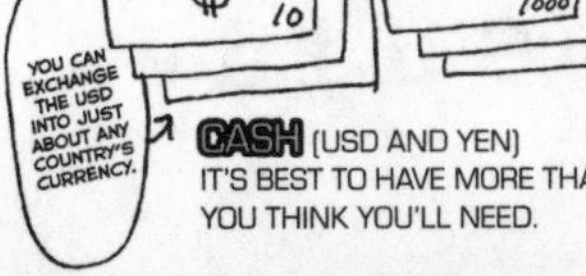

10
$
10
1000
YEN
1000
YOU CAN EXCHANGE THE USD INTO JUST ABOUT ANY COUNTRY'S CURRENCY.

CASH (USD AND YEN)
IT'S BEST TO HAVE MORE THAN YOU THINK YOU'LL NEED.

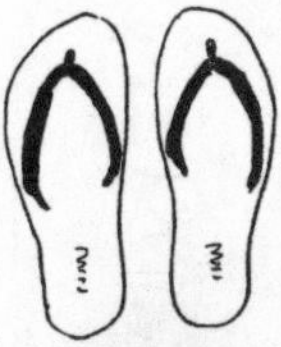

FLIP FLOPS
THERE ARE DEFINITELY TIMES YOU'LL BE GLAD YOU HAD THESE IN YOUR HOTEL, DURING YOUR FLIGHT, IN THE SHOWER (DEPENDING ON YOUR HOTEL), AND ON RAINY DAYS, ETC.

RECENTLY EVEN IN JAPAN, CUSTOMERS ARE BEING CHARGED FOR PLASTIC BAGS FOR GROCERIES AND OTHER ITEMS. YOU CAN ALSO BUY AN ECO BAG WHILE VISITING AS A MEMENTO.

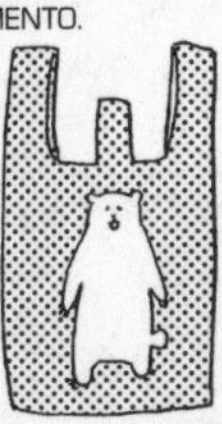

MULTI-PLUG ADAPTER

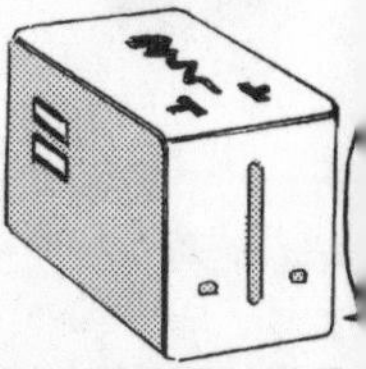

THESE ADAPTERS CAN BE USED IN MANY DIFFERENT COUNTRIES SO THEY ARE A MUST. YOU CAN USE THEM CHARGE YOUR CELL PHON AND LAPTOP!

ECO BAG
THERE'S NOTHING WRONG W ALWAYS CARRYING ONE ARO

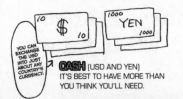

Our ^{not-so} Lonely Planet
Travel Guide
. . . .

A GENTLE NOBLE'S VACATION RECOMMENDATION, VOLUME 1

Misaki, Momochi & Sando

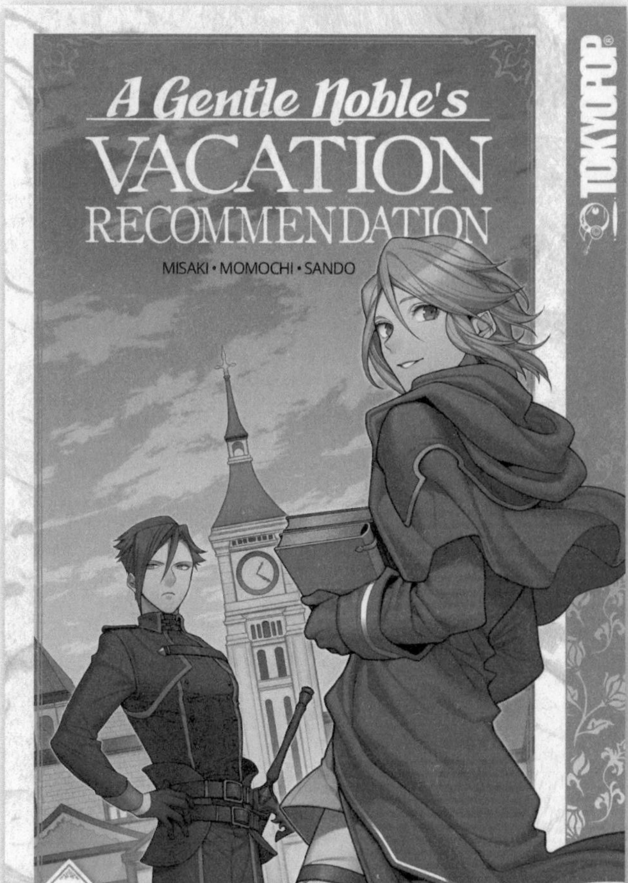

A Gentle Noble's
VACATION
RECOMMENDATION
MISAKI • MOMOCHI • SANDO
TOKYOPOP
1

FANTASY

When Lizel mysteriously finds himself in a city that bears odd similarities to his own but clearly isn't, he quickly comes to terms with the unlikely truth: this is an entirely different world. Even so, laid-back Lizel isn't the type to panic. He immediately sets out to learn more about this strange place, and to help him do so, hires a seasoned adventurer named Gil as his tour guide and protector. Until he's able to find a way home, Lizel figures this is a perfect opportunity to explore a new way of life adventuring as part of a guild. After all, he's sure he'll go home eventually... might as well enjoy the otherworldly vacation for now!

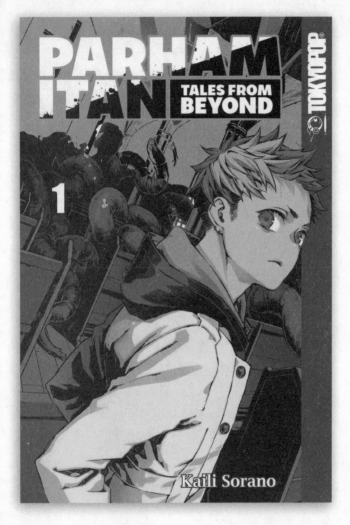

PARHAM ITAN
TALES FROM BEYOND
TOKYOPOP
1
Kaili Sorano

PARHAM ITAN: TALES FROM BEYOND, VOLUME 1
Kaili Sorano

SUPERNATURAL

Yamagishi and Sendo are schoolmates, and that's about all they have in common: one is a down-to-earth guy in the boxing club, while the other is a brainy, bookish conspiracy nut. But when they stumble across something weird and inexplicable after class one evening, it seems they'll have to set their differences aside in order to uncover the truth behind the mysterious creatures and strange figure prowling the school grounds.

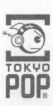